T0281514

Lecture Notes in Computer Science   13387

More information about this series at https://link.springer.com/bookseries/558

Hartwig Anzt · Amanda Bienz · Piotr Luszczek ·
Marc Baboulin (Eds.)

High Performance Computing

ISC High Performance 2022
International Workshops

Hamburg, Germany, May 29 – June 2, 2022
Revised Selected Papers

 Springer

Editors
Hartwig Anzt
University of Tennessee
Knoxville, TN, USA

Piotr Luszczek 🄳
University of Tennessee
Knoxville, TN, USA

Amanda Bienz
University of New Mexico
Albuquerque, NM, USA

Marc Baboulin
Université Paris-Saclay
Orsay, France

ISSN 0302-9743   ISSN 1611-3349 (electronic)
Lecture Notes in Computer Science
ISBN 978-3-031-23219-0   ISBN 978-3-031-23220-6 (eBook)
https://doi.org/10.1007/978-3-031-23220-6

This Springer imprint is published by the registered company Springer Nature Switzerland AG
The registered company address is: Gewerbestrasse 11, 6330 Cham, Switzerland

Preface

The ISC High Performance 2022 conference was held in Hamburg, Germany. Due to the lingering effects of the COVID-19 pandemic and the ongoing changes in the corresponding regulations for travel restrictions, the 37th edition of ISC was conducted in a hybrid fashion with both in-person and online components during the period from May 29 to June 2, 2022.

In the organization and execution of this edition of the conference, the organizing team benefited heavily from the lessons learned during the ISC 2021 digital edition as well as the countless virtual meetings that have become the cornerstone of ISC communities' collaboration in the recent years. These experiences resulted in tapering the steep learning curve and the hard work of the committees paid off because the HPC community responded enthusiastically as manifested by over 3,000 attendees from over 50 countries.

As in past years, ISC 2022 was accompanied by the ISC High Performance workshop series. In total, 7 workshops chose the option to contribute to this edition of proceedings: Compiler-assisted Correctness Checking and Performance Optimization for HPC, HPC on Heterogeneous Hardware (H3), Malleability Techniques Applications in High Performance Computing, the Fifth Workshop on Interactive High Performance Computing, the 3rd ISC HPC International Workshop on Monitoring & Operational Data Analytics, the 6th International Workshop on In Situ Visualization, and the 17th Workshop on Virtualization in High Performance Cloud Computing. Also, even more workshops opted for a presentation-only format.

In total, 27 high-quality papers were accepted that all underwent thorough review by their respective workshops' Program Committees. Each of the 43 submitted papers received on average almost 4 reviews, either single- or double-blind. Each chapter of this proceedings book contains the accepted and revised papers for a single workshop. For some workshops, an additional preface describes the review process and provides a summary of the outcomes.

We hope that with the effects of the COVID-19 pandemic fading away, we will gather next year in Hamburg, Germany, for another successful ISC High Performance workshops series with the majority of participants attending in person. Until then, we want to thank our workshop committee members, workshop organizers, and all contributors and attendees of the ISC 2022 workshops, and we are proud to present the latest findings on the topics related to the research, development, and applications of large-scale, high-performance systems.

September 2022

Hartwig Anzt
Amanda Bienz
Piotr Luszczek
Marc Baboulin

Organization

Workshops Committee

Hartwig Anzt (Chair)	Karlsruhe Institute of Technology, Germany; University of Tennessee, USA
Amanda Bienz (Deputy Chair)	University of New Mexico, USA
Cody Balos	Lawrence Livermore National Laboratory, USA
Harun Bayraktar	NVIDIA, USA
Natalie Beams	University of Tennessee, USA
Luc Berger-Vergiat	Sandia National Laboratories, USA
George Bosilca	University of Tennessee, USA
Lisa Claus	Lawrence Berkeley National Laboratory, USA
Terry Cojean	Karlsruhe Institute of Technology, Germany
Anthony Danalis	University of Tennessee Knoxville, USA
Edoardo Di Napoli	Jülich Supercomputing Centre, Germany
Markus Goetz	Karlsruhe Institute of Technology, Germany
Aditya Kashi	Karlsruhe Institute of Technology, Germany
Sarah Knepper	Intel, USA
Andreas Knuepfer	Technische Universität Dresden, Germany
Martin Kronbichler	Technical University of Munich, Germany
Weifeng Liu	China University of Petroleum, Beijing, China
Simone Pezzuto	Università della Svizzera italiana, Switzerland
Enrique S, Quintana-Orti	Universitat Politècnica de València, Spain
Estela Suarez	Jülich Supercomputing Centre, Germany
Nico Trost	AMD, Germany
Markus Wittmann	Friedrich-Alexander-Universität Erlangen-Nürnberg, Germany

Proceedings Chairs

Piotr Luszczek (Chair)	University of Tennessee, USA
Marc Baboulin (Deputy Chair)	Université Paris-Saclay, France

Contents

Compiler-Assisted Correctness Checking and Performance Optimization for HPC

Compiler-Assisted Instrumentation Selection for Large-Scale C++ Codes 5
Sebastian Kreutzer, Christian Iwainsky, Jan-Patrick Lehr,
and Christian Bischof

Lightweight Array Contraction by Trace-Based Polyhedral Analysis 20
Hugo Thievenaz, Keiji Kimura, and Christophe Alias

Detecting Scale-Induced Overflow Bugs in Production HPC Codes 33
Justs Zarins, Michèle Weiland, Paul Bartholomew, Leigh Lapworth,
and Mark Parsons

HPC on Heterogeneous Hardware (H3)

AI Benchmarking for Science: Efforts from the MLCommons Science
Working Group 47
Jeyan Thiyagalingam, Gregor von Laszewski, Junqi Yin, Murali Emani,
Juri Papay, Gregg Barrett, Piotr Luszczek, Aristeidis Tsaris,
Christine Kirkpatrick, Feiyi Wang, Tom Gibbs, Venkatram Vishwanath,
Mallikarjun Shankar, Geoffrey Fox, and Tony Hey

Performance Analysis of Matrix Multiplication for Deep Learning
on the Edge 65
Cristian Ramírez, Adrián Castelló, Héctor Martínez,
and Enrique S. Quintana-Ortí

Strategies for Efficient Execution of Pipelined Conjugate Gradient Method
on GPU Systems 77
Manasi Tiwari and Sathish Vadhiyar

A Multi-Level Platform-Independent GPU API for High-Level
Programming Models 90
Akihiro Hayashi, Sri Raj Paul, and Vivek Sarkar

Precise Energy Consumption Measurements of Heterogeneous Artificial
Intelligence Workloads 108
  René Caspart, Sebastian Ziegler, Arvid Weyrauch, Holger Obermaier,
  Simon Raffeiner, Leon Pascal Schuhmacher, Jan Scholtyssek,
  Darya Trofimova, Marco Nolden, Ines Reinartz, Fabian Isensee,
  Markus Götz, and Charlotte Debus

Malleability Techniques Applications in High Performance Computing

Detecting Interference Between Applications and Improving
the Scheduling Using Malleable Application Proxies 129
  Alberto Cascajo, David E. Singh, and Jesus Carretero

An Emulation Layer for Dynamic Resources with MPI Sessions 147
  Jan Fecht, Martin Schreiber, Martin Schulz, Howard Pritchard,
  and Daniel J. Holmes

Exploiting OpenMP Malleability with Free Agent Threads and DLB 162
  Joel Criado, Victor Lopez, Joan Vinyals-Ylla-Catala,
  Guillem Ramirez-Miranda, Xavier Teruel, and Marta Garcia-Gasulla

QR Factorization Using Malleable BLAS on Multicore Processors 176
  Adrián Castelló, Sandra Catalán, Francisco D. Igual,
  Enrique S. Quintana-Ortí, and Rafael Rodríguez-Sánchez

IMSS: In-Memory Storage System for Data Intensive Applications 190
  Javier Garcia-Blas, David E. Singh, and Jesus Carretero

On the Convergence of Malleability and the HPC PowerStack: Exploiting
Dynamism in Over-Provisioned and Power-Constrained HPC Systems 206
  Eishi Arima, A. Isaías Comprés, and Martin Schulz

The Fifth Workshop on Interactive High Performance Computing

Interactive, Cloud-Native Workflows on HPC Using KNoC 221
  Evangelos Maliaroudakis, Antony Chazapis, Alexandros Kanterakis,
  Manolis Marazakis, and Angelos Bilas

Workflows to Driving High-Performance Interactive Supercomputing
for Urgent Decision Making 233
  Nick Brown, Rupert Nash, Gordon Gibb, Evgenij Belikov,
  Artur Podobas, Wei Der Chien, Stefano Markidis, Markus Flatken,
  and Andreas Gerndt

The 3rd ISC HPC International Workshop on Monitoring and Operational Data Analytics

Data Center Facility Monitoring with Physics Aware Approach 251
  Hilary Egan, Avi Purkayastha, and David Sickinger

Rule-Based Thermal Anomaly Detection for Tier-0 HPC Systems 262
  Mohsen Seyedkazemi Ardebili, Andrea Bartolini, Andrea Acquaviva, and Luca Benini

The 6th International Workshop on In Situ Visualization

In Situ Analysis and Visualization of Extreme-Scale Particle Simulations 283
  Soumya Dutta, Dan Lipsa, Terece L. Turton, Berk Geveci, and James Ahrens

Insite: A Pipeline Enabling In-Transit Visualization and Analysis
for Neuronal Network Simulations 295
  Marcel Krüger, Simon Oehrl, Ali C. Demiralp, Sebastian Spreizer, Jens Bruchertseifer, Torsten W. Kuhlen, Tim Gerrits, and Benjamin Weyers

The Need for Pervasive In Situ Analysis and Visualization (P-ISAV) 306
  David Pugmire, Jian Huang, Kenneth Moreland, and Scott Klasky

Interactive Visualization of Large-Scale Oil and Gas Reservoir Simulation
Models 317
  Pavel Novikov, Denis Sabitov, Nikita Bukhanov, Marwan Charara, Michel Cancelliere, Fahad Rashed, and Abdulaziz Baiz

Cinema Transfer: A Containerized Visualization Workflow 324
  Isaac Nealey, Nicola Ferrier, Joseph Insley, Victor A. Mateevitsi, Michael E. Papka, and Silvio Rizzi

The 17th Workshop on Virtualization in High Performance Cloud Computing

Virtual Clusters: Isolated, Containerized HPC Environments in Kubernetes 347
  George Zervas, Antony Chazapis, Yannis Sfakianakis, Christos Kozanitis, and Angelos Bilas

Analyzing Unikernel Support for HPC: Experimental Study of OpenMP ....,... 358
  Pierre Jacquot, Pierre Olivier, Christian Perez, and Abdulrahman Azab

On the Use of Linux Real-Time Features for RAN Packet Processing
in Cloud Environments 371
Luca Abeni, Tommaso Cucinotta, Balázs Pinczel, Péter Mátray,
Murali Krishna Srinivasan, and Tobias Lindquist

eBPF-based Extensible Paravirtualization 383
Luigi Leonardi, Giuseppe Lettieri, and Giacomo Pellicci

Correction to: Compiler-Assisted Instrumentation Selection
for Large-Scale C++ Codes C1
Sebastian Kreutzer, Christian Iwainsky, Jan-Patrick Lehr,
and Christian Bischof

Author Index 395

Compiler-Assisted Correctness Checking and Performance Optimization for HPC

Preface to the Third Workshop on Compiler-Assisted Correctness Checking and Performance Optimization for HPC (C3PO'22)

Julien Jaeger[1,2] and Emmanuelle Saillard[3]

[1] CEA, DAM, DIF, 91297 Arpajon, France

[2] Universite Paris-Saclay, CEA, Laboratoire en Informatique Haute Performance pour le Calcul et la simulation, 91680 Bruyeres-le-chatel, France

julien.jaeger@cea.fr

[3] Inria Bordeaux Sud-Ouest Talence, France

emmanuelle.saillard@inria.fr

1 Introduction

Changing HPC architecture and software stack create enormous challenges for HPC application developers that need to write performance portable code and keep existing applications up to speed. Purely manual solutions are cost prohibitive. Source-to-source translators are poised to address these challenges automatically or with user input semi-automatically. Practical compiler-enabled programming environments, applied analysis methodologies, and end-to-end toolchains are crucial to performance portability in the exascale era.

C3PO is a workshop at the intersection of compilers/translators, HPC middleware, and HPC applications. The workshop brings together researchers with a shared interest in applying compilation and source-to-source translation methodologies to enhance parallel programming, including explicit programming models such as MPI, OpenMP, and hybrid models.

2 Organization

Five papers were submitted, and after a double-blind review process, three papers were accepted. The workshop took place on June 2, 2022.

2.1 Organizing Committee

Julien Jaeger	French Alternative Energies and Atomic Energy Commission
Emmanuelle Saillard	Inria Bordeaux Sud-Ouest
Anthony Skjellum	University of Tennessee at Chattanooga
Martin Ruefenacht	University of Edinburgh
Purushotham	Bangalore University of Alabama at Birmingham

Peter Pirkelbauer	Lawrence Livermore National Laboratory and University of Central Florida
Peter Thoman	University of Innsbruck

2.2 Program Committee

Hadia Ahmed	Bodo.ai
Patrick Carribault	French Alternative Energies and Atomic Energy Commission
Chunhua Liao	Lawrence Livermore National Laboratory
Reed Milewicz	Sandia National Laboratories
Amalee Wilson	Stanford University
Sara Royuela	Barcelona Supercomputing Center
Benson Muite	Kichakato Kizito
Markus Schordan	Lawrence Livermore National Laboratory
Aravind Sukumaran Rajam	Washington State University

3 Program

The workshop content was built on two tracks: invited talk and research paper presentations. The invited talk was performed virtually using zoom while the research paper presentations were performed live.

3.1 Invited Talk

Software has become indispensable in our daily lives, but if a software system fails it can have considerable human or economical consequences. Dynamic and static analysis tools can aid developers in establishing and maintaining correctness of such software systems.

Software has become indispensable in our daily lives, but if a software system fails it can have considerable human or economical consequences. Dynamic and static analysis tools can aid developers in establishing and maintaining correctness of such software systems.

One concern regarding the correctness of HPC applications is the existence of data races. Markus described his design decisions in the development of his data race benchmark suite DataRaceBench and reflected on how his design principles may have contributed to its acceptance by the community. He also summarized his own experience as participants in software verification competitions and what contributed to his error-free submissions throughout several years, also discussing the challenges in achieving the correctness of correctness tools.

3.2   Research Papers

The first speaker was Hugo Thievenaz from Inria. He presented a four steps process to reduce the storage requirements of a temporary array of a given scheduled program. He used an algorithm to deduce array access functions for which bounds are modulos of affine functions of parameters of the program.

In the next presentation, Justs Zarins from EPCC talked about an extension of an existing algorithm that can find scaling bugs in complex real applications.

Finally, Sebastian Kreutzer from TU Darmstadt described a new instrumentation tool called CaPI (short for Compiler-assisted Performance Instrumentation) that can instrument large-scale scientific codes.

The workshop program information, including the keynote presentation slides is available under https://c3po-workshop.github.io/2022/program.

Compiler-Assisted Instrumentation Selection for Large-Scale C++ Codes

Sebastian Kreutzer[1]([✉])[ID], Christian Iwainsky[2][ID], Jan-Patrick Lehr[1][ID], and Christian Bischof[1][ID]

[1] Scientific Computing, Department of Computer Science, Technical University of Darmstadt, Darmstadt, Germany
{sebastian.kreutzer,jan-patrick.lehr,christian.bischof}@tu-darmstadt.de
[2] Hessian Competence Center for High Performance Computing (HKHLR), Darmstadt, Germany
christian.iwainsky@tu-darmstadt.de

Abstract. Code instrumentation is the primary method for collecting fine-grained performance data. As instrumentation introduces an inherent runtime overhead, it is essential to measure only those regions of the code which are most relevant to the analysis. In practice, the typical approach is to define filter lists manually. Prior projects aim to automate this process using static analysis. Specifically, InstRO enables tailored instrumentation via sophisticated user-defined selection of code regions. However, due to the need for whole-program call-graph analysis, its application on large-scale scientific codes is currently impractical. In this work, we present the new instrumentation tool CaPI (short for "Compiler-assisted Performance Instrumentation"), which is targeted towards such large-scale applications. We demonstrate its application on the CFD framework OpenFOAM. Our evaluation shows that a hybrid approach of CaPI and existing profile-guided filtering outperforms profile-guided filtering alone. Furthermore, we identify correctness and usability issues and propose possible avenues to improve CaPI, as well as compiler-assisted instrumentation tools in general.

Keywords: Instrumentation · Score-P · Static analysis · OpenFOAM

1 Introduction

Collecting performance data to examine the run-time behavior of a program is essential for identifying regions in the code that benefit most from optimization or parallelization [14]. Traditionally, this data is collected using either sampling or instrumentation techniques. For use cases that require a more in-depth analysis, such as the creation of performance models [4,5] for specific functions, accurate measurements are essential. Hence, instrumentation is better suited, as it guarantees that every function invocation is recorded accurately.

However, instrumenting all functions in a program typically generates a large overhead, which can increase the execution time by orders of magnitude [18].

The original version of this chapter was revised: this chapter was previously published non-open access. The correction to this chapter is available at
https://doi.org/10.1007/978-3-031-23220-6_28

H. Anzt et al. (Eds.): ISC High Performance 2022 Workshops, LNCS 13387, pp. 5–19, 2022.
https://doi.org/10.1007/978-3-031-23220-6_1

This is in large part caused by frequently-called, short-running functions. Additionally, the insertion of measurement hooks can prohibit optimization in some cases [25].

For this reason, a filtering approach is typically necessary to instrument only those functions which are most relevant w.r.t. a user-defined metric, e.g. execution time. Excluding all other functions reduces the total number of calls to the measurement tool and, thus, the execution overhead. We refer to the set of instrumented functions as the instrumentation configuration (IC).

The simplest way to create a suitable IC is to define filter lists manually. The typical workflow involves first profiling a fully-instrumented version of the code. Subsequently, the user examines the resulting profile and selects the functions that should be excluded from the measurement. The drawback with this approach is that the user has to manually select the functions to instrument, which may require multiple iterations of compiling the code, executing it to generate a profile, and refining the IC. Hence, different tools to automate the selection process have been proposed and mainly differ in whether they use runtime data or rely on source-code features to determine a suitable IC. Unfortunately, the application of current compiler-assisted static selection tools is tedious and error prone, despite their general advantages in expressiveness and overhead reduction.

In this paper, we focus on the composable instrumentation selection mechanism introduced by the InstRO [10] project. In the context of the exaFOAM project,[1] we investigated its applicability for the instrumentation of the computational fluid dynamics (CFD) framework OpenFOAM [26]. However, due to the scale and structure of OpenFOAM, we found that the current implementation of InstRO is not suited to this task.

We present the *Compiler-assisted Performance Instrumentation* (CaPI) tool, which adopts ideas from InstRO and makes them applicable for the selective instrumentation of large-scale codes. We make the following contributions: **(1)** Present a new instrumentation tool based on key principles of InstRO. **(2)** Demonstrate its application on large-scale scientific software and identify specific usability and validation impediments. **(3)** Identify key challenges for improving CaPI specifically, as well as compiler-assisted selection tools in general.

The paper is structured as follows: Sect. 2 gives an overview of related work. Section 3 explains particularities of OpenFOAM and how they stress limitations of InstRO. Section 4 presents the CaPI toolchain to address these limitations. Thereafter, CaPI is evaluated on OpenFOAM in Sect. 5. Usability and validation impediments are highlighted in Sect. 6. The results are subsequently discussed in Sect. 7. Finally, Sect. 8 summarizes the paper and gives a brief outline on how remaining challenges may be addressed.

2   Related Work

Several tools have been developed to help automate the process of constructing ICs for performance measurements, or reduce the overhead by filtering runtime

---

[1] https://exafoam.eu/.

events. Their function selection methods can be divided into three categories, for which we list some representative tools.

Profile-guided selection uses previously recorded profile data to determine which functions to exclude or include in a subsequent measurement. An example is the *scorep-score* utility of the Score-P measurement infrastructure [12]. It enables the user to define a set of threshold values for, e.g., execution time per invocation, which need to be exceeded by a function to be considered for instrumentation. PerfTaint [6] applies a taint analysis to determine which parts of the application depend on a given set of input parameters, and only instruments dependent functions, as all others are considered to have constant runtime w.r.t. the set of input parameters.

Compiler-assisted selection tools aim to semi-automatically determine a suitable IC with the help of static code analysis. Tau [25] enables the selective instrumentation of functions via the use of its intermediate representation called PDT [19]. Cobi [21] requires the user to specify which points in a program to instrument in an XML-based format. It relies on binary instrumentation using the DynInst API [3], and, since it operates at the binary level, ignores C++ virtual functions or function pointers for any path analysis. The InstRO project [10] gives the user the ability to define selection passes that filter out functions based on statically collected information. Notably, a static call graph (CG) is generated that gives information about the call context of the respective function. This information can be used to decide if the function is relevant for overall performance.

Hybrid selection tools combine profile- and static data for the creation of IC files. PIRA [16] employs a static statement aggregation scheme [11] to estimate the amount of work per function for an initial IC. Subsequently, the IC is iteratively refined using profile information or empirically constructed performance models [15]. X-Ray [1] instrumentation uses instruction-level heuristics to estimate if a function should be instrumented, and, if so, inserts no-op sleds into the binary. At runtime, the sleds can be patched to enable or disable the recording of events, which may also be filtered based on their occurrence or available memory.

3   Tailored Instrumentation for OpenFOAM

While the utility of compiler-assisted selection tools has been successfully demonstrated on smaller applications, large scientific codes pose particular challenges.

OpenFOAM, a modular CFD framework, is a prime example of such a code. It is comprised of a multitude of individual solvers, and applicable to a wide variety of problems. OpenFOAM v2106 [22] consists of over 5000 C++ source files and ≈1.2 million lines of code (counted with `cloc` [7]).

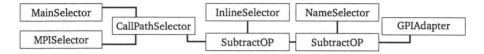

Fig. 1. Example InstRO pass pipeline, adapted from [10]. `MainSelector` and `MPISelector` select the `main` and all `MPI_*` functions, respectively. `CallPathSelector` identifies the paths between the functions selected. The `SubtractOP` removes functions which match either the `InlineSelctor` (all `inline`-marked functions) or the `NameSelector` (functions matching a certain regular expression). Finally, the `GPIAdapter` inserts the instrumentation hooks.

Its philosophy centers around an extendable toolbox for physics simulation. Hence, OpenFOAM provides many libraries that implement different solver algorithms, preconditioners, and other utilities required to develop simulation software. These libraries are employed in various solvers for specific use cases and physical phenomena, e.g., multi-phase flows or fluid-structure interaction, requiring a high degree of flexibility and configurability in the code base. One of OpenFOAM's very particular properties is the use of the project-specific build system `wmake`. Build systems, particularly custom and niche ones, commonly pose challenges in their application [8], e.g., maintaining multiple configurations. For such systems, the application of static analysis and instrumentation tools can be challenging.

The following section outlines how these features of OpenFOAM make the application of the existing InstRO tool impractical.

3.1 Design and Limitations of InstRO

InstRO provides a configurable set of passes, which can be combined by the user to perform customized source-to-source code transformations on selected code regions. Passes can be divided into three categories: *Selectors* select code regions for instrumentation based on code features. *Transformers* perform necessary source code transformations, e.g., to canonicalize certain constructs for instrumentation. Finally, *Adapters* implement the actual instrumentation of the code. Figure 1 provides an example of how passes may be combined for selective instrumentation of functions related to MPI [20] usage.

This abstract pass design makes InstRO highly configurable, and, together with its whole-program analysis, a powerful instrumentation tool. Moreover, the layered design of InstRO makes many parts of the tool—theoretically at least—independent of the compiler technology used underneath. However, most of InstRO's features have been implemented on top of the ROSE source-to-source translator. A Clang-based implementation exists, but provides, in comparison, only limited functionality.

For the application to OpenFOAM, both versions proved unsuitable. The main issue is the need for a global CG analysis in order to enable the selection of specific call-paths. In the ROSE implementation, this requires the parsing and merging of all 5000 source files at once, which is impractical due to time and memory constraints. The Clang implementation lacks global CG analysis capabilities altogether.

To overcome this obstacle, we developed the new CaPI tool based on the InstRO paradigms, but capable for application to large-scale codes. We demonstrate its capabilities on OpenFOAM and construct a low-overhead IC that focuses on analyzing functions that use MPI communication.

4   The CaPI Instrumentation Toolchain

In this section, the CaPI workflow and its implementation are introduced and explained in further detail.

We reworked the InstRO toolchain in order to make it applicable for the OpenFOAM use case. Most notably, we switched from a source-to-source transformation to a more flexible compiler instrumentation approach. This necessitated moving from the abstract pass formulation to a more concrete workflow comprised of analysis, selection and instrumentation steps. CaPI employs MetaCG [17] for global CG analysis, which was developed for a similar purpose in the automatic instrumentation refinement tool PIRA [16]. We use a custom domain-specific language (DSL) to implement the user-defined selection mechanism, designed with a focus on ease-of-use and conciseness.

4.1   Instrumentation Workflow

The toolchain consists of two main phases: In the analysis and selection phase the code is analyzed statically and relevant code regions are selected for instrumentation. We employ a stand-alone selection tool to process the collected data and generate the IC. The final instrumentation step is implemented using a custom LLVM [13] optimizer plugin. During compilation, hooks are inserted into the selected functions to interface with the measurement library. These steps are illustrated in Fig. 2.

4.2   Implementation

The implementation distinguishes between the selection phase, which is implemented in a stand-alone tool, and the compilation phase, in which an LLVM plugin is used to insert the instrumentation hooks. We provide a more detailed explanation on how the selection is implemented and how different selection passes are combined. Thereafter, we briefly explain the compilation phase.

Analysis and Selection. The selection is applied to the whole-program CG representation provided by MetaCG. Hence, selectors can match function names, or structural properties of functions within the CG. The whole-program view enables the selectors to maintain full context information for the functions selected, when desired.

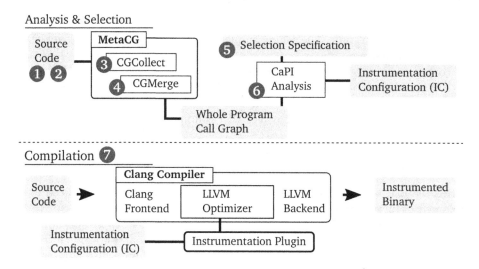

Fig. 2. Our instrumentation toolchain consists of these steps: (1) Preparation of the target code's build system, in case it is required. (2) Generation of a compilation data base for Clang-based tools. (3) Translation-unit local CG construction, given the MetaCG workflow. (4) Whole-program CG construction, manually combining relevant source files. (5) Definition of the selection specification. (6) Execution of the CaPI analysis to create the IC. (7) Compilation of target code with IC instrumentation.

One of the fundamental paradigms of InstRO is the composability of its selector modules. We realize this composability via a lightweight DSL. This DSL enables the user to easily instantiate a nested sequence of parameterized selectors. We found that, compared to an alternative XML or JSON based format, this approach results in a much more concise and comprehensible specification. A simplified grammar definition is shown in Fig. 3.

A selection specification consists of a sequence of selector definitions, which may be named or anonymous. The last of these definitions serves as the entry point to the selection pipeline. Each definition starts with the name of the selector module, followed by a list of arguments enclosed in parentheses. Aside from basic data types, i.e. strings, booleans, integers and floating-point numbers, selector modules may accept other selector definitions as input. These can be defined in-place or passed as a reference to a previously defined (named) selector instance. Such references are marked with a leading %, followed by the identifier. The reference %% is pre-defined and corresponds to the set of all functions.

Listing 1 shows an example for a call-path selection pipeline that instruments functions on paths to MPI calls.

The user can choose from a set of predefined selectors that can be customized for the specific use case. The following selectors are currently available:

$\langle spec \rangle$ ::= $\langle selectorDecl \rangle$ | $\langle spec \rangle$ $\langle selectorDecl \rangle$

$\langle selectorDecl \rangle$ ::= $\langle selectorName \rangle$ '=' $\langle selectorDef \rangle$ | $\langle selectorDef \rangle$

$\langle selectorDef \rangle$ ::= $\langle selectorType \rangle$ '(' $\langle params \rangle$ ')' | $\langle selectorType \rangle$ '(' ')'

$\langle selectorRef \rangle$ ::= '%' $\langle selectorName \rangle$ | '%%'

$\langle selectorType \rangle$ ::= $\langle identifier \rangle$

$\langle selectorName \rangle$ ::= $\langle identifier \rangle$

$\langle params \rangle$ ::= $\langle param \rangle$ | $\langle params \rangle$ ',' $\langle param \rangle$

$\langle param \rangle$ ::= $\langle string \rangle$ | $\langle int \rangle$ | $\langle float \rangle$ | $\langle bool \rangle$ | $\langle selectorRef \rangle$ | $\langle selectorDef \rangle$

Fig. 3. BNF grammar of the CaPI DSL. Some nonterminals related to the parsing of literals have been omitted for brevity. The full, up-to-date grammar is available in the project repository (https://github.com/tudasc/CaPI).

Include/exclude lists: Select functions by name based on regular expressions.

Specifier selection: Select functions w.r.t. specifiers, e.g., the `inline` keyword.

Call-path selection: Select all functions that are in the call chain below or above a previously selected function.

Unresolved call selection: Select functions that contain calls via function pointers, which may not be statically resolvable.

Set operations: Merge selection sets using basic operations such as union, intersection and complement.

The selection pipeline is applied to all functions in the CG, resulting in the final IC file. This file consists of the list of functions to be instrumented and is compatible with the Score-P filter file format. Hence, Score-P can be used as an alternative to our compiler plugin for the instrumentation step.

Compilation. We use the Clang/LLVM compiler toolchain to build the target code and perform the instrumentation. A custom LLVM plugin reads the IC file and identifies all functions in the current translation unit that are contained in the IC. These functions are then marked with LLVM function instrumentation attributes. Subsequently, the instrumentation attributes are consumed by the existing `post-inline` LLVM pass and the measurement hooks are inserted accordingly. We apply the instrumentation after inlining, in order to pre-emptively reduce instrumentation overhead. The enter and exit hooks conform to the GNU profiling interface, which is used by GCC compatible compilers for function instrumentation via the `-finstrument-functions` flag [9].

4.3 Score-P Integration

In principle, CaPI is compatible with any measurement tool that supports the GNU interface. Our main target, however, is the Score-P measurement infras-

```
1  mpi      = onCallPathTo(byName("MPI_.*", %%))
2  exclude = join(byPath(".*\/OpenFOAM\/db\/.*", %%),
3                 inlineSpecified(%%))
4  subtract(%mpi, %exclude)
```

Listing 1. The selector `mpi` selects all functions that match the name `"MPI_*"`, uses the result to select all functions that are on a path through the CG to an MPI function, and finally subtracts all inlined functions and those defined in a certain directory from the result.

tructure, which is commonly available in HPC environments. While Score-P provides support for the GNU profiling interface as well as defining its own measurement API, the GNU version is limited to recording only statically linked functions. This is due to the fact that only symbols with statically known addresses are collected from the main executable. As a result, the corresponding function names of calls to shared libraries cannot be identified and are thus ignored in the measurement.

We have developed the *Score-P symbol injector* library to identify and register these missing symbols [24]. Linked into the instrumented executable, it queries the `/proc/self/maps` pseudo-file at start-up to obtain information about the memory mapping of the loaded shared libraries. Each of these libraries is then analyzed with `nm`. Using the previously-collected information, each symbol is mapped to its address in the running program. Functions that are included in the IC are then registered in Score-P's internal address-resolution hash map.

5   Evaluation on OpenFOAM

In this section, we demonstrate the presented CaPI toolchain on OpenFOAM and examine the obtained measurement results.

We evaluated the ICs with two OpenFOAM test cases: 3-D Lid-driven cavity (`cavity`), a well-known benchmark problem for incompressible flow [2], and HPC_Motorbike (`motorbike`), a simulation of flow around a motorbike model [23]. The executables applied in the main solve phase are `icoFoam` and `simpleFoam`, respectively. We measured the execution time for the Score-P profiling mode on a single node of the Lichtenberg 2 cluster, running with 4 MPI processes.[2]

The compatibility of CaPI with the Score-P filter file format enables the comparison of various combinations of the available selection and instrumentation methods. This is illustrated in Fig. 4.

The full specification of the evaluated variants is shown in Table 1. All instrumented variants rely on Score-P's compile-time filtering method, using an IC generated by either scorep-score or CaPI. The `scorep-full` variant corresponds to Score-P's default full instrumentation, which does not perform any explicit

[2] https://www.hhlr.tu-darmstadt.de/.

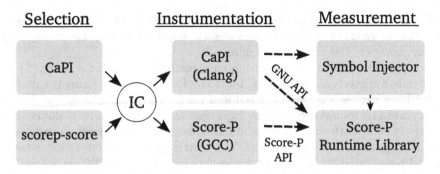

Fig. 4. Interoperability of Score-P and CaPI selection and instrumentation methods. The IC generated by CaPI or scorep-score can be combined with CaPI's Clang-based instrumenter or the GCC-based Score-P instrumenter. Note that using the GNU interface requires the inclusion of the symbol injector library to record calls to shared libraries.

filtering but excludes all functions declared as `inline`. The `hybrid` variant combines both selection methods by performing additional runtime filtering. All variants were compiled with `-02` optimization.

Table 1. Build configurations used in the evaluation.

Name	Compiler	Instrumentation interface	Filter	
			Compile-time	Run-time
vanilla-gcc	GCC	–	–	–
vanilla-clang	Clang	–	–	–
scorep-full	GCC	Score-P	–	–
scorep-filt	GCC	Score-P	scorep-score	–
capi-gnu	Clang	GNU	CaPI	–
capi-scorep	GCC	Score-P	CaPI	–
hybrid	GCC	Score-P	CaPI	scorep-score

For the `scorep-score` IC, we filtered out all functions that are called at least a million times and take less than 10 μs to execute. This yielded a filter file that excludes 17 functions for `cavity` and 38 functions for `motorbike` that are responsible for a majority of the overhead.

For the CaPI variants, we used the selection specification shown in Listing 1, which selects all call paths performing MPI communication. Additionally, we filtered out functions defined in files from a directory that contains mostly code related to I/O operations, as well as functions specified as `inline`.

We manually validated these ICs by comparing the resulting profiles with the results from `scorep-full`. Both profiles represented the behavior of the program accurately and preserved the call paths comprising hot spots.

Figure 5 shows the execution time measured for each variant. For both benchmarks, `vanilla-gcc` performed slightly better than `vanilla-clang`. For `cavity`, however, this difference is miniscule.

Compared to `vanilla-gcc`, the unfiltered instrumentation `scorep-full` produced only 8% overhead for `cavity`, but 135% for `motorbike`. Using the profile-guided filter variant `scorep-filt` reduced the overhead significantly to 3% for `cavity` and 44% for `motorbike`. The `capi-gnu` variant, however, was slower than `scorep-filt` in both cases. This is in part due to the initial look-up and registration of the shared library symbols. This step is quite time consuming because the CaPI-generated IC consists of an include list of about $110k$ entries, which have to be cross-checked with the found symbols. In the `capi-scorep` variant, the performance penalty due to the initialization overhead is eliminated, thus showing better results in both cases. The discrepancy in the execution time of `main` between `capi-gnu` and `capi-scorep` are likely due to the differences in compilers and the Score-P measurement API.

The `hybrid` variant showed the most promising results. For `cavity`, it reduces the instrumentation overhead to below 1%. Similarly, `hybrid` yielded the overall best results for `motorbike` with an overhead of 30% compared to `vanilla-gcc`.

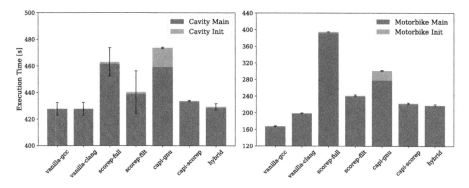

Fig. 5. Mean execution time of the instrumentation variants for the `cavity` and `motorbike` benchmarks over 5 runs. The total time is split into contributions from initialization and the execution of the `main` function. The error bars indicate the standard deviation. Note that the lower limits of the y-axes have been adjusted for better visibility.

6   Usability and Validation Impediments

In this section, we highlight some of the usability impediments that we had to overcome in the instrumentation of OpenFOAM.

As mentioned earlier, dealing with the particularities of uncommon build systems can be cumbersome and tedious. As such, OpenFOAM's `wmake` made certain aspects of the tool application more difficult. We do not consider it as a separate issue in this list. Nonetheless, it should be noted that the chosen build system heavily influences the ease-of-use of any instrumentation workflow.

Whole-Program CG. The generation of the whole-program CG is the most time-consuming part of our toolchain, and took several hours for OpenFOAM. The main difficulty, however, lies in setting up the analysis correctly. It has to be executed as a preprocessing step and is therefore not easily applied via the build system. This makes it difficult to identify which source files should be included.

For the initial local CG analysis, it is sufficient to search the code base for C++ files. The subsequent merging into a whole-program CG, however, requires additional care. OpenFOAM builds a large number of individual solver executables. Merging them all together is not sensible, as their behavior varies significantly. Hence, to generate the CG for each solver, we first merge all local CGs of the OpenFOAM libraries into a large library CG. We then identify the source files specific to the solver and merge the corresponding CGs with the library CG.

In general, this requires the user to have detailed knowledge about the build process of the target application. In its current form, the setup of the CG analysis therefore constitutes a significant barrier.

Limitations of Static Analysis. Due to the inherent limitations of static analysis, some call paths cannot be correctly identified by MetaCG. The resulting CG is therefore not guaranteed to be complete. A common reason for missed call edges is the use of function pointers [17]. For OpenFOAM, this played a minor role. In general, however, we cannot guarantee that there are no other issues that lead to missed calls, e.g., due to bugs in the analysis or misconfigured selection specifications. Unfortunately, there is no direct way to reliably check that a recorded profile is complete. Hence, it is the responsibility of the user to manually verify that no major parts of the code are missing.

To mitigate the issue, MetaCG provides a tool that compares the statically constructed CG with one constructed from a full-instrumentation profile and adds missing edges. This approach, however, introduces additional steps into the instrumentation workflow and requires a fully-instrumented build of the target. Furthermore, the resulting CG is only valid for the specific program inputs used to generate the profile. In order to guarantee completeness, this validation step must be repeated every time the program calling behavior changes based on inputs. For large code bases, this is impractical.

Managing Multiple Configurations. In the use case of OpenFOAM, it is sensible to create separate ICs for different solvers, as they may use completely different parts of the main library. As the instrumentation of the selected functions happens at compile-time, every new IC requires a rebuild of the program. Moreover, for multiple, different ICs, a separate build folder per IC is required.

This is especially tedious in OpenFOAM because the build system is designed to have only one build for each compiler configuration. Maintaining multiple instrumented builds is doable, but requires tedious configuration work. In addition, the user needs to keep track of the purpose of each build and document the configuration steps. If this is done poorly, the wrong build may be used, potentially leading to incomplete profiling data.

Furthermore, having multiple builds of a large program can waste significant amounts of disk space, despite the binaries being virtually identical.

In order to avoid these issues altogether, Score-P provides an option for run-time filtering. Using this method, all functions are initially instrumented. At run-time, the entry/exit hooks are still called, but measurements are only recorded for functions that pass the filter. As a result, the overhead is generally bigger compared to compile-time filtering, which may lead to skewed measurements. This is especially apparent with our toolchain, which generates a filter list containing ≈29k entries for the `cavity` case. We observed a significant increase in overhead using run-time filtering with this CaPI-generated filter, compared to the compile-time filtering method.

7   Discussion

We have demonstrated that our tool is capable of generating instrumentation configurations for large-scale codes. The results show that a hybrid approach, which combines the tailored CaPI selection with run-time filtering to remove remaining high-overhead functions, proved to be especially effective in mitigating the overhead, while preserving relevant call paths. This demonstrates that the compiler-assisted instrumentation workflow is in principle feasible to apply and beneficial w.r.t. overhead reduction.

In practice, however, the application on OpenFOAM proved to be quite time-consuming and required a good understanding of the code base and build system. We can therefore conclude that for most cases, the use of existing profile-guided filtering techniques with manual adjustments is preferable, as they require far less configuration overhead. The issues we identified are in large part applicable to other compiler-assisted instrumentation tools that rely on prior static analysis. This relates to PIRA in particular, which uses the same CG analysis workflow. In order for compiler-assisted instrumentation tools to be a viable alternative, the following key challenges must be addressed:

Simplification of the Analysis Workflow: The global static CG analysis is a requirement for the presented selection techniques. Currently, this step is very time-consuming. In order to simplify the workflow, the manual set-up must be reduced, by providing better integration into the compilation process.

Management of Build Configurations: Different instrumented versions of a code currently require maintaining multiple program builds. Instrumentation tools should aid in organizing and identifying them. Ideally, the need for separate builds should be eliminated altogether by providing an alternative run-time adaptation method that introduces little overhead.

Detection of Missed Calls: Currently, the user is unable to tell if function calls are missing due to limitations in the static analysis. A manual comparison with a complete instrumentation of the same program is possible, but requires extra steps that have to be repeated for every input configuration. Ideally, the static analysis phase should detect situations where such problems might occur and insert run-time checks to detect missed calls.

8   Conclusion and Future Work

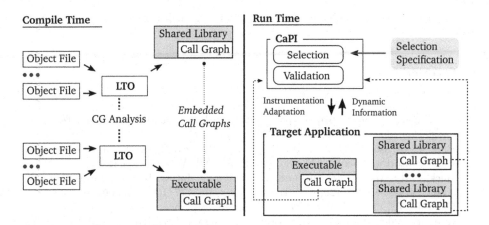

Fig. 6. Envisioned workflow with embedded CG: The CG analysis is performed as link-time-optimization (LTO) on all object files of a shared library or executable and the CG is embedded into it. At run time, the CaPI runtime library queries the objects for their respective CGs and merges them to construct the whole-program CG.

We presented the Compiler-assisted Performance Instrumentation tool for user-defined selective program instrumentation. CaPI was demonstrated by creating tailored instrumentation for the CFD framework OpenFOAM. Our evaluation showed that a hybrid selection approach, comprised of static selection and run-time filtering, is effective in eliminating overhead. However, the amount of required manual work for CaPI is undesirable. Hence, we identified key areas for improvement to make such techniques more accessible.

Currently, the biggest usability issue for CaPI and similar tools is the requirement for a separate analysis phase. This issue could be mitigated by shifting the whole-program CG construction to link-time and embedding the CG into the generated binary, as illustrated in Fig. 6. In this proposed toolchain, a suitable dynamic instrumentation method enables the selection and instrumentation steps at program start. This opens up opportunities for dynamic instrumentation refinement based on collected run-time information, as employed by PIRA, without the need to rebuild the program. In addition, the availability of the CG at run-time would enable the assessment of the IC's completeness. Further work is required to assess the feasibility of this approach.

CaPI is available at https://github.com/tudasc/CaPI under the BSD 3-Clause license.

Acknowledgments. This work was funded by the Bundesministeriums für Bildung und Forschung (BMBF) - 16HPC023, and by the Hessian LOEWE initiative within the Software-Factory 4.0 project and the Deutsche Forschungsgemeinschaft (DFG, German Research Foundation) - Project-ID 265191195 - SFB 1194.

The exaFOAM project has received funding from the European Union's Horizon 2020/EuroHPC research and innovation program under grant Agreement number: 956416.

Calculations were conducted on the Lichtenberg high-performance computer of Technical University of Darmstadt.

References

1. Berris, D.M., Veitch, A., Heintze, N., Anderson, E., Wang, N.: XRay: a function call tracing system (2016). https://static.googleusercontent.com/media/research.google.com/en//pubs/archive/45287.pdf
2. Bnà, S., Spisso, I., Olesen, M., Rossi, G.: PETSc4FOAM: a library to plug-in PETSc into the OpenFOAM Framework. PRACE White paper (2020)
3. Buck, B.R.: An API for runtime code patching. Int. J. High Perform. Comput. Appl. **14**(4), 317–329 (2000). https://doi.org/10.1177/109434200001400404
4. Calotoiu, A., et al.: Fast multi-parameter performance modeling. In: 2016 IEEE International Conference on Cluster Computing (CLUSTER), pp. 172–181. IEEE, September 2016. https://doi.org/10.1109/CLUSTER.2016.57
5. Calotoiu, A., Hoefler, T., Poke, M., Wolf, F.: Using automated performance modeling to find scalability bugs in complex codes. In: Proceedings of the International Conference on High Performance Computing, Networking, Storage and Analysis, SC 2013, pp. 45:1–45:12. ACM, New York (2013). https://doi.org/10.1145/2503210.2503277
6. Copik, M., Calotoiu, A., Grosser, T., Wicki, N., Wolf, F., Hoefler, T.: Extracting clean performance models from tainted programs. In: Proceedings of the 26th ACM SIGPLAN Symposium on Principles and Practice of Parallel Programming, PPoPP 2021, pp. 403–417. ACM, New York (2021). https://doi.org/10.1145/3437801.3441613
7. Daniel, A.: Contributors: CLOC (2006–2020). https://github.com/AlDanial/cloc
8. Dubois, P., Epperly, T., Kumfert, G.: Why Johnny can't build [portable scientific software]. Comput. Sci. Eng. **5**(5), 83–88 (2003). https://doi.org/10.1109/MCISE.2003.1225867
9. Free Software Foundation Inc: GCC Program Instrumentation Options (2022). https://gcc.gnu.org/onlinedocs/gcc/Instrumentation-Options.html
10. Iwainsky, C.: InstRO: a component-based toolbox for performance instrumentation. Ph.D. thesis, TU Darmstadt (2015). https://doi.org/10.2370/9783844045628
11. Iwainsky, C., Bischof, C.: Calltree-controlled instrumentation for low-overhead survey measurements. In: Proceedings - 2016 IEEE 30th International Parallel and Distributed Processing Symposium, IPDPS 2016, pp. 1668–1677. IEEE, July 2016. https://doi.org/10.1109/IPDPSW.2016.54
12. Knüpfer, A., et al.: Score-P: a joint performance measurement run-time infrastructure for Periscope, Scalasca, TAU, and Vampir. In: Proceedings of the 5th International Workshop on Parallel Tools for High Performance Computing 2011, pp. 79–91 (2012). https://doi.org/10.1007/978-3-642-31476-6_7
13. Lattner, C., Adve, V.: LLVM: a compilation framework for lifelong program analysis & transformation. In: International Symposium on Code Generation and Optimization, CGO 2004, pp. 75–86 (2004). https://doi.org/10.1109/CGO.2004.1281665

14. Lehr, J.P., Bischof, C., Dewald, F., Mantel, H., Norouzi, M., Wolf, F.: Tool-supported mini-app extraction to facilitate program analysis and parallelization. In: 50th International Conference on Parallel Processing. ACM, New York (2021). https://doi.org/10.1145/3472456.3472521

15. Lehr, J.P., Calotoiu, A., Bischof, C., Wolf, F.: Automatic instrumentation refinement for empirical performance modeling. In: Proceedings of ProTools 2019: Workshop on Programming and Performance Visualization Tools - Held in conjunction with SC 2019: The International Conference for High Performance Computing, Networking, Storage and Analysis, pp. 40–47. IEEE, November 2019. https://doi.org/10.1109/ProTools49597.2019.00011

16. Lehr, J.P., Hück, A., Bischof, C.: PIRA: performance instrumentation refinement automation. In: AI-SEPS 2018 - Proceedings of the 5th ACM SIGPLAN International Workshop on Artificial Intelligence and Empirical Methods for Software Engineering and Parallel Computing Systems, Co-located with SPLASH 2018, pp. 1–10. ACM, New York, November 2018. https://doi.org/10.1145/3281070.3281071

17. Lehr, J.P., Hück, A., Fischler, Y., Bischof, C.: MetaCG: annotated call-graphs to facilitate whole-program analysis. In: TAPAS 2020 - Proceedings of the 11th ACM SIGPLAN International Workshop on Tools for Automatic Program Analysis, Co-located with SPLASH 2020, pp. 3–9. ACM, New York, November 2020. https://doi.org/10.1145/3427764.3428320

18. Lehr, J.P., Iwainsky, C., Bischof, C.: The influence of HPCToolkit and score-p on hardware performance counters. In: Proceedings of the 4th ACM SIGPLAN International Workshop on Software Engineering for Parallel Systems, SEPS 2017, pp. 21–30. ACM, New York (2017). https://doi.org/10.1145/3141865.3141869

19. Lindlan, K.A., et al.: A tool framework for static and dynamic analysis of object-oriented software with templates. In: Proceedings of the ACM/IEEE 2000 Conference on Supercomputing, p. 49, November 2000. https://doi.org/10.1109/SC.2000.10052

20. Message Passing Interface Forum: MPI: a message-passing interface standard version 3.1 (2015). https://www.mpi-forum.org/docs/mpi-3.1/mpi31-report.pdf

21. Mußler, J., Lorenz, D., Wolf, F.: Reducing the overhead of direct application instrumentation using prior static analysis. In: Jeannot, E., Namyst, R., Roman, J. (eds.) Euro-Par 2011. LNCS, vol. 6852, pp. 65–76. Springer, Heidelberg (2011). https://doi.org/10.1007/978-3-642-23400-2_7

22. OpenCFD: OpenFOAM v2106. https://develop.openfoam.com/Development/openfoam/-/tree/OpenFOAM-v2106

23. OpenFOAM Project: OpenFOAM benchmark problems. https://develop.openfoam.com/committees/hpc/-/tree/develop/

24. Sebastian Kreutzer: Score-P Symbol Injector Library (2022). https://github.com/sebastiankreutzer/scorep-symbol-injector

25. Shende, S.S.: The TAU parallel performance system. Int. J. High Perform. Comput. Appl. **20**(2), 287–311 (2006). https://doi.org/10.1177/1094342006064482

26. Weller, H.G., Tabor, G., Jasak, H., Fureby, C.: A tensorial approach to computational continuum mechanics using object-oriented techniques. Comput. Phys. **12**(6) (1998). https://doi.org/10.1063/1.168744

Lightweight Array Contraction
by Trace-Based Polyhedral Analysis

Hugo Thievenaz[1]([✉]), Keiji Kimura[2], and Christophe Alias[1]

[1] CNRS, ENS-Lyon, Inria, University of Lyon, Lyon, France
{hugo.thievenaz,christophe.alias}@ens-lyon.fr
[2] Waseda University, 3-4-1 Okubo, Shinjuku-ku, Tokyo 169-8555, Japan
Keiji@waseda.jp

Abstract. Array contraction is a compilation optimization used to reduce memory consumption, by reducing the size of temporary arrays in a program while preserving its correctness. The usual approach to this problem is to perform a static analysis of the given program, creating overhead in the compilation cycle. In this work, we take a look at exploiting execution traces of programs of the polyhedral model, in order to infer reduced sizes for the temporary arrays used during calculations. We designed a four step process to reduce the storage requirements of a temporary array of a given scheduled program, in which we used an algorithm to deduce array access functions for which bounds are modulos of affine functions of parameters of the program. Our results show memory reductions of an order of magnitude on several benchmarks examples from PolyBench, a collection of programs from the polyhedral community. Execution time is compared to a baseline implementation of a static algorithm, and results show speed-up factors up to 20.

Keywords: Compilation · Array contraction · Polyhedral model · Dynamic analysis · Memory allocation

1 Introduction

The problem of temporary memory allocation is a challenge for programs meant to be running on platforms that have limited computing resources. Such temporary arrays manipulate results of intermediate computations that are disposed of at the end of the program. They are therefore sometimes oversized, when array cells are left unused and not overwritten by following computation despite their value no longer being used. Array contraction is a program transformation whose goal is to detect such unused array cells and replace a write to another cell to an unused one, in order to reduce the effective memory footprint of the array and shrink its maximum size, allocating less memory to the buffer while keeping program correctness intact.

Figure 1 introduces two direct applications of this method. Both the local memories used by the CPUs, and the buffer(s) used for communicating between

Supported by Inria through the polytrace exploratory action.

H. Anzt et al. (Eds.): ISC High Performance 2022 Workshops, LNCS 13387, pp. 20–32, 2022.
https://doi.org/10.1007/978-3-031-23220-6_2

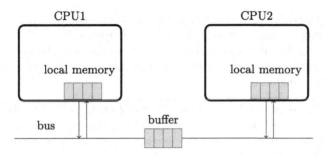

Fig. 1. Two CPUs perform computations on local memories and communicate data through a buffer

themselves, benefit from allocating smaller arrays. More precisely, many computing units require or may use on-the-fly memory sizing to exploit their structure (scratchpad memories, systems on chips). The class of programs studied for this optimization are affine loop kernels manipulating arrays (SCoPs, static control parts [2]), and this form of loop nest is the most common in many High-Performance Computing examples. The polyhedral model provides the necessary mathematical foundations to develop compiler optimizations such as array contraction, that focuses on compute-intensive scientific kernels containing such SCoPs. In this context, compilers rely on static analysis of the program to reduce the memory footprint of the program. Static analysis has been the basis of many works in the field [1–3,5,7,13]. However, dynamic analysis outclass static compiler ones when small execution traces can be efficiently produced and analysed. Static methods use polyhedral projections and Integer Linear Programming, which can be expensive depending on the shape of the code.

It would seem that no approach to this problem, to our knowledge, has explored the option of using dynamic analysis of the program in order to infer compilation optimizations. In this work, we contradict this habit and study the problem of determining a buffer allocation function from analysis of several execution traces. The problem can be formulated as follows: given a program manipulating a temporary array A, we want to infer allocations functions σ_A, of minimal image cardinal, such that any access $A[i]$ can be safely replaced by $\hat{A}[\sigma_A(i)]$. Our general approach is then to apply a lightweight analysis on a few offline execution traces, with the assumption that the input parameter instances chosen for those traces are small enough that the execution time is significantly smaller.

In this paper, we make the following contributions:

- We present a new method for storage optimization, a dynamic approach that uses offline execution trace analysis. In particular, we describe a liveness algorithm from such execution trace, and another to compute the maximum number of variables alive alongside a dimension, from which we get our scalar modular mappings.

- We show, through the use of interpolation, that we can identify parameters from said modulo and deduce a generalized mapping.
- We implement this method on several benchmarks from the polyhedral community and show reductions both in implementation execution time and storage mappings deduced.

Our paper is structured as follows. Section 2 outlines the polyhedral model and the array contraction problem. Section 3 discusses related work. Section 4 describes our trace-based approach. Section 5 presents experimental results. Finally, Sect. 6 concludes this paper and draws research perspectives.

2   Background

We present the necessary background to the problem. We define the *polyhedral model*, and what is an usual polyhedral compilation flow. Then, we define the problem at hand, *array contraction*, and the related notions.

2.1   Polyhedral Model

```
for (y=0; y<2; y++)
    for (x=0; x<N; x++)
S:    blurx[x,y] = in[x,y] +
        in[x+1,y] + in[x+2,y];
for (y=2; y<N; y++)
    for (x=0; x<N; x++)
T:    blurx[x,y] = in[x,y] +
        in[x+1,y] + in[x+2,y];
U:    out[x,y] = blurx[x,y-2] +
        blurx[x,y-1] + blurx[x,y];
```

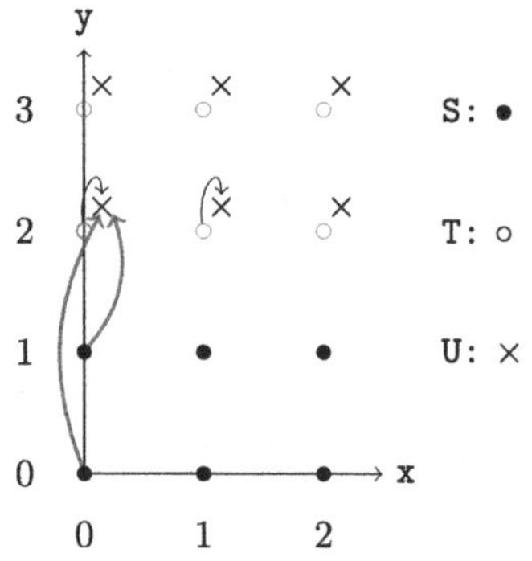

Fig. 2. Motivating example: 2D Blur filter

The *polyhedral model* defined by [8] is an intermediate representation of a loop nest as a graph over points of $\mathbb{Z}^n$. The class of programs that can be represented in this model, and therefore are subject to polyhedral optimizations, is polyhedral programs. These are (sequences of, possibly nested) *for* loops where all loop bounds and conditions are affine functions of the surrounding loop iterators and program parameters. Each execution of a statement S, nested in a n-depth loop, namely an *instance* or *operation*, can be represented by $\langle S, i \rangle$ where i is a n-dimensional *iteration vector* of the surrounding loop indices. Its *iteration domain* D, the set of all possible iteration vectors for S, forms a graph over points of $\mathbb{Z}^n$.

Running Example. We illustrate our algorithm on the 2D Blur filter illustrated with its iteration domains on Fig. 2. This is a well-known example of the polyhedral community, that applies two consecutive elementary convolutions on the input signal in. We have represented the iteration domains of S, T and U as colored symbols.

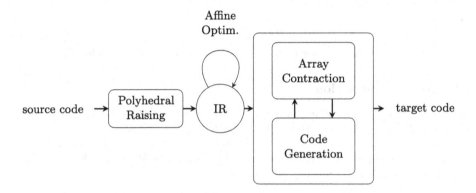

Fig. 3. Simplified polyhedral compilation flow of our method

Polyhedral Compilation Flow. Compilation flows usually produce an in-between form of the program at hand, named Intermediate Representations (IR), on which transformations can be applied more easily to optimize its execution. Polyhedral compilation is no different, and in the case of our method, we produce those IRs as a pre-analysis step, separated from the algorithm. Figure 3 describes our simplified polyhedral compilation flow. Source code gets transformed once to an intermediate representation through *polyhedral raising*, who is then subject to possibly multiple affine transformations in order to optimize execution of the target code. The focus of our algorithm, and its performance, is therefore focused entirely on the application of such polyhedral optimization, for which ours is Array Contraction.

Affine Transformations. At the heart of a polyhedral compiler, code transformations are expressed by affine mappings specifying a new execution order:

Definition 1 (Affine Scheduling). *A schedule maps each execution instance $\langle S, i \rangle$ to an execution date $\theta_S(i)$. In the polyhedral model, schedules are affine per statement, i.e. $\theta_S(i) = A_S i + b_S$, and dates are vectors of $\mathbb{Z}^p$ ordered with the lexicographic ordering $\ll$. A schedule maps each iteration vector to its counterpart in the transformed, scheduled program.*

A possible schedule for our motivating example is the *canonical sequential schedule* θ, which is the order specified by the original for statements of the program: $\theta_S(y, x) = (0, y, x, 0), \theta_T(y, x) = (1, y, x, 0), \theta_U(y, x) = (1, y, x, 1)$.

Correctness. In the polyhedral model, data dependencies might be expressed between iterations. In the computation of the blur-interleaved example, for any instance where $y \geq 3$, we have that an instance of $\langle U, x, y \rangle$ of the second convolution depends (flow) on the preceding instances $\langle T, x, y \rangle$, $\langle T, x, y-1 \rangle$, $\langle T, x, y-2 \rangle$ of the first convolution. Anti- and output- dependencies are expressed in the same way. The dependence relation is denoted by $\rightarrow$. Of course, the schedule is constrained by data dependencies:

$$\langle S, i \rangle \rightarrow \langle T, j \rangle \Rightarrow \theta_S(i) \ll \theta_T(j) \tag{1}$$

This gives affine constraints which allow to compute affine schedules [8].

2.2 Array Contraction

The problem of array contraction, given a temporary array A, consists in finding a mapping $A[i] \rightarrow \hat{A}[\sigma_A(i)]$ reducing or matching the unknown required size of A, minimal size for which the correctness of the program is intact. In our case, we seek memory mappings of the form $\sigma_A(i) = i \bmod b(N)$, where b is an affine function of program's structure parameters N (e.g. array size).

Definition 2 (Conflict Relation). *A conflict relation $\bowtie_\theta$ is defined as the set of array cells whose lifetimes intersect during the execution of the program for the schedule θ.*

The conflict relation induces a correctness condition on array contraction, as conflicting array cells might be mapped to different places:

$$a[i] \bowtie_\theta a[j] \wedge i \neq j \Rightarrow \sigma_a(i) \neq \sigma_a(j) \tag{2}$$

Running Example (cont'd). With the original loop schedule, the temporary array `blurx` might be contracted with the mapping $(y, x) \mapsto (y \bmod 3, x \bmod N)$, when $N \geq 3$. Indeed, `blurx` bufferizes the first convolution (`S`,`T`) before applying the next convolution (`U`) which only needs three rows y. This way, the footprint is reduced to $3 \times N$ array elements.

The *successive minima technique* [10] is the state-of-the-art approach to compute such mappings. The method of this work by Lefebvre and Feautrier can be boiled down to the following process. The conflict relation is represented as a difference set $\Delta_a = \{i - j \mid a[i] \bowtie a[j]\}$ for each array a; Then, for each array dimension k, the modulos are computed with $b_k(N) = 1 + \max\{\delta_k \mid (\delta_1, \ldots, \delta_n) \in \Delta_a\}$. Finally, resolved conflicts are removed before iterating on the next array dimension : $\Delta_a := \Delta_a \cap \{\delta \mid \delta_k = 0\}$.

Our contribution, as we will show later, consists in a lightweight instantiation of this algorithm on several small execution traces, followed by an interpolation to obtain a general mapping. We show experimentally that *our results are obtained way faster than with the Lefebvre-Feautrier method, the latter dealing with costly parametric Integer Linear Programming (ILP).* More fundamentally, **this work is a proof-of-concept that costly polyhedral analysis might be rephrased as lightweight trace analysis. This opens new perspectives to scale polyhedral compilers.**

3   Related Work

We quickly go over the multiple works related to our subject. We first present defining works on the subject. We then go over closely related work on the subject of array contraction. Finally, we present loosely related work on trace manipulation and analysis, but no work on dynamic array contraction by trace analysis has crossed our eyes.

Affine Array Contraction. As described by [3,10], and again in this work, the successive modulo technique seeks to reduce the memory storage requirements of an already scheduled program, by performing static analysis in order to construct a conflict set. The array dimensions are reduced by finding contraction moduli along the array's axes. While recalling that the method of Lefebvre and Feautrier [10] obtains on the example *blur-interleaved* a storage mapping $(y, x) \mapsto (y \bmod 3, x \bmod N)$, the more advanced work of Bhaskaracharya et al. [3] infers a more refined mapping $(y, x) \mapsto 2x - y \bmod (2N + 1)$, because their approach consider the change to a better basis for the contraction vectors.

Inter-array and Intra-array Contraction. The type of optimization we are looking for in this paper is an *intra-array optimization* as designed by [3], and references such as [1,8,11] focus on this intra-array analysis. This means that the analysis performed is done on a per-array basis. [3,4] build a technique for intra-array as well as inter-array optimization, a technique that consider the reduction of multiple temporary arrays, allowing them to find even more reduced mapping by changing (often reducing) the dimensionality of the array(s) considered for the analysis. [6] calculate the memory requirements of a program by approaching them as a polynomials in the parameters of the program, but their method has to relax the solutions as rational instead of integer, and only give an upper bound of the memory consumption.

Trace Analysis. In terms of trace analysis, some work has already covered similar topics such as loop recognition and trace prediction [9] and trace-based affine loop reconstruction [12]. The former compresses traces (as sequences of scalars) and constructs a loop nest producing such sequence of numbers. The latter focuses on reconstructing loops based on their predictable affine behavior, from the addresses of the memory accesses, and presents a terminating algorithm to reconstruct the loop function entirely. These works, therefore, focus only on rebuilding incomplete traces, and not on the usage of traces in a compilation process.

4   Our Approach

This section presents the contributions made to the problem of array contraction, and detail our method of offline trace execution and analysis to infer a general mapping.

4.1 Overview of the Approach

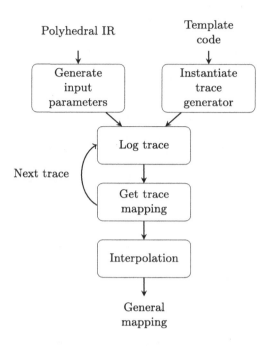

Fig. 4. Our approach

Figure 4 depicts our approach. We start with an input Intermediate Representation, comprised of the program, its schedule θ, and its Dependence Graph. We also input the code generated from θ (Template code), which will allow to produce traces.

First, we compute the input parameter instances on which running the program to obtain interesting traces. We also instrument the template code to prepare the trace generation. Then, for each input parameter instance N, we generate the trace (Log trace) and we apply a *lightweight instance* of the successive minima method (Get trace mapping). We end up with a collection of trace mappings. Finally, we infer the general mapping (working for any input parameter) from an interpolation between each input parameter instance and its corresponding output modulo mapping (Interpolation). All these steps are detailed thereafter.

4.2 Generating Input Parameter Instances

Our trace analysis operates on execution traces of programs, meaning we have to instantiate our kernel program with scalar values for its parameters N. Since we would like to interpolate modulos as an affine forms of parameters $N \mapsto b_k(N)$, we need $|\boldsymbol{N}| + 1$ parameter instances. Also, the parameter instances must be independent to enforce a unique interpolation. We first explain how the first parameter instance is computed. Then, we explain how we get the remaining parameter instances.

First parameter instance, $\mathcal{O}$ We derive the set of parameters covering all the dependencies by projecting the dependency constraints of the program on each of the parameters. Then, we compute a minimum value for each of the parameters. Usually the constraints are of the form $N \geq \ell$ with ℓ some constant lower bound. Hence, we may infer a lower bound for each parameter with a simple syntactic heuristic without using expensive linear programming techniques. This gives the first parameter instance, denoted as $\mathcal{O}$ (for "origin").

This heuristic assumes that in the main program execution, all the dependencies are reached. However, this is not always the case, and if we deal with imperfect loop nests, then the result is an upper bound, giving potential additional overhead by operating on traces with bigger parameter instances than needed. How to extend this heuristic to the general case is left to future work. In our running example, the intersection of all the dependence constraints boils down to the polyhedron $\{N|N \geq 3\}$. Hence $\mathcal{O} = (3)$, denoting the parameter instance $N = 3$.

Remaining Parameter Instances. One set of parameter values is not sufficient to establish an interpolation. For each parameter N_i, $1 \leq i \leq p$, we create a new parameter instance, linearly independent from the rest. A straightforward way to compute such new instances is to build the set of increments by each canonical vector $\boldsymbol{e}_i$: $\mathcal{I} = (\mathcal{O}, \mathcal{O} + e_1, \ldots, \mathcal{O} + e_p)$, where $\mathcal{O} + \boldsymbol{e}_i = (N_1, ..., N_i + 1, ..., N_p)$. These parameter instances will lead to a unique affine interpolation, as we will see later. On our example, we would obtain $(3, 4)$, denoting the parameter instances $N = 3$ and $N = 4$.

4.3   Inferring a Mapping on a Trace

The following Algorithm 1 describes our lightweight instance of the successive minima method to compute a mapping from an execution trace.

We apply a direct liveness analysis on the trace to compute the difference set Δ_a we defined earlier, then each modulo is computed as the maximum difference measured alongside each array dimension i, following the lines of the successive minima algorithm. Since we deal with finite (and small) integer sets, no ILP is required.

This method is an instance of the Lefebvre-Feautrier algorithm [10] since we produce the same mapping while operating on a trace, i.e. an instantiated program. Since the mapping is affine, we can directly apply a linear interpolation to deduce a generalized parametrized mapping, as we will describe in the next section.

Algorithm 1: Find the mapping for the array a on the trace T

Result: mapping $i \mapsto i \bmod m$
function GETMAPPING(T,a)
$(In, Out) \leftarrow$ LIVENESS(T)
$CS \leftarrow \bigcup_p \{(a[i], a[j]) \mid a[i], a[j] \in In(p)\}$
$\Delta_a \leftarrow \{i - j \mid (a[i], a[j]) \in CS\}$
for *each array dimension i, starting from 0, in increasing order* **do**
$\quad \mid \quad m_i \leftarrow 1 + max\{\delta_i \mid (0, ..., 0, \delta_i, ...) \in \Delta_a\}$
end

Running Example (cont'd). For our blur-interleaved example, such analysis would show, on the trace for $N = 3$, for the `blurx` array, that the biggest width alongside the y axis is 2, so there are a maximum of 2+1 array cells in conflict at any given control point p. The observation on x is similarly done, and again we measure a width of 2, and so a number of conflicts of 3. Hence, we obtain $(y, x) \mapsto (y \bmod 3, x \bmod 3)$. This is repeated for the trace with $N = 4$ where we obtain $(y, x) \mapsto (y \bmod 3, x \bmod 4)$.

4.4 Interpolation

From the mapping instances deduced, we show how to interpolate a generalized mapping that depends on program parameters. We retrieve mappings of the form $i \mapsto i \bmod b(N)$ by a direct affine interpolation from the pairs of inputs (parameter instances) and outputs (modulo scalars found). We realise this by solving the following systems of equations. Let p be the number of program parameters ($N = (N_1, \ldots, N_p)$), and k the number of array indices ($i = (i_1, \ldots, i_k)$). Then:

$$\sigma_a(i) = \begin{pmatrix} i_1 \bmod f_1(N_1, ..., N_p) \\ \vdots \\ i_k \bmod f_k(N_1, ..., N_p) \end{pmatrix} \tag{3}$$

This system of Eq. (3) defines the f_ℓ functions that we are determining. Expecting to deal with affine functions, each f_ℓ can be written in the homogeneous form:

$$f_\ell(N) = \tau_\ell \cdot \begin{pmatrix} N \\ 1 \end{pmatrix} \tag{4}$$

where τ_ℓ is a vector of size $p + 1$, τ_i being the coefficient of N_i, for $1 \leq i \leq p$, and τ_{p+1} being the constant coefficient.

We have collected sample values from these affine functions, for each array index ℓ, represented by:

$$\begin{cases} f_\ell(\mathcal{O}) = m_0 \\ \quad \vdots \\ f_\ell(\mathcal{O} + e_p) = m_p \end{cases} \tag{5}$$

Which can be written as $A\boldsymbol{\tau}_\ell = \boldsymbol{m}$:

$$\begin{pmatrix} \mathcal{O} & 1 \\ \mathcal{O} + e_1 & 1 \\ \vdots & \vdots \\ \mathcal{O} + e_p & 1 \end{pmatrix} \boldsymbol{\tau}_\ell = \begin{pmatrix} m_0 \\ \vdots \\ m_p \end{pmatrix} \tag{6}$$

We now show that this system has always a unique solution in $\mathbb{Z}^{p+1}$:

Theorem 1. *A is unimodular.*

Proof. We apply the Gaussian elimination method to express the determinant of A. We may subtract from each of the first p columns that we label each a_i, the last column a_{p+1} multiplied by N_i without changing the determinant. The resulting matrix is as such:

$$\det A = \begin{vmatrix} 0 & \cdots & \cdots & 0 & 1 \\ 1 & 0 & \cdots & 0 & 1 \\ 0 & 1 & \cdots & 0 & 1 \\ \vdots & \ddots & \ddots & \vdots & \vdots \\ 0 & \cdots & 0 & 1 & 1 \end{vmatrix}$$

It immediately follows that the determinant of this matrix is $(-1)^{p+1} \times \det I_p$, the permutation of the $p + 1$-th and the first column leading to the $(-1)^{p+1}$ factor, and $\det I_p$ the determinant of the lower-left matrix which is the identity. Therefore, $\det A = \pm 1$ and so A is unimodular.   □

Because A is unimodular, the linear equation system always has integer solutions. Therefore, for any given program with p parameters, $p+1$ traces are both necessary and sufficient to produce an interpolation.

Running example (cont'd) On traces, we obtained the *trace mappings* $(y, x) \mapsto (y \bmod 3, x \bmod 3)$ for $N = 3$, and $(y, x) \mapsto (y \bmod 3, x \bmod 4)$ for $N = 4$. Denoting $(y, x) \mapsto (y \bmod b_1(N), x \bmod b_2(N))$ the general mapping, we have $b_1(3) = 3$ and $b_1(4) = 3$. Hence we solve: $A\boldsymbol{\tau}_1 = \begin{pmatrix} 3 & 1 \\ 4 & 1 \end{pmatrix} \boldsymbol{\tau}_1 = \begin{pmatrix} 3 \\ 3 \end{pmatrix}$ from which we deduce $\boldsymbol{\tau}_1 = \begin{pmatrix} 0 \\ 3 \end{pmatrix}$. Hence $b_1(N) = \boldsymbol{\tau}_1 \cdot \begin{pmatrix} N \\ 1 \end{pmatrix} = 3$.

Also, $b_2(3) = 3$ and $b_2(4) = 4$. Hence we solve: $A\boldsymbol{\tau}_2 = \begin{pmatrix} 3 & 1 \\ 4 & 1 \end{pmatrix} \boldsymbol{\tau}_2 = \begin{pmatrix} 3 \\ 4 \end{pmatrix}$ from which we deduce $\boldsymbol{\tau}_2 = \begin{pmatrix} 1 \\ 0 \end{pmatrix}$. Hence $b_2(N) = \boldsymbol{\tau}_2 \cdot \begin{pmatrix} N \\ 1 \end{pmatrix} = N$.

Hence, we get the *parametrized program mapping* $(y, x) \mapsto (y \bmod 3, x \bmod N)$.

5   Experimental Results

This section presents our implementation and the results obtained with our approach, and make a comparison with the successive minima approach.

5.1   Experimental Setup

We have implemented our method as an automatic code generator in C++ named PoLi. Our tool takes as input an intermediate representation of a kernel and first outputs a C program where its statements have been swapped out with calls to trace generation methods. Then, the lifetime analysis is performed on several execution traces, from a remote compilation and execution of the modified kernel. Finally, the deduced mapping is directly applied by modifying the access functions of the temporary arrays to the ones deduced.

The baseline implementation, used to compare our analysis time and storage requirement measurements with, is an implementation of the successive modulo technique [10]. The C kernels have been compiled using gcc 9.3.0 with flags "-fPIC -O3", while the implementation itself has been compiled using g++ 9.3.0 using flags "-O3 -ldl -lstdc++fs". Every compilation and execution of the kernels, and so their time measurements have been done on an Intel Core i5-1135G7 CPU running at 2.40GHz. No HPC computer is required, as we deal with *compilation*, not execution. The LF method is compiled with the same directives. We list the examples present in our benchmarks, which are part of the PolyBench test suite[1]:

- **fibonacci** computes the n-th term of the fibonacci sequence. It showcases very low runtime because of a very simple single loop nest.
- **pc-2d** and **pc-2d-line**, two examples of a producer-consumer mechanic in two dimensions, respectively without and with the last 2 rows of A explicitly being output dependencies. Those show the relevance of the method to only temporary memory.
- **blur-interleaved** and **blur-tiled**, two examples of the 2D blur filter, respectively with producer-consumer statements interleaved (motivating example), and tiled scheduling. Together, they highlight the versatility of the method, matching the Lefebvre-Feautrier approach for the interleaved case, but outpaces it when the loop nest gets more complex with more loop counters added for the tiling.
- **2 mm**, example of two successive matrix multiplication and assignment. This example shows that the Lefebvre-Feautrier method also suffers from the multiplicity of arrays in the program, which skyrockets its runtime compared to our approach.

5.2   Results

Table 1 depicts the kernels and their targeted temporary array, alongside its original size, and the mapping found is the reduced size inferred from our algorithm. Parameter instance represents the starting parameter values chosen for the analysis. The execution times shown are not the ones of the modified kernels' executions, as the mappings found are the same for both methods. Rather, the first average runtime describes, for our method PoLi, the sum of the measured

---

[1] Available at https://web.cse.ohio-state.edu/ pouchet.2/software/polybench/.

Table 1. Mappings and runtimes obtained using our approach (PoLi) compared to the baseline successive modulo method (LF) [10]

Kernel	Mapping found	Parameters	PoLi time (ms)	LF time (ms)	Speed-up
fibonacci	i mod 2	$N = 2, 3$	0.00103	0.024221	**23.5**
pc-2d	i mod N j mod N	$N = 2, 3$	0.00284	0.045513	**16.0**
pc-2d-line	i mod 2 j mod N	$N = 3, 4$	0.01022	0.064114	**6.3**
blur-2d	y mod 3 x mod N	$N = 5, 6$	0.15636	0.187037	**1.2**
blur-tiled	y mod 3 x mod 4	$N = 5, 6$	0.166067	4.041242	**24.3**
2 mm	i mod N j mod N	$N = 2, 3$	0.096936	2.228872	**23.0**

time spent on the generation of the parameter instance, the time spent instantiating the trace and the time spent interpolating the resulting mappings. This is compared to the baseline runtime which represents the time spent applying the instance of the Lefebvre-Feautrier approach we have implemented, and we show the speed-up factor between the two methods ran successively. We can observe that the `fibonacci` example has a speedup of more than 20, explained by the small trace parameters chosen, as the runtime of PoLi on this example is noticeably the lowest out of all. `blur-tiled` and 2 mm have respectively bigger iteration dimension and a greater overall number of arrays, meaning the Lefebvre-Feautrier approach irremediably takes more time projecting over those several dimensions, whereas our method takes advantage of the smallness of the parameter instances selected and suffers way less from more arrays and array dimensions. The complexity of the LF method is directly tied to the iteration dimension in an exponential fashion, while our approach is less sensitive to it. `blur-interleaved` and `pc-2d-line` both present smaller speed-up factors, as our parameter instance generation gives an upper bound too big, while the dependencies can still be respected with lower parameter values. Therefore, more carefulness is required in the selection of the starting parameter instance, meaning that a better method to infer parameter instances is also of the essence. On these two examples, our approach still manages to match or outperform the Lefebvre-Feautrier method while having unnecessarily large starting parameter instances.

6 Conclusion

In this paper, we have presented a novel lightweight method for array contraction in the polyhedral model. This work is the very first step towards a new paradigm of trace-based analysis to scale polyhedral compilation and demonstrate a promising proof of concept on the array contraction problem. We design and implement an automatic array contraction tool, that takes as input the source code of the kernel and outputs optimized target code in regards to storage space consumption. We present the algorithms and methodology used in our tool. Execution times are compared to those of the Lefebvre and Feautrier method and shows promising speed-up factors. Results answers positively to the question of the possibility of generalization from a subset of execution traces.

In the future, we seek to apply another methodology to the starting parameter instance deduction, in order to choose minimal parameters regardless of the form of the loop. We also look forward to deduce more complex mappings, of the form $i \mapsto Ai \bmod b(N)$, similarly to [1,3]. More generally, we seek to apply the paradigm of trace analysis to other problems of the polyhedral compilation, to further study the potential yield of trace analysis in the compilation process. Finally, we plan to address the interaction of array contraction and other optimizations passes by integrating our implementation in an automatic parallelizer.

References

1. Alias, C., Baray, F., Darte, A.: Bee+ Cl@ k: an implementation of lattice-based array contraction in the source-to-source translator rose. ACM SIGPLAN Notices **42**(7), 73–82 (2007)
2. Bastoul, C., Cohen, A., Girbal, S., Sharma, S., Temam, O.: Putting polyhedral loop transformations to work. In: Rauchwerger, L. (ed.) LCPC 2003. LNCS, vol. 2958, pp. 209–225. Springer, Heidelberg (2004). https://doi.org/10.1007/978-3-540-24644-2_14
3. Bhaskaracharya, S.G., Bondhugula, U., Cohen, A.: Automatic storage optimization for arrays. ACM Trans. Program. Lang. Syst. (TOPLAS) **38**(3), 1–23 (2016)
4. Bhaskaracharya, S.G., Bondhugula, U., Cohen, A.: SMO: an integrated approach to intra-array and inter-array storage optimization. In: Proceedings of the 43rd Annual ACM SIGPLAN-SIGACT Symposium on Principles of Programming Languages, pp. 526–538 (2016)
5. Bondhugula, U., Hartono, A., Ramanujam, J., Sadayappan, P.: A practical automatic polyhedral parallelizer and locality optimizer. In: Proceedings of the 29th ACM SIGPLAN Conference on Programming Language Design and Implementation, pp. 101–113 (2008)
6. Clauss, P., Fernández, F.J., Garbervetsky, D., Verdoolaege, S.: Symbolic polynomial maximization over convex sets and its application to memory requirement estimation. IEEE Trans. Very Large Scale Integr. VLSI Syst. **17**(8), 983–996 (2009)
7. Darte, A., Schreiber, R., Villard, G.: Lattice-based memory allocation. IEEE Trans. Comput. **54**(10), 1242–1257 (2005)
8. Feautrier, P., Lengauer, C.: Polyhedron model. In: Encyclopedia of Parallel Computing, vol. 1, pp. 1581–1592 (2011)
9. Ketterlin, A., Clauss, P.: Prediction and trace compression of data access addresses through nested loop recognition. In: Proceedings of the 6th Annual IEEE/ACM International Symposium on Code Generation and Optimization, pp. 94–103 (2008)
10. Lefebvre, V., Feautrier, P.: Automatic storage management for parallel programs. Parallel Comput. **24**(3–4), 649–671 (1998)
11. Quilleré, F., Rajopadhye, S.: Optimizing memory usage in the polyhedral model. ACM Trans. Program. Lang. Syst. (TOPLAS) **22**(5), 773–815 (2000)
12. Rodríguez, G., Andión, J.M., Kandemir, M.T., Touriño, J.: Trace-based affine reconstruction of codes. In: Proceedings of the 2016 International Symposium on Code Generation and Optimization, pp. 139–149 (2016)
13. Simbürger, A., Apel, S., Größlinger, A., Lengauer, C.: PolyJIT: polyhedral optimization just in time. Int. J. Parallel Program. **47**(5), 874–906 (2018). https://doi.org/10.1007/s10766-018-0597-3

Detecting Scale-Induced Overflow Bugs in Production HPC Codes

Justs Zarins[1]([⊠]) [iD], Michèle Weiland[1] [iD], Paul Bartholomew[1] [iD],
Leigh Lapworth[2] [iD], and Mark Parsons[1] [iD]

[1] EPCC, University of Edinburgh, Edinburgh, UK
j.zarins@epcc.ed.ac.uk
[2] Rolls-Royce plc, Derby, UK

Abstract. Scaling bugs – errors that only manifest at large scale simulations, in terms of number of parallel workers or input size – are critical to detect early in the testing of HPC codes. If missed, these bugs can cause applications to either crash at runtime during production runs or, even worse, silently continue and corrupt results. This results in wasting vast amounts of resources and the crash might not provide any useful debugging information. Laguna et al. presented a method for solving this in [13] using an approach where scale variables are traced throughout an application statically and potentially overflowing instructions are detected, with further refinements done by running a few small scale experiments. However, their algorithm is not able to trace multiple code patterns found in production HPC applications, for example code modularity, and has not been applied to Fortran applications. We present an extension to their algorithm which addresses these issues thus enabling us to find scaling bugs in complex real applications where they could not be found before. The key features that enable this are backward/forward tracing and optimistic GEP comparison.

Keywords: Scaling bugs · Correctness · LLVM

1 Introduction

Verifying the correctness of supercomputing applications is a significant challenge, not least due to the ever increasing scale that these applications run at. The majority of testing is done with either serial or small scale parallel runs, with the largest scales reserved for production jobs. This approach of testing at small scale cannot catch "scaling bugs" – errors that occur as the number of processes used by a program, or the size of the simulation, increases. As a result, an application that is deemed to be correct may fail only on a large scale production run, at which point the cost of the failure is huge and debugging information likely unavailable. It is therefore desirable to be able to anticipate and report such issues based on small scale testing only.

A promising approach was presented by Laguna and Schulz [13] to predict integer overflow bugs and pinpoint their location in an application's code. In

H. Anzt et al. (Eds.): ISC High Performance 2022 Workshops, LNCS 13387, pp. 33–43, 2022.
https://doi.org/10.1007/978-3-031-23220-6_3

their method, an application is analysed at the LLVM bitcode level, marking scale dependent variables (such as the number of MPI ranks or the size of the input) and identifying integer arithmetic instructions that are influenced directly or indirectly by the scale variables. The marked instructions are narrowed down to the most likely to cause overflow bugs by running an instrumented version of the application at small scales and logging the relationship between the resulting values of the instructions and the scale of each run. Their method proved to be successful in finding many scaling bugs in multiple C/C++ test applications and benchmarks, as well as the widely used MPICH library [10].

We adopted their method to analyse the scaling behaviour of supercomputing applications of interest to our research. However we encountered a number of significant limitations in the power of the method, most importantly the ability to verify Fortran applications (which continue to represent a very large fraction of applications run on supercomputers). Additionally, the complexity of production applications, which caused no instructions to be traced at all (see Sect. 3), also needed to be addressed in order for the approach to be viable for our purposes. Real world supercomputing applications are often structured in a modular way, which precludes straight-forward tracing between scale variables and the affected instructions, but this can be disentangled with "optimistic" analysis. In this paper we present OFT,[1] the Overflow Tool, which includes an extension to the tracing algorithm first presented in [13] to handle modular code, with a view to support Fortran applications in particular, and significantly expand the ability to find scaling bugs in production codes.

Our specific contributions presented in this paper are:

- Enable the tracing of integer overflow bugs in Fortran-based applications;
- Present an extension to the tracing algorithm that uses a *backwards/forwards* approach to support tracing of modular code;
- Enable tracing of complex data structures, such as allocatable arrays in Fortran and heap allocated structures in C.

2 Tracing Algorithm Extension

OFT is implemented as an LLVM Module pass and analyses an application in two steps, a static and a dynamic one. The static step detects scale variables that are marked either by MPI communicator size functions or by the user in a whole-application bitcode. These variables are traced to find all 32-bit integer arithmetic operation instructions that are influenced by the scale variables. The user is presented with a list of these instructions, including their location in the source code. Additionally, a modified version of the bitcode is generated, where all scale affected instructions are instrumented to record their maximum value encountered at runtime.

---

[1] The code is available at https://github.com/asimovpp/oft.

Listing 1.1. Limited backward tracing used in [13]. A scale variable is marked on line 5, and influences a potentially overflowable instruction on line 8.

```
1 %rank_299 = alloca i32, align 4
2 ...
3 %2 = bitcast i32* %rank_299 to i8*
4 %3 = bitcast void (..)* @oft_mark_ to void (i8*, ..)*
5 call void (i8*, ..) %3(i8* %2)
6 ...
7 %15 = load i32, i32* %rank_299, align 4
8 %16 = mul nsw i32 %15, 3
```

The user may run the instrumented application to perform the dynamic part of the analysis to reduce the number of false positives. This can be done by running the instrumented application at a few small scales and passing the output to our analysis tool. The tool fits a linear or polynomial function to the max-value versus scale-size relationship of each recorded instruction. The fitted lines can then be extrapolated to scales relevant to each application and it can be seen whether any instruction will overflow. The amount of overhead introduced by instrumentation depends on the number of instructions instrumented, but this can be significantly reduced by focusing on instructions most likely to overflow [13]. Note that multiple test cases may be required in order to exercise every part of a codebase.

Listing 1.2. Common pattern that requires advanced tracing.

```
1 struct my_mpi { int rank; int size; };
2
3 void set_scale_var(struct my_mpi *sv) {
4     MPI_Comm_size(MPI_COMM_WORLD, &(sv->size))
5     MPI_Comm_rank(MPI_COMM_WORLD, &(sv->rank))
6 }
7
8 int main() {
9     struct my_mpi *sv = malloc(sizeof(struct my_mpi));
10     set_scale_var(sv);
11     return sv->rank * 3 + sv->size * 7;
12 }
```

In the method presented in [13] scale variables can only be traced if the emitted instructions are close in scope, for example the scale variable has to be declared, set and then used in subsequent instructions (see Listing 1.1). However, more complicated patterns are often used in real applications, for example to organise the information pertaining to the configuration of a simulation (see Listing 1.2). In such a scenario there may be an initialisation function that sets the MPI environment and other scale variables in a container data structure, which is accessed later in the application's code. As a result, there will be a local pointer in an initialisation function which is set as the scale variable; its tracing is contained within the initialisation function and the rest of the application cannot be reached when tracing. Examples such as the one in Listing 1.3 were not traceable prior to the extensions we introduced as part of OFT.

Listing 1.3. An example of extended tracing enabled by the method presented in this paper. A scale variable is marked on line 10, and influences a potentially overflowable instruction on line 20.

```
1  %.Z0632_306 = alloca i32*, align 8
2  ...
3  %16 = load i32*, i32** %.Z0632_306, align 8
4  %17 = bitcast i32* %16 to i8*
5  %18 = getelementptr i8, i8* %17, i64 4
6  %19 = load i64, i64* %z_b_3_302, align 8
7  %20 = mul nsw i64 %19, -4
8  %21 = getelementptr i8, i8* %18, i64 %20
9  %22 = bitcast void (..)* @oft_mark_ to void (i8*, ..)*
10 call void (i8*, ..) %22(i8* %21)
11 ...
12 %48 = load i32*, i32** %.Z0632_306, align 8
13 %49 = bitcast i32* %48 to i8*
14 %50 = getelementptr i8, i8* %49, i64 4
15 %51 = load i64, i64* %z_b_3_302, align 8
16 %52 = mul nsw i64 %51, -4
17 %53 = getelementptr i8, i8* %50, i64 %52
18 %54 = bitcast i8* %53 to i32*
19 %55 = load i32, i32* %54, align 4
20 %56 = mul nsw i32 %55, 3
```

To address this scenario, it is necessary to trace the scale variable back to its "root", i.e. the first instruction defining the variable: we call this part of the analysis "backward tracing". If GetElementPointer (GEP) instructions[2] are involved, additional steps are required to find instructions performing equivalent memory accesses to the one of the original scale variable. This can result in multiple instructions from which to start tracing the rest of the application.

There are three stages in the backward/forward tracing method:

1. Trace the scale variable *backwards* to its root and record a track.
2. Analyse the track, resolving the root and GEPs in the track, to identify accesses equivalent to the one made by the originally marked scale variable.
3. Trace the accesses *forwards* to the rest of the application.

Stage 1. Firstly, marked scale variables are traced backwards as far as possible in order to find the originally allocated variable. This tracing is done by following bitcast, load, store and GEP operators, as well as function arguments.

---

[2] GEP instructions calculate addresses of sub-elements of data structures based on a base pointer and one or more indices into the data structure [2].

All encountered instructions form a list and are stored as a *trace*. Traced backward, one scale variable may result in multiple traces due to the possibility of a function being called from multiple locations in the analysed application.

Stage 2. Secondly, the traces produced in stage 1 are analysed to find all instructions that access the marked scale variable either directly or via a GEP instruction. The trace is iterated through and the GEP instructions are added to a list. The iteration stops when an stack allocation or global variable, or a call instruction to a predefined function (e.g. malloc), are encountered. The terminating instruction is recorded as the "root" of the trace. The "transitional" instructions like bitcasts and loads/stores are skipped while traversing the trace.

Next, the reduced traces are used to generate a list of scale instructions that indirectly connect to the originally traced scale variable.

1. If a root has been recorded without any GEPs, the root is returned.
2. If a root and a single GEP have been recorded, find and return all equivalent GEPs to the one that was recorded.
3. If a root and multiple GEPs have been recorded, find equivalent GEPs for each recorded GEP in reverse order (resetting the root at each level to the intermediate GEP), and return the last level of equivalent GEPs.

In order to connect a scale variable set via a GEP to further uses of that scale variable, we must find equivalent GEPs to the source GEP. We do this by first finding all GEPs that use the same base pointer as the source GEP by following the define-use relationship chain of the base pointer, including through store and call instructions. The search stops on each branch when the first GEP operation is encountered on that branch, or if there are no further instructions to follow.

Each discovered GEP is compared to the source GEP by comparing the indices of both instructions (the base pointers have already been established to be equal due being results of tracing). Supported types of indices are simple integers, results of load instructions and results of arithmetic operations. For indices that are the results of other instructions, the comparison is applied recursively, thus supporting a sequence of arithmetic operations which computes an index. Nested GEPs with complex index calculations can be generated by Fortran applications that use allocatable arrays which are supported by array descriptors.

Listing 1.3 shows an example where GEP comparison is required, resulting from a Fortran array descriptor. A scale variable is marked on line 10 and can be traced backwards through two GEP instructions (including index calculations) to an `alloca` instruction root. The same variable is accessed (and used thereafter) on line 17, which can be seen by comparing lines 3–8 with lines 12–17.

The GEPs found in this way are not guaranteed to resolve to the same memory accesses in runtime because we do not consider all possible memory interactions that could have happened between the accesses. Doing a definitive trace statically is expensive and impossible for most complex applications. Hence we call these GEPs equivalent, not equal. However, scale variables are normally set at the beginning of an application run and remain unchanged and are not overwritten. Therefore, performing "optimistic" GEP comparisons will produce the correct results in this use case.

Stage 3. Finally, the list of scale instructions are passed on to forward tracing where their influence on the rest of the application is established, as in [13]. Scale instructions are iteratively traced via define-use relationships, including store and load pairs, up to function calls and those calls expanded until no more changes occur.

2.1 Fortran Support

In principle, performing analysis at bitcode level should allow Fortran support automatically. However, in practice, there are key differences between how Fortran bitcode and, for example, C bitcode is generated, which prevent tracing. In Fortran bitcode function calls are performed with an intermediate bitcast operation, which obscures the function name and thus the starting points of tracing cannot be identified. Also, global variables stored in modules are accessed like structure elements, not directly. These issues can be overcome, but they require special cases in the analysis code. However, dynamic arrays in Fortran are significantly more challenging to handle, due to the reliance on array descriptors, and require multi-step processing, such as backwards/forwards tracing described in this paper.

3   Evaluation

To evaluate OFT, we compare its results in two configurations: one that replicates the functionality of the original tool in [13], and the second where we extend its functionality with backward/forward tracing.

The evaluated applications were compiled using LLVM 12.0.0 clang and classic flang [1] without optimisations (-O0). We chose to use -O0 to retain a close link between generated bitcode and the source code, which facilitates identification of scale bugs in the analysed application. Whole-application bitcode was generated at link time using the LLVM gold linker plugin by adding -flto to compilation steps and -fuse-ld=gold -Wl,-plugin-opt=emit-llvm to the linking step. OFT analyses the bitcode and detects functions that set MPI rank and size automatically for tracing. User defined scale variables are detected if they are passed to a function called oft_mark_(variable); the function does not perform any actions, OFT merely registers arguments passed to it for tracing. Note that constant variables defined using macros (e.g. #define in C) cannot be marked in this way. Also, dynamically linked libraries, where the bitcode has not been generated and linked during compilation, are not traced.

Xcompact3d. Xcompact3d [5,14,15] is an open source [4] solver for the incompressible and low Mach number Navier-Stokes equations focused on Large Eddy and Direct Numerical Simulations (LES and DES) of turbulent flows. It is based on a fractional step method for time advancement with a direct Poisson solver based on FFTs for the enforcement of the velocity divergence constraint [5,15]. Combined with 6th order accurate compact finite difference schemes [17] for derivative approximations a quasi-spectral accuracy is achieved. Both the FFTs for the Poisson solver and the compact finite difference schemes map naturally to a 2D pencil-based parallel decomposition as provided by the 2DECOMP&FFT library [18]. As the FFTs and compact finite differences operate in a single pencil at a time the data must be transposed between different decompositions for each spatial dimension, these are implemented using `MPI_ALLTOALL(V)` and the code makes multiple MPI calls per time step.

Implemented in approximately 50k lines of Fortran the resulting whole-application bitcode for the analysis is about 1M lines long. The program accepts as input numerous parameters related to the problem to be studied, in terms of scale-dependence these include the mesh size $n_x \times n_y \times n_z$ and the $p_{row} \times p_{col} = np$ pencil decomposition where np is the number of MPI ranks.

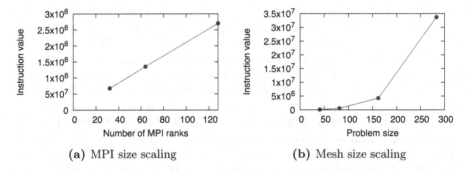

(a) MPI size scaling   (b) Mesh size scaling

Fig. 1. Potentially overflowable instruction values at small scale in Xcompact3d. When extrapolated, (a) will overflow when MPI ranks exceed around 1,000 and (b) when the problem size exceeds 1,291. The problem size is defined as $\sqrt[3]{nx \times ny \times nz}$.

It was found that without backward/forward tracing no tracing was possible at all for Xcompact3d, resulting in no marked overflowable instructions. The reason is that in Xcompact3D the scale variables are stored in a module separate from where they are initialised. With our new backward/forward tracing enabled, OFT reported around 1,000 potentially overflowable instructions. Among these, the value of two calculations grew rapidly in the dynamic part of the analysis, as shown in Fig. 1. These corresponded to two code locations, one initialising random number generator seeds based on the MPI rank and the other printing the total size of the problem. Based on the rate of growth of the values observed in small scale runs, the value in Fig. 1a extrapolated linearly would overflow at around 1,000 MPI ranks and the value in Fig. 1b extrapolated exponentially would overflow with a $1,291^3$ problem size. These values are representative of real-world code use: production runs of 1,000 MPI ranks or more are very common, with scaling demonstrated well beyond this [5,15], and problems in excess of $1,000^3$ mesh nodes have been used to assess performance at extreme scales [8]. While the two bugs that we identified are not critical to the application's successful execution *per se* (it will run and produce correct results), detecting them demonstrates the necessity for our tracing extensions for production HPC applications. The random seed-related overflow bug in particular has potentially serious implications for reproducibility and validation of results in the future. It is worth noting that it only took a few hours to analyse Xcompact3d, with most of that time spent compiling code and running small scale experiments, thus this is an efficent method for assessing application correctness.

OPlus Parallel Library. The Oxford Parallel Library for Unstructured Solvers (OPlus) [6] aims to ease the development of parallel solvers for unstructured grids written in Fortran by insulating the programmer from the burden of writing parallel code. To do so OPlus introduces parallel abstractions such as op_par_loop which allow the application to be written as though serial and executed in parallel by the OPlus framework. By abstracting the parallel execution a program written in the OPlus framework may be executed in a distributed or shared memory context without changes to the source code [6]. This not only allows application experts to focus on their problem domain but also opens the possibility for significant impact through optimisations to the OPlus framework benefiting the whole ecosystem of OPlus programs. The library has been applied to real world problems, for example Crumpton et al [7] show results obtained using a multigrid solver parallelised with OPlus to perform aerodynamic calculations of an aircraft and it has been used in developing industrial CFD codes [16]. The success of this approach has led to the development of a follow on OP-DSL effort [3] which will be the focus of future work. Also studied as part of this work is the ParMETIS [11] parallel graph partitioning library that can be used by OPlus to decompose and reorder the input mesh for parallel processing. It is written in C and parallelised using MPI.

Our analysis shows that without backward/forward tracing some scale instructions are marked, but many more are identified with our extensions to tracing (see Table 1). This shows better code coverage and increases the confidence in the program's correctness after analysis.

We used a 3D Poisson solver which uses multigrid with Jacobi smoothing as a test case to drive the OPlus library for the dynamic part of the analysis. No MPI size related issues were found in OPlus, even when projecting out to 500,000 MPI ranks. However, problem scaling (which is defined by the size of the finest grid) revealed potential overflow bugs related to checking buffer sizes (shown with coloured lines in Fig. 2) which may be triggered with problem size of 1024 and greater. Multiple other instructions (shown in grey in Fig. 2) would overflow if extrapolated exponentially further to 2048. Unfortunately, the test program does not exercise ParMETIS code so we plan to investigate this in future work, in addition to the instructions that may overflow at very large scales.

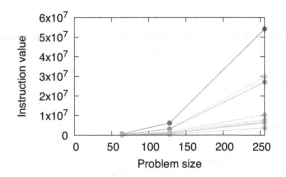

Fig. 2. Potentially overflowable instruction values at small scale in OPlus. When extrapolated, the coloured instruction lines will overflow when the problem size exceeds 1,024 and the gray instruction lines when the problem size exceeds 2,048. The problem size is defined by the size of the finest grid.

Table 1. OFT static analysis result summary. *Lines of Bit Code are given for a test application which includes both OPlus and ParMETIS.

Application	LoBC	Instructions marked (old)	Instructions marked (new)
Xcompact3d	1,167,461	0	1,058
OPlus	154,109*	121	1,156
ParMETIS	154,109*	48	130

4 Related Work

Verification and validation are two intensely studied areas in software development. In the world of scientific and large-scale parallel computing, they have added layers of complexity: will the answer remain correct for an arbitrary level of parallelism, will the application complete successfully when it is scaled up, and are the scale and level of parallelism themselves potential sources of incorrectness? The "Report of the HPC Correctness" summit [9] provides a comprehensive overview of these different topics.

Laguna et al. [12] discuss the general challenges when it comes to trying to address errors at scale. Aside from it being technically challenging, with poor support from debugging tools at very large scales, it is also expensive and time consuming. The conclusion is that ideally it should be possible to predict errors that occur when running at scale based on much smaller job sizes. In [13], the paper that describes the method on which OFT is based, the authors take this learning and apply it to scaling bugs using tracing and dynamic analysis.

Another approach for detecting scaling bugs is presented in [19]. The authors favour a statistical approach, building and applying models of known bug free behaviour at small scale. When an application is run at larger-scale, the behaviour should remain the same; if an error is detected, the correlation will break. A follow-on paper [20] extends the method by adding automatic pinpointing of errors to a region of the code, which was previously not possible. Although both approaches can make use of small-scale runs, and are implementation language agnostic, they rely on data from larger scales in order to detect and locate issues with the application.

5   Conclusion

We have presented an extension to the scale variable tracing algorithm presented in [13]. The backward/forward tracing algorithm enables us to detect more integer oveflow bugs than was possible before as well as to analyse modular Fortran-based applications. For the first time, we were able to evaluate the correctness of Xcompact3d application, finding two scaling bugs, and greatly expanded the analysis coverage for the OPlus and ParMETIS libraries. We plan to expand the capabilities of OFT to detect other kinds of scaling issues, for example memory usage scaling.

Acknowledgements. This research forms part of the Rolls-Royce led EPSRC Prosperity Partnership (Grant Ref: EP/S005072/1) entitled "Strategic Partnership in Computational Science for Advanced Simulation and Modelling of Virtual Systems - AsiMoV". The permission of Rolls-Royce to publish this paper is gratefully acknowledged.

References

1. Classic Flang. https://github.com/flang-compiler/flang. Accessed 27 Feb 2022
2. LLVM Language Reference Manual. https://llvm.org/docs/LangRef.html# getelementptr-instruction. Accessed 25 Feb 2022
3. Oxford Parallel Domain Specific Languages. https://op-dsl.github.io/. Accessed 26 Feb 2022
4. Xcompact3d GitHub repository. https://github.com/xcompact3d/Incompact3d. Accessed 25 Feb 2022
5. Bartholomew, P., Deskos, G., Frantz, R.A., Schuch, F.N., Lamballais, E., Laizet, S.: Xcompact3D: an open-source framework for solving turbulence problems on a Cartesian mesh. SoftwareX **12**, 100550 (2020)
6. Burgess, D.A., Crumpton, P.I., Giles, M.B.: A parallel framework for unstructured grid solvers. Technical Report NA-95/20. Oxford University Numerical Computing Laboratory, Numerical Analysis Group (1994). https://people.maths.ox.ac.uk/gilesm/files/NA-95-20.pdf
7. Crumpton, P.I., Giles, M.B.: Multigrid aircraft computations using the OPlus parallel library. In: Parallel Computational Fluid Dynamics 1995, pp. 339–346. Elsevier (1996)

8. Giannenas, A.E., Laizet, S.: A simple and scalable immersed boundary method for high-fidelity simulations of fixed and moving objects on a cartesian mesh. Appl. Math. Model. **99**, 606–627 (2021)
9. Gopalakrishnan, G., et al.: Report of the HPC Correctness Summit (2017)
10. Gropp, W., Lusk, E., Doss, N., Skjellum, A.: A high-performance, portable implementation of the MPI message passing interface standard. Parallel Comput. **22**(6), 789–828 (1996)
11. Karypis, G.: METIS and ParMETIS. In: Padua, D.A. (ed.) Encyclopedia of Parallel Computing, pp. 1117–1124. Springer, Cham (2011). https://doi.org/10.1007/978-0-387-09766-4_500
12. Laguna, I., et al.: Debugging high-performance computing applications at massive scales. Commun. ACM **58**(9), 72–81 (2015). https://doi.org/10.1145/2667219
13. Laguna, I., Schulz, M.: Pinpointing scale-dependent integer overflow bugs in large-scale parallel applications. In: SC 2016: Proceedings of the International Conference for High Performance Computing, Networking, Storage and Analysis, pp. 216–227. IEEE (2016)
14. Laizet, S., Lamballais, E.: High-order compact schemes for incompressible flows: a simple and efficient method with quasi-spectral accuracy. J. Comput. Phys. **228**(16), 5989–6015 (2009)
15. Laizet, S., Li, N.: Incompact3d: a powerful tool to tackle turbulence problems with up to O(105) computational cores. Int. J. Numer. Meth. Fluids **67**(11), 1735–1757 (2011)
16. Lapworth, L.: Hydra-CFD: a framework for collaborative CFD development. In: International Conference on Scientific and Engineering Computation (IC-SEC), vol. 30 (2004)
17. Lele, S.K.: Compact finite difference schemes with spectral-like resolution. J. Comput. Phys. **103**(1), 16–42 (1992)
18. Li, N., Laizet, S.: 2DECOMP&FFT-a highly scalable 2D decomposition library and FFT interface. In: Cray User Group 2010 Conference, Edinburgh, UK (2010)
19. Zhou, B., Kulkarni, M., Bagchi, S.: Vrisha: using scaling properties of parallel programs for bug detection and localization, pp. 85–96 (2011). https://doi.org/10.1145/1996130.1996143
20. Zhou, B., Too, J., Kulkarni, M., Bagchi, S.: WuKong: automatically detecting and localizing bugs that manifest at large system scales, pp. 131–142 (2013). https://doi.org/10.1145/2462902.2462907

HPC on Heterogeneous Hardware (H3)

AI Benchmarking for Science: Efforts from the MLCommons Science Working Group

Jeyan Thiyagalingam[1]([⊠]), Gregor von Laszewski[2], Junqi Yin[3], Murali Emani[4],
Juri Papay[1], Gregg Barrett[5], Piotr Luszczek[6], Aristeidis Tsaris[3],
Christine Kirkpatrick[7], Feiyi Wang[3], Tom Gibbs[8], Venkatram Vishwanath[4],
Mallikarjun Shankar[3], Geoffrey Fox[2]([⊠]), and Tony Hey[1]

[1] Rutherford Appleton Laboratory, Harwell Campus, Didcot OX11 0QX, UK
t.jeyan@stfc.ac.uk
[2] University of Virginia, Charlottesville, VA 22904-4298, USA
vxj6mb@virginia.edu
[3] Oak Ridge National Laboratory, Oak Ridge, TN 37831, USA
[4] Argonne National Laboratory, Lemont, IL 60439, USA
[5] Cirrus AI, Johannesburg, South Africa
[6] University of Tennessee, Knoxville, TN 37996, USA
[7] SDSC, 10100 Hopkins Dr, La Jolla, CA 92093, USA
[8] NVIDIA, Santa Clara, USA

Abstract. With machine learning (ML) becoming a transformative tool for science, the scientific community needs a clear catalogue of ML techniques, and their relative benefits on various scientific problems, if they were to make significant advances in science using AI. Although this comes under the purview of benchmarking, conventional benchmarking initiatives are focused on performance, and as such, science, often becomes a secondary criteria.

In this paper, we describe a community effort from a working group, namely, MLCommons Science Working Group, in developing science-specific AI benchmarking for the international scientific community. Since the inception of the working group in 2020, the group has worked very collaboratively with a number of national laboratories, academic institutions and industries, across the world, and has developed four science-specific AI benchmarks. We will describe the overall process, the resulting benchmarks along with some initial results. We foresee that this initiative is likely to be very transformative for the AI for Science, and for performance-focused communities.

Keywords: Machine learning · Benchmarks · Science · AI for Science

1 Introduction

Recently, owing to the advances in deep learning, the AI, has been transformational in various aspects of our life. These advances have resulted in machine

© Springer Nature Switzerland AG 2022
H. Anzt et al. (Eds.): ISC High Performance 2022 Workshops, LNCS 13387, pp. 47–64, 2022.
https://doi.org/10.1007/978-3-031-23220-6_4

learning being one of the effective techniques for scientific data analysis, covering a number of domains of sciences, such as material, life, and environmental sciences, particle physics and astronomy [1,9–11,13,22,24]. With AI becoming one of the underpinning technologies for science, there is a considerable amount of attention on several aspects of AI, including, but not limited to, understanding the general applicability of AI/ML to various scientific problems, role of high performance computing on AI/ML, datasets, explainability and robustness of AI/ML techniques, role of small-scale devices on AI/ML, AI/ML-specific algorithms, and scalability of AI/ML techniques with varying volumes of data or varying computational capabilities. With each of these areas being considerably large, it is a substantial undertaking for any single organization or community for developing an overall understanding of various initiatives and their corresponding impacts, particularly across different domains of applications. Ideally, multiple communities should join forces to understand these issues and to make relevant progresses in AI.

MLCommons is one such global initiative with the mission being *accelerate machine learning innovation and increase its positive impact on society*. Although MLCommons™ initiatives were legally setup in 2020, the initiatives originated along with the MLPerf™ benchmarking efforts in 2018. The overarching strands are: benchmarks, datasets, and best practice systems and usage. The current MLCommons initiatives retain the core activities of MLPerf across six distinct focus areas: Training, Training HPC, Inference Datacenter, Inference Edge, Inference Mobile, and Inference Tiny. With application and impact of AI being rather broad, MLCommons is setup along with a number of research working groups with the vision of creating an open *"AI for Research"* ecosystem that is driven by the community for the community.[1] These groups are open to the public, including academics and researchers. The philosophy of MLCommons is to support open-source "AI for Research". The MLCommons Research organization is responsible for overseeing new activities that can lead to new scientific methods in ML, as well as new applications of ML, and currently houses a number of working groups that focus on various areas of ML. These include: ML algorithms (Algorithms), dataset benchmarking (DataPerf), building shared resource infrastructure (Dynabench), benchmarking and best practices for healthcare (Medical), storage benchmarking for ML (Storage), and AI benchmarking for science (Science) [6].

In this paper, we describe the benchmarking initiatives of the Science Working Group, covering our initial set of benchmarks, datasets, policies that govern our benchmarks and benchmarking, rules around submitting new benchmarks or datasets, and some initial results on the evaluation of these benchmarks.

The rest of this paper is organized as follows: In Sect. 2, we describe the working group, goals of the group, and policies adopted by the working group towards science benchmarking. This is then followed by Sect. 3, where we describe the initial set of benchmarks curated by the working group. In Sect. 4, we provide some initial evaluations and discuss the results, and we conclude the paper with future directions in Sect. 5.

---

[1] https://mlcommons.org/en/groups/research/.

2   MLCommons Science Working Group

2.1   About the Working Group

The Science working group [6] was an early member of MLCommons Research, created by the international community working on AI for Science, such as various national laboratories, large-scale experimental facilities, universities and commercial entities, to advance AI for Science along with other national and international level initiatives (e.g., [2]). The overarching drive of the WG is to support various scientific communities that are trying to leverage AI for advancing scientific discoveries. Since the inception, the WG has expanded to include almost 120 members, located across various organizations. The group also works with a number of other working groups within MLCommons, such HPC WG [5], where there are a number of overlapping issues of interest. The overall mission of the group entails collaborative engagements across different domains of sciences.

2.2   Science Benchmarking

Achieving the overall goals of the working group requires a number of sub-aspects to be covered by the WG, such as, (a)identifying a number of representative scientific problems where AI can make a difference, (b) engineering at least one ML solution to the problem, to be considered as a baseline implementation, (c) identifying relevant datasets upon which the ML models can be trained or tested, (d) identifying a scientifically-driven metric that can help recognizing the scientific advancement to the problem, (e) curating and publishing those relevant datasets, (f) publishing the scientific results that can help the communities to develop improve these solutions, and (g) fostering collaborations and scientific achievements across multidisciplinary communities. All these activities are akin to conventional benchmarking, but with a major difference of focusing on scientific merits than pure performance, and hence the notion of science benchmarking. Since the formation, the WG has consulted a large number of scientific organizations, and worked with scientists in achieving some of the sub-aspects listed above. In particular, the WG has succeeded in identifying four science benchmarks derived from different branches of sciences, namely, (a) Cloud masking (`cloud-masking`) [23]—atmospheric sciences, (b) Space group classification of solid state materials from Scanning Transmission Electron Microscope (STEM) data using Deep Learning (`stemdl`) [14]—solid state physics, (c) Time evolution operator (`tevelop`) [7] exemplified using predicting earthquakes—earth sciences and (d) predicting tumor response to drugs (`candle-uno`)—healthcare.

We discuss these benchmarks in detail in Sect. 3. The key aspect here is that a single benchmark is actually a combination of a baseline or reference implementation and one or more datasets. The scientific data here requires a special attention. Although scientific datasets are widespread and common, curating, maintaining, and distributing large-scale, scientific datasets for public consumption is a challenging process, covering various aspects, from abiding by the FAIR principles [26] to distribution to versioning of the datasets. These benchmarks have a multitude of purpose, which are discussed at length in [11, 24]. However, it is worth highlighting that these scientific benchmarks serve one important purpose to the wider AI community: offering an unprecedented pedagogical value across domain boundaries.

2.3 Policies for Benchmarking

Benchmarking is an art and can be very subjective. Without clear policies, the benchmarking results can be subjectively and differently interpreted, leading to the whole initiative not serving the intended purpose. As such, establishing a set of policies, rules and guidelines for evaluating and reporting results for the benchmarks is an important step. The Science WG is in the process of drafting a detailed policy statement, and, here, we mention some of the key points for the reasons of brevity. The overarching policy will cover training and inference benchmarks, with a number of sub-policies focusing on each and every benchmark, as no two benchmarks are the same. In general, the policies will cover the evaluation of benchmarks under two divisions, namely, Open and Closed divisions. Benchmark evaluation under the former will focus on achieving better scientific results (using the established scientific metric). As such, the community has considerable amount of freedom to enhance the underlying ML models or pre- or post-processing aspects of the benchmarks, including data augmentation, wherever that is possible or sensible. Evaluation under the Closed division, on the other hand, limits the freedom and often will list permissible changes for each and every benchmark. In general, pre- and/or post-processing, and data aspects are often kept fixed, with flexibility to change or fine-tune the underling ML model. Similarly, policies around submission of results may also vary across benchmarks. For example, some benchmarks may insist on certain set of measurements to be submitted, such as power or network performance, while some may rely on generic details along with scientific metrics.

3   Benchmarks for the First Release

As outlined in Sect. 2, the WG has consolidated four different benchmarks from four different branches of sciences, namely, `cloud-mask`, `stemdl`, `candle-uno` and `tevelop`. We describe each of these benchmarks in detail, covering the science case, objectives, metrics, data and outline the baseline reference implementation. The aim here is to ensure that the community is aware of these challenges, and can develop techniques outperforming the baseline cases.

3.1   Cloud Masking (`cloud-mask`)

Sea and land surface temperatures (SST and LST), have a significant influence on the Earth's weather, and as such, estimation of SST from space-borne sensors, such as satellites, is crucial for a number of applications in environmental sciences. Satellites are often equipped with special sensors for this purpose, such as the Sea and Land Surface Temperature Radiometer (SLSTR) on board the Sentinel-3 satellite. In principle, it is possible to make direct measurements of surface temperature from these satellites everywhere, except when clouds are present. Clouds can really affect the signals measured by satellites making it much harder to retrieve the temperature measurements. One of the aspects that underpins the derivation of SST is cloud screening, which is a step that marks each pixel of thousands of satellite images as containing cloud or clear sky. This has been, historically, performed using either thresholding or Bayesian method. The purpose of this benchmark is to perform this using machine learning. An example input and output images are given in Fig. 1. We also summarize the key features of this benchmark in Table 1. Details around objective of the benchmark, description of relevant datasets, and reference implementation are given below.

Table 1. Summary of the `cloud-mask` Benchmark.

Description	Image classification at pixel level of satellite imagery
Objective	Classification of pixels of satellite images into cloud and clear sky categories using machine learning
Challenge Stream	Image Segmentation
Domain	Atmospheric Sciences
Metrics	Classification accuracy
Data	Type: Images ($[2400 \times 3000 \times 6]$ and $[1200 \times 1500 \times 3]$)
	Size: 180 GB
	Source: CEDA
	Location: STFC Servers [23]
Reference implementation	SciML-Bench Cloudmask Benchmark [12]

Benchmarking Objectives and Metrics: The scientific objective of the problem is to develop a segmentation model for classifying the pixels in satellite images. This classification allows determining whether the given pixel belongs to a cloud or to a clear sky. The Bayesian techniques [17] used conventionally can lead to sub-optimal outputs in a number of cases, and hence the scope of the `cloud-mask` benchmark is to explore whether ML-driven algorithms can outperform the Bayesian techniques. Although various options are there, in its present form, the `cloud-mask` benchmark is set as a supervised learning problem, with cloud images are treated as inputs. However, like all science cases, the "true" ground truth (or labels), are never available for this case. Hence, the benchmark uses the Bayesian masks, supplied by the provider of the satellite images, as the ground truth. While this is arguable, we believe that in the absence of any ground truth, this is a valid and perfect choice. However, with Bayesian masks not always being accurate or not offering a gold-standard for masks, the resulting model is likely to suffer from learnability issues, which sets the perfect challenge for an ML-driven case. The benchmark can be considered as both

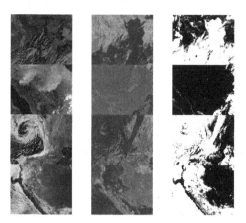

Fig. 1. Cloud mask example. The left column shows the raw images from the Sentinel-3 satellite while the images on the right column shows the predicted probability that a particular pixel is cloud.

training and inference focused, where the science metric is same as the classification accuracy—number of pixels classified correctly. The performance metric, can be inference timing and scalability on the training across a number of GPUs.

Data: The masking can be performed across different satellite imaging modalities. This particular benchmark relies on satellite imagery obtained from the SLSTR sensors equipped as part of the Sentinel-3 satellite. More specifically, the benchmark operates on multi-spectral image data. The overall dataset identified for this benchmark is split into two distinct sets: training set (163 GB) and an inference set (1.7 GB). Each dataset inside these sets is made up of two parts: reflectance and brightness temperature. The reflectance is captured across six channels with the resolution of 2400 × 3000 pixels, and the brightness temperature is captured across three channels with the resolution of 1200 × 1500 pixels. Although the raw satellite images are free to download from the CEDA archive,[2] the curated datasets are available as part of this benchmark, located in object store within the STFC servers. The exact instructions for securing these datasets are outlined in the WG pages.

Reference Implementation: The current reference implementation is variation of the U-Net deep neural network [20], implemented using TensorFlow and Keras, with the support for distributed training using TensorFlow's native library, Distributed Mirrored Strategy. The model represents a U-Net network and consists of 39 layers with two million trainable parameters. Further details can be found in [23].

---

[2] https://www.ceda.ac.uk/.

3.2   STEMDL (stemdl)

State of the art Scanning Transmission Electron Microscopes (STEM) produce
focused electron beams with atomic dimensions, and allow capturing diffraction
patterns arising from the interaction of incident electrons with nano-scale material volumes. Backing out the local atomic structure of said materials requires
compute- and time-intensive analyses of these diffraction patterns (known as
convergent beam electron diffraction or CBED). Traditional analyses of CBED
requires iterative numerical solutions of partial differential equations and comparison with experimental data to refine the starting material configuration. This
process is repeated anew for every newly acquired experimental CBED pattern
and/or probed material (Table 2).

Table 2. Summary of the stemdl benchmark.

Description	Classification and reconstruction of convergent beam electron diffraction, CBED
Objectives	Classification for crystal space groups and reconstruction for local electron density using machine learning
Challenge Stream	Classification
Domain	Solid-state Physics
Metrics	Classification accuracy and/or F1-score
Data	Type: Images
	$[512 \times 512 \times 3]$, label: $[200]$ (Classification)
	$[256 \times 256 \times 256]$, label: $[256 \times 256]$ (Reconstruction)
	Size: 548.7 GB for Classification
	Training samples: 138.7K
	Validation samples: 48.4
	Reconstruction: 10 TB
	Source: Oak Ridge National Laboratory (ORNL)
	Location: OSTI Servers [14]
Reference Implementation	AAIMS repository [21]
	Model: ResNet-50
	Run Instructions: [21]
	Time-to-solution: 40 min on 60 V100 GPUs
References	[14, 15, 19]

Benchmark Objectives and Metrics: The scientific objective of the benchmark is to develop a universal classifier for space group of solid state materials,
and reconstruction of local electron density. As stated before, this is conventionally performed using expensive simulations. The goal here is to use explore the
suitability of ML algorithms for performing advanced analysis of CBED. This
benchmark aims to quantify this using a classification task. As such, the benchmark is set with the supervised learning focus where both the scientific metric

is reflected by the classification accuracy of the ML model. The benchmark also desires to achieve better top-1 classification accuracy and/or F1-score compared to the reference implementation.

Data: A single data sample [14] from this dataset is given by a three-dimensional array formed by stacking various CBED patterns simulated from the same material at different distinct material projections (i.e. crystallographic orientations). Each CBED pattern is a two-dimensional array with 32-bit floating-point image intensities. Associated with each data sample in the dataset is a host of material attributes or properties which are, in principle, retrievable via analysis of this CBED stack. The dataset has (1) 200 crystal space groups out of 230 unique mathematical discrete space groups and (2) local electron density which governs material's property. A more detailed description of the data can be found in CBED database [14]. The dataset is divided into three distinct sets, split across training (148,006 files), testing (18,749 files), and development (20,400 files). The distinct nature of these sets ensures that the model learns the generic symmetry based on space groups instead of memorizing a particular pattern for a material.

Reference Implementation: A detailed description of the baseline implementation method can be found in [19] and [15] along with the reference implementation deposited into the AAIMS repository [21].

3.3   CANDLE-UNO (candle-uno)

The CANDLE (Exascale Deep Learning and Simulation Enabled Precision Medicine for Cancer) project[3] aims to implement deep learning architectures that are relevant to problems in cancer research, addressing problems at three biological scales: cellular (Pilot1 or P1), molecular (Pilot2 or P2), and population (Pilot3 or P3), resulting three mainstreams of benchmarks covering these pilots. The UNO version of the CANDLE suite is a P1 benchmark, which is formed out of problems and data at the cellular level. The high level goal of the problems behind the P1 benchmarks is to predict drug response based on molecular features of tumor cells and drug descriptors. We summarize the key aspects of this benchmark in Table 3, and a detailed description of the objectives, metrics, data and the reference implementation below.

Benchmarking Objectives and Metrics: The goal is to predict tumor response to single and paired drugs, based on molecular features of tumor cells across multiple data sources. It aims to accelerate the scientific goal of establishing the effectiveness of drugs. The ML component aims to accelerate this aspect using ML-based prediction of response values. As such, it is a regression problem, with the science metric being mean absolute error (MAE) between the predicted and ground truth values. On the performance front, the metric is responses predicted per second for a given batch size.

---

[3] https://github.com/ECP-CANDLE/Benchmarks.

Table 3. Summary of the `candle-uno` benchmark.

Description	The Pilot 1 Unified Drug Response Predictor benchmark, Uno to enable drug discovery, drug response prediction from cell lines
Objectives	Predictions of tumor response to drug treatments, based on molecular features of tumor cells and drug descriptors
Challenge Stream	Regression
Domain	Healthcare
Metrics	Validation loss with a minimum score of 0.0054
Data	Type:
	Size: 6.4 GB
	Training samples: 423,952
	Validation samples: 52,994
	Location: ALCF Servers [25]
Reference implementation	Model: Multi-task Learning-based custom model
	Code & Instructions: [4] (see README)
	Ideal performance: 10,667 samples/sec on a single A100 GPU for a batch size of 64

Data: Combined dose response data relies on a number of sources that are specific drug responses to cancer conditions. These include The Cancer Therapeutics Response Portal (CTRP), The Genomics of Drug Sensitivity in Cancer (GDSC), The NCI Sarcoma (SCL), The NCI Small Cell Lung Cancer (SCLC), The NCI-60 Human Cancer Cell Line Screen single drug response (NCI60), A Large Matrix of Anti-Neoplastic Agent Combinations drug pair response (ALMANAC.FG, ALMANAC.FF, ALMANAC.1A), The Genentech Cell Line Screening Initiative (gCSI) and The Cancer Cell Line Encyclopedia (CCLE). The ML model can be trained on any subset of a dataset obtained from these dose response data sources. The benchmark relies on a dataset that includes both single drug dose response measurements pair dose response measurements. More specifically, there are 27,769,716 single drug dose response measurements and 3,686,475 drug pair dose response measurements. The combined raw dose response data has 3,070 unique samples and 53,520 unique drugs. For the scope of this work, we used the AUC configuration of Uno that utilizes a single data source, namely, CCLE. We show the data distribution between the samples in Table 4. The training can be accelerated by using a pre-staged dataset file. This static dataset can, however, be pre-built. The datasets are publicly available from the CANDLE site [25]. These are directly downloadable with relevant download scripts, including a pre-built static dataset to simplify the deployment.

Reference Implementation: The reference implementation implements a deep learning architecture with 21 M parameters in TensorFlow framework in Python. The code is publicly available on GitHub. It can be run in both training and inference modes. However, this benchmark is defined to be training focused.

Table 4. The data distribution between the single and pair drug samples.

	Growth	Sample	Drug1	Drug2	MedianDose
ALMANAC.1A	208,605	60	102	102	7.000000
ALMANAC.FF	2,062,098	60	92	71	6.698970
ALMANAC.FG	1,415,772	60	100	29	6.522879
CCLE	93,251	504	24	0	6.602060
CTRP	6,171,005	887	544	0	6.585027
GDSC	1,894,212	1,075	249	0	6.505150
NCI60	18,862,308	59	52,671	0	6.000000
SCL	301,336	65	445	0	6.908485
SCLC	389,510	70	526	0	6.908485
gCSI	58,094	409	16	0	7.430334

A dedicated script in the repository downloads all required datasets. The primary metric to evaluate for this application is the model throughput (samples per second). The model is said to converge when the validation loss reaches a certain threshold, for example 0.0054. The throughput is then measured for the last epoch when the model converges. With the required packages in the software stack, Uno can be run on diverse systems. More details on running Uno can be found in the repository (Table 4).

3.4   Time Series Evolution Operator (tevelop)

Time series capture the variation of values against time, and common to a number of scientific problems. Time series can be multiple dimensions. For example geospatial datasets are two-dimensional series, based both on time and spatial position. One of the common tasks when dealing with time series is the ability to predict or forecast them in advance. Such a task is considerably easier if the underlying time series has a clear evolution structure across dimensions. For example, if the evolution structure can be established on the spatial aspects (i.e. there is a strong correlation between nearby spatial points), estimating the evolution becomes relatively easier. The problem chosen is termed as a spatial bag where there is spatial variation, but it is not clearly linked to the geometric distance between spatial regions. In contrast, traffic-related time series have a strong spatial structure. As such, identifying the evolution in time series is a common problem across a number of domains. This particular benchmark focuses on extracting the evolution, using earthquake as the driving example. We summarize the key features of the benchmark in Table 5.

Benchmarking Objectives and Metrics: The scientific objective is to extract the evolution of a time series, exemplified using earthquake forecasting. To make the benchmarking exercise more focused, this forecasting is done

Table 5. Summary of the `tevelop` Benchmark

Description	Earthquake Forecasting [3, 7, 8, 16]
Objectives	Improve the quality of Earthquake forecasting in a region of Southern California.
Metrics	Normalized Nash-Sutcliffe model efficiency coefficient (NNSE) with $0.8 \leq NNSE \leq 0.99$
Data	Type: Richter Measurements with spatial and temporal information (Events)
	Input: Earthquakes since 1950
	Size: 11.3 GB (Uncompressed), 21.3 MB (Compressed)
	Training samples: 2,400 spatial bins
	Validation samples: 100 spatial bins
	Source: USGS Servers [3]
Reference Implementation	[8]

on a subset of the overall earthquake dataset for the region of Southern California. Conventional methods for forecasting relies on statistical techniques. Here, the aim is to use ML for not only extracting the evolution, but also to test the effectiveness using forecasting. The exact scientific metric for quantifying the benefit of the forecasting is the Nash Sutcliffe Efficiency (NSE) [18]. It is also possible to qualitatively asses prediction by comparing the observed earthquake, if one desires, but the benchmarks relies on the former [7].

Data: The benchmark relies on a very small subset of the earthquake data from United States Geological Survey (USGS) focused between the regions of Southern California (latitude: 32°N to 36°N, longitude: −120°S to −114°S). The subset of the data for this region covers all earthquakes in that region since 1950. There are four measurements per record, namely, magnitude, spatial location, depth from the crust, and time. The curated dataset is organized to cover this in different temporal and spatial bins. Although the actual time lapse between measurements is one day, we accumulate this into a fortnightly data. The region is then divided into a grid of 40 × 60 with each pixel covering actual zone of 0.1° × 0.1 or 11 km × 11 km grid. The dataset also includes an assignment of pixels to known faults, and a list of the largest earthquakes in that region from 1950. We have chosen various samplings of the dataset to provide both input and predicted values. These include time ranges from a fortnight up to four years. Furthermore, we calculate summed magnitudes and depths and counts of significant quakes (magnitude < 3.29).

Reference Implementation: The benchmark includes three distinct deep learning-based reference implementations. These are Long short-term memory (LSTM)-based model, Google Temporal Fusion Transformer (TFT) [16]-based model, and a custom hybrid transformer model. The TFT-based model uses two distinct LSTMs, covering a an encoder a decoder with a temporal attention-based transformer. The custom model includes a space-time transformer for the Decoder and a two-layer LSTM for the encoder. Each model predicts NSE and generates visualizations illustrating the TFT for interpretable multi-horizon time series forecasting [16]. Details of the current reference models can be found in [7].

4   Results from Initial Evaluations

In this section, we present some of the early results obtained initial evaluations of our benchmarks. As this is the first time we are presenting these findings, it is worth noting that the initial evaluations are far from being complete or perfect, especially when lacking any relative measures to benchmark against. However, these initial evaluations are likely to provide more insight into how these evaluations should be tuned or scoped in future releases. We outline these aspects in Table 6. We relied on three different platforms, namely, Pearl,[4] Summit[5] and Theta,[6] along with other architectures, for our evaluations.

Table 6. Summary of the Evaluation.

Benchmark	Platforms/(architectures)	Science metric(s)	Performance metric(s)
cloud-mask	Pearl (V100) Summit (V100)	Accuracy	Scalability
stemdl	Summit (V100)	Accuracy, F1	–
candle-uno	Theta (A100)	–	Throughput
tevelop	K80, P100, V100 A100, RTX3080, RTX3090	NNSE	Training time

4.1   Results for the cloud-mask Benchmark

We show the masking accuracy for the training and validation cases in Fig. 2a, and the scalability results in Fig. 2b. We show two different performance results. In the former, we show how the accuracy of the classification varies against the number of epochs, either trained or tested. The latter shows how the benchmark training scales (average time per epoch) on the Pearl and Summit platforms when the number of GPUs are varied up to 32. There are a number of observations here:

- The accuracy improves with the number of epochs (both testing and training), but they do not exceed 95% of the accuracy shows by the Bayesian mask-based ground truth. However, this has to be interpreted very carefully. The

---

[4] https://www.turing.ac.uk/research/asg/pearl.

[5] https://www.olcf.ornl.gov/summit/.

[6] https://www.alcf.anl.gov/alcf-resources/theta.

Bayesian-based mask is not necessarily the best either [17]. Hence the sub-optimal outputs does not mean, the ML model is not being effective. We are exploring different means for verifying the real accuracy of the model (such as using data from LIDAR and ground sensors).

– Pearl offers better scalability when more than two GPUs are used, while for Summit this has to be four GPUs. However, interestingly, both Pearl and Summit are based on V100 GPUs with totally two different configurations. However, there are performance differences between these platforms when a few GPUs are used. A more detailed investigation is needed both on the scalability and why few GPUs offer sub-optimal performance.

It is very important to note that these conclusions would not have been possible without these initial evaluations.

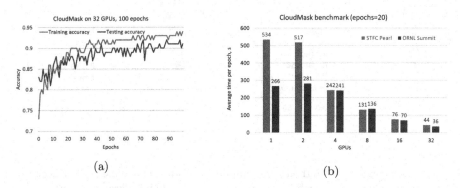

(a)   (b)

Fig. 2. Performance of `cloud-mask`. The classification accuracy against the number of epochs (on Pearl), and the training scalability of benchmark both on Pearl and Summit platforms are shown in (a) and (b), respectively.

4.2   Results for the `stemdl` Benchmark

We used the Namsa simulation code[7] on the Summit to generate CBED patterns for well over 60,000 solid-state materials, representing nearly every known crystal structure, on which we used the reference implementation. Although the classification accuracy is the ultimate metric, this is influenced by a number of hyper-parameters that underpin our network architecture. As such, it is important to ensure that the best classification is achieved through hyper-parameter search. Although various techniques exist for hyper-parameter search, and that itself can be a separate benchmarking challenge, here we show the validation accuracy and F1-score for various hyper-parameter sets. There are a number of observations here, but to highlight two: first, as expected, hyper-parameters have an overall influence on the rate and best performance of the benchmark, and secondly the performance converges rapidly for some of the hyper-parameter

---
[7] https://www.osti.gov/biblio/1631694.

settings, namely, for the ResNet-101 model. We also show how the accuracy can further be improved from baseline performance in Fig. 4, where the raw performance is marked as (1), along with various optimizations, including, pre-processing (2), time augmentation (3), regularization (4), and by using deeper models (5). These optimizations improve the accuracy from 14% to 57% through these optimizations (Fig. 3).

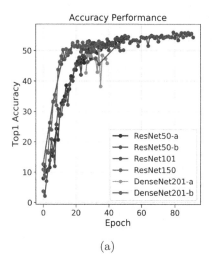 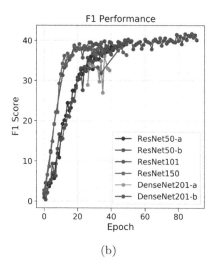

(a)   (b)

Fig. 3. Performance of `stemdl` on the Summit platform. The classification accuracy and F1-Score against the number of epochs for various hyper-parameter settings are shown in (a) and (b), respectively. See text for more details.

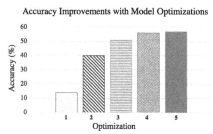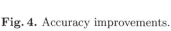 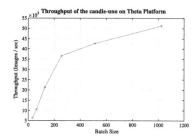

Fig. 4. Accuracy improvements.   **Fig. 5.** Throughput of `candle-uno`.

4.3   Results for the `candle-uno` Benchmark

We used the reference implementation on the ThetaGPU platform. As stated before, our metric is throughput (i.e., number of samples processed per second) for varying batch sizes on a single GPU. We present the results in Fig. 5. The results show that the overall throughput increases with the batch size, showing a trend of saturation, and highlights that more investigation is needed to qualify future implementations, especially across different platforms.

4.4   Results for the `tevelop` Benchmark

The `tevelop` benchmark is evaluated by using it to predict earthquakes over the Southern Californian region. The earthquake data is often binned to generate the spatial time series, and for this evaluation, we consider the bin size of two-weeks. With this, we used our reference model with three baseline implementations, namely, LSTM, TFT and Transformer-based models. We first present the performance results of the LSTM-based model focused on science metric in Fig. 6. The results show that ML can, indeed, offer significant benefits. Additional examples ranging from a week to a year are presented in [7].

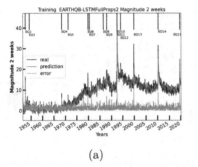 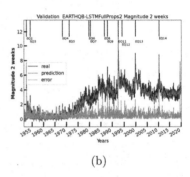

(a)   (b)

Fig. 6. Performance of the `tevelop` in predicting earthquakes, for two-week window periods. The training performance and the validation accuracy are shown in (a) and (b), respectively covering real and predicted values and the error.

To compare and contrast the performance of different baseline models, we use a subset of the full dataset (which has 2,400 pixels) consisting of 500 most active pixels, divided at the ratio of 4:1 for training and validation. We then compare these models, across a number of time periods, ranging from two-weeks to four years, and compare their normalized NSE (NNSE) values, with the interpretation of increasing NNSE values imply better predictions. We show the resulting performance in Table 7. A more detailed set of examples, and illustrations can be found in [7]. Finally, we compare the performance of this benchmark on different architectures, and show the results in Fig. 7.

Table 7. Comparison of different models for earthquake prediction.

Period	LSTM		TFT		Transformer	
	Train	Test	Train	Test	Train	Test
2 weeks	0.902	0.869	0.931	0.885	0.893	0.856
4 weeks	0.896	0.883	–	–	0.866	0.883
2 months	0.887	0.881	–	–	0.865	0.881
3 months	0.925	0.893	0.976	0.922	0.919	0.881
6 months	0.950	0.900	0.972	0.882	0.954	0.896
1 year	0.923	0.865	0.976	0.853	0.955	0.876
2 years	0.928	0.830	–	–	0.855	0.830
4 years	0.937	0.770	–	–	0.817	0.770

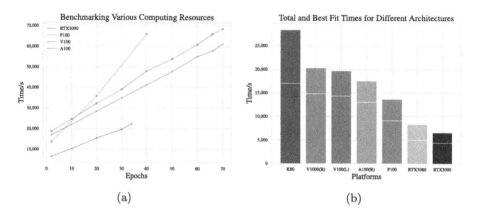

(a)   (b)

Fig. 7. Evaluation of the `tevelop` benchmark across a range of architectures and storage systems. Figure (a) shows the training performance while (b) shows the impact of different storage systems (such as, local HDD, local NVMe, NFS).

5   Conclusions

In this paper, we have discussed the initiatives of the MLCommons Science Working Group for advancing the AI for Science through science-specific benchmarks. By collaboratively working with multiple communities, covering various international laboratories, academic institutes and industries, the working group has succeeded in identifying a number of key scientific problems, and developed benchmarks for them. While this is a notable step forward for AI benchmarking, it is significant step for AI benchmarking focused on science. The working group is also actively working on a number of future benchmarks, drawing expertise from various domains. These future benchmarks will cover additional domains, and will also include a variety of classes of ML algorithms, such as surrogate models, inference- and training-based evaluations, and generative models, to mention a few. The future work will also give emphasis to the FAIR aspects of the data, ensuring that all our datasets are FAIR compliant. The working group is aspiring to support submissions of evaluations, so that the community is aware of performance benefits of different systems.

We are very hopeful that this initiative becomes beneficial to the scientific community in a number of different ways, such as supporting easy selection of ML algorithms for a given scientific problem, or for pedagogical purposes. With such purposes, we are hopeful the combined effect of MLCommons is likely to make a significant difference in the AI community.

Acknowledgements. We would like to thank Samuel Jackson from the Scientific Machine Learning Group at the Rutherford Appleton Laboratory (RAL) of the Science and Technology Facilities Council (STFC)(UK) for his contributions towards the Cloud Masking benchmark. This work was supported by Wave 1 of the UKRI Strategic Priorities Fund under the EPSRC grant EP/T001569/1, particularly the 'AI for Science' theme within that grant, by the Alan Turing Institute and by the Benchmarking for AI for Science at Exascale (BASE) project under the EPSRC grant EP/V001310/1, along with the Facilities Funding from Science and Technology Facilities Council (STFC) of UKRI, NSF Grants 2204115 and 2204115, and DOE Award DE-SC0021418. This manuscript has been authored in part by UT-Battelle, LLC, under contract DE-AC05-00OR22725 with the US Department of Energy (DOE). The publisher acknowledges the US government license to provide public access under the DOE Public Access Plan (http://energy.gov/downloads/doe-public-access-plan). This research also used resources from the Oak Ridge and Argonne Leadership Computing Facilities, which are DOE Office of Science user facilities, supported under contracts DE-AC05-00OR22725 and DE-AC05-00OR22725, respectively, and from the PEARL AI resource at the RAL, STFC. This work would not have been possible without the continued support of MLCommons and MLCommons Research, and in particular, we thank Peter Mattson, David Kanter and Vijay Janapa Reddi for their leadership and help.

References

1. Callaway, E.: It will change everything: DeepMind's AI makes gigantic leap in solving protein structures. Nature **588**, 203–204 (2020)
2. Department of Energy: Artificial Intelligence for Science in the US Department of Energy. https://science.osti.gov/Initiatives/AI. Accessed 30 June 2022
3. Earthquake Data. https://github.com/laszewsk/mlcommons-data-earthquake. Accessed 30 June 2022
4. ECP-CANDLE: Benchmarks. GitHub. https://github.com/ECP-CANDLE/Benchmarks/tree/master/Pilot1/Uno. Accessed 30 June 2022
5. Farrell, S., et al.: MLPerf HPC: a holistic benchmark suite for scientific machine learning on HPC systems (2021). arXiv:2110.11466
6. Fox, G., Hey, T., Thiyagalingam, J.: Science data working group of MLCommons research. Web Page. https://mlcommons.org/en/groups/research-science/. Accessed 30 June 2022
7. Fox, G., Rundle, J., Donnellan, A., Feng, B.: Earthquake nowcasting with deep learning. Geohazards **3**(2), 199 (2022)
8. Fox, G.C., von Laszewski, G., Knuuti, R., Butler, T., Kolesar, J.: MLCommons science benchmark earthquake code. https://bityl.co/COro

9. Henghes, B., Pettitt, C., Thiyagalingam, J., Hey, T., Lahav, O.: Benchmarking and scalability of machine-learning methods for photometric redshift estimation. Mon. Notices Royal Astron. Soc. **505**(4), 4847–4856 (2021)

10. Henghes, B., Thiyagalingam, J., Pettitt, C., Hey, T., Lahav, O.: Deep learning methods for obtaining photometric redshift estimations from images. Mon. Notices Royal Astron. Soc. **512**(2), 1696–1709 (2022)

11. Hey, T., Butler, K., Jackson, S., Thiyagalingam, J.: Machine learning and big scientific data. Philos. Trans. Ser. A Math. Phys. Eng. Sci. **378**(2166), 20190054 (2020)

12. Jackson, S., Cox, C., Thiyagalingam, J., Hey, T.: SciML-Bench: SciML benchmarking suite for AI for science: cloud masking benchmark. GitHub (2021). https://github.com/stfc-sciml/sciml-bench/tree/master/sciml_bench/benchmarks/slstr_cloud. Accessed 30 June 2022

13. Jumper, J., Evans, R., Pritzel, A., et al.: Highly accurate protein structure prediction with AlphaFold. Nature **596**, 583–589 (2021)

14. Laanait, N., Borisevich, A., Yin, J.: A database of convergent beam electron diffraction patterns for machine learning of the structural properties of materials (2019). https://www.osti.gov/servlets/purl/1510313/

15. Laanait, N., et al.: Exascale deep learning for scientific inverse problems (2019). arXiv:1909.11150

16. Lim, B., Arık, S.Ö., Loeff, N., Pfister, T.: Temporal fusion transformers for interpretable multi-horizon time series forecasting. Int. J. Forecast. **37**(4), 1748–1764 (2021)

17. Merchant, C.J., Harris, A.R., Maturi, E., Maccallum, S.: Probabilistic physically based cloud screening of satellite infrared imagery for operational sea surface temperature retrieval. Q. J. R. Meteorol. Soc. **131**(611), 2735–2755 (2005)

18. Nash, J., Sutcliffe, J.: River flow forecasting through conceptual models part I - a discussion of principles. J. Hydrol. **10**(3), 282–290 (1970)

19. Pan, J.: Probability flow for classifying crystallographic space groups. In: Nichols, J., Verastegui, B., Maccabe, A.B., Hernandez, O., Parete-Koon, S., Ahearn, T. (eds.) SMC 2020. CCIS, vol. 1315, pp. 451–464. Springer, Cham (2020). https://doi.org/10.1007/978-3-030-63393-6_30

20. Ronneberger, O., Fischer, P., Brox, T.: U-Net: convolutional networks for biomedical image segmentation. In: Navab, N., Hornegger, J., Wells, W.M., Frangi, A.F. (eds.) MICCAI 2015. LNCS, vol. 9351, pp. 234–241. Springer, Cham (2015). https://doi.org/10.1007/978-3-319-24574-4_28

21. STEMDL Benchmark: STEMDL Benchmark. GitHub. https://github.com/at-aaims/stemdl-benchmark. Accessed 30 June 2022

22. Tanaka, A., Tomiya, A., Hashimoto, K.: Deep Learning and Physics. Springer, Singapore (2021). https://doi.org/10.1007/978-981-33-6108-9

23. Thiyagalingam, J., et al.: SciML-bench: SciML benchmarking suite for AI for science. GitHub (2021). https://github.com/stfc-sciml/sciml-bench. Accessed 30 June 2022

24. Thiyagalingam, J., Shankar, M., Fox, G., Hey, T.: Scientific machine learning benchmarks. Nat. Rev. Phys. **4**, 413–420 (2022)

25. Index of Pilot1 CANDLE-UNO Benchmark. https://ftp.mcs.anl.gov/pub/candle/public/benchmarks/Pilot1/combo. Accessed 30 June 2022

26. Wilkinson, M.D., et al.: The FAIR guiding principles for scientific data management and stewardship. Sci. Data **3**(1) (2016)

Performance Analysis of Matrix Multiplication for Deep Learning on the Edge

Cristian Ramírez[1]([✉])[iD], Adrián Castelló[1][iD], Héctor Martínez[2][iD], and Enrique S. Quintana-Ortí[1]([✉])[iD]

[1] Universitat Politècnica de València, Valencia, Spain
crirabe@upv.es, {adcastel,quintana}@disca.upv.es
[2] Universidad de Córdoba, Córdoba, Spain
el2mapeh@uco.es

Abstract. The devices designed for the Internet-of-Things encompass a large variety of distinct processor architectures, forming a highly heterogeneous zoo. In order to tackle this, we employ a simulator to estimate the performance of the matrix-matrix multiplication (GEMM) kernel on processors designed to operate at the edge. Our simulator adheres to the modern implementations of GEMM, advocated by GotoBLAS2, BLIS, OpenBLAS, etc., to carefully account for the amount of data transfers across the memory hierarchy of different algorithmic variants of the kernel. A small collection of experiments provide the necessary data to calibrate the simulator and deliver highly accurate estimations of the execution time for a given processor architecture.

Keywords: Performance analysis · Matrix multiplication · High performance · IoT processors

1 Introduction

Deep learning (DL) technologies are currently being deployed at the edge in order to improve safety and privacy, reduce the latency for the end-user, and/or decrease energy consumption [4,7,12]. The IoT (Internet-of-Things) appliances operating in this scenario comprise a myriad of different processor designs, facing limited computational and memory capacities as well as strict restrictions in power supply and, sometimes, time-to-response. As a consequence, the software running on these devices has to be carefully optimized.

The general matrix-matrix multiplication (GEMM) is a key kernel for the realization of the convolutional deep neural networks (DNNs) employed in signal processing and computer vision, as well as for the transformers applied to natural language processing tasks [10]. However, developing an efficient realization of GEMM is a time-consuming chore, aggravated by the heterogeneity of IoT architecture designs, which requires a good expertise on high performance computing and computer architecture.

H. Anzt et al. (Eds.): ISC High Performance 2022 Workshops, LNCS 13387, pp. 65–76, 2022.
https://doi.org/10.1007/978-3-031-23220-6_5

In this paper we contribute toward dealing with the development of optimized realizations of GEMM for IoT processors leveraging a performance simulator to experiment with different algorithmic alternatives for this kernel, prior to actually implementing and testing them. Our simulator, built upon the GotoBLAS2 ideas [2] and the BLIS framework [5,11], mimics the algorithm behavior in order to capture the data transfers across the memory hierarchy, and requires only a few experimental data which can be collected via simple calibration experiments. The result delivers highly accurate estimations of the execution time on an GAP8 parallel-ultra-low power processor (PULP).

2   Blocked Algorithms for GEMM

2.1   The Baseline Algorithm for GEMM

Consider the GEMM $C \mathrel{+}= AB$, where the dimensions of the matrix operands A, B and C are $m \times k$, $k \times n$ and $m \times n$, respectively. Many current high performance realizations of this kernel, in open-source as well as commercial linear algebra libraries, adhere to the GotoBLAS ideas [2] to implement it as a collection of five nested loops around a *micro-kernel* that performs a tiny GEMM. In rough detail, the instances of GEMM in these libraries apply tiling (blocking) to the matrix operands so that 1) a $k_c \times n_c$ block of B is packed into a buffer B_c that is intended to reside in the L3 cache memory; 2) an $m_c \times k_c$ block of A is packed into a buffer A_c for the L2 cache memory; and 3) a specific $k_c \times n_r$ block of B_c, say B_r, is expected to reside in the L1 cache memory during the execution of the micro-kernel. Furthermore, 4) the micro-kernel performs all the arithmetic, retrieving the data of A_c from the L2 cache, B_r from the L1 cache, and C directly from memory; see Fig. 1. These techniques are adopted, for example, in BLIS [11], OpenBLAS [6], AMD BLIS and, presumably, Intel MKL, among others.

The baseline algorithm for GEMM presented in this section, hereafter referred to as B3A2C0,[1] features a micro-kernel that comprises a sixth loop, and is usually encoded directly in assembly (or in C with vector intrinsics). At each iteration, this loop updates an $m_r \times n_r$ micro-tile of C, say C_r, by performing an outer product involving (part of) one row of A_c and one column of B_r, as illustrated by loop L6 in Fig. 1. The cost of loading/storing C_r can be expected to be amortized over the k_c iterations of this loop, as $m_r, n_r \ll k_c$ in practice. Furthermore, a specialized packing of A_c and B_c ensures that their entries are retrieved with unit stride from the micro-kernel; see Fig. 2.

2.2   A Family of Algorithms for GEMM

A different re-ordering of the GEMM loops, combined with an appropriate selection of the loop strides, result in other variants for GEMM, which favor that the

---

[1]   The notation introduced in [9] refers to the baseline algorithm as B3A2C0, where each letter denotes one of the matrix operands, and the subsequent number indicates the cache level where that operand resides (with 0 referring to the processor registers). The same matrix operand resides in both the L1 and L3 caches.

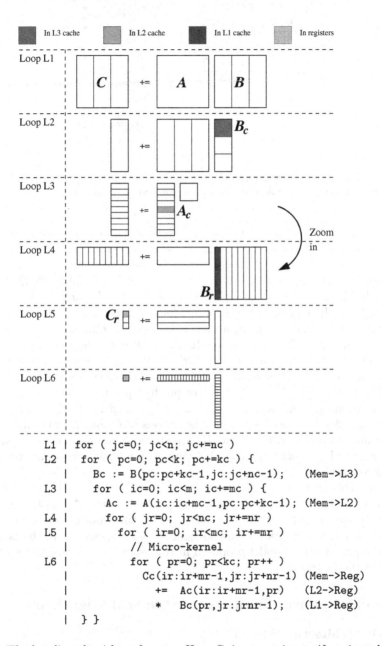

```
L1 | for ( jc=0; jc<n; jc+=nc )
L2 |   for ( pc=0; pc<k; pc+=kc ) {
   |     Bc := B(pc:pc+kc-1,jc:jc+nc-1);    (Mem->L3)
L3 |     for ( ic=0; ic<m; ic+=mc ) {
   |       Ac := A(ic:ic+mc-1,pc:pc+kc-1);  (Mem->L2)
L4 |       for ( jr=0; jr<nc; jr+=nr )
L5 |         for ( ir=0; ir<mc; ir+=mr )
   |           // Micro-kernel
L6 |           for ( pr=0; pr<kc; pr++ )
   |             Cc(ir:ir+mr-1,jr:jr+nr-1)   (Mem->Reg)
   |             +=  Ac(ir:ir+mr-1,pr)       (L2->Reg)
   |              *  Bc(pr,jr:jrnr-1);       (L1->Reg)
   | } }
```

Fig. 1. The baseline algorithm of GEMM. Here C_c is a notation artifact, introduced to ease the presentation of the algorithm while A_c and B_c are actual buffers that maintain copies of certain blocks of A and B.

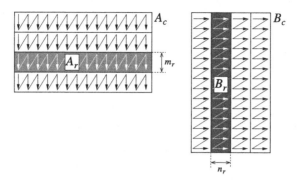

Fig. 2. Packing in the baseline algorithm of GEMM. Note how the entries of A, B are re-organized into A_c, B_c in micro-panels of m_r rows, n_r columns, respectively.

matrix blocks of A, B, C reside in specific levels of the memory hierarchy, from the main memory to the cache(s) and processor registers. This was analyzed in [3,9], and more recently, in the context of DL inference, in [1].

Figure 3 shows the algorithms for two of these variants: C3B2A0 and B3C2A0. In the former case, 1) an $m_c \times n_c$ block of C is packed into a buffer C_c for the L3 cache memory; 2) a $k_c \times n_c$ block of B is packed into a buffer B_c for the L2 cache memory; and 3) an $m_r \times n_c$ block of C_c, say C_r, is intended to reside in the L1 cache memory. In the B3C2A0 case, the roles of C and B are swapped. Furthermore, 4) in both variants the micro-kernel operates with a $m_r \times k_r$ micro-tile of A, streamed directly from the memory to the registers, performing a small, $m_r \times k_r$ matrix-vector product per iteration of Loop L6 (n_c iterations), each involving a single column of C_r and (part of) B_c; see Fig. 3. In addition, in order to ensure accessing the entries of C and B with unit stride from the micro-kernel, both C_c and B_c are stored following the same pattern shown for A_c in Fig. 2, with C_c also re-organized in micro-panels of m_r rows but B_c in micro-panels of k_r rows.

To close this section, we note that swapping the roles of A and B in the three previous algorithms, yields three alternative variants: A3B2C0, C3A2B0, A3C2B0 [1]. However, given the symmetric role of the input operands of GEMM (A, B), these other variants present no significant differences from the point of view of the performance model proposed in this work and, therefore, we do not consider in the following.

3   A Performance Simulator for GEMM Algorithms

3.1   IoT Architecture Model

We make the following considerations with respect to the target IoT processor:

- The processor is equipped with a single core, with a SIMD (single instruction multiple data) arithmetic units capable of working with 32 vector registers of width 32 bits (4 INT8 numbers).

```
L1 | for ( jc=0; jc<n; jc+=nc )
L2 |   for ( ic=0; ic<m; ic+=mc ) {
   |     Cc = C(ic:ic+mc-1,jc:jc+nc-1);          (Mem->L3)
L3 |     for ( pc=0; pc<k; pc+=kc ) {
   |       Bc := B(pc:pc+kc-1,jc:jc+nc-1);        (Mem->L2)
L4 |       for ( ir=0; ir<mc; ir+=mr )
L5 |         for ( pr=0; pr<kc; pr+=kr )
L6 |           for ( jr=0; jr<nc; jr++ )
   |             Cc(ir:ir+mr-1,jr)                (L1->Reg)
   |               += Ac(ir:ir+mr-1,pc:pc+kr-1)  (Mem->Reg)
   |                * Bc(pc:pc+kr-1,jr);          (L2->Reg)
   |       }
   |     C(ic:ic+mc-1,jc:jc+nc-1) = Cc;          (L3->Mem)
   |   }

------------------------------------------------------------------

L1 | for ( jc=0; jc<n; jc+=nc )
L2 |   for ( pc=0; pc<k; pc+=kc ) {
   |     Bc := B(pc:pc+kc-1,jc:jc+nc-1);          (Mem->L3)
L3 |     for ( ic=0; ic<m; ic+=mc ) {
   |       Cc := C(ic:ic+mc-1,jc:jc+nc-1);        (Mem->L2)
L4 |       for ( pr=0; pr<kc; pr+=kr )
L5 |         for ( ir=0; ir<mc; ir+=mr )
L6 |           for ( jr=0; jr<nc; jr++ )
   |             Cc(ir:ir+mr-1,jr)                (L2->Reg)
   |               += Ac(ir:ir+mr-1,pc:pc+kr-1)  (Mem->Reg)
   |                * Bc(pc:pc+kr-1,jr);          (L1->Reg)
   |       C(ic:ic+mc-1,jc:jc+nc-1) := Cc;        (L2->Mem)
   | } }
```

Fig. 3. Variants of the family of algorithms for GEMM with A resident in the processor registers: C3B2A0 (top) and B3C2A0 (bottom).

- The memory comprises four levels, from fastest/smallest to slowest/largest referred to as R (for processor registers), L1, L2, and M (for main memory).
- There is a strict control of the data transfers between memory levels. The L1 and L2 levels can thus be viewed as "scratchpad" memories instead of conventional caches.
- The capacity of each memory level will be denoted as C_L, with L denoting the corresponding level.
- The transfer rates between two levels will be referred to as $T_{O,D}$, with the subindices O/D specifying the origin/destination memory levels.

From the point of view of the algorithms, for simplicity we assume that computation is not overlapped with data transfers involving the scratchpad memories.

3.2   Validation

Hardware Platform. For the validation of our performance simulator, in this work we target the GAP8 PULP, from GreenWaves Technologies. This system

Table 1. Transfers rates in the GAP8 FC. The packing/unpacking rates (three first rows) were measured when transferring chunks of $r = 4$ elements at a time.

	Transfer	Mbytes/s	B3A2C0	C3B2A0	B3C2A0
Packing	$T_{\mathrm{M,M}}$	1.62E + 00	B to B_c	C to C_c	B to B_c
Packing	$T_{\mathrm{M,L2}}$	5.30E − 01	A to A_c	B to B_c	C to C_c
Unpacking	$T_{\mathrm{L2,M}}$	6.54E − 01	–	–	C_c to C
Copy	$T_{\mathrm{M,L1}}$	8.81E + 00	B_c to B_r	C_c to C_r	B_c to B_r
Stream from	$T_{\mathrm{M,R}}$	4.87E − 01	C to reg.	A to reg.	A to reg.
Micro-	$T_{\mathrm{L1,R}}$	1.78E + 02	B_r to reg.	C_r to reg.	B_r to reg.
Kernel	$T_{\mathrm{L2,R}}$	7.18E + 00	A_c to reg.	B_c to reg.	C_c to reg.

comprises 1) a fabric controller (FC) core for control, communications, and security functions; 2) a cluster of 8 cores designed for the execution of parallel algorithms; and 3) a specialized accelerator (HWCE). All these components share the same 512-KB L2 *memory area* (MA). Furthermore, the FC has a 16-KB L1 MA while the cluster cores and HWCE share a 64-KB multi-banked TCDM L1 (data/instruction) MA. Several DMA (direct memory access) units allow fast transfers between MAs. The banks of the shared L1 MA can be accessed from the cluster cores in a single cycle. In comparison, accessing data in external MAs (referred to as L3 memory,) incurs a very high cost and, therefore, should be avoided whenever possible. The GAP8 relies on DMA units to transfer data to/from peripherals and in between the internal L1 and L2 MAs, which can be viewed as "scratchpads". The DMA unit is used to transfer data to/from peripherals, including the L3 memory.

Following our assumptions on the IoT processor, we only target the FC core, and associated MAs, for the validation and experimentation in the remainder of the paper. Repeating the analysis for the GAP8 cluster, using a multi-threaded version of GEMM, is left as part of future work.

Calibration. We conducted a series of experiments to estimate the data transfer rates between the MAs in the GAP8 FC, with the results offered in Table 1. The first block-row there comprises the packing/unpacking operations associated with blocking (tiling) and are performed by the three outermost loops of the algorithms. They all involve the L3 MA (M in the model), and the results were obtained using DMA programmed transfers of $r = 4$ elements "at a time". This type of calibration is required because packing/unpacking the matrix operands into their corresponding buffers, requires a reorganization that copies the data in "chunks" of r consecutive elements in memory; see Fig. 2. We could also verify that, when multiplying r by a factor s, the transfer rate also increased in the same proportion. For example, for algorithm B3A2C0, B is packed into the buffer B_c taking into account the dimension $n_r = 4$ of the micro-kernel, and proceeds at a rate of 1.62 MBytes/s. If the micro-kernel for this algorithm is modified to use $n_r = 8$, we experimentally observed that the rate was doubled, to 3.24 MBytes/s. Our simulator takes this consideration into account.

The second block-row in the table (consisting of a single row) corresponds to the copy between the L3 and L1 MAs. This copy is implicit in the case of the conventional GEMM algorithms, which assume a cache system (and therefore, they do not appear reflected in the formulation of the algorithms), but they need to be explicitly programmed in the case of scratchpads.

The third block-row of results are for the data streaming performed from inside the micro-kernel.

A separate experiment with a micro-kernel designed for the GAP8 FC, with A resident in the processor registers and the two other operands placed in the proper MAs, showed an arithmetic performance of 5.64 billions of INT8 arithmetic operations per second (INT8 GOPS).

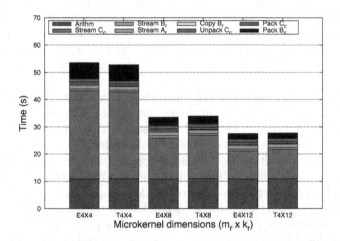

Fig. 4. Distribution of costs among the different components of the B3C2A0 algorithm using micro-kernels of dimension 4×4, 4×8, and 4×12. The labels starting with "E" and "T" below each bar distinguish between results from experimentation and the simulator, respectively.

Validation. We next leveraged our implementation of the C3B2A0 algorithm for the GAP8 FC described in [8] in order to assess the accuracy of our simulator. For this purpose, we selected a GEMM of moderate dimensions: $m, n, k = 256, 784, 2304$. (These particular dimensions were chosen because they arise when applying the lowering approach [10] to transform the convolution operator in layer #10 of MobileNetV1 DNN into a GEMM.) Once we fixed the micro-kernel dimension ($m_r \times k_r$, for this particular variant), we then set the scratchpad configuration parameters (m_c, n_c, k_c) so that C_r, B_c respectively maximize the occupancy of the L1, L2 MAs of the GAP8 FC.

Figure 4 shows that the simulator, tuned with the calibrated transfer and arithmetic rates, estimates the execution time of the actual implementation remarkably well. Overall, the relative errors of the simulator in all these tests remained below 2%.

4   Performance Analysis

As argued in the introduction of this paper, the ultimate goal of our performance simulator for GEMM is to experiment with different algorithmic alternatives for the kernel, prior to going through the effort of implementing and testing any of them on a specific IoT processor.

In this section we evaluate the three algorithmic variants for GEMM discussed earlier: B3A2C0, C3B2A0 and B3C2A0, comparing their estimated performance as a function of the dimension of the internal micro-kernel ($m_r \times n_r$ for the first variant; and $m_r \times k_r$ for last two), and initially leveraging the same problem case from the previous section: $m, n, k = 256,784,2304$. The size of the selected micro-kernels was determined following the assumptions on the width of the SIMD arithmetic unit (32 bits) and number of vector registers (32) made in Sect. 3.

Figure 5 shows the distribution of the arithmetic and data/transfer costs, for the three variants, using the performance simulator calibrated for the GAP8 platform. An assumption of our basic simulator is that the arithmetic rate is independent of the micro-kernel dimension and this results in all cases reporting the same cost due to arithmetic. (This assumption may be reasonable for very simple IoT processor designs, but we will discuss this aspect further at the end of this section.) In contrast, for this particular GEMM shape, the distribution of costs and the global execution time is highly dependent on the algorithmic variant and micro-kernel dimensions. Thus, for this particular layer of MobileNetV1, both B3A2C0 and B3C2A0 tend to favor "low-and-fat" micro-kernels, such as 4×24, while C3B2A0 yields better performance for "squarish" ones: 8×12 and 12×8.

Finally, Fig. 6 compares the estimated execution time for the GEMM resulting from the application of lowering to all the convolution layers of MobileNetV1. The particular dimensions of these layers are specified in Table 2, together with the optimal micro-kernel dimension for each algorithmic variant and layer dimensions. (Layer #28 is skipped because it does not correspond to a convolution operator.)

The results in this final experiment show that a high variability of the execution time, in accordance with the heterogeneity of the GEMM shapes for the distinct layers, but also a general advantage of the B3A2C0 variant. This was not totally unexpected as B3A2C0 mimics the baseline algorithm in BLAS instances such as those in GotoBLAS2, OpenBLAS and BLIS, and presents the advantage of reducing the number of stores in memory during the update of the result C. However, we note that this variant depends on the underlying architecture offering an efficient SIMD support for the outer product, which may not be the case for all Iot processors. For example, the GAP8 architecture is especially

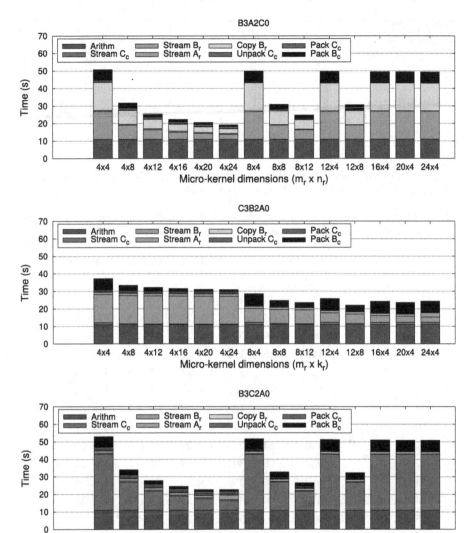

Fig. 5. Execution time of the three algorithms for the GEMM in layer #10 of MobileNetV1 estimated using the performance simulator calibrated for the GAP8.

designed to deliver high performance for the scalar (or dot) product, which favors the GEMM variants with A resident in the processor registers (C3B2A0 and B3C2A0). This would be reflected in a different (INT8) GOPS rates in our simulator, depending on the type of micro-kernel and architecture design. This architecture-specific adaptation of the simulator to the arithmetic units in the target processor is left as part of future work.

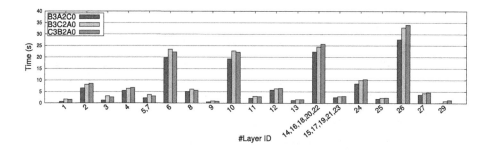

Fig. 6. Execution time of the three algorithms for the GEMM in MobileNetV1 estimated using the performance simulator calibrated for the GAP8.

Table 2. GEMM operations in the convolution layers arising in MobileNetV1 transformed via lowering, and dimension of the optimal micro-kernel.

#Layer ID	m	n	k	B3A2C0	C3B2A0	B3C2A0
1	32	12544	27	4×24	24×4	8×12
2	32	12544	288	4×24	8×12	4×24
3	64	12544	32	4×24	24×4	12×8
4	64	3136	576	4×24	12×8	4×24
5,7	128	3136	128	4×24	24×4	4×24
6	128	3136	1152	4×24	12×8	4×24
8	128	784	1152	4×24	12×8	4×24
9	256	784	128	4×24	24×4	8×12
10	256	784	2304	4×24	12×8	4×24
11	256	784	256	4×24	12×8	4×20
12	256	196	2304	4×24	12×8	4×24
13	512	196	256	4×24	24×4	4×24
14, 16, 18, 20, 22	512	196	4608	4×24	12×8	4×24
15, 17, 19, 21, 23	512	196	512	4×24	12×8	4×24
24	512	49	4608	8×12	12×8	4×24
25	1024	49	512	8×12	12×8	4×24
26	1024	49	9216	8×12	12×8	4×24
27	1024	49	1024	8×12	12×8	4×24
29	1024	1000	1	4×24	24×4	24×4

5   Discussion and Future Work

In order to address the heterogeneous zoo of IoT processor designs for edge computing, we have leveraged a performance simulator for estimating the execution costs of GEMM that offers very useful information about which algorithmic variant can better fit a particular architecture.

At the same time, we recognize this work needs to be extended and improved along several paths. As part of future work, we plan to explore several avenues:

- Micro-kernels with A/B or C resident in registers are usually cast in terms of distinct assembly SIMD (single instruction, multiple data) instructions. This needs to be taken into account in the calibration experiments.
- Also, most current processors architectures are equipped with DMA controllers. This complicates programming in order to orchestrate asynchronous transfers with computation, and requires double buffering thus reducing the amount of memory for the buffers in the intermediate memory levels.
- Finally, we plan to modify the memory model to take into account actual cache memories instead of scratchpads. This introduces challenges associated with modeling the effects of cache associativity, cache eviction, and replacement policies.

Acknowledgments. This work was supported by the research project PID2020-113656RB-C22 of MCIN/AEI/10.13039/501100011033. C. Ramírez is a "Santiago Grisolía" fellow supported by *Generalitat Valenciana*. Adrián Castelló is a FJC2019-039222-I fellow supported by MCIN/AEI/10.13039/501100011033. H. Martínez is a "Ayuda Postdoctoral" fellow supported by *Consejería de Transformación Económica, Industria, Conocimiento y Universidades de la Junta de Andalucía*.

This project has received funding from the European High-Performance Computing Joint Undertaking (JU) under grant agreement No 955558. The JU receives support from the European Union's Horizon 2020 research and innovation programme, and Spain, Germany, France, Italy, Poland, Switzerland, Norway.

References

1. Castelló, A., Igual, F.D., Quintana-Ortí, E.S.: Anatomy of the BLIS family of algorithms for matrix multiplication. In: 2022 30th Euromicro International Conference on Parallel, Distributed and Network-based Processing (PDP) (2022, to appear)
2. Goto, K., van de Geijn, R.A.: Anatomy of a high-performance matrix multiplication. ACM Trans. Math. Softw. **34**(3), 12:1–12:25 (2008)
3. Gunnels, J.A., Henry, G.M., van de Geijn, R.A.: A family of high-performance matrix multiplication algorithms. In: Alexandrov, V.N., Dongarra, J.J., Juliano, B.A., Renner, R.S., Tan, C.J.K. (eds.) ICCS 2001. LNCS, vol. 2073, pp. 51–60. Springer, Heidelberg (2001). https://doi.org/10.1007/3-540-45545-0_15
4. Hazelwood, K., et al.: Applied machine learning at Facebook: a datacenter infrastructure perspective. In: IEEE International Symposium on High Performance Computer Architecture, pp. 620–629 (2018)
5. Low, T.M., Igual, F.D., Smith, T.M., Quintana-Ortí, E.S.: Analytical modeling is enough for high-performance BLIS. ACM Trans. Math. Softw. **43**(2) (2016)
6. OpenBLAS (2012). http://xianyi.github.com/OpenBLAS/
7. Park, J., et al.: Deep learning inference in Facebook data centers: characterization, performance optimizations and hardware implications. arXiv:1811.09886 (2018)
8. Ramírez, C., Castelló, A., Quintana-Ortí, E.S.: A BLIS-like matrix multiplication for machine learning in the RISC-V ISA-based GAP8 processor. J. Supercomput. **78**, 18051–18060 (2022). https://doi.org/10.1007/s11227-022-04581-6

9. Smith, T.M., van de Geijn, R.A.: The MOMMS family of matrix multiplication algorithms. CoRR arXiv:1904.05717 (2019)
10. Sze, V., Chen, Y.H., Yang, T.J., Emer, J.S.: Efficient processing of deep neural networks: a tutorial and survey. Proc. IEEE **105**(12), 2295–2329 (2017). https://doi.org/10.1109/JPROC.2017.2761740
11. Van Zee, F.G., van de Geijn, R.A.: BLIS: a framework for rapidly instantiating BLAS functionality. ACM Trans. Math. Softw. **41**(3), 14:1–14:33 (2015)
12. Wu, C., et al.: Machine learning at Facebook: understanding inference at the edge. In: IEEE International Symposium on High Performance Computer Architecture (HPCA), pp. 331–344 (2019)

Strategies for Efficient Execution of Pipelined Conjugate Gradient Method on GPU Systems

Manasi Tiwari[✉] and Sathish Vadhiyar

Department of Computational and Data Sciences, Indian Institute of Science, Bangalore, India
{manasitiwari,vss}@iisc.ac.in

Abstract. The Preconditioned Conjugate Gradient (PCG) method is widely used for solving linear systems of equations with sparse matrices. A recent version of PCG, Pipelined PCG (PIPECG), eliminates the dependencies in the computations of the PCG algorithm so that the non-dependent computations can be overlapped with communication. In this paper, we develop three methods for efficient execution of the Pipelined PCG algorithm on GPU accelerated heterogeneous architectures. The first two methods achieve task-parallelism using asynchronous executions of different tasks on multi-core CPU and a GPU. The third method achieves data parallelism by decomposing the workload between multi-core CPU and GPU based on a performance model. We performed experiments on both the K40 and V100 GPU systems and our methods give up to 8x speedup and on average 3x speedup over PCG CPU implementation of Paralution and PETSc libraries. They also give up to 5x speedup and on average 1.45x speedup over PCG GPU implementation of Paralution and PETSc libraries. The third method also provides an efficient solution for solving problems that cannot be fit into the GPU memory and gives up to 6.8x speedup for such problems.

Keywords: Preconditioned conjugate gradient · Pipelined methods · Heterogeneous architectures · GPU · Asynchronous executions

1 Introduction

Conjugate Gradient (CG) [7] is one of the most widely used iterative methods for finding the solution of linear systems $Ax = b$ with symmetric positive definite sparse matrices. A preconditioner can be applied to the system to condition the input system and to improve convergence.

Today's HPC systems have accelerators like GPUs along with traditional multi-core CPUs. The programming models for these accelerators are different from that of the multi-core processors as well. In order to use all the resources available within a compute node efficiently, we must interleave the features in the programming models in such a way that we achieve the best possible performance from the platform.

H. Anzt et al. (Eds.): ISC High Performance 2022 Workshops, LNCS 13387, pp. 77–89, 2022.
https://doi.org/10.1007/978-3-031-23220-6_6

The main computational kernels in the PCG method are Sparse Matrix Vector Product (SPMV), Preconditioner Application (PC), Vector-Multiply-Adds (VMAs) and Dot Products. For distributed memory systems, the bottleneck in PCG is the synchronization that occurs on all cores due to the allreduce in the dot products of the algorithm. **Pipelined PCG (PIPECG)** proposed by Ghysels et al. [6], on which this work is based, has one allreduce per iteration. By introducing extra VMAs, they eliminate the dependencies between the dot products and PC+SPMV of PCG. The aim of doing this is to overlap the communication introduced by dot products with PC and SPMV. The resulting algorithm offers another advantage which makes it a perfect candidate for our hybrid executions on a single node-single GPU system. As the PC and SPMV in PIPECG do not depend on results of the previous dot products, we can execute them simultaneously on multi-core CPU and GPU. This would require communicating data between CPU and GPU, thus introducing additional costs. We show that by using asynchronous streams efficiently, we can hide the complete time for data movement between CPU and GPU.

We develop three methods for efficient execution of PIPECG on a single node-single GPU system. The first two methods, **Hybrid-PIPECG-1** and **Hybrid-PIPECG-2**, achieve task-parallelism by simultaneous execution of the dot products on multi-core CPU and PC and SPMV on the GPU. They are different in the amount of data that needs to be moved between the CPU and GPU in every iteration of PIPECG. The third method, **Hybrid-PIPECG-3**, achieves data parallelism by decomposing the workload between multi-core CPU and GPU based on a performance model and then using asynchronous data transfers for PIPECG iterations. We use CUDA streams for asynchronous data transfers between CPU and GPU. We performed experiments on both the K40 and V100 GPU systems and our methods give up to 8x speedup and on average 3x speedup over PCG CPU implementation of Paralution and PETSc libraries. Our methods give up to 5x speedup and on average 1.45x speedup over PCG GPU implementation of Paralution and PETSc libraries. Hybrid-PIPECG-3 method also provides an efficient solution for solving problems that cannot be fit into the GPU memory and gives up to 6.8x speedup for such problems.

2   Related Work

To achieve optimum performance of the PCG method on GPU systems, many works have concentrated on efficient GPU implementation of the PC kernel. Algebraic Multigrid GPU implementations are presented in [3]. Incomplete LU and Cholesky factorizations on GPUs are presented in [9]. Research works also concentrate on optimizing the most time consuming kernel in PCG, the SPMV kernel [5]. Different sparse matrix formats have been proposed in [4] to improve SPMV performance on GPUs. All the works mentioned above concentrate on kernel executions only on the GPUs. They do not utilize the multi-core CPU present in the system. Our work is different from all the works described above since we aim to utilize all the available resources of the system and accelerate the performance of the PCG method as a whole. Furthermore, our work can be used in conjunction with the enhanced kernels on the GPUs mentioned above.

3   Background

PCG: PCG introduced by Hestenes [7] is given in Algorithm 1. The computational kernels in PCG are SPMV in line 10, PC in line 15, VMAs in lines 9, 13 and 14 and dot products in lines 11, 16 and 17. In PCG, we can see that the operation in every line depends on the operation in the previous line. There are no independent computations in each iteration which can be executed simultaneously.

PIPECG: PIPECG was proposed by Ghysels et al. [6]. As shown in Algorithm 2, PIPECG introduces extra VMAs (on lines 11, 12, 13, 17, 18) to remove the dependencies between the dot products (lines 19, 20, 21) and PC (line 22) and SPMV (line 23) so that PC and SPMV can be computed while dot products are being computed. We can use PIPECG for our hybrid executions as the dot products can be executed on the CPU while PC+SPMV can be executed simultaneously on GPU as they are not dependent on each other. This strategy helps us utilize all the resources in the GPU accelerated node and achieve optimum performance.

Algorithm 1 PCG Method
1: $r_0 = b - Ax_0$; $u_0 = M^{-1}r_0$;
2: $\gamma_0 = (u_0, r_0)$; $norm_0 = \sqrt{(u_0, u_0)}$
3: **for** i=0,1... **do**
4:    **if** $i > 0$ **then**
5:        $\beta_i = \gamma_i/\gamma_{i-1}$
6:    **else**
7:        $\beta_i = 0$
8:    **end if**
9:    $p_i = u_i + \beta_i p_{i-1}$
10:    $s = Ap_i$
11:    $\delta = (s, p_i)$
12:    $\alpha = \gamma_i/\delta$
13:    $x_{i+1} = x_i + \alpha p_i$
14:    $r_{i+1} = r_i - \alpha s$
15:    $u_{i+1} = M^{-1}r_{i+1}$
16:    $\gamma_{i+1} = (u_{i+1}, r_{i+1})$;
17:    $norm_{i+1} = \sqrt{(u_{i+1}, u_{i+1})}$
18: **end for**

Algorithm 2 PIPECG Method
1: $r_0 = b - Ax_0$; $u_0 = M^{-1}r_0$; $w_0 = Au_0$;
2: $\gamma_0 = (r_0, u_0)$; $\delta = (w_0, u_0)$; $norm_0 = \sqrt{(u_0, u_0)}$
3: $m_0 = M^{-1}w_0$; $n_0 = Am_0$
4: **for** i=0,1... **do**
5:    **if** $i > 0$ **then**
6:        $\beta_i = \gamma_i/\gamma_{i-1}$;
7:        $\alpha_i = \gamma_i/(\delta - \beta_i\gamma_i/\alpha_{i-1})$;
8:    **else**
9:        $\beta_i = 0$; $\alpha_i = \gamma_i/\delta$
10:    **end if**
11:    $z_i = n_i + \beta_i z_{i-1}$
12:    $q_i = m_i + \beta_i q_{i-1}$
13:    $s_i = w_i + \beta_i s_{i-1}$
14:    $p_i = u_i + \beta_i p_{i-1}$
15:    $x_{i+1} = x_i + \alpha_i p_i$
16:    $r_{i+1} = r_i - \alpha_i s_i$
17:    $u_{i+1} = u_i - \alpha_i q_i$
18:    $w_{i+1} = w_i - \alpha_i z_i$
19:    $\gamma_{i+1} = (r_{i+1}, u_{i+1})$
20:    $\delta = (w_{i+1}, u_{i+1})$
21:    $norm_{i+1} = \sqrt{(u_{i+1}, u_{i+1})}$
22:    $m_{i+1} = M^{-1}w_{i+1}$
23:    $n_{i+1} = Am_{i+1}$
24: **end for**

4   Methodology

4.1   Hybrid-PIPECG-1 Method

In the standard GPU implementation of PCG, the CPU launches CUDA kernels for VMAs, dot products, PC and SPMV on the GPU and then remains idle. In PIPECG, we have independent kernels and thus, we can make use of the idle CPU cores. We show the execution flow of Hybrid-PIPECG-1 in Fig. 1(a).

The rectangular boxes show the operation performed and the number within the bracket is the line number of Algorithm 2 that the box executes. The solid thick arrow represents data movement and its direction shows the source and destination of the data movement. The matrix A, the vectors b and x have been moved to the GPU prior to this execution flow.

The implementation starts with executing the initialization steps on the GPU. After this, the *for* loop starts which iterates until the preconditioned residual norm becomes smaller than the user defined tolerance. In each iteration, α and β are calculated on the CPU. Then the Vector Operations are executed on the GPU which update the vectors w, r and u among others. We know that dot products γ, δ and $norm$ can be executed simultaneously with PC and SPMV. For executing these dot products on the CPU cores, the CPU needs to have the vectors w, u and r but as the updated vectors are on the GPU, we have to copy them to the CPU at every iteration. So here, we define a stream which asynchronously copies w, r and u while GPU carries on with its kernel executions. The CPU waits on this stream till the copy is completed and then proceeds to calculate γ, δ and $norm$ by using all available cores. Thus, in Hybrid-PIPECG-1, PC and SPMV computations on the GPU are overlapped with the data movement from GPU to CPU and the dot product calculation on the CPU cores.

4.2   Hybrid-PIPECG-2 Method

Hybrid-PIPECG-1 requires copy of 3N elements from GPU to CPU in every iteration which can become costly for linear systems with vectors with large N, as the time for copying will exceed the PC + SPMV times thus degrading the overall performance. Therefore, we develop Hybrid-PIPECG-2 shown in Fig. 1(b) to reduce the number of vectors to be copied from GPU to CPU in every iteration.

If we want to compute the dot products γ, δ and $norm$ on the CPU, we need to have w, u and r vectors on the CPU. Instead of copying the updated vectors from the GPU at every iteration, we can update them on the CPU itself. In PIPECG method in Algorithm 2, we see that we can update w, u and r on the CPU using the vectors z, q and s. In turn, we would need n and m for updating z and q. This means the CPU should have a copy of z, q, s, n, m, w, u and r. For updating these vectors on the CPU, we can copy only n from the GPU to CPU. As shown in Fig. 1(b), in the for loop, after calculating α and β, the vector n is copied from the GPU to the CPU on the user defined stream. While the copy is progressing, both CPU and GPU perform their operations. GPU proceeds with

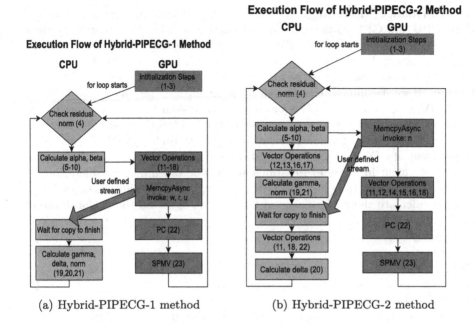

(a) Hybrid-PIPECG-1 method   (b) Hybrid-PIPECG-2 method

Fig. 1. Task parallel algorithms

its Vector Operations, PC and SPMV kernels. On the CPU, we observe that for updating the vectors z, w and m, CPU needs the vector n. While n is being copied, CPU can proceed with the update of vectors q, s, r and u as they don't need n. After vector updates, γ and $norm$ can be calculated. Then the CPU waits on the user defined stream until the copy is copied. After n is successfully received, CPU can proceed to update z, w and m vectors and compute δ.

Thus, with Hybrid-PIPECG-2, we are able to reduce the number of vector copies to one per iteration. Moreover, the data movement is hidden by computations on the CPU so the CPU doesn't have to be idle while the copy proceeds.

4.3 Hybrid-PIPECG-3 Method

Hybrid-PIPECG-1 and Hybrid-PIPECG-2 achieve task parallelism by executing independent kernels on CPU and GPU simultaneously. But for linear systems with even larger N, executing redundant computations for complete vectors of length N on both CPU and GPU proves to be counter-productive. Thus, we propose a data parallel version of PIPECG, Hybrid-PIPECG-3, where the matrix and vectors are decomposed between the CPU and GPU and both these entities carry out PIPECG on their data with communication between each other for important data. This method can also be used for problems that cannot fit in the GPU memory. Hybrid-PIPECG-3 consists of 3 parts: Performance modelling, Data decomposition, and the actual PIPECG iterations.

1. Performance Modelling: We want to calculate the relative performances of the CPU and GPU so that we can decompose data between them according to these relative performances. For this, we execute the SPMV kernel for the complete matrix A (nnz elements) on CPU and GPU separately. We select the SPMV kernel because that is the most time dominating kernel in the PIPECG iteration. If we decompose the data in a way such that the time taken by CPU for SPMV kernel on its data is equal to the time taken by GPU for the SPMV kernel on its data, then complete overlap of the most time consuming kernel is achieved. Hence, we perform five executions of SPMV on both CPU and the GPU for nnz elements. We perform five executions so that effects of cache locality that become prevalent in the later iterations are also be taken into consideration.

Once we have the time taken by CPU cores, t_{cpu} and the time taken by GPU, t_{gpu}, we calculate the performance of CPU cores, s_{cpu} and the performance of GPU, s_{gpu} as follows:

$s_{cpu} = nnz/t_{cpu}$

$s_{gpu} = nnz/t_{gpu}$

Then, we calculate the relative performance r_{cpu} and r_{gpu} as follows:

$r_{cpu} = s_{cpu}/(s_{cpu} + s_{gpu})$

$r_{gpu} = s_{gpu}/(s_{cpu} + s_{gpu})$

After we obtain r_{cpu} and r_{gpu}, we now divide the nnz into two parts, nnz_{cpu} and nnz_{gpu} as follows:

$nnz_{cpu} = nnz * r_{cpu}$

$nnz_{gpu} = nnz - nnz_{cpu}$

For ease of implementation, we do not assign exact nnz_{cpu} elements to CPU and nnz_{gpu} elements to GPU. Instead, we find out the number of rows to be assigned to the CPU, N_{cpu}, which would contain either equal to or slightly less number of non-zeroes than nnz_{cpu}. This gives a 1-D decomposition of the A matrix. N_{gpu} is then obtained by $N - N_{cpu}$.

2. Data Decomposition: Now that we have N_{cpu} and N_{gpu}, we assign N_{cpu} rows to the CPU and N_{gpu} rows to the GPU. We also divide the vectors between the CPU and GPU using same parameters. The division of vectors ensures that there are no redundant computations as both CPU and GPU will be acting on just their local elements. But in every iteration, the SPMV kernels of both CPU and GPU will require the full m vector. After 1-D decomposition, the CPU has N_{cpu} elements of the m vector and the GPU has the other N_{gpu} elements. It is clear that we need to copy these partial vectors from their home device to the other device.

In order to hide the time taken for this copy, we perform a further decomposition of the nnz_{cpu} into $nnz1_{cpu}$ and $nnz2_{cpu}$ in such a way that all the nnz's in $nnz1_{cpu}$ need only the local N_{cpu} elements of m for the SPMV. When SPMV kernel acts on just $nnz1_{cpu}$ elements, we call it SPMV part 1. After the copy of N_{gpu} elements of m is complete, we will then commence SPMV part 2 on $nnz2_{cpu}$ elements which will complete the entire SPMV. We perform the same for nnz_{gpu}. So, through this further local decomposition, we are able to achieve better overlap of computations with communication. In effect, we have achieved the 2-D decomposition of the matrix A. This is illustrated in Fig. 2.

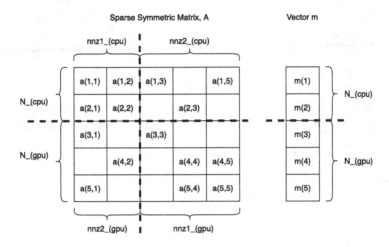

Fig. 2. 2-D decomposition of Matrix A

3. Execution Flow of Hybrid-PIPECG-3 Method: Fig. 3 shows the execution flow of the Hybrid-PIPECG-3 method.

For Performance Modelling, we execute the SPMV kernel on CPU and GPU simultaneously. After we get N_{cpu} and N_{gpu}, we perform 2-D decomposition of the matrix A and also decompose the vectors. After the decomposition step, the PIPECG method starts. Both CPU and GPU perform the initialization steps on their data except the computation of n vector. Then the for loop starts. After checking the residual norm, CPU calculates α and β. Then asynchronous copy of m vector is started from CPU to GPU as well as GPU to CPU. These two Copy's are executed simultaneously using two user defined streams, Stream 1 and Stream 2. Similar to Hybrid-PIPECG-2 method, while CPU and GPU wait for m vector to be copied so that they can calculate vector n, the vectors that do not depend on n can be updated. This results in vector operations for q, s, p, x and r. After these vector updates, γ and $norm$ can be computed. To further use the waiting time, CPU and GPU can compute SPMV part 1 as described in Sect. 4.3. Both CPU and GPU then wait for the Copy's to finish. With proper data decomposition, this wait is negligible as the data movement time is completely overlapped with useful computations. Then, CPU and GPU execute SPMV part 2 and obtain the vector n. They update the vectors that depend on n and apply PC. Finally, they compute δ and follow the same steps iteratively.

Thus, with Hybrid-PIPECG-3, we achieve data parallelism by decomposing data between CPU and GPU and the simultaneous operations on CPU and GPU are overlapped with the asynchronous data movement.

Execution Flow of Hybrid-PIPECG-3 Method

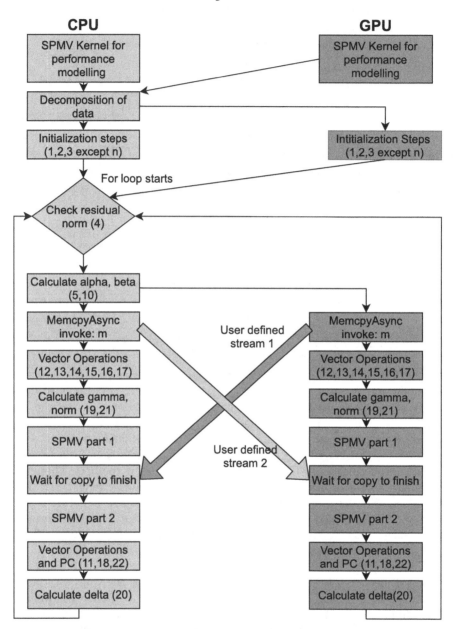

Fig. 3. Execution flow of Hybrid-PIPECG-3 method

5   Experiments and Results

Experimental Setup: We run our tests on two systems: first, a Tesla K40 GPU with 15 Streaming Multiprocessors (SMX), 5 GB memory, 16 core Intel CPU and second, a Volta V100 GPU with 80 SMX, 32 GB memory and 32 core Intel CPU. We employ OpenMP for using all CPU cores and we employ CUDA kernels, cublas and cusparse libraries for GPU. We run experiments on matrices from the SuiteSparse Matrix Collection [1] as well our own generated Poisson matrices shown in Table 1. N is the number of rows and nnz is the number of non-zeroes in the matrix. We solve a linear system of equations $Ax = b$ with the exact solution $x_0 = 1/\sqrt{N}$, where N is the number of rows of A and $b = Ax_0$. We set the absolute tolerance to 10^{-5}, maximum number of iterations to 10000 and use Jacobi preconditioner. We run all tests to convergence and compare the total execution times of Hybrid-PIPECG-1, Hybrid-PIPECG-2 and Hybrid-PIPECG-3 with the PCG CPU and GPU implementations in the widely used Paralution [8] and PETSc [2] libraries. We also compare our methods with the CPU and GPU implementations of PIPECG method. Here, we note that the total execution time for the Hybrid-PIPECG-3 method always includes the time consumed for performance modelling and data decomposition.

Table 1. Matrices used for Experiments

System	Matrix	N	nnz
K40	bcsstk15	3,948	117,816
	gyro	17,361	1,021,159
	boneS01	127,224	6,715,152
	hood	220,542	10,768,436
	offshore	259,789	4,242,673
	Serena	1,391,349	64,531,701
	Queen_4147	4,147,110	329,499,284
K40	4.5 M Poisson	4,492,125	549,353,259
	5 M Poisson	4,913,000	601,211,584
	6 M Poisson	5,929,741	726,572,699
V100	17.5 M Poisson	17,576,000	2,166,720,184
	20 M Poisson	19,902,511	2,454,911,549
	25 M Poisson	24,897,088	3,073,924,664

Figure 4 compares the performance of our hybrid methods with CPU implementations of PCG in Paralution and PETSc, and with our CPU implementation of PIPECG method on a single node with 16 CPU cores and a K40 GPU. We present the speedups obtained by each method wrt to our PIPECG-OpenMP implementation. We observe that PIPECG-OpenMP performs the worst for every matrix. This is because the PIPECG method introduces extra VMAs to remove the dependencies. This VMA overhead is less pronounced for distributed memory systems but more pronounced for multi-core CPU in a single node. We see that PETSc-PCG-MPI always performs worse than Paralution-PCG-OpenMP. Finally, we observe that our hybrid methods perform better than all the CPU versions for all matrices because we use GPU cores as well.

For bcsstk15 and gyro, Hybrid-PIPECG-1 performs the best. The same behaviour is observed for matrices with N from 100 to 36000. The other hybrid methods don't perform well for these matrices with small N as Hybrid-PIPECG-2 has redundant computations on the CPU cores and Hybrid-PIPECG-3 has extra overhead of performance modelling and data decomposition. For boneS01, hood and offshore, Hybrid-PIPECG-2 performs the best. The same behaviour is observed for matrices with N from 36000 to 260,000. Hybrid-PIPECG-1 doesn't perform well for larger matrices because copying 3N elements becomes costly for large N. Hybrid-PIPECG-2 copies only N elements. Hybrid-PIPECG-3 performs worse than Hybrid-PIPECG-2 because in Hybrid-PIPECG-2, the vector copy is overlapped by the full SPMV kernel, whereas in Hybrid-PIPECG-3 method, it is overlapped by only SPMV part 1 kernel. For Serena and Queen_4147, Hybrid-PIPECG-3 performs the best. Similar behavior is observed for matrices with N from 260,000 to 4M. Hybrid-PIPECG-1 copies 3N elements in every iteration and hence performs poorly for matrices with very large N. Hybrid-PIPECG-2 copies N elements but performs redundant computations on CPU and GPU which provide great overhead for very large N. So, for very large N (and consequently large nnz), Hybrid-PIPECG-3 provides almost perfect overlap of operations on the CPU and GPU and is the best suited. Thus, we find that different hybrid methods give the best performance for different matrix size ranges.

Figure 5 compares the performance of our hybrid methods with GPU implementations of PCG in Paralution, PCG in PETSc and PIPECG method in PETSc. We present the speedups obtained by each method wrt to PETSc-PIPECG-GPU implementation. Similar trends as the CPU comparison are observed here as well and we observe that different hybrid methods give the best performance for different matrix size ranges.

Until now, we have presented results on matrices from the SuiteSparse collection that can be fit in K40's memory. Queen_4147 is the largest matrix size that we are able to run on a single K40 GPU. We now analyse Poisson matrices that cannot be fit in K40 and V100 memory (shown in the last 6 rows of Table 1). Hybrid-PIPECG-1 and Hybrid-PIPECG-2 launch the SPMV kernel on only the GPU and thus require the complete matrix to be on the GPU. Hence, these methods cannot be used for these cases. We can use Hybrid-PIPECG-3 method because it decomposes data between multi-core CPU and GPU. We compare Hybrid-PIPECG-3 with CPU-only implementations of our PIPECG, PETSC PCG and Paralution PCG methods. We show the performance comparisons on various Poisson Matrices in Figure 6. We find that our Hybrid-PIPECG-3 method gives 2–2.5 times speedup over the other methods on K40 and 2.5–6.8 times speedup on V100.

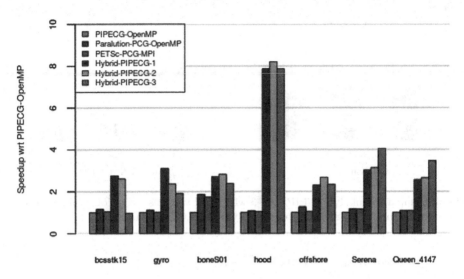

Fig. 4. Comparison of Hybrid methods with various CPU versions on a single node with 16 CPU cores and K40 GPU. Speedup presented wrt PIPECG-OpenMP.

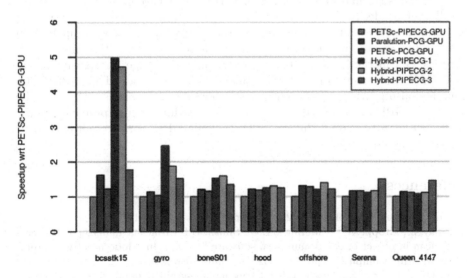

Fig. 5. omparison of Hybrid methods with various GPU versions on a single node with 16 CPU cores and K40 GPU. Speedup presented wrt PETSc-PIPECG-GPU.

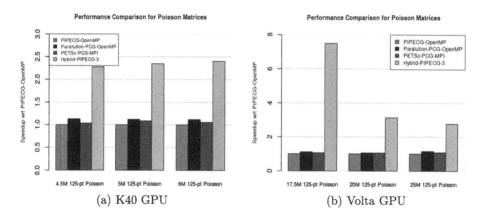

(a) K40 GPU   (b) Volta GPU

Fig. 6. Comparison of Hybrid-PIPECG-3 with CPU versions for various Poisson problems on K40 and V100. Speedup presented wrt PIPECG-OpenMP.

6   Conclusion and Future Work

In this work, we proposed three methods for efficient execution of PIPECG method on GPU accelerated systems. Hybrid-PIPECG-1 and Hybrid-PIPECG-2 methods achieve task parallelism by executing dot products on the CPU while GPU executes PC and SPMV kernels. Hybrid-PIPECG-3 method achieves data parallelism by decomposing the workload between multi-core CPU and GPU based on a performance model. Our methods give up to 8x speedup and on average 3x speedup over PCG CPU implementation of Paralution and PETSc libraries. Our methods give up to 5x speedup and on average 1.45x speedup over PCG GPU implementation of Paralution and PETSc libraries. Hybrid-PIPECG-3 method also provides an efficient solution for solving problems that cannot be fit into the GPU memory and gives up to 6.8x speedup for such problems. In the future, we plan to extend this single node single GPU work to multiple nodes with multiple GPUs.

References

1. Suitesparse matrix collection (2020). https://sparse.tamu.edu/
2. Balay, S., Gropp, W.D., McInnes, L.C., Smith, B.F.: Efficient management of parallelism in object oriented numerical software libraries. In: Modern Software Tools in Scientific Computing, pp. 163–202. Birkhäuser Press (1997)
3. Bell, N., Dalton, S., Olson, L.N.: Exposing fine-grained parallelism in algebraic multigrid methods. SIAM J. Sci. Comput. **34**(4), C123–C152 (2012)
4. Bell, N., Garland, M.: Efficient sparse matrix-vector multiplication on CUDA (2008)
5. Bell, N., Garland, M.: Implementing sparse matrix-vector multiplication on throughput-oriented processors. In: SC 2009, pp. 1–1 (2009)
6. Ghysels, P., Vanroose, W.: Hiding global synchronization latency in the preconditioned conjugate gradient algorithm. Parallel Comput. **40**(7), 224–238 (2014)

7. Hestenes, M.R., Stiefel, E.: Methods of conjugate gradients for solving linear systems. J. Res. Natl. Bureau Stand. **49**, 409–436 (1952)
8. Labs, P.: Paralution v1.1.0 (2020). http://www.paralution.com/
9. Li, R., Saad, Y.: GPU-accelerated preconditioned iterative linear solvers. J. Supercomput. **63**(2), 443–466 (2013)

A Multi-Level Platform-Independent GPU API for High-Level Programming Models

Akihiro Hayashi[1]([⊠]), Sri Raj Paul[2], and Vivek Sarkar[1]

[1] Georgia Institute of Technology, Atlanta, GA 30332, USA
{ahayashi,vsarkar}@gatech.edu
[2] Intel Corporation, Austin, USA
sriraj.paul@intel.com

Abstract. While there has been a growing interest in supporting accelerators, especially GPU accelerators, in large-scale systems, the user typically has to work with low-level GPU programming models such as CUDA along with the low-level message passing interface (MPI).

We believe higher-level programming models such as Partitioned Global Address Space (PGAS) programming models enable productive parallel programming at both the intra-node and inter-node levels in homogeneous and heterogeneous nodes. However, GPU programming with PGAS languages in practice is still limited since there is still a big performance gap between compiler-generated GPU code and hand-tuned GPU code; hand-optimization of CPU-GPU data transfers is also an important contributor to this performance gap. Thus, it is not rare that the user eventually writes a fully external GPU program that includes the host part -i.e., GPU memory (de)allocation, host-device/device-host data transfer, and the device part - i.e., GPU kernels, and calls it from their primary language, which is not very productive.

Our key observation is that the complexity of writing the external GPU program comes not only from writing GPU kernels in the device part, but also from writing the host part. In particular, interfacing objects in the primary language to raw C/C++ pointers is tedious and error-prone, especially because high-level languages usually have a well-defined type system with type inference.

In this paper, we introduce the GPUAPI module, which offers multiple abstraction levels of low-level GPU API routines for high-level programming models with a special focus on PGAS languages, which allows the user to choose an appropriate abstraction level depending on their tuning scenarios. The module is also designed to work with multiple standard low-level GPU programming models: CUDA, HIP, DPC++, and SYCL, thereby significantly improving productivity and portability.

We use Chapel as the primary example and our preliminary performance and productivity evaluations show that the use of the GPUAPI module significantly simplifies GPU programming in a high-level programming model like Chapel, while targeting different multi-node CPUs+GPUs platforms with no performance loss.

Keywords: GPUs · Chapel · PGAS languages · Distributed programming model · GPU API library

H. Anzt et al. (Eds.): ISC High Performance 2022 Workshops, LNCS 13387, pp. 90–107, 2022.
https://doi.org/10.1007/978-3-031-23220-6_7

1   Introduction

There has been a growing interest in accelerators, especially GPU accelerators, in large-scale systems. In the Top 500 list, one can see that a significant number of systems consist of heterogeneous nodes with GPUs. As with homogeneous systems, software productivity and portability is still a profound issue for heterogeneous systems. We believe that the use of PGAS (Partitioned Global Address Space) languages [2,5,15] including Chapel, is a scalable and portable way to achieve high-performance without sacrificing productivity.

As for GPU support in PGAS languages, some of the past approaches [6, 13] aim at compiling high-level parallel constructs (e.g., Chapel's `forall`) to GPUs. Also, from Chapel 1.24 onwards, a preliminary full automatic approach is available [4,12]. However, in general, there is still a big performance gap between compiler-generated GPU code and hand-tuned GPU code. Thus, it is possible that the user ends up writing a low-level GPU program that includes the host part—i.e., GPU memory (de)allocation, host-device/device-host data transfer, and the device part—i.e., GPU kernels, and call it from their primary language.

Our key observation is that there are only two ultimate GPU programming approaches in PGAS languages: fully automatic and fully manual, and there is no "intermediate" approach. Also, our another key observation is that the complexity of the fully manual approach comes not only from writing GPU kernels in the device part, but also from writing the host part. In particular, interfacing objects in the primary language to raw C/C++ pointers is tedious and error-prone, especially because PGAS languages have a well-defined type system with type inference.

In this paper, we propose the GPUAPI module, which offers "medium-level (MID-level)" abstraction of low-level GPU API routines for high-level programming models with a special focus on PGAS languages, which fills the gap between the fully automatic approach (we call it HIGH-level) and fully manual approach (we call it LOW-level). In our design, MID-level includes two sub-levels:

- **MID-level:** Provides GPU API that is more natural to the user of the primary language -i.e., use the `new` keyword to allocate GPU memory.
- **MID-LOW-level:** Provides simple wrapper functions for raw GPU API functions -i.e., use the `Malloc` function to allocate GPU memory.

This multi-level design allows the user to choose an appropriate one depending on their tuning scenarios. Specifically, the user has the option of 1) providing a high-level specification (HIGH-level) and letting the compiler do the job, and 2) diving into lower-level details to incrementally evolve their implementations for improved performance (MID-level → MID-LOW-level → LOW-level). Also, the module is designed to work with multiple standard low-level GPU programming models: CUDA, HIP, DPC++, and SYCL, thereby significantly improving productivity and portability.

To the best of our knowledge, this paper is the first paper that discusses the design and implementation of "intermediate-level" GPU API for multiple CPUs+GPUs platforms.

This paper makes the following contributions:

- The design and implementation of multi-level platform-independent GPU API for high-level languages.
- Performance evaluations and productivity discussion using different distributed mini applications and a real-world application [1] on different CPU+GPU systems.

While we use Chapel as the primary language, our discussion should apply to other PGAS languages.

2   Background

2.1   Chapel

Chapel has been one of the most active PGAS languages for decades. Chapel is designed to express parallelism as part of language rather than include it as libraries or language extensions such as compiler directives or annotations. Due to this design, many of the constructs that support parallelism are treated as first-class citizens of the language. Since locality is also important in achieving performance in parallel programs, the locality constructs are also included as a first-class citizen in the Chapel language. Chapel allows expressing parallelism at various granularity for a wide range of platforms without the need for code specialization. This expressiveness of parallelism helps programmers to create portable parallel programs, thereby improving their productivity.

Also, Chapel's "global-view" programming model allows the user to easily write a multi-node program as if they are writing a program for a single-node. For example, suppose D is a distributed domain, which is an iteration space that is distributed across multiple nodes, one can write the following code to create a distributed array A with the length of n and assign 1 to it:

```
1  // D is a block distributed domain, n is a big number
2  var D: domain(1) dmapped Block(boundingBox = {1..n}) = {1..n};
3  var A[D]: int;
4  forall i in D {
5    A[i] = 1;
6  }
```

Space limitations prevent us from including more details on Chapel. For more details, see [3].

2.2   Chapel's GPUIterator Module

In our past work [9], we introduced the GPUIterator module, which facilitates the invocation of a user-written low-level GPU program. The module provides a parallel iterator for a forall loop, in which the iteration space is divided into two spaces: a CPU and GPU space. The original forall iterating over the CPU

Listing 1.1. A Chapel program with the `GPUIterator` module.

```
1  use GPUIterator;
2  proc GPUCallBack(lo: int, hi: int, nElems: int) {
3    // The GPU portion (lo, hi, nElems) is automatically computed
4    // even in multi-node + multi-GPUs settings.
5    // Also, hi-lo+1 == nElems
6    myGPUCode(...);
7  };
8  var CPUpercent = x; // X% goes to the CPU
9                      // (100 - X)% goes to the GPU
10  // D can be a distributed domain
11  forall i in GPU(D, GPUCallBack, CPUPercent) {...}
```

space is executed on the CPUs. Similarly, for the GPU space, it invokes a user-written callback function where a low-level GPU program is invoked with the divided GPU space.

Listing 1.1 shows an example of a Chapel program with the module. The domain D is wrapped in the `GPU()` iterator. The `GPUCallBack()` is invoked once the module has computed a CPU and GPU space, and the user is supposed to write the invocation of low-level GPU code (`myGPUCode()`) in the callback. Also, the user can tweak the CPU/GPU percentage by changing the `CPUPercent` (100% goes to the GPU if the user omits the argument).

Let us emphasize that the module is designed to facilitate multi-node, multi-GPUs, plus hybrid execution in a portable way. This feature is significant because many of the past approaches that tackle GPU execution in PGAS languages do not support such a feature. To handle multi-GPUs per node, the module automatically computes a subspace for each GPU and implicitly calls the callback function multiple times - i.e., the number of GPUs per node × the number of nodes. Because the module implicitly sets the device ID for each GPU, all the user has to do is 1) to write a code snippet that gets a local portion of a distributed array in the Chapel part, 2) to make the device part flexible to change in iteration spaces -i.e., making it aware of `lo`, `hi`, `nElems`, and 3) not to put a device setting call.

Listing 1.2 and Listing 1.3 illustrate an example distributed implementation of the STREAM benchmark (`A = B + alpha*C`) that enables distributed hybrid execution on multple CPUs+GPUs nodes. On line 16 in Listing 1.2, in the `GPUCallBack` function, it obtains a local portion of the distributed array A, B, and C using the `localSlice()` API, which is fed into the external C function `cudaSTREAM()` along with a subspace for each GPU (`lo`, `hi`, and `nElems`). The GPU part in Listing 1.3 includes a typical host program including device memory (de)allocation, data transfer, and kernel invocation. Note that the kernel (line 3 in Listing 1.3) is flexible to change in iteration space because it only iterate over 0 to `nElems-1` that is given by the Chapel part. Also, since `localSlice(lo..hi)`[1] returns a pointer to the head of the local slice, it is safe to assume that `&A[0]`,

---

[1] In Chapel, `lo..hi` means a range starting with `lo` and ending in `hi` (inclusive).

Listing 1.2. An example distributed implementation of STREAM (The Chapel part).

```
1  /* stream.chpl */
2  use BlockDist; use GPUIterator; use GPUAPI;
3
4  extern proc cudaSTREAM(A: [] real(32), B: [] real(32), C: [] real(32),
5                         alpha: real(32), lo: int, hi: int, nElems: int);
6
7  config const n = 1024: int;
8  config const CPUPercent = 0: int;
9  var D: domain(1) dmapped Block(boundingBox={0..#n}) = {0..#n};
10 // distributed arrays (A, B, C) with the domain D
11 var A: [D] real(32); var B: [D] real(32); var C: [D] real(32);
12 var alpha: real(32) = 0.5;
13
14 proc GPUCallBack(lo: int, hi: int, nElems: int) {
15   // lo, hi, nElems plus device ID is automatically set here
16   cudaSTREAM(A.localSlice(lo..hi), B.localSlice(lo..hi),
17             C.localSlice(lo..hi), alpha, lo, hi, nElems);
18 };
19 ...
20 forall i in GPU(D, GPUCallBack, CPUPercent) { A[i] = B[i] + alpha * C[i]; }
```

Listing 1.3. An example distributed implementation of STREAM (The GPU part)

```
1  /* stream.cu */
2  // the kernel part
3  __global__ void stream(float *dA, float *dB, float *dC,
4                         float alpha, int nElems) {
5    int id = blockIdx.x * blockDim.x + threadIdx.x;
6    if (id < nElems) dA[id] = dB[id] + alpha * dC[id];
7  }
8  // the host part
9  extern "C" {
10 void cudaSTREAM(float* A, float *B, float *C, float alpha,
11                 int64_t start, int64_t end, int64_t nElems) {
12   assert((end-start+1) == nElems);
13   float *dA, *dB, *dC; size_t nBytes = sizeof(float) * nElems;
14   cudaMalloc(&dA, nBytes);
15   cudaMalloc(&dB, nBytes);
16   cudaMalloc(&dC, nBytes);
17   cudaMemcpy(dB, B, nBytes, cudaMemcpyHostToDevice);
18   cudaMemcpy(dC, C, nBytes, cudaMemcpyHostToDevice);
19   stream<<<ceil(((float)nElems)/)1024, 1024>>>(dA, dB, dC, alpha, nElems);
20   cudaDeviceSynchronize();
21   cudaMemcpy(A, dA, nBytes, cudaMemcpyDeviceToHost);
22   cudaFree(dA);
23   cudaFree(dB);
24   cudaFree(dC);
25 }}
```

&B[0], and &C[0] in the host part point to A[lo], B[lo], and C[lo] in the Chapel part respectively.

For completeness, for the CPU space, it is possible to optimize the CPU part for multiple sub-nodes such as NUMA domains thanks to Chapel. Specifically, the user may let Chapel's tasking runtime map sub-nodes to NUMA domains by doing export CHPL_LOCALE_MODEL=numa.

3 Design

3.1 Motivation

While the GPUIterator module provides a portable way to perform distributed, hybrid, and multi-GPU execution, in terms of productivity, there is room for further improvements. As shown in Listing 1.3, most of the host part includes device memory (de)allocation and host-to-device/device-to-host transfer, which is relatively larger than the kernel invocation and the kernel itself. Note that the complexity of the host part can significantly grow as the kernel part grows. More importantly, in this low-level program, the user has to deal with raw C pointers and the size of the allocated memory regions, which is abstracted away in the main Chapel program. This motivates us to design and implement a set of Chapel-level GPU API which mitigates the complexity of handling the low-level host part, thereby improving productivity.

As discussed in Sect. 1, our main focus is to develop MID-level/MID-LOW-level explicit GPU API. We believe this level of abstraction is still important even when fully automatic approaches (the HIGH-level abstraction) are available because 1) compiler-generated kernels would not always outperform user-written kernels or highly-tuned GPU libraries, and 2) it would not be always trivial for the compiler to perform data transfer optimizations such as data transfer hoisting. Therefore, MID-level/MID-LOW-level GPU API comes in portions that remain as performance bottlenecks even after automatic compilation approaches.

Also, related to the point on data transfer optimizations, it is worth noting that, while the calls to our GPU API routines are inside the callback function in the code examples below, this does not necessarily mean that these calls should be placed there. The user has the option of placing these calls outside of the callback function to optimize data transfers.

3.2 MID-LOW-level API: Thin Wrappers for Raw GPU Routines

At the MID-LOW-level, most of the low-level 1) device memory allocation, 2) device synchronization, and 3) data transfer can be written in Chapel. This level of abstraction only provides thin wrapper functions for the CUDA/HIP/SYCL-level API functions, which requires the user to directly manipulate C types like c_void_ptr and so on. The MID-LOW level API is helpful, particularly when the user wants to fine-tune the use of GPU API but still wants to stick with Chapel.

Listing 1.4. An example distributed implementation of STREAM (The MID-LOW version).

```
1  /* steram-mid-low.chpl */
2  use BlockDist; use GPUIterator; use GPUAPI; use CTypes;
3  proc GPUCallBack(lo: int, hi: int, nElems: int) {
4    var dA, dB, dC: c_void_ptr; // device memory pointers
5    ref lA = A.localSlice(lo..hi);
6    ref lB = B.localSlice(lo..hi);
7    ref lC = C.localSlice(lo..hi);
8    const size: c_size_t = (lA.size:c_size_t * c_sizeof(lA.eltType));
9    Malloc(dA, size);
10   Malloc(dB, size);
11   Malloc(dC, size);
12   Memcpy(dB, c_ptrTo(lB), size, H2D);
13   Memcpy(dC, c_ptrTo(lC), size, H2D);
14   cudaSTREAM_kernel(dA, dB, dC, alpha,
15                     lo, hi, nElems);
16   DeviceSynchronize();
17   Memcpy(c_ptrTo(lA), dA, size, D2H);
18   Free(dA);
19   Free(dB);
20   Free(dC);
21 };
22 ...
23 /* stream-kernel.cu or equivalent (HIP, DPC++, ...) */
24 void cudaSTREAM_kernel(float* dA, float *dB, float *dC, float alpha,
25                        int start, int end, int nElems) {
26   // the kernel code remains the same
27   stream<<<ceil(((float)nElems)/1024), 1024>>>(dA, dB, dC, alpha, start, end, nElems);
28 }
```

Listing 1.4 is an example program written with the MID-LOW-level API. On line 2, `use GPUAPI;` is added to use the GPUAPI module. Also, since this version manipulates raw C pointers, `use CTypes;`[2] is also required. From line 9 to line 20, there is a sequence of the host code including `Malloc()`, `Memcpy()`, a kernel invocation, `DeviceSynchronize()`, and `Free()`. Each GPU API routine is essentially a thin wrapper for the corresponding CUDA API (e.g., `cudaMalloc()`, `cudaMemcpy()`, `cudaDeviceSynchronize()`, and `cudaFree()`).

Now that all of the host part except for the kernel invocation is done at the Chapel level, the low GPU program part only includes a CUDA kernel invocation (see line 24). Note that the user has the option of writing the kernel part in another language (e.g., HIP, DPC++, and so on). For more details, please see Sect. 4. While this MID-LOW-level abstraction simplifies the host code compared to the original host part in Listing 1.3, notice that the user still needs to handle C pointers explicitly (e.g., `c_void_ptr`, `c_sizeof`, and `c_ptrTo()`).

Pitched Memory Allocation and 2D Data Transfer: In addition to `Malloc()` and `Memcpy()`, which are linear memory allocation and data transfer, the `GPUAPI` module also supports pitched memory allocation (`MallocPitch()`) and 2D data transfer (`Memcpy2D()`). The pitched memory allocation API takes 2D shape information - i.e., `width` and `height`, and the underlying raw routine

---

[2] In Chapel 1.27, 1) SysCTypes is replaced with `CTypes`, and 2) `size_t` is replaced with `c_size_t`.

Listing 1.5. Allocating pitched memory and perform 2D memcpy

```
1  var D = {0..255, 0..255};
2  var A: [D] real(32) = 1.0;
3  var widthInBytes: c_size_t = D.dim(1).size:c_size_t * c_sizeof(A.eltType);
4  var spitch = widthInBytes;
5  var dA: c_void_ptr;
6  var dpitch: c_size_t;
7  MallocPitch(dA, dpitch, widthInBytes, D.dim(0).size:c_size_t);
8  Memcpy2D(dA, dpitch, c_ptrTo(A), spitch, widthInBytes,
9           D.dim(0).size:c_size_t, 0);
```

Listing 1.6. An example distributed implementation of STREAM. (The MID version)

```
1  use BlockDist; use GPUIterator; use GPUAPI; /* use CTypes; is no longer required */
2  proc GPUCallBack(lo: int, hi: int, nElems: int) {
3    // nElems * sizeof(int) will be automatically allocated onto the device
4    var dA = new GPUArray(A.localSlice(lo..hi));
5    var dB = new GPUArray(B.localSlice(lo..hi));
6    var dC = new GPUArray(C.localSlice(lo..hi));
7    dB.toDevice();
8    dC.toDevice();
9    cudaSTREAM_kernel(dA.dPtr(), dB.dPtr(), dC.dPtr(), alpha, lo, hi, nElems);
10   DeviceSynchronize();
11   dA.fromDevice();
12   // allocate GPU memory automatically deallocated
13 }
```

may add a fixed pad (`pitch`) to ensure high memory bandwidth on the device. The 2D data transfer API is a variant of `Memcpy()`, which is aware of the pad information.

Listing 1.5 shows a standalone example program with the pitched memory allocation and 2D data transfer. First, the 2D domain (`D`) on line 1 is used to construct the 2D array (`A`) on line 2. The arguments to `MallocPitch()` on line 7 are as follows: `dA` is a `ref` variable that stores a pointer to allocated device memory, `dpitch` is also a `ref` variable that stores pitch on the device, `hpitch` is the width of the Chapel array in bytes, and the last argument is the height of the Chapel array (# of elements).

3.3   MID-level API: A Chapel Programmer Friendly GPU API

At the MID-level, as with the MID-LOW-level, most of the low-level 1) device memory allocation, 2) device synchronization, and 3) data transfer can be written in Chapel. The key difference between the MID-LOW and the MID levels is that the MID-level API utilizes Chapel features so the programming style can be more Chapel programmer-friendly. For example, the user can allocate GPU memory using the `new` keyword and no longer need to manipulate C types explicitly.

Listing 1.6 shows an example program written with the MID-level API. As shown on line 4–6, device memory allocation can be done using `new GPUArray()`. The corresponding device pointer can be obtained by invoking `dPtr()` (line 9).

Host-to-device and device-to-host transfer can be done by using `toDevice()` and `fromDevice()` respectively (line 7, 8, and 11) Note that no device memory deallocation is required because the deinitializer of `GPUArray` is automatically invoked to handle the deallocation as with typical Chapel class objects. In case the user wants to manually manage device memory, this can be done by doing `var dA = new unmanaged GPUArray(A);` and `delete dA;`.

Comparing Listing 1.6 with Listing 1.4 and Listing 1.3, one can see that the use of the MID-level API significantly simplifies the host part.

The following discusses the details of API provided at the MID level.

`class GPUArray`: This class encapsulates the allocation, deallocation, and transfer of device memory. It can accept a multi-dimensional Chapel array and internally allocates linear memory for it. For 2D Chapel arrays, the user has the option of using pitched memory by adding `pitched=true` to the constructor call, and the allocated pitch can be obtained using `pitch()` method.

`class GPUJaggedArray`: This class encapsulates the allocation, deallocation, and transfer of jagged device memory. We introduce this class because a real-world Chapel program [10] heavily uses this pattern. Let us discuss our motivation using a simple Chapel program. Consider the Chapel code shown in Listing 1.7. There is a declaration of `class C` (line 1–5), which includes an array (x). Also, on line 7, an array of C, namely `Cs`, is created. When mapping `Cs` onto the device, since `Cs` is a heterogeneous array, it is required to create an array of an array using `Malloc()`. Line 10 shows an example implementation using the MID-LOW level API. Essentially, it first performs `Malloc()` and `Memcpy()` for each `Cs[0].x` and `Cs[1].x`, then performs another `Malloc()` and `Memcpy()` for allocating a device memory region that stores pointers to the device counterpart of `Cs[0].x` and `Cs[1].x`. On the other hand, the MID-level version (line 24) saves a lot of lines. Essentially like the `GPUArray` class, all the user has to do is put `Cs.x` into the constructor of `GPUJaggedArray`. Thanks to the promotion feature of Chapel, `Cs.x` is promoted to `Cs[0..#2].x` and the jagged array class internally performs the same thing as the MID-LOW version does.

3.4   Supporting Asynchrony

While the current implementation of the `GPUAPI` module does not directly support asynchronous calls, one can asynchronously invoke GPU-related routines using Chapel's `async` API. Listing 1.8 shows an example of an asynchronous GPU invocation. Line 1 creates a lambda function that performs the boiler-plate GPU invocation code with the MID-level API routines. First, the `async` API returns a *future* variable (F) immediately after the lambda function is asynchronously spawned. Then, the completion of F can be detected by calling `F.get()` (on Line 9). Note that `F.get()` blocks until the returning value is available.

We also plan to directly support asynchronous GPUAPI routines in the future.

Listing 1.7. A jagged array example.

```
 1 class C {
 2   var n: int;
 3   proc init(_n: int) { n = _n; }
 4   var x: [0..#n] int;
 5 }
 6
 7 var Cs = [new C(256), new C(512)];
 8 const N = Cs.size;
 9
10 // MIDLOW
11 {
12     var dA: [0..#N] c_void_ptr;
13     var dAs: c_ptr(c_void_ptr);
14     for i in 0..#N {
15         const size = Cs[i].x.size:c_size_t*c_sizeof(int);
16         Malloc(dA[i], size);
17         Memcpy(dA[i], c_ptrTo(Cs[i].x), size, 0);
18     }
19     const size = N: c_size_t * c_sizeof(c_ptr(c_void_ptr));
20     Malloc(dAs, size);
21     Memcpy(dAs, c_ptrTo(dA), size, 0);
22     // kernel invocation
23 }
24 // MID
25 {
26     var dAs = new GPUJaggedArray(Cs.x);
27     dAs.toDevice();
28     // kernel invocation
29 }
```

Listing 1.8. An asynchronous GPU invocation example.

```
 1 var F = async(lambda () {
 2         writeln("GPU Ctrl Thread");
 3         var dA = new GPUArray(A);
 4         dA.toDevice();
 5         kernel(dA.dPtr());
 6         dA.fromDevice();
 7         return 1;
 8     });
 9 if (F.get() == 1) { // F is done }
```

4 Implementation

4.1 Library Implementation

We implemented the GPUAPI module as an external Chapel module. The module can be used either standalone or with the GPUIterator module. The actual implementation and the detailed documentation can be found at [11].

In the current implementation, the module mainly supports NVIDIA CUDA-supported GPUs, AMD ROCm-supported GPUs, Intel DPC++ (SYCL) supported GPUs (and FPGAs) through different vendor-provided libraries/frameworks as shown in Fig. 1. One of the interesting aspects of our implementation is that there is only a CUDA implementation of the GPUAPI module. We utilize the hipify from AMD and dpct from Intel to convert the CUDA implementation to a HIP and DPC++ version respectively. Also, for Intel platforms, it is possible to run the hipifyed code with hipLZ [14]. More specifically, at the time

Table 1. How user-written kernels work on different GPU platforms.

	CUDA	HIP	SYCL
NVIDIA	✓	✓	✓
AMD	✓ (via `hipify`)	✓	✓
Intel	✓ (via `dpct`)	✓ (via `hipLZ`)	✓

of installation, our cmake-based build system identifies installed GPUs and generates an appropriate static (.a) and/or shared (.so) library with the conversion. (Fig. 2).

Because the cmake-generated library (.a and/or .so) includes all of the MID-LOW-level API routines and we provide a cmake file that helps an external cmake project to find this module, it is technically possible to link the MID-LOW-level library from other languages than Chapel. Also, while the MID-level API is tightly-coupled with Chapel, we believe it is feasible to port our module to other PGAS languages.

4.2 The GPU Kernel Part by the User

As we discussed, the user is supposed to write the kernel part using vendor-provided GPU libraries/frameworks such as CUDA, HIP, SYCL, and so on. The user can simply write their kernels using their favorite framework and link it with the corresponding version of GPUAPI library (`libGPUAPICUDA.so`, and so on). If there is any conversion required, the user can also utilize our cmake-based build system. Table 1 summarizes how user-written kernels work on different GPU platforms.

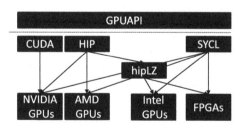

Fig. 1. Multi-platform support in the `GPUAPI` module.

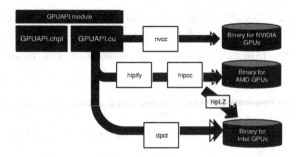

Fig. 2. The implementation of the GPUAPI module.

Also, it is also worth noting that this auto-conversion approach works very well even with real-world applications. For example, while the kernel part of the distributed tree search application in Sect. 5 was originally implemented in CUDA, the `hipify` tool was able to produce the HIP version flawlessly. Similarly, in [10], we were able to produce the HIP version of a computational fluid dynamics (CFD) application.

5   Performance and Productivity Evaluations

Purpose: In this evaluation we validate our GPUAPI implementation on different CPU+GPU platforms. We mainly discuss the performance and productivity of different levels of GPU API (LOW, MID-LOW, MID) with the GPUIterator module. The goal is to demonstrate 1) there is no significant performance difference between the LOW, MID-LOW, and MID versions, and 2) the use of a higher-level API improves the productivity in terms of lines of code.

Machine: We present the performance results on three platforms: a GPU cluster and a supercomputer. The first platform is the Cori GPU nodes at NERSC, each node of which consists of two sockets of 20-core Intel Xeon Gold 6148 running at 2.40 GHz with a total main memory size of 384 GB and 8 NVIDIA Tesla V100 GPUs, each with 16 GB HBM2 memory, connected via PCIe 3.0[3]. The second platform is the Summit supercomputer at ORNL, which consists of the IBM Power System AC922 nodes. Each node contains two IBM POWER9 running at 3.45 GHz with a total main memory size of 512 GB and 6 NVIDIA Tesla V100 GPUs, each with 16 GB HBM2 memory, connected via NVLink. The third platform is a single-node AMD server, which consists of 12-core Ryzen9 3900X running at 3.8 GHz and a Radeon RX570 GPU with 8 GB memory.

Benchmarks: We use four distributed mini-applications (Stream, BlackScholes, Matrix Multiplication, and Logistic Regression) and a distributed Tree Search implementation as a real-world example. We use an input data size of $n = 2^{30}$ (Stream, BlackScholes), $n \times n = 4096 \times 4096$ (MM), $nFeatures =$

---
[3] Interconnection network between the GPUs is NVLink.

$2^{18}, nSamples = 2^4$ (Logistic Regression), and $n = 2^{18}$ (Tree Search). We report the average performance number from 5 runs.

Experimental Variants: Each benchmark is evaluated by comparing the following variants:

- **Chapel-CPU:** Implemented in Chapel using a `forall` with the default parallel iterator that is executed on CPUs.
- **Chapel-GPU:** Implemented using a `forall` with the `GPUIterator` module with `CPUPercent=0`.
  - **MID-level:** All the GPU part except for GPU kernels is implemented using the MID-level API, which is a Chapel class based abstraction of GPU arrays.
  - **MID-LOW-level:** All the GPU part except for GPU kernels is implemented using the MID-LOW-level API, which is a set of thin wrappers for raw GPU API routines.
  - **LOW-level:** The GPU part is fully implemented in CUDA (on NVIDIA GPUs) or HIP (on AMD GPUs).

5.1   Distributed Mini Applications

Figure 3, 4, and 5 show speedup values relative to the Chapel-CPU version on a log scale. In the figures *GPU(M)*, *GPU(ML)*, *GPU(L)* refers to MID-level, MID-LOW-level, and LOW-level respectively. While we use the Chapel compiler version 1.20 with the `-fast` option, `CHPL_COMM=gasnet`, `CHPL_COMM_SUBSTRATE=ibv`, and `CHPL_TASK=qthreads` in this evaluation, we believe the performance trend will not change when the latest Chapel version is used.

As shown in these figures, for all the benchmarks, there is no significant performance difference between the MID, MID-LOW, and LOW versions, which indicates that the overhead of the `GPUAPI` module can be ignored.

Table 2 shows source code additions and modifications required for using the GPUAPI. We measure the productivity in term of source lines of code[4]. The goal of this productivity experiment is to demonstrate SLOC for both the Chapel part and the host part are reduced when the MID-level API is used. Note that the CUDA kernel part is out of the scope of this paper. The results show 1) the MID-LOW level version requires almost the same lines of code as the LOW-level version, and 2) the use of the MID-level API significantly decreases the lines of code. Let us reiterate that the MID-level simplifies the host part more than what it appears as the lines of code reduction because it avoids the explicit manipulation of raw C pointers.

---

[4] Our definitions of source code "lines" is based on common usage.

Table 2. Source code additions and modifications required for using the `GPUAPI` module in terms of source lines of code (SLOC).

Application	Level	Chapel	Host (CUDA)	Kernel (CUDA)
Stream	LOW	4	13	6
	MID-LOW	16	1	6
	MID	8	1	6
BlackScholes	LOW	4	13	68
	MID-LOW	16	1	68
	MID	8	1	68
Matrix multiplication	LOW	3	12	10
	MID-LOW	14	1	10
	MID	8	1	10
Logistic regression	LOW	2	15	13
	MID-LOW	16	1	13
	MID	10	1	13
Tree search	LOW	2	16	71
	MID-LOW	13	4	71
	MID	9	4	71

In terms of performance improvements over Chapel-CPU, for Blackscholes, Matrix Multiplication, and Logistic Regression, the kernels have enough workloads, and the GPU variants significantly outperform the Chapel-CPU. Specifically, the results show a speedup of up to 21k × on the Cori supercomputer, 20k × on the Summit supercomputer. For Stream, the Chapel-CPU outperforms the GPU variants because the data transfer time is significantly larger than the kernel time. Note that if we only compare the kernel times, the GPU kernel is faster. However, let us reiterate that our primary focus is to prove that there is no significant performance difference between the three Chapel-GPU variants. Also, the use of the `GPUIterator` can help the user to easily switch back and forth between the Chapel-CPU and the Chapel-GPU versions.

5.2   Real-world Example: Distributed Tree Search

Here we present the performance and productivity of the `GPUAPI` module using a real-world application: distributed tree search [1]. In this evaluation, we use the latest Chapel compiler version 1.24 with the `-fast` option, `CHPL_COMM=gasnet`, `CHPL_COMM_SUBSTRATE=ibv`, and `CHPL_TASK=qthreads`. Note that there is no Chapel-CPU version of this application.

Figure 6a, 6b, and 6c show speedup values relative to the LOW version on a single node of each platform with the 95% confidence intervals. Note that, on the Summit supercomputer, 6 GPUs/node are used without any modifications to the source code thanks to the `GPUIterator` module, while the use of multiple

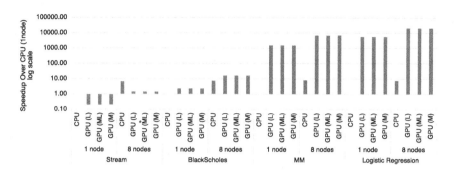

Fig. 3. Performance improvements of mini applications on the Cori GPUs (log scale, multi-nodes: 1GPU/node)

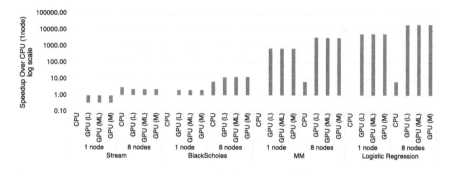

Fig. 4. Performance improvements of mini applications on the Summit supercomputer (log scale, multi-nodes: 1GPU/node)

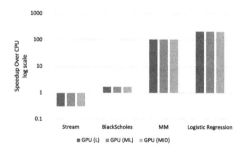

Fig. 5. Performance improvements of mini applications on the AMD server (log scale, single-node:1GPU/node)

GPUs gives an error that is unrelated to our modules on the Cori GPUs. Also, in Fig. 6c, the intervals are not very visible because the numbers are very stable. As with the mini applications discussed in Sect. 5.1, while there are slight performance differences, the use of the 95% confidence intervals indicates that there is no statistically significant performance difference between the LOW, MID-LOW, and MID versions. Because this application is highly irregular, the strong scalability is not as good as that of the mini applications. However, improving the scalability is orthogonal to this work.

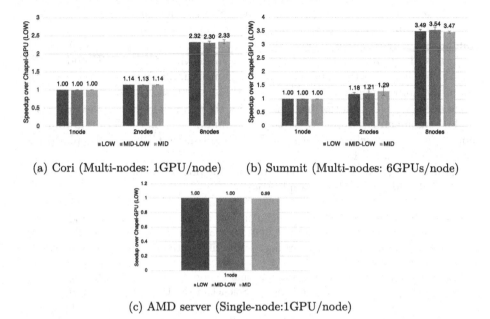

(a) Cori (Multi-nodes: 1GPU/node)   (b) Summit (Multi-nodes: 6GPUs/node)

(c) AMD server (Single-node:1GPU/node)

Fig. 6. Performance improvements of the distributed tree search application.

Also, the last row of Table 2 shows source code additions and modifications required for this application. The results also show the same trends as the other mini-applications, where a higher-level GPU API simplifies the Chapel and host parts.

6   Related Work

In the context of compiling PGAS langauges to GPUs, X10CUDA [7] uses the concept of *places* to map a nested parallel loop to blocks and threads on a GPU. It also provides thin wrappers for low-level GPU API routhines, which is analogous to our MID-LOW API.

For Chapel, while Sidelnik et al. [13], Chu et al. [6], and recent versions of Chapel compiler compile Chapel's `forall` constructs to GPUs, it is unfortunate that these approaches are still early and do not support multi-node GPUs or multiple GPUs on a single node. Also, Ghangas [8] compiles a Chapel statement containing multiple arrays GPUs with a single kernel. However, performance results have not been demonstrated yet.

In contrast, our approach is designed to facilitate manual CPU-GPU programming for multi-node platforms with Chapel, while keeping Chapel constructs as much as possible.

7 Conclusions

In this paper, we introduced the `GPUAPI` module, which allows PGAS programmers to have the option of explicitly manipulating device memory (de)allocation API, and data transfer API in their primary language. While it can be used standalone, when it is used with the `GPUIterator` module [9], it significantly facilitates distributed and hybrid execution on multiple CPU+GPU nodes.

We use Chapel as the primary example. Our preliminary performance evaluation using mini-applications and a real-world application is conducted on a wide range of CPU+GPU platforms. The results show that the use of the GPUAPI module significantly simplifies GPU programming in a high-level programming model like Chapel, while targeting different multi-node CPUs+GPUs platforms with no performance loss.

In future work, we plan to explore further the possibility of using our modules in different real-world Chapel applications.

Acknowledgement. The authors would like to thank Tiago Carneiro and Nouredine Melab for giving feedback on the `GPUIterator` and using it in their distributed tree search application. Also, the authors would like to thank Josh Milthorpe for his contribution to our code base.

This research used resources of the National Energy Research Scientific Computing Center, which is supported by the Office of Science of the U.S. Department of Energy under Contract No. DE-AC02-05CH11231. Also, this research used resources of the Oak Ridge Leadership Computing Facility at the Oak Ridge National Laboratory, which is supported by the Office of Science of the U.S. Department of Energy under Contract No. DE-AC05-00OR22725.

References

1. Carneiro, T., Melab, N., Hayashi, A., Sarkar, V.: Towards chapel-based exascale tree search algorithms: dealing with multiple GPU accelerators. In: HPCS 2020 - The 18th International Conference on High Performance Computing & Simulation. Barcelona/Virtual, Spain (2021). https://hal.archives-ouvertes.fr/hal-03149394
2. Chamberlain, B.L.: Chapel (cray inc. HPCS language). In: Encyclopedia of Parallel Computing, pp. 249–256 (2011). https://doi.org/10.1007/978-0-387-09766-4_54
3. Chapel: Chapel documentation (2022). https://chapel-lang.org/docs/index.html
4. the Chapel team: GPU programming in chapel documentation (2022). https://chapel-lang.org/docs/latest/technotes/gpu.html
5. Charles, P., et al.: X10: An object-oriented approach to non-uniform cluster computing. Acm Sigplan Not. **40**(10), 519–538. OOPSLA 2005. ACM, New York, NY (2005). https://doi.org/10.1145/1094811.1094852
6. Chu, M.L., Aji, A.M., Lowell, D., Hamidouche, K.: GPGPU support in Chapel with the Radeon Open Compute Platform (Extended Abstract). CHIUW 2017 (2017)
7. Cunningham, D., Bordawekar, R., Saraswat, V.: GPU programming in a high level language: compiling X10 to CUDA. In: Proceedings of the 2011 ACM SIGPLAN X10 Workshop. X10 2011. Association for Computing Machinery, New York, NY, USA (2011). https://doi.org/10.1145/2212736.2212744

8. Ghangas, R., Milthorpe, J.: Chapel on accelerators. In: 2020 IEEE International Parallel and Distributed Processing Symposium Workshops, IPDPSW 2020, New Orleans, LA, USA, 18–22 May 2020, pp. 679–679. IEEE (2020). https://doi.org/10.1109/IPDPSW50202.2020.00121

9. Hayashi, A., Paul, S.R., Sarkar, V.: GPUIterator: bridging the gap between chapel and GPU platforms. In: Proceedings of the ACM SIGPLAN 6th on Chapel Implementers and Users Workshop, pp. 2–11. CHIUW 2019. Association for Computing Machinery, New York, NY, USA (2019). https://doi.org/10.1145/3329722.3330142

10. Hayashi, A., Paul, S.R., Sarkar, V.: Accelerating CHAMPS on GPUs. CHIUW 2022 (2022). https://chapel-lang.org/CHIUW/2022/Hayashi.pdf

11. Hayashi, A., et al.: GPUIterator and GPUAPI repository. https://github.com/ahayashi/chapel-gpu (2019)

12. Kayraklioglu, E., Stone, A., Iten, D., Nguyen, S., Ferguson, M., Strout, M.: Targeting GPUs Using Chapel's Locality and Parallelism Features. CHIUW 2022 (2022). https://chapel-lang.org/CHIUW/2022/Kayraklioglu.pdf

13. Sidelnik, A., Maleki, S., Chamberlain, B.L., Garzarán, M.J., Padua, D.: Performance portability with the chapel language. In: Proceedings of the 2012 IEEE 26th International Parallel and Distributed Processing Symposium, pp. 582–594. IPDPS 2012, IEEE Computer Society, Washington, DC, USA (2012). https://doi.org/10.1109/IPDPS.2012.60

14. Zhao, J., et al.: hipLZ repository (2021). https://github.com/jz10/anl-gt-gpu

15. Zheng, Y., et al.: UPC++: a PGAS extension for C++. In: 2014 IEEE 28th International Parallel and Distributed Processing Symposium, Phoenix, AZ, USA, 19–23 May 2014, pp. 1105–1114. IPDPS 2014 (2014). https://doi.org/10.1109/IPDPS.2014.115

Precise Energy Consumption Measurements of Heterogeneous Artificial Intelligence Workloads

René Caspart[1]([⊠]), Sebastian Ziegler[2], Arvid Weyrauch[1], Holger Obermaier[1], Simon Raffeiner[1], Leon Pascal Schuhmacher[1], Jan Scholtyssek[2], Darya Trofimova[2], Marco Nolden[2], Ines Reinartz[1], Fabian Isensee[2], Markus Götz[1], and Charlotte Debus[1]

[1] Karlsruhe Institute of Technology (KIT), Karlsruhe, Germany
{rene.caspart,arvid.weyrauch,holger.obermaier,simon.raffeiner,
leon.schuhmacher,ines.reinartz,markus.goetz,charlotte.debus}@kit.edu
[2] German Cancer Research Centre (DKFZ), Heidelberg, Germany
{sebastian.ziegler,jan.scholtyssek,darya.trofimova,
marco.nolden,fabian.isensee}@dkfz-heidelberg.de

Abstract. With the rise of artificial intelligence (AI) in recent years and the subsequent increase in complexity of the applied models, the growing demand in computational resources is starting to pose a significant challenge. The need for higher compute power is being met with increasingly more potent accelerator hardware as well as the use of large and powerful compute clusters. However, the gain in prediction accuracy from large models trained on distributed and accelerated systems ultimately comes at the price of a substantial increase in energy demand, and researchers have started questioning the environmental friendliness of such AI methods at scale. Consequently, awareness of energy efficiency plays an important role for AI model developers and hardware infrastructure operators likewise. The energy consumption of AI workloads depends both on the model implementation and the composition of the utilized hardware. Therefore, accurate measurements of the power draw of respective AI workflows on different types of compute nodes is key to algorithmic improvements and the design of future compute clusters and hardware. Towards this end, we present measurements of the energy consumption of two typical applications of deep learning models on different types of heterogeneous compute nodes. Our results indicate that 1. contrary to common approaches, deriving energy consumption directly from runtime is not accurate, but the consumption of the compute node needs to be considered regarding its composition; 2. neglecting accelerator hardware on mixed nodes results in overproportional inefficiency regarding energy consumption; 3. energy consumption of model training and inference should be considered separately – while training on GPUs outperforms all other node types regarding both runtime and energy consumption, inference on CPU nodes can be comparably efficient. One advantage of our approach is the fact that the information on energy consumption is available to all users of the supercomputer and not just those with administrator rights, enabling an easy transfer to other workloads alongside a raise in user-awareness of energy consumption.

© Springer Nature Switzerland AG 2022
H. Anzt et al. (Eds.): ISC High Performance 2022 Workshops, LNCS 13387, pp. 108–121, 2022.
https://doi.org/10.1007/978-3-031-23220-6_8

Keywords: Energy measurement · Artificial intelligence · Green AI ·
Energy efficiency · High performance computing · GPUs

1   Introduction

In the past decade, artificial intelligence (AI) methods have yielded great advances in many areas of science and technology. However, growing complexity in prediction tasks is followed by an equally growing size and complexity in the AI models. Training such large models requires an enormous amount of compute resources, as demonstrated by recent publications [1,9]. In addition, the development process usually includes multiple test runs and hyperparameter optimization, further increasing the needed compute time. While modern accelerator hardware and large-scale computer clusters allow AI researchers to implement such models, the extraordinary need for electricity of these IT-infrastructures poses an increasing challenge, especially with regards to climate change. Recent studies have therefore placed a focus not only on the predictive accuracy of modern AI models, but also on their environmental friendliness in terms of energy consumption and CO_2 footprint [23]. Yet, current efforts rely mainly on estimating electricity consumption from training and prediction (inference) runtimes [26]. Such approaches can only give a rough approximation and do not factor in consumption differences of specific hardware components or executed tasks. To properly gauge the gain in prediction accuracy versus the additional model complexity, as well as raise user awareness on the energy consumption of their AI applications accurate measurements of AI workload energy consumption are needed.

In conventional high-performance-computing, measuring energy consumption of computer code has been investigated thoroughly. Several studies have used either external or internal power meters for assessing the power consumption of commonly used numeric algorithms [5]. For AI models, however, there exists little work on actual measurements of electricity consumption.

Modern deep learning models are increasingly trained on large computer clusters, where measurements via external power meters are not feasible. An alternative is investigating electricity draw of a single device, e.g. a single GPU via NVIDIAs management library (NVML). However, AI workloads are typically run on entire compute nodes, which host nodes with more than one accelerator device or multiple thereof, connected via a fabric. Thus, the energy consumption of the entire training pipeline cannot be precisely captured by linear scaling with the number of GPUs utilized as this would neglect the consumption of the enclosing environment of the accelerator, e.g. CPU, RAM, local disks, fabric, and so forth. Furthermore, despite the tremendous success of GPUs for deep learning applications, access to accelerator hardware is still limited, and many super-computers still host mainly CPU-only nodes.

In order to assess the energy consumption of large-scale neural network training as well as raising user awareness on the carbon footprint of extensive, and potentially inefficient, AI workloads, comprehensive, easily accessible and yet precise assessment of the nodes energy consumption is needed. However, the information on hardware power draw usually requires root access to the system and is therefore not available to common users. Towards this end, the following study presents whole node energy measurements of two use cases representing typical deep learning applications, an image classification problem and a time series forecasting problem. Energy profiles and consumption of these workloads were evaluated in a way that is available to all users of the system. To highlight the differences in heterogeneous hardware compositions, model training and prediction is run on different compute node types with and without GPUs. For all of the experiments, we limit ourselves to measuring the energy consumption in an as-is state of the worker nodes of the HPC cluster. We explicitly do not optimize the node configuration, power limits and CPU frequencies to the specific use case, to imitate the usage scenario of a typical user of an HPC system.

The remainder of the paper is organized as follows: Sect. 2 discusses prior work on the topic of measuring power consumption of compute hardware and energy-efficient AI. Section 3 introduces the use cases, including model architectures and datasets, as well as the compute environment and energy measurement tools utilized in the study. Results of the energy measurements are presented in Sect. 4. Finally, Sect. 5 discusses the found results and future studies.

2   Related Work

Power Aware Computing. Energy Efficient HPC is an important topic for the HPC community, specifically in the light of exascale clusters. Many efforts to study and improve the overall energy efficiency of HPC clusters and corresponding aspects are coordinated and conducted as part of the "Energy Efficient High Performance Computing Working Group" [29].

Many studies are conducted on the energy consumption of HPC systems to guide the design and develop strategies to improve the energy efficiency of an HPC clusters as a whole, e.g. [4,16,18]. Additional studies consider optimizing the energy distribution in an HPC cluster [6,31]. These focus on improving the overall performance of a cluster, while respecting an overall power limit. Patel et al.[20,21] and Shin et al. [24] studied the power consumption and behaviour of an HPC center across many different jobs. Our work shares commonalities with these studies, however, we focus ourselves on AI/ML workflows and aim at providing a view of the energy consumption of typical workloads in this domain, as they are performed by users of HPC clusters on a daily basis. We explore and compare different possible usage options for these jobs on the cluster, aiming to incentivise energy efficiency considerations among the users in this domain.

Several authors have published studies on energy measurements utilizing power meters, which can be categorized into two different approaches: internal or external ones. Among others Suda et al. [27] used external power meters via clamp probes with the aim of verifying a power model for workloads. On their own, these types of measurement are not practical, since their implementation requires substantial efforts and the approach is hardly suited for larger cluster setups, such as high-performance computing clusters. Internal power meters can be further subdivided based on which parts of a system are measured by it. On most nowadays available NVIDIA and AMD GPUs internal power meters are available. These can be read out using high-level libraries and tools, such as NVML [17] or corresponding tools for AMD. Using NVML to provide real-time power measurement data for GPUs has been studied and compared to a proposed power model used for predicting power demands of linear algebraic kernels on GPUs [10]. However, utilizing libraries and tools like NVML yield only power metrics for the GPUs in a system, which makes out only one part of the energy consumption of the full system. Other components such as CPU, memory or local disk, are not taken into account with this approach. Considering the power draw of all components of a node becomes particularly important for scientists having the choice of different compute nodes to run their computation on, e.g. CPU-only nodes and nodes also equipped with GPU accelerators.

Many system vendors are integrating internal solutions for measuring the power demand of a system, which provide important information to HPC operators. A study to make information relying on these tools also available to users of the systems is for example the joint HDEEM project between Bull and Technical University Dresden (TUD), which aims to provide high resolution and accurate power consumption metrics [8]. The approach is also used in production at TUD enabling users to gain information on the energy consumption of their workloads.

Energy Efficiency in AI. Recently, awareness on the energy consumption and eco-friendliness of modern AI methods has been raised [23]. Yet, there are only few reports studying the actual energy consumption of modern day AI algorithms. In general, it is assumed that a reduction in runtime, especially for training, and/or number of parameters results in more energy efficient networks. Several authors rely on estimating power consumption based on the number of used floating point operations per second (FLOPs), e.g. Brown et al. [1]. To reduce training time, authors employ approaches like pre-training and few-shot learning [3]. To reduce the parameter count, sparsity is extensively explored in the literature. So far, these approaches are mostly limited to inference models, i.e. pruning fully trained models to smaller sizes for deployment on low-energy (embedded) hardware, e.g. FPGAs or ASICs [14]. However, direct measurements of the entire energy consumption including all hardware components is rarely performed. Strubell et al. [26] estimated electricity usage and carbon dioxide footprint of training, tuning and inference of several well-known large deep learning models. Their method is based on the runtime of these models, also factoring in the effects of hyperparameter tuning. In an attempt to further raise awareness around the carbon emissions of machine learning methods Lacoste et al. [12] presented a *Machine Learning Emissions Calculator*, that estimates the CO_2 emission of a given model based on the geographical location of the utilized server, the type of utilized accelerator and the overall training time of the model.

Li et al. [13] evaluated the power behavior and energy efficiency of convolutional neural networks (CNN) in commonly used deep learning frameworks on

Table 1. Summary of the computational properties of the use cases *Health* and *Energy*.

Use case	Model	Parameters	FLOPs/sample
Health	CNN	20.4M	10.14G
Energy	LSTM	9.79K	16.13K

both, CPUs and GPUs, namely Intel Xeon CPUs, NVIDIA K20 and Titan X GPUs. Power draw of different CNNs were assessed via Intel's Running Average Power Limit (RAPL) interface for CPU and VRAM [2], and via the NVIDIA System Management Interface for GPUs. Our work is similar to that performed by Hodak et al. [7]. In their study, the authors perform measurements of the total consumed energy as well as relative CPU, GPU and other hardware contributions in a typical image recognition task. They ran training of an ImageNet-based Tensorflow benchmark on multi-GPU-Servers, comprising four 32 GB NVIDIA V100 GPUs and two Intel Xeon Gold 6142 CPUs, and measured both AC and DC draw over the entire AI workload through power meters embedded in the servers power supplies as well as through NVML.

3   Experimental Evaluation

In order to evaluate energy consumption of different AI workloads on heterogeneous hardware nodes, we performed experimental runs of two types of deep learning applications (use cases) on different types of compute nodes on a high-performance computer cluster.

3.1   Workloads

For the use cases, two common types of AI tasks were chosen: a computer vision classification task and a time series regression task. With the aim of measuring energy consumption of AI workloads representing typical scientific applications of deep neural networks, real-world datasets for these two tasks were selected from the research fields *Health* and *Energy*. For both use cases, training and prediction runs with realistic model configurations were conducted on different types of large scale compute nodes, and the overall energy consumption was measured. Table 1 shows a high-level summary of the computational characteristics of the used deep learning models.

Use Case *Energy*. For the use case *Energy*, we chose the task of predicting future electricity consumption (load) over a 7-day period based on historic data. In terms of AI workloads, this corresponds to a classical time-series forecasting, i.e. regression problem. The dataset was derived from the Western Europe Power Consumption Dataset [22], which consists of five years of load data of 15 European countries. The datasets was prepared to be continuous and complete, i.e.

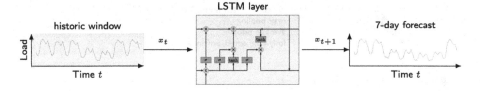

Fig. 1. Schematic LSTM architecture for the use case *Energy* to forecasting electrical load for a 7-day period.

NaNs were removed and all load curves were brought to a temporal resolution of 1 h through averaging. Samples were normalized separately for each country to the interval $[0, 1]$. Training data covers the years 2014–2017, validation and test data was taken from the years 2018 and 2019, respectively.

A single layer long-short term memory (LSTM) architecture (cf. Fig. 1) with 48 hidden nodes was used to forecast the hourly electric demand for the next seven days based on the prior seven days load profiles as input [11,15]. The resulting 48 output features were mapped to the required single output feature with one fully-connected layer, i.e. each recurrent loop of the model produces a one-week ahead forecast. While the model itself is rather small in terms of trainable parameters (cf. Table 1) the recurrence in sequence processing results in a substantial computation workload.

The model was trained for 30 epochs with the Adam optimizer at a learning rate of 10^{-3} and a batch size of 64. Loss was calculated as the mean squared error (MSE). All related scripts can be found on GitHub[1].

Use Case *Health*. The second use case *Health* covered the task of predicting a COVID-19 infection based on an lung x-ray images, i.e. an image classification problem. The dataset was taken from the COVID-Net Open Initiative [30] on Kaggle [32]. It comprises 2,358 images of COVID-19-positive patients and 13,993 images of COVID-19-negative patients, collected from various sources. We employed a different data split than the one provided by Kaggle, to prevent data sources in training and test data from overlapping. The training set contains 2,088 positive and 13,696 negative samples, the validation set contains 74 positive and 76 and negative samples and the test set contains 196 positive and 221 negative samples. Images were transformed by applying a logarithmic transform and random blurring. For the prediction model we followed the VGG-19 architecture [25], adding batch normalization and replacing the three fully connected layers in the end by an average pooling and one fully connected layer. The model was trained for 250 epochs using the SGD optimizer with a Cosine Annealing learning rate scheduler at an initial learning rate of 0.1 and a batch size of 64. Data was augmented during training by resizing, applying random horizontal flips and random rotations, taking a random crop of 224×224 pixels and finally normalizing the image. For validation and testing the images only

---

[1] https://github.com/Helmholtz-AI-Energy/AI-HERO-Energy.

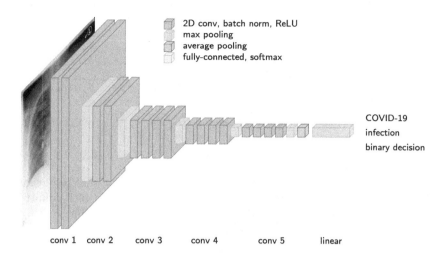

2D conv, batch norm, ReLU
max pooling
average pooling
fully-connected, softmax

COVID-19
infection
binary decision

conv 1   conv 2   conv 3   conv 4   conv 5   linear

Fig. 2. VGG model architecture for the use case *Health* to predict a COVID-19 infection based on the x-ray input images.

got resized to the respective size and normalized. The entire code used to run the model can be found on GitHub[2].

3.2 Computation Environment

All experiments are conducted on the Tier-2 *HoreKa* supercomputing system, an innovative hybrid cluster with nearly 60 000 Intel Xeon "Ice Lake" processor cores, more than 220 terabytes of main memory, and nearly 700 NVIDIA A100 Tensor Core GPUs. The system is designed as an energy efficient system, peaking at rank 25 in the Green500 [28]. HoreKa consists of two partitions, a CPU-only partition (HoreKa-Blue) designed for highly parallel MPI applications with large memory bandwidth and an accelerated partition (HoreKa-Green) equipped with state-of-the-art accelerators for extremely data- and compute-intensive applications in machine learning. Each of the nodes is a two socket system with Intel Xeon Platinum 8368 CPUs, 38 cores per socket, and two threads per core. It has 64 KB L1 and 1 MB L2 cache per core and 57 MB shared L3 cache per CPU. Horeka-Blue nodes feature 256 GB of main memory and one 960 GB NVMe SSD each. HoreKa-Green nodes are equipped with 512 GB of main memory and four NVIDIA A100-40 GPUs. The operating system of the nodes is Red Hat Enterprise Linux 8.2 with kernel version 4.18.0-193.60.2.el8_2.x86_64, with NVIDIA driver version 470.57.02, and CUDA version 11.4 for the nodes equipped with A100 accelerators. Our use cases are implemented in Python 3.8.0 compiled with GCC 8.3.1 20191121 (Red Hat 8.3.1–5) using the PyTorch framework [19] versioned 1.11.0.dev20210929+cu111. For the interactive access to the compute resources, we utilize the available Jupyterhub service, which uses jupyterlab 3.3.2 and jupyter_server 1.16.0.

---

[2] https://github.com/Helmholtz-AI-Energy/AI-HERO-Health.

3.3 Measurement Setup

AI workloads, containing the full pipeline of either model training or inference for the two different use cases, were run as batch jobs on the HoreKa system. For measuring energy consumption, we consider four different cases of run setups, depending on the utilized hardware:

- *GPU*: The workload was run as exclusive on one A100 GPU of a HoreKa-Green node, while the other three GPUs were kept idle

- *CPU-mix*: The workload was run on all 76 CPU cores of a HoreKa-Green node, while all of the four GPUs were kept idle

- *CPU-only*: The workload was run on all 76 CPU cores of a HoreKa-Blue node, which do not contain any GPUs

- *Jupyter*: Additionally, an entire analysis pipeline including data exploration and plotting was created in a Jupyter notebook and run on one GPU of a HoreKa-Green node.

Energy consumption of the workloads was assessed via two different sources. For one, internal power sensors of the HoreKa nodes were used to measure whole node energy consumption of the entire workflow. These sensors are part of Lenovo's XClarity Controller (XCC), which can be read via IPMI. To enable access to the energy consumption information without requiring root access on the nodes or sharing of access credentials to the management interfaces of the nodes, a slurm plugin is used. This plugin queries the information from XCC and stores it in slurm's accounting database as accumulated energy consumption. To facilitate a reproducibility of our results and applicability of the method also to other workloads, we rely solely on information which can easily be accessed by any user of the HoreKa system. For the evaluation, we query the average and total energy consumption for the jobs from slurm. As a second source of information, we utilize NVML to assess the individual energy consumption of the GPUs for the workloads *GPU* and *Jupyter* running on accelerator hardware. In order to profile the power draw on the GPUs, NVML was queried every 500 ms. For statistical assessment, runs were repeated five times. We report average measurement parameters for job wall-clock time, average node power draw and overall workload energy consumption.

4 Results

Use Case Energy. The LSTM model achieved a mean absolute percentage error (MAPE) of 5.65% on the unnormalized test dataset within the 30 epochs. Since the test dataset is comparably small and would result in very short inference runtimes with consequently little to no noticeable energy consumption above baseline, measurements of prediction energy consumption were conducted on a separate dataset containing five copies of the training dataset.

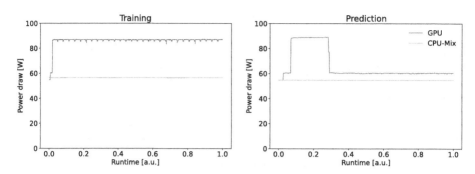

Fig. 3. Jobprofile of the Energy use case, as acquired via NVML.

Table 2. Results of the Energy use case.

	Node	Consumption [kJ]	Average power draw [W]	Runtime
Training	GPU	680.7 ± 6.7	665.8 ± 9.7	00:17:02
	CPU-mix	$4\,856.0 \pm 43.6$	644.4 ± 9.9	02:05:37
	CPU-only	$2\,821.5 \pm 70.8$	374.1 ± 11.0	02:05:42
Prediction	GPU	156.9 ± 3.4	606.6 ± 8.8	00:04:18
	CPU-mix	320.2 ± 5.9	621.5 ± 7.9	00:08:35
	CPU-only	189.5 ± 4.8	370.6 ± 8.7	00:08:31
Jupyter	GPU	701.9	–	00:17:26

Figure 3 shows the power draw of the LSTM training and inference workload on HoreKa-Green nodes both with (green, *GPU*) and without (blue, *CPU-Mix*) usage of the GPU, as measured by NVML. As expected, when running the model on the nodes CPU-partition, the GPU stagnates at an idle consumption of roughly 55 W. For running the model, the GPU consumes an additional energy of ≈30 W, with small drops between epochs being visible. For prediction, a similar increment in energy consumption can be observed (between 0.05 and 0.3 of the fractional runtime), with the much longer low-energy idle time towards the end of the inference run attributed to result saving.

Results of the overall node energy consumption, average power draw and runtimes of the workload on different node types are given in Table 2. Training of the LSTM network on one NVIDIA A100 GPU is superior to running it on 76 CPU cores with respect to both runtime and energy efficiency: While *GPU* runs consumed only one quarter of the energy the *CPU-only* runs required, they was faster by a factor of ≈7.4. Although the average power draw of the *GPU* runs is almost twice as much as that of the *CPU-only* runs, the immense speed-up achieved through vector processing of the GPU still results in a reduced energy consumption, even for a inherently sequential problem that is a recurrent neural network. Interestingly, while runtimes on were very similar for the *CPU-only* and the *CPU-Mix* runs, the additional idle consumption of the GPUs on mixed nodes

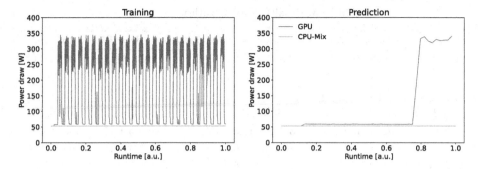

Fig. 4. Jobprofile of the Health use case, as acquired via NVML.

led to a significant increase in energy consumption by a factor of 1.7. Results
for the inference runs however show, that even though jobs utilizing the GPUs
run faster by a factor of 2, *CPU-only* provides comparable energy consumption.
Again, runtimes on both *CPU-only* and *CPU-mix* were comparable, but the
additional power draw of the idle GPUs leads to a higher energy consumption of
the mixed nodes. Furthermore, we find that running a full analysis pipeline (data
exploration, training and inference) in a Jupyter notebook on an A100 of the
HoreKa-Green nodes results in similar energy consumption and runtimes as bash
processing. However, this is under the assumption, that all cells of the notebook
are executed immediately one after another, with no idle-time in between. Since
this is usually not the utilization mode of Jupyter notebooks, additional baseline
consumption of $\approx$300 W for notebook idle time will be added for real-world
applications.

Use Case Health. The VGG model of the use case *Health* achieved an accuracy
of 63.79% on the test set. Training the model to full convergence (250 epochs)
took 2 h and 34 min on one A100 GPU, with an overall energy consumption
of 7723.958 kJ and an average node power draw of 835.4W. Since running full
training on CPUs of an entire node would have taken several weeks to complete,
we conducted shortened experiments of 25 epochs to train the VGG model. Due
to the small size of the test dataset and the subsequent difficulties in accurately
assessing inference power draw, prediction runs were modified such that each
sample in the test set was used 10 times for prediction. Results are presented
in Fig. 4 and Table 3. The GPU power draw profile exhibits a similar behavior
as previously the *Energy* use case: While for the *CPU-Mix* run on mixed nodes
the GPU stagnates at an idle consumption around 55 W, the training workload
with individual epochs can be clearly seen in the *GPU* run. With this use case
however being much more compute intensive due to the processing of images
instead of single-value time-series, the additional power draw from the workload
amounts to about 300 W on top of the baseline consumption. For prediction,
a major fraction of the job runtime was used for data loading, which resulted
only in a small increase in energy consumption. The largest contribution to the

Table 3. Results of the Health use case.

	Node	Consumption [kJ]	Average power draw [W]	Runtime
Training	GPU	761.7 ± 17.0	835.6 ± 6.8	00:15:11
	CPU-mix	$109\,477.1 \pm 1\,104.9$	651.7 ± 7.4	1-22:39:43
	CPU-only	$65\,796.7 \pm 4\,899.4$	392.1 ± 28.8	1-22:36:31
Prediction	GPU	46.7 ± 2.0	549.5 ± 14.3	00:01:25
	CPU-mix	367.8 ± 10.2	644.5 ± 17.1	00:09:30
	CPU-only	213.5 ± 8.6	377.4 ± 15.6	00:09:25
Jupyter	GPU	783.6	−	00:16:06

power draw budget stems from running model predictions towards the end of the workflow.

Total node energy consumption and runtime of *GPU* runs is superior to runs using only CPUs in training as well as inference, even though the *CPU-only* runs provide a much lower average power draw. Runs on *CPU-only* require about 86 times more energy for training than those on *GPU*, and 4.5 times more energy for inference. The increase in consumed energy of runs on CPUs is not directly proportional to the increase in runtime, since prediction runs on CPUs take ≈ 6.3 times as long as runs on the GPU and training runs took about 194 times as long as on the GPU. Hence the electricity demand of workloads cannot safely be extrapolated from runtime alone, but there is a hardware specific component, making *CPU-only* nodes still relatively efficient in terms of energy consumption. In any case, runs on *CPU-mix* yielded the poorest results with respect to energy consumption as well as runtime.

Running the full training and inference pipeline in a Jupyter notebook results again in similar values for runtime and energy consumption as the batch job on a GPU. The power draw resulting from data exploration and plotting appears to be negligible in comparison to the training workload of the model.

5   Conclusion

In this study, we presented high-precision measurements of whole-node energy consumption of two different AI workloads run on different heterogeneous node types of a large scale supercomputer. Our results show that for image-related deep learning models, running training and inference on a single GPU provides both shorter runtimes and lower power draw than multi-core CPU nodes. The massively parallel processing capabilities of the A100 lead to higher energy efficiency due to the significant reduction in runtime. For non-imaging workloads such as recurrent neural networks for sequential data, inference on CPU yields a comparably low energy consumption as the GPU runs, providing a valid alternative for production runs if there are no runtime constraints.

Our results further demonstrate that energy consumption of composite compute nodes cannot be estimated accurately from linear scaling in runtime of GPU consumption. Especially for sequential data problems, a significant contribution of the energy consumption originates from the baseline of the entire node, e.g. CPU usage and memory access.

From our experiments, it is further evident that GPU idle time results in a non-negligible portion of energy consumption. Hence, GPUs should be utilized for deep learning workflows when available, even if the problem size or network architecture do not demand it straight away. This aspect also makes a strong argument for data parallel multi-GPU training, leveraging the compute power of all accelerators on a node. Finally, we showed that running AI workloads in Jupyter provides comparable energy consumption to submission via batch jobs, thereby facilitating the usage of GPUs and allowing for rapid prototyping while still maintaining energy efficiency.

A major advantage of our approach is the fact that access to metrics of node power consumption measurements is not restricted to users with administration rights, but can be queried by every user of the system for his or her workloads. With this, AI model developers will be sensitized towards the energy footprint of their models and are able to include considerations on energy efficiency into every step of the development process. In future studies, we aim to further map out the energy consumption of different parts of AI workflows through accurately profiling entire node power draw, as well as investigate the energy efficiency of modern AI models, namely self-attention-based architectures. Furthermore, studies taking into account system-level optimization for the power consumption are foreseen.

Acknowledgment. This work was performed on the HoreKa supercomputer funded by the Ministry of Science, Research and the Arts Baden-Württemberg and by the Federal Ministry of Education and Research.

This work is supported by the Helmholtz Association Initiative and Networking Fund under the Helmholtz AI, HIDSS4Health, Helmholtz Imaging and the Helmholtz Metadata Collaboration platform grants and the HAICORE@KIT partition.

References

1. Brown, T., et al.: Language models are few-shot learners. Adv. Neural Inf. Process. Syst. **33**, 1877–1901 (2020)
2. David, H., Gorbatov, E., Hanebutte, U.R., Khanna, R., Le, C.: RAPL: memory power estimation and capping. In: 2010 ACM/IEEE International Symposium on Low-Power Electronics and Design (ISLPED), pp. 189–194. IEEE (2010)
3. Devlin, J., Chang, M.W., Lee, K., Toutanova, K.: BERT: Pre-training of Deep Bidirectional Transformers for Language Understanding (2018). https://doi.org/10.48550/ARXIV.1810.04805, URL https://arxiv.org/abs/1810.04805
4. Endrei, M., et al.: Energy efficiency modeling of parallel applications. In: SC18: International Conference for High Performance Computing, Networking, Storage and Analysis, pp. 212–224 (2018). https://doi.org/10.1109/SC.2018.00020
5. Ezzatti, P., Quintana-Ortí, E.S., Remón, A., Saak, J.: Power-aware computing (2019)

6. Gholkar, N., Mueller, F., Rountree, B., Marathe, A.: Pshifter: feedback-based dynamic power shifting within HPC jobs for performance. In: Proceedings of the 27th International Symposium on High-Performance Parallel and Distributed Computing, pp. 106–117, HPDC 2018, Association for Computing Machinery, New York, NY, USA (2018). ISBN 9781450357852, https://doi.org/10.1145/3208040.3208047

7. Hodak, M., Gorkovenko, M., Dholakia, A.: Towards power efficiency in deep learning on data center hardware. In: 2019 IEEE International Conference on Big Data (Big Data), pp. 1814–1820. IEEE (2019)

8. Ilsche, T., et al.: Power measurement techniques for energy-efficient computing: reconciling scalability, resolution, and accuracy. SICS Softw.-Intens. Cyber-Phys. Syst. **34**(1), 45–52 (2018). https://doi.org/10.1007/s00450-018-0392-9

9. Jumper, J., et al.: Highly accurate protein structure prediction with AlphaFold. Nature **596**(7873), 583–589 (2021)

10. Kasichayanula, K., Terpstra, D., Luszczek, P., Tomov, S., Moore, S., Peterson, G.D.: Power aware computing on GPUs. In: 2012 Symposium on Application Accelerators in High Performance Computing, pp. 64–73. IEEE (2012)

11. Kong, W., Dong, Z.Y., Jia, Y., Hill, D.J., Xu, Y., Zhang, Y.: Short-term residential load forecasting based on LSTM recurrent neural network. IEEE Trans. Smart Grid **10**(1), 841–851 (2019). ISSN 1949–3061, https://doi.org/10.1109/TSG.2017.2753802

12. Lacoste, A., Luccioni, A., Schmidt, V., Dandres, T.: Quantifying the carbon emissions of machine learning. arXiv preprint arXiv:1910.09700 (2019)

13. Li, D., Chen, X., Becchi, M., Zong, Z.: Evaluating the energy efficiency of deep convolutional neural networks on CPUs and GPUs. In: 2016 BDCloud-SocialCom-SustainCom, pp. 477–484. IEEE (2016)

14. Montgomerie-Corcoran, A., Venieris, S.I., Bouganis, C.S.: Power-aware FPGA mapping of convolutional neural networks. In: 2019 International Conference on Field-Programmable Technology (ICFPT), pp. 327–330. IEEE (2019)

15. Muzaffar, S., Afshari, A.: Short-term load forecasts using LSTM networks. Energy Procedia **158**, 2922–2927 (2019). ISSN 1876–6102, https://doi.org/10.1016/j.egypro.2019.01.952, https://www.sciencedirect.com/science/article/pii/S1876610219310008

16. Nonaka, J., Hanawa, T., Shoji, F.: Analysis of cooling water temperature impact on computing performance and energy consumption. In: 2020 IEEE International Conference on Cluster Computing (CLUSTER), pp. 169–175 (2020). https://doi.org/10.1109/CLUSTER49012.2020.00027

17. NVIDIA Corporation: NVML API Reference. https://docs.nvidia.com/deploy/nvml-api/index.html (2022). Accessed 03 Apr 2022

18. Pakin, S., et al.: Power usage of production supercomputers and production workloads. Concurr. Comput. Pract. Exper. **28**(2), 274–290 (2016). https://doi.org/10.1002/cpe.3191,https://onlinelibrary.wiley.com/doi/abs/10.1002/cpe.3191

19. Paszke, A., Gross, S., Massa, F., Lerer, A., et al.: Pytorch: an imperative style, high-performance deep learning library. Adv. Neural Inf. Process. Syst. **32**, 8024–8035, Curran Associates, Inc. (2019). http://papers.neurips.cc/paper/9015-pytorch-an-imperative-style-high-performance-deep-learning-library.pdf

20. Patel, T., Liu, Z., Kettimuthu, R., Rich, P.M., Allcock, W.E., Tiwari, D.: Job characteristics on large-scale systems: long-term analysis, quantification, and implications. In: SC20: International Conference for High Performance Computing, Networking, Storage and Analysis, pp. 1–17 (2020)

21. Patel, T., Wagenhäuser, A., Eibel, C., Hönig, T., Zeiser, T., Tiwari, D.: What does power consumption behavior of HPC jobs reveal?: demystifying, quantifying, and predicting power consumption characteristics. In: 2020 IEEE International Parallel and Distributed Processing Symposium (IPDPS), pp. 799–809 (2020). https://doi.org/10.1109/IPDPS47924.2020.00087

22. Raucent, F.: Western Europe Power Consumption Dataset. https://www.kaggle.com/datasets/francoisraucent/western-europe-power-consumption (2020)

23. Schwartz, R., Dodge, J., Smith, N.A., Etzioni, O.: Green AI. Commun. ACM **63**(12), 54–63 (2020)

24. Shin, W., Oles, V., Karimi, A.M., Ellis, J.A., Wang, F.: Revealing power, energy and thermal dynamics of a 200pf pre-exascale supercomputer. In: Proceedings of the International Conference for High Performance Computing, Networking, Storage and Analysis, SC 2021, Association for Computing Machinery, New York, NY, USA (2021). ISBN 9781450384421, https://doi.org/10.1145/3458817.3476188, https://doi.org/10.1145/3458817.3476188

25. Simonyan, K., Zisserman, A.: Very deep convolutional networks for large-scale image recognition. arXiv preprint arXiv:1409.1556 (2014)

26. Strubell, E., Ganesh, A., McCallum, A.: Energy and policy considerations for deep learning in NLP. arXiv preprint arXiv:1906.02243 (2019)

27. Suda, R., et al.: Accurate measurements and precise modeling of power dissipation of CUDA kernels toward power optimized high performance CPU-GPU computing. In: 2009 International Conference on Parallel and Distributed Computing, Applications and Technologies, pp. 432–438. IEEE (2009)

28. TOP500.org: Green500 List - June 2022. https://www.top500.org/lists/green500/2022/06/ (2022). Accessed 01 July 2022

29. WG, E.H.: Energy Efficient High Performance Computing Working Group. https://eehpcwg.llnl.gov/ (2022). Accessed 01 July 2022

30. Wong, A.: COVID-Net Open Initiative. https://alexswong.github.io/COVID-Net/ (2020). Accessed 29 Mar 2022

31. Zhang, H., Hoffmann, H.: Podd: power-capping dependent distributed applications. In: Proceedings of the International Conference for High Performance Computing, Networking, Storage and Analysis, SC 2019, Association for Computing Machinery, New York, NY, USA (2019). ISBN 9781450362290, https://doi.org/10.1145/3295500.3356174

32. Zhao, A.: COVIDx CXR-2 (2021). https://www.kaggle.com/datasets/andyczhao/covidx-cxr2/

.

Malleability Techniques Applications in
High Performance Computing

Malleability Techniques and Applications in High-Performance Computing (HPCMALL 2022)

Jesús Carretero[1] ⓘ, Martin Schulz[2,3] ⓘ, and Estela Suarez[4,5] ⓘ

[1] University Carlos III of Madrid, Spain
jcarrete@inf.uc3m.es
[2] Technical University of Munich, Germany
schulzm@in.tum.de
[3] Leibniz Supercomputing Centre (LRZ), Germany
[4] Juelich Supercomputing Centre, Forschungszentrum Juelich GmbH, Germany
e.suarez@fz-juelich.de
[5] University of Bonn, Germany

Abstract. The continuously growing complexity and heterogeneity of system architectures, together with the increased usage of complex and dynamic workflow, makes the current static usage model of HPC systems increasingly inefficient. Malleability techniques that allow dynamically increasing or reducing the hardware allocation of a given application promise a much more flexible usage mode, in which the use of resources in a shared system can be maximized. This ISC 2022 workshop has presented current research and challenges in the area of malleability.

Keywords: Malleability · Resource management · Dynamic allocation

1 Motivation and Objectives

The current static usage model of HPC systems is becoming increasingly inefficient. This is driven by the continuously growing complexity and heterogeneity of system architectures, in combination with the increased usage of coupled applications, the need for strong scaling with extreme scale parallelism, and the increasing reliance on complex and dynamic workflows. Therefore, we see a rise in research on malleable systems, middleware software and applications, which can adjust resources usage dynamically in order to extract a maximum of efficiency. By providing an intelligent global coordination of resources usage, through runtime scheduling of computation, network usage and I/O across all components of the system architecture, malleable HPC systems can maximize the exploitation of their resources, while at the same time minimizing the makespan of applications in many, if not most, cases.

Of particular concern is the emerging class of data-intensive applications and their interaction with classic simulation workloads, driven by the growing need to process extremely large data sets. However, uncoordinated file access in combination with limited bandwidth make the I/O system a serious bottleneck. Emerging multi-tier storage hierarchies come with the potential to remove this barrier, but maximizing performance still requires careful control to avoid congestion. Malleability allows systems to dynamically adjust the computation and storage needs of applications, on the one side, and the global system on the other.

Such malleable systems, however, face a series of fundamental research challenges, including: who initiates changes in resource availability or usage? How is it communicated? How to compute the optimal usage? How can applications cope with dynamically changing resources? What should malleable programming models and abstractions look like? How to design resource management frameworks for malleable systems? Which resources benefit from malleability, and which (if any) should still be managed statically?

In order to address these challenges, the HPCMALL workshop brought together researchers from diverse areas of HPC that are impacted or actively pursuing malleability concepts, from application developers to system architects, from programming model to system software researchers. The workshop also provided a lively discussion forum for researchers working in HPC and pursuing the concepts of and around malleability topics shown below.

2 Topics

The workshop targeted original high-quality research and position papers on applications, services, and system software for malleable high-performance computing systems. Topics of interest included:

- System and system architecture considerations in designing malleable architectures.
- Emerging software designs to achieve malleability in high-performance computing.
- High-level parallel programming models and programmability techniques to improve applications malleability.
- Run-time techniques to provide malleable execution models for computation, communication and I/O.
- Resource management frameworks and interfaces supporting malleable scheduling, resource allocations and application execution.
- Computing and I/O scheduling algorithms providing and/or exploiting static or dynamic malleability.
- Use of AI and ML techniques to steer malleability in systems and applications.
- Ad-hoc storage systems and I/O scheduling techniques helping I/O malleability.
- Support for malleable execution of applications in performance, debugging and correctness tools.
- Energy efficiency and malleability (applications, over-provisioned systems wrt. power/energy, storage systems, etc.).
- Experiences and use cases applying malleability to HPC applications.

Regular 10-12 page research papers, as well as 6-7 page short or position papers were considered, in order to cover both more mature approaches in the area as well as hot and novel concepts in their early stages.

3 Contributions

The workshop received 10 papers. All of them went through a peer-review process with at least 3 reviewers. After the review process, 7 good quality papers were accepted:

- IMSS: In-Memory Storage System for Data Intensive Applications. Javier Garcia Blas, David E. Singh, and Jesús Carretero.
- *An Emulation Layer for Dynamic Resources with MPI Sessions.* Jan Fecht, Martin Schreiber, and Martin Schulz, Howard Pritchard, and Daniel J. Holmes.
- On the Convergence of Malleability and the HPC PowerStack: Exploiting Dynamism in Over-Provisioned and Power-Constrained HPC Systems. Eishi Arima, Isaías Comprés, and Martin Schulz.
- *Exploiting OpenMP malleability with free agent threads and DLB.* Joel Criado, Victor Lopez, Joan Vinyals-Ylla-Catala, Guillem Ramirez-Miranda, Xavier Teruel, and Marta Garcia-Gasulla.
- Detecting interference between applications and improving the scheduling task using malleable proxies based on application models. Alberto Cascajo, David E. Singh, and Jesus Carretero.
- *QR factorization using Malleable BLAS on Multicore Processors.* Adrian Castelló, Sandra Catalán, Francisco D. Igual, Enrique S. Quintana-Ortí, and Rafael Rodríguez-Sánchez.

4 Workshop organization

4.1 Workshop Chairs

The chairs of this workshop are the three authors of this introduction paper.

- Prof. Jesus Carretero, University Carlos III of Madrid, Spain.
- Prof. Martin Schulz, Technical University of Munich, Germany.
- Prof. Estela Suarez, Juelich Supercomputing Centre, Forschungszentrum Juelich GmbH, Germany

4.2 Program Committee

The workshop program committee was composed of the following members:

- Fabio Affinito. Cineca. Italy
- Alexander Antonov. Moscow State University, Russia
- Jean-Baptiste Besnard. ParaTools SAS. France
- Andre Brinkmann. Johannes Gutenberg-Universität Mainz. Germany
- Iacopo Colonnelli, University of Totino. Italy.
- Norbert Eicker. JSC and Univ. Wuppertal. Germany.
- Hamid Mohammadi Fard. Technical University of Darmstadt. Germany
- Hal Finkel, Department of Energy, USA.
- Javier Garcia Blas. Carlos III University. Spain
- Michael Gerndt. Technical University of Munich. Germany.

- Balazs Gerofi. RIKEN. Japan.
- Emmanuel Jeannot. INRIA. France.
- Michael Klemm. AMD. Germany.
- Masaki Kondo. Keio University. Japan.
- Erwin Laure. MPCDF. Germany.
- Stefano Markidis. KTH. Sweden.
- Ramon Nou. Universitat Politécnica de Catalunya. Spain
- Ariel Oleksiak. Poznan Supercomputing and Networking Center. Poland.
- David E. Singh. Universidad Carlos III de Madrid. Spain
- Martin Schreiber University of Grenoble-Alpes. France
- Sameer Shende. ParaTools SAS. USA.
- Miwako Tsuji. RIKEN AICS. Japan.
- Marc André Vef. Johannes Gutenberg-Universität Mainz. Germany.
- Carlos A. Varela. Rensselaer Polytechnic Institute. USA.
- Vladimir Voevodin. Moscow State University. Russia.
- Mohamed Wahib. AIST/TokyoTech. OIL Japan.
- Josef Weidendorfer. Technical University of Munich. Germany
- Michele Weiland. EPCC- The University of Edinburgh. UK.
- Roman Wyrzykowski. Czestochowa University of Technology. Poland.
- Shahbaz Memon. Juelich Supercomputing Centre, Forschungszentrum Juelich GmbH, Germany.

5   Workshop background and perspective

This was the first edition of this workshop, but the intention is to make this an active workshop over many years. The topic of malleability is under investigation in many projects and research groups and is seen by many experts as one of the key challenges to operate systems at Exascale and beyond.

This proposal is a joint effort of the EuroHPC projects ADMIRE, REGALE, DEEP-SEA, and TIME-X.

6   Acknowledgements

The **ADMIRE project** have received funding from EuroHPC Programme call H2020-JTI-EuroHPC-2019-1, under Grant Agreement n° 956748. The EuroHPC Joint Undertaking (JU) receives support from the European Union's Horizon 2020 research and innovation programme and Spain, Germany, France, Spain, Italy, Sweden, and Poland.

The **DEEP Projects** have received funding from the European Commission's FP7, H2020, and EuroHPC Programmes, under Grant Agreements n° 287530, 610476, 754304, and 955606. The EuroHPC Joint Undertaking (JU) receives support from the European Union's Horizon 2020 research and innovation programme and Germany, France, Spain, Greece, Belgium, Sweden, United Kingdom, Switzerland

The **REGALE project** have received funding from EuroHPC Programme call H2020-JTI-EuroHPC-2019-2, under Grant Agreement n° 956560. The EuroHPC Joint

Undertaking (JU) receives support from the European Union's Horizon 2020 research and innovation programme and Greece, Germany, France, Spain, Austria, and Italy.

The **TIME-X project** have received funding from EuroHPC Programme call H2020-JTI-EuroHPC-2019-1, under Grant Agreement n° 955701. The EuroHPC Joint Undertaking (JU) receives support from the European Union's Horizon 2020 research and innovation programme and Belgium, Germany, France, and Switzerland.

Detecting Interference Between Applications and Improving the Scheduling Using Malleable Application Proxies

Alberto Cascajo$^{(\boxtimes)}$, David E. Singh, and Jesus Carretero

Computer Science and Engineering Department, Universidad Carlos III de Madrid, Madrid, Spain
`acascajo@inf.uc3m.es`

Abstract. LIMITLESS is a lightweight and scalable framework that provides a holistic view of the system employing the combination of both platform and application monitoring. This paper presents a novel feature for improving the scheduling process based on the performance prediction and the detection of interference between real applications. This feature consists of using malleable synthetic benchmark clones (proxies) for the applications executed in the system with two objectives: (1) build large and representative datasets that can be used to train the machine learning algorithms for predicting, and (2) evaluate if two applications can share the same compute node in order to leverage the unused node resources.

Other related works use detailed micro-architecture independent metrics obtained from functional simulators, which are hard to generate in many new applications. The results are proxies that preserve many of the original features of the applications (control flow, memory access pattern, etc.), and their code needs obfuscation to make impossible the use of reverse engineering. LIMITLESS generates application proxies based on generic-purpose performance information collected from monitoring. It means that other methods may obtain more accurate execution behaviours. However, LIMITLESS' proxies generate similar performance without extracting data from the binaries, without the necessity of managing code or data from the applications, and they can be shared securely because they have not been generated using any piece of the original code.

LIMITLESS leverages the generated proxies to execute them offline. Each execution increases the datasets of the machine learning algorithms to improve the application scheduling. Besides, the executions between proxies are combined to detect performance degradation (interference) without the necessity of waiting for the execution of the real applications, which depends on the users. In this work, we evaluate the proposed proxy generation approach on a set of benchmarks and applications. We compare the performance obtained during the execution of the proxies and

---

This work has been partially funded by the European High-Performance Computing Joint Undertaking (JU) under the ADMIRE project (grant agreement No 956748) and the Spanish Ministry of Science and innovation Project DECIDE (Ref. PID2019-107858GB-I00.).

H. Anzt et al. (Eds.): ISC High Performance 2022 Workshops, LNCS 13387, pp. 129–146, 2022.
https://doi.org/10.1007/978-3-031-23220-6_9

the applications to show their similarity. Finally, we include an evaluation of the interference detection using this approach. As far as we know,
this is the first work that uses malleable proxies.

Keywords: Malleable proxy · Malleable synthetic benchmarks ·
Performance cloning · Interference detection · Application scheduling

1   Introduction

One of the key challenges in large-scale clusters is to determine as accurately as
possible the status of the system. In this work, we combine system and application monitoring in order to provide, not only a more accurate cluster monitoring
but also a scheme that permits to model the application behaviour. The goal
is to generate proxies that can be used as benchmarks and to use those proxies to generate more information to improve the application scheduling in two
ways: by predicting the performance of the applications and by detecting interference between applications. Initially, we depend on the user and the executions
he wants to run. However, LIMITLESS can perform different actions without
waiting for the original executions due to the proxies.

The use of benchmarks is one of the keys for assessing computer systems performance. Researchers and engineers need to quantify the performance of their
applications by running them many times and in different architectures. Some
uses of those benchmarks are to compare the design alternatives during development, test computer systems for guiding development, or enable a fair evaluation
of the performance in different architectures. For example, SPEC, CPU2006,
ImplanBench, PARSEC, etc., are benchmarks that provide suites for evaluating
the performance of general-purpose processors. These standard benchmarks are
generally generated based on open-source programs. Their main limitation is
that they are not representative of real-life applications, and usually, they are
very different from the applications of interest to the developers and researchers.
The alternative consists of using real-life applications, but the code are typically
proprietary. The industry could benefit from the researchers because they can
improve their applications: the computer systems could be designed to provide a
good performance of these applications, or by applying new optimizations. And
the researchers could benefit from the industry by using their real applications to
find better design solutions or studying new research lines based on the results.

This paper presents a new alternative for proxies creation based on the generic
performance information obtained by the LIMITLESS system monitor. The monitor collects the performance metrics during the execution of an application in a
compute node and stores them in a database. Then, the analytic component processes those metrics to generate a malleable proxy (using FlexMPI [10]) that reproduces the same performance metrics and can be reconfigured in run time.

The proposed proxy generation features three key properties: (1) no information of the proprietary application is revealed, (2) the performance metrics
obtained by executing the proxy are similar to the original application so that
the proxy can serve as a benchmark to evaluate possible performance behaviours

in whatever architecture, and (3) related to the last point, an intelligent scheduler could combine executions of proxies, and applications and proxies, to check
if there is interference between them, allowing the system to share nodes between
non-conflicting applications. Note that the malleability in already implemented
in the proxies due to their integration with FlexMPI.

The main contributions of this work are:

- A proxy generation feature to provide synthetic malleable micro-benchmarks
  based on the collected performance behaviour.
- An improvement in the application scheduling employing machine learning
  algorithms trained with proxies executions.
- A methodology to improve the application scheduling through the malleable
  proxies, combining them with the real applications to identify interference.
  In this context, malleability means that the system can use a single proxy for
  evaluating different configurations (number of processes) at run-time.

The structure of the paper is as follows: Sect. 2 describes the architecture
organization; Sect. 3 describes LIMITLESS's features for providing proxy generation, Machine Learning training algorithms, and the studies of the interference
between applications; Sect. 4 provides a practical evaluation of the performance
metrics obtained from the proxy executions, the accuracy of the prediction algorithms, and the results of the studies related to the interference between applications; Sect. 5 shows relevant works related to our proposal. Finally, Sect. 6
summarizes the main conclusions and future work.

2 Monitor Architecture

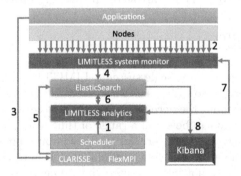

Fig. 1. General overview of the system architecture and interrelation with other components.

LIMITLESS is a light-weight scalable monitor that operates on each compute
node and provides information about available system resources and the performance of the applications that are being executed. Figure 1 shows a general

overview of the LIMITLESS architecture. It is integrated with other components like the application scheduler, FlexMPI and CLARISSE runtimes to extend its capabilities, for example, including features for application-level monitoring. LIMITLESS includes four main modules: a *System monitor* that collects the performance metrics from the cluster, an *ElasticSearch* database [6] that provides persistent storage, Kibana, a *GUI* for displaying the cluster information in a user-friendly format, and an *Analytic* component that analyses and models the executing applications, and generates proxies.

LIMITLESS Analytics (LAN) is the component that deals with the storage, visualization, communication with the scheduler and is responsible of the application performance prediction. It stores and manages the application models, generates the predictors, trains and executes the machine learning algorithms, and it generates the malleable proxies.

In order to explain the system dataflow, the arrows in Fig. 1 include numbers. When one application is executed, the scheduler notifies LIMITLESS Analytics (arrow 1) about the application characteristics (which is used to identify and classify the application). After that, when the applications are executed two different metrics are collected simultaneously: at node level to the monitor (arrow 2) and application level to FlexMPI and CLARISSE (arrow 3). Then, both metrics are processed by the respective runtimes and are written into Elastic search (arrows 4 and 5). Then, the LIMITLESS analytics creates an application model using the information stored in ElasticSearch (arrow 6). Once the application model is generated, the analytics also creates the proxy associated with the application, which can be used to generate more performance metrics to increase the size of the dataset. Then, the predictors are refined using this offline information. And finally, the prediction model (arrow 7) is sent to LIMITLESS to predict the performance of the applications on each node. During all these processes, Kibana may be used to visualize (arrow 8) the cluster status.

2.1   System Monitor

The LIMITLESS monitor is designed to provide performance information of the nodes and applications in large scale systems. LIMITLESS allows to change the the monitoring period (also called *sample interval*) online, having one different for each node, and without the necessity of restarting the system or the monitor. The monitoring interval can be set in a range of time from hours to seconds and also sub-second. Moreover, the overhead in the compute nodes is low ($<1\%$ in CPU consumption and a memory footprint of 3890 KB in resident), which means that the monitoring does not interfere with the applications.

The system monitor consists of one *LIMITLESS Daemon Monitor* (LDM) per node, which periodically collects the performance metrics; a set of *LIMITLESS DaeMon Aggregators* (LDAs), that forwards the information from the LDMs to other aggregators or servers; and the *LIMITLESS DaeMon Server* (LDS) that gathers and stores the monitoring information in ElasticSearch. The deployment over the architecture is done hierarchically, generating a data flow from the nodes (LDMs) to the main server (LDS) and the database. The user

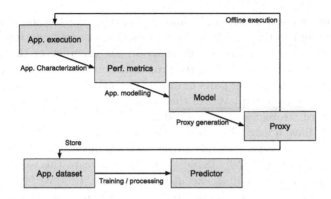

Fig. 2. Designed methodology to create the proxy benchmarks based on the monitoring data, and how that new data is used to produce more accurate predictors.

defines the hierarchy, but the optimal design consists of mapping the hierarchy with the network topology.

3   Building Synthetic Micro-benchmarks

The proposed proxy generation process can be seen in Fig. 2. The first step is the application characterization. This process consists of collecting the performance metrics associated with the running applications. The LIMITLESS Monitor is in charge of providing this collection of metrics. The execution time is also obtained from the scheduler. The second step consists of storing the performance metrics associated with each application in the database. Then, the analytic component generates a model of each application based on the collected performance metrics. Finally, the last step is to generate the proxy based on that model, resulting in an executable that tries to reproduce the same performance metrics as the original application.

The LIMITLESS Analytic component uses the performance models to generate the proxy benchmark. We extend the previous works by a new lightweight proxy generation that do not contain proprietary information, can be shared without any issue, do not need input data, and it is malleable. However, there are also some weaknesses. Note that the resulting proxies are not as accurate as other proposals due to the general-purpose source data.

The LIMITLESS' scheduling policies have been designed for clusters that use shared nodes. They can be applied to clusters with exclusive resource allocations, but they have no potential for improvement. There are three strategies to schedule the applications: the first one is based on monitoring information, the second one is based on prediction, and the last one is based on proxies utilization. The first alternative was implemented in [2] and uses the monitoring information to make decisions about the application schedule depending on the available resources, the performance of the running applications and other user-defined metrics. The second alternative uses the generated application models to predict the future performance of the applications to make decisions about application scheduling in advance, which is a process that does not consume resources or CPU. However, this alternative depends on the accuracy of the predictors. The third strategy consists of using the proxies to combine their executions with other applications to identify pairs of applications that can run concurrently in the same compute node (to leverage the unused resources). The concepts of the second and third strategies are explained below.

In order to have a large dataset for the training and test phases, the framework executes the proxies multiple times until the accuracy of the prediction algorithms enhanced until 85%. Typically, during our tests, this value is achieved when the applications have been executed three times. However, the proxies are not as much accurate as the original application, which means that the training with proxies needs more executions. During our tests, we achieved that accuracy with 10 executions. Instead, LIMITLESS uses the compute-nodes to execute the proxies when there are free computational resources, and the scheduler does not have tasks ready to be run.

3.1   Application for Improving Machine Learning Algorithms

Deep-learning networks perform automatic feature extraction from the datasets independently. Most traditional machine-learning algorithms need to analyze large amounts of data in order to provide accurate predictions, and those datasets has to be large and representative enough of the features that the users want to extract.

The feature extraction process can take a long time to accomplish using statistical analysis by hand. Besides, there is no applications for generating well datasets for training, validating and processing. However, the more data a net can train on, the more accurate it is likely to be. So, the fact of having large datasets with representative data for each feature is directly related to the accuracy improvement.

Following this idea, LIMITLESS uses the proxy generator to produce new synthetic micro-benchmarks to execute at non critical hours and generate more data. Each execution of an application proxy is stored as a model of the original application, increasing the dataset for that application. Then, this dataset is used by the prediction algorithms to predict the performance of the running applications. Predicting the performance behaviour permits the scheduler to improve its policies, making decisions based on possible future scenarios. This proposal is the continuation of a previous work [2] and [3], in which LIMITLESS uses monitoring information to schedule the jobs dynamically. The proxies allow the scheduler to predict possible future states of the nodes and applications. Currently, this information is used to perform dynamic application scheduling based on predicting the future states of the cluster.

Note that this scheduling strategy can be used when an application has run one time because LIMITLESS generates the proxy. Then, the proxy model is used to train and predict. This process substitutes the human action of executing the applications by hand, saving time until the users re-run their applications, and without consuming resources.

3.2   Application for Application Interference Analysis

One of the main objectives to generate these proxies based on application monitoring is the interference evaluation when two applications are running in the same node (note that one application could use more than one node with a different number of processes). This situation can occur when the scheduler allocates the jobs in non-exclusive nodes in order to perform a better utilization of the resources. With this configuration, depending on the available resources of a certain compute node, another application can share the unused ones. However, there is a potential risk of performance degradation (interference) between them. To improve the scheduling task, we propose the use of our malleable proxies to generate a *profiling study* under different workloads while a real application is running in the system.

To know if there is interference between two jobs (two applications, an application and a proxy, or two proxies), the system collects the performance metrics of the applications at the beginning, during a short period of time when the application is running exclusively in the node. Then, when another application is allocated in the same compute node the same performance counters are collected. By comparing the *exclusively-collected* and the *shared-collected* metrics, the system can identify if there is performance degradation. Using this information, the scheduler can make decisions about the scheduling, for instance migrating one of them to avoid the interference, or evaluating if that interference is mitigated when the number of processes is increased or decreased.

The collected information results in three performance counters: RTIME indicates the CPU time per group of iterations, CTIME is the communication time per group of iterations, and finally the execution time TIME. The execution time indicates if there is generic interference between two applications: if the execution time of an application is lower than the obtained when another application is running in the same node, it means that the second application is interfering with the first one. However, using the other counters, the system can identify more details about the reasons behind the performance degradation. This information contributes to making decisions to avoid it. For instance, if the interference is produced at CPU-level, the second application could reduce its processes to mitigate it, or the scheduler could move the second application to another compute node. FlexMPI performs these operations of expanding, reducing and migrating. It allows the application to increase or decrease its processes and redistribute the data every reconfiguration. Note that there is no necessity to kill the job and restart it with the new configuration. In the case of communication-based interference, the solution could be the reduction of the number of processes to reduce the communication between them.

Currently, the malleable proxies are relevant because, during the execution of the real application, the proxies can be run with different configurations: the scheduler, employing FlexMPI, can reconfigure a proxy from 2 processes to n to collect information about the performance and the interference. The objective is to evaluate different configurations to generate a scalability model that could support the scheduler with the scheduling making decisions. Note that, different from the last strategy, this one consumes computational resources due to the concurrent execution of the proxy and the applications. However, the interference evaluation is done with only one execution of the original application and one execution with the proxy to evaluate the different scenarios, which is faster than executing the original application and every configuration of the proxy.

4   Evaluation

We have implemented a proof-of-concept of application proxy generation based on CPU, memory and communication usage. We do not use profilers or perform reverse engineering like other related works.

The evaluation has been divided into three sections. The first one shows a comparison between the original benchmark and the proxy based on it. The original benchmarks used come from the Princeton Application Repository for Shared-Memory Computers (PARSEC) [14], which is a benchmark suite composed of multi-threaded programs that are focused on emerging workloads, and NASA Advance Supercomputing (NAS) Parallel Benchmarks (NPB) [11], which consists of a small set of applications designed to evaluate the performance of parallel supercomputers. The second section consists of a brief evaluation of the predictors when LIMITLESS uses the proxies to train the algorithms instead of the original applications. Finally, the third section corresponds to the evaluation of the interference produced between applications and proxies.

The evaluation has been done in a physical platform that consists of eight compute nodes. One partition of the cluster contains six nodes with Intel(R) Xeon(R) E7 with 12 cores and 128 GB of RAM in the other. The second partition contains two nodes with Intel(R) Xeon(R) Gold 6212U CPU @ 2.40 GHz with 24 cores and 315 GB of RAM. The connection between nodes is a 10 Gbps Ethernet. The I/O is based on Gluster parallel file system.

4.1   Proxy Accuracy

The different benchmarks used for this evaluation includes, as we have indicated before, a set of applications from PARSEC, NPB and the Jacobi method. The used benchmarks are:

- Jacobi: This is an algorithm for determining the solutions of a diagonally dominant system of linear equations. Each diagonal element is solved for, and an approximate value is plugged in. The process is then iterated until it converges.
- Integer-Sort: This is a kernel that performs random memory access. It belongs to the class of bucket sort algorithms which perform an all-to-all communication pattern (through OpenMP in this case).

- Multi-grid: This benchmark solves a 3D Poisson equation using a V-cycle multigrid method. It exhibits structured, long range communications.
- Bodytrack: This application tracks a human body with multiple cameras through an image sequence.
- Blackscholes: This application calculates the prices for a portfolio of European options analytically with the Black-Scholes partial differential equation (PDE). There is no closed-form expression for the Black-Scholes equation and as such it must be computed numerically [13].

Figure 3a shows the performance behavior of the Jacobi method. It exhibits characteristic CPU, memory and communication patterns. The CPU phases are correlated to the memory and the communication phases. Once LIMITLESS has modelled the application, the LAN component generates its proxy, which produces the performance behavior that can be seen in Fig. 3b.

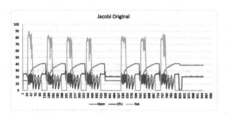 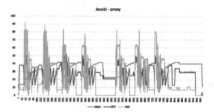

(a) Original 1. Jacobi I/O (JIO) executing with six parallel threads. (b) Proxy 1. Jacobi I/O (JIO) proxy executing with six parallel threads.

Fig. 3. Jacobi I/O model. The X-axis represents the time in seconds while the Y-axis represents the usage percentage.

The next two figures (Figs. 4a and 4b show the performance behavior of Integer-sort (IS) and Multi-grid (MG) benchmarks from the NAS Parallel Benchmarks. Figure 4a shows the performance behavior of the Integer-sort benchmark. In this case, the execution performs a series of computations, including a gradual increase in memory usage until the data load is complete (the first 30 s of the execution). Figure 4b corresponds to the performance behavior obtained from the proxy execution. In this case, the CPU usage is a bit higher as the original due to the overhead of the memory replication.

Figure 5a shows the performance behavior of the Multi-Grid benchmark. This use case is similar to the last one (and similar to the rest of the benchmarks of the NPB 1). MG also performs a series of computations keeping the CPU and the memory barely constant along the execution time. Figure 5b corresponds to the performance behaviour obtained from the proxy execution, which is reproduced with high fidelity.

Figures 6a and 6b show the performance behavior of Bodytrack and Blackscholes benchmarks from the PARSEC Benchmarks. The first one corresponds

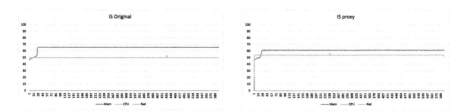

(a) Original 2. Integer-Sort (IS) executing with 12 parallel threads.

(b) Proxy 2. Integer-Sort (IS) proxy executing with 12 parallel threads.

Fig. 4. Integer-Sort model. The X-axis represents the time in seconds while the Y-axis represents the usage percentage.

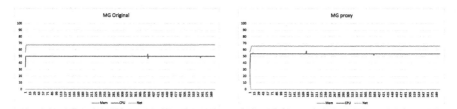

(a) Original 3. Multi-Grid (MG) executing with 12 parallel threads.

(b) Proxy 3. Multi-Grid (MG) proxy executing with 12 parallel threads.

Fig. 5. Multi-Grid model. The X-axis represents the time in seconds while the Y-axis represents the usage percentage.

to a computer vision workload, which performs medium working sets of computation. The second one is the simplest of all PARSEC workloads because it performs small working sets with no communication until execution end. The first one shows the performance behavior of Bodytrack benchmark. It consists of seventeen computation phases that are well replicated by the proxy in the second figure. There are no significant changes in the memory consumption, and it keep constant along the time.

The performance of the last original use case can be seen in Fig. 7a, which corresponds to Blackscholes benchmark. It performs an unique computation (but longer) phase at the middle of the executions. At the end of the execution there is a peak of communication. The performance metrics obtained from the proxy execution can be seen in Fig. 7b.

As it can be seen, in all the cases the proxy program is able to reproduce the original workload, despite the fact of existing small differences between the original program and the proxy. It is due to LIMITLESS does not perform deep profiling of the applications to produce 100% accurate proxies. Instead, LIMITLESS tries to build generic proxies that reproduce, with certain accuracy, the performance behaviour, the computation phases, the memory consumption and the network traffic. Taking all into account, LIMITLESS uses these proxies offline to generate new data to refine faster the performance predictors. It is important

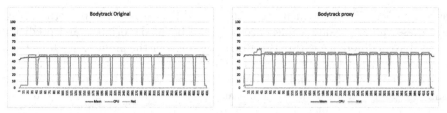

(a) Original 4. Bodytrack (BT) executing with 12 parallel threads.

(b) Proxy 4. Bodytrack (BT) proxy executing with 12 parallel threads.

Fig. 6. Bodytrack model. The X-axis represents the time in seconds while the Y-axis represents the usage percentage.

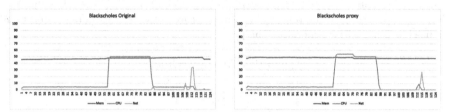

(a) Original 5. Blackscholes (BS) executing with 12 parallel threads.

(b) Proxy 5. Blackscholes (BS) proxy executing with 12 parallel threads.

Fig. 7. Blackscholes model. The X-axis represents the time in seconds while the Y-axis represents the usage percentage.

to highlight that the predictors are re-built every time new model is stored in the LIMITLESS database, so the proxy programs improve their accuracy over the time.

4.2 Prediction Algorithms Improvement

LIMITLESS includes one analysis method to predict the performance of the applications. It is based on multi-variable analysis, and uses a federation of machine learning algorithms: Nearest Neighbour (NN), AdaBoost and Support Vector Machines (SVM). The purpose of having this prediction feature is to improve the application scheduling by means of evaluating possible future states of the system. If the scheduler needs to schedule an application *App*, it can predict the complete behaviour of *App*, select better nodes to run *App*, or decide if any of the current running applications could share a node with *App*.

Regarding the accuracy by using proxies, Table 1 shows the accuracy of the predictors using the five use cases previously described. Only the first execution stores real data in the dataset. Hence, another 20 execution patterns are stored using proxies. At first, it is important to know that these machine learning algorithms showed an average accuracy of 97% by using real executions and patterns. As it can be seen in Table 1, the average accuracy for all these use cases is 87.5% (77.6% for memory patterns and 97.4% for CPU patterns). Note that these values include a tolerance of 3% (if both, the original and predicted values, have a difference within this range, we consider the prediction a hit). CPU is better predicted because generating CPU loads is easier than other factors. However, memory, I/O, and communications are harder to replicate without using the same code structure and operations, as [8] and [17] suggest. In our case, we do not try to consider the memory pattern, the execution flow, the system calls used, etc., which should improve the accuracy. Instead, we try to generate generic algorithms to provide similar proxies to replicate the performance of the original applications.

Table 1. Accuracy of the machine learning algorithms using datasets without real application executions, taking into account a tolerance of $+/-3\%$. Note that the first execution is provided by the real application (first execution in the system), and then it is used as a model for generating the proxies.

Application	Memory	CPU
BS	55%	97%
BT	92%	98%
IS	50%	99%
MG	99%	99%
JIO	92%	94%

4.3 Interference Detection Using Malleable Proxies

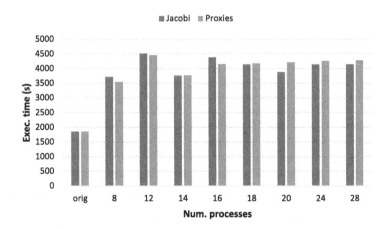

Fig. 8. Use case Jacobi - comparison between the execution time of Jacobi instances running concurrently in the same compute node and the same executions using proxies. The interference is directly related to the execution time.

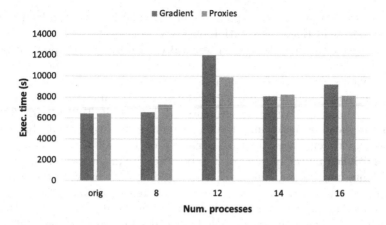

Fig. 9. Use case Gradient - comparison between the execution time of Conjugate Gradient instances running concurrently in the same compute node and the same executions using proxies. The interference is directly related to the execution time.

In this section we show two examples of how the system studies the interference between two applications using the malleable proxies. With the information related to the interference analysis, the scheduler is able to make more precise decisions for future executions, knowing which applications are compatible (i.e. both can share a node without performance degradation). The following tests have been focused on the second partition of the cluster. Note that the applications can be run in more compute nodes, however only the last allocated node could have available resources to share with other applications. For example, *App1* requires 28 processes and *App2* 20 in a cluster with two nodes with 24 cores each. The scheduler will allocate 24 processes in the first node and the other 4 processes in the second node for *App1*. As there are enough free resources in the second compute node, the scheduler can allocate *App2* on them.

Following this idea, the first use case corresponds to the Jacobi I/O application. The second use case corresponds to the Conjugate Gradient algorithm. Figure 8 shows the execution time of the Jacobi use case under different conditions. The experiments start with the execution time of the Jacobi application running in an exclusive node. Then, each experiment corresponds to a Jacobi instance with 12 processes (in blue) combined with another instance with processes from 8 to 28 (in orange). The objective is to quantify the interference under different scenarios. As it can be seen, the interference reaches the maximum value with 12 processes per application because all the cores are in use, and both instances are performing the same operations.

The same scenario is proposed in Fig. 9 with the Conjugate Gradient use case. In this scenario, the evaluation is done between 8 and 16 processes due to the size of the problem. There is no possibility to increase the processes because of the data redistribution. The same behaviour can be observed in the 12-processes experiment. Before and after this, the interference is lower because the interfere operations overlap in a lower percentage in the time because the load changes on each experiment (load distribution between processes).

The last scenarios have been done statically, with the proxies previously configured with the concrete number of processes. However, due to the malleability, the same experiments can be done in a row, executing one instance of Jacobi or Gradient, and a malleable proxy that increases its number of processes periodically. The results of these experiments can be seen in Tables 2 and 3. They show the overhead of performing the interference study using malleability. Note that each experiment takes the time per iteration instead of the execution time (which multiplied by the number of iterations results in the estimated execution time). Taking into account the overheads, the difference between the static and the malleable evaluation is the time needed to get the results: *32,734* s for the first use case and *44,868* s for the second one with the static model. In the case of the malleable mode, the time needed is *3850* s for the first one, and *6003* s for the second one. Note that the executions start with 8 processes. Malleability generates overheads for process creation/destruction, but it is compensated by the time saved when the application is running with more processes.

Table 2. Jacobi use case - Interference evaluation using malleability with one proxy, from 8 processes to 28.

N. procs	Expand/shrink time (s)	Data redistribution
8 to 12	0.891120	0.121103
12 to 14	0.949042	0.116333
14 to 16	0.898925	0.114143
16 to 18	0.901130	0.120974
18 to 20	0.908145	0.114886
20 to 24	0.909972	0.104716
24 to 28	0.907456	0.104094
28 to 8	0.017645	0.131265
Total overhead	**6.383435**	**0.927514**

Table 3. Gradient use case - Overhead using malleability with one proxy, from 8 processes to 16.

N. procs	Expand/shrink time	Data redistribution time
8 to 12	0.087823	0.125488
12 to 14	0.088597	0.105049
14 to 16	0.935568	0.115070
16 to 8	0.002273	0.158980
Total overhead	**1.111978 s.**	**0.5048587 s.**

5   Related Work

In this section we introduce some related works that are relevant in fields of monitoring, application proxy generation and scheduling. Unfortunately, it does not contains any related work about malleable proxies, because, as far as we know, our proposal is a novelty.

The main goal of the authors in [9] is to provide easy-to-use, portable, transparent, and efficient instrumentation tools (called Pintools) that are written in C/C++ using Pin's rich API. They provide different instrumentation than other similar tools, for example, Valgrind and dynamoRIO. The instrumentation does not interfere with the loads/stores in the registers. The authors provide a comparison between PIN, Valgrind and dinamoRIO, where we can observe that PIN and dinamoRIO outperform Valgrind without instrumentation, and PIN outperforms both Valgrind and dinamoRIO when we consider performance with instrumentation.

In [4] the authors proposed a synthetic proxy generation to (1) reduce the simulation time employing these proxies generated instead of the original applications, and (2) share these proxies for computer architects, as some of the specific target applications are proprietary, and vendors hesitate to share them. They provided the synthetic clones for CPU2006 and ImplanBench workloads. The metrics used include the Memory Level Parallelism (MLP) of those workloads to estimate the burstiness of accesses to the main memory, and the features needed to characterize a benchmark are: a Statistical Flow Graph (SFG) that is used to capture the control flow behaviour; a branch prediction algorithm based on the branch transition rate; the Instruction Level Parallelism (ILP) in the workload; and the memory access pattern. Instead of capturing data to get the memory access pattern, the authors used a stride base memory access (because Joshi et al. concluded previously in [7] that most of the load and store instructions in CPU200 workloads have that pattern).

Later, in [5], the authors proposed a framework that can generate proxies for real-world multi-threaded applications based on: shared caches, coherence logic, out-of-order cores, interconnection network and DRAM. This framework is evaluated by generating proxies from the PARSEC benchmark suite and comparing their results in terms of performance. Their solution consists of extracting performance information from the applications and then generating the code for the proxies based on a C template with some options. The main benefit of creating and using these proxies is that they have used a simulator to calculate the energy consumption of different workloads and different parameters, and the simulations are four magnitude orders faster using the proxies due to the number of instructions executed (millions versus thousands of instructions).

In [16] the authors proposed code mutation (to generate application proxies), a technique that mutates the original code of a real application to make harder/impossible reverse engineering. Their objective consists of allowing the distribution of those proxies that have the same behaviour (in terms of performance) as the original. To test the results, they use the SPEC CPU2000 and MiBench benchmarks. They also provide a comparison between the different related works for code mutation, because the approaches differ in the way to preserve the proprietary application's memory accesses and control flow behaviour. The code mutation uses the same code structure by maintaining the execution flow but using different instructions, operations and registers. In these cases, the mutant code has the same execution time as the original application, which is one of the main objectives.

In [15] the same authors as the last related work propose a framework to generate synthetic benchmarks based on real applications. To do that, the framework performs different profiling analyses, similar to reverse engineering. Based on that set of instructions, data and code information, the framework generates an application in a high-level programming language (C) that fulfils the performance requirements. Finally, the framework performs a semi-random obfuscation for avoiding the possibility of generating similar code as the original application, but with smaller number of instructions.

Clone morphing [17] is different from Clone workloads. The second one tries to copy in an application its performance behaviour, without providing real information about the original application. The first one proposes systematic changes to clone the behaviour of the application focusing on certain features. In this case, this program copies the cache/memory patterns for each application. Their main contribution is the systematic method for producing new proxies with performance behaviours that are the result of the combination of more than one application. The main weakness of this work is that the authors focus their work on the cache and memory patterns.

In [12] the authors proposed PerfProx, another alternative to build proxies based on real applications. However, this related work differs from other previous works because their proxy generator tries to replicate the performance of the applications based on the performance counters (similar to our proposal), and it is only focused on database processes. PerfProx directly genetares a general-purpose proxy executable. They have evaluated their proposal on Casandra, MongoDB and MySQL running both the data-serving and data-analysis on different platforms.

In [1] the authors proposed SynFull, a synthetic traffic generator that captures both applications and cache coherence behaviour to evaluate NoCs (Networks on chips). SynFull provides a novel technique for modelling real application traffic without the need for expensive, detailed simulation of all levels of the system. The authors determined the key traffic attributes that a cache-coherent application-driven traffic model must capture, including coherence-based message dependencies, application phase behaviour and injection process. So, this work is focused on modelling the network and the cache coherence traffic. As a result, SynFull attains an overall accuracy of 10.5% across the three configurations for all benchmarks relative to full-system simulation.

In contrast to the previous related works, the objective of this proposal is not to replicate the applications accurately. Instead, our goal is to reproduce the performance of the applications without extracting data from the binaries, without the necessity of dealing with code or data from the applications, and without a big penalty in terms of overhead. However, this research line is relevant because more accurate proxies will produce more accurate performance counters, and they will increase the accuracy of the predictors. Moreover, the LIMITLESS' proxies are malleable using FlexMPI, which allows dynamic reconfiguration of the number of processes in run time. Due to this, the system is able to analyze different configurations of the same application proxy to discover its scalability and its impact on other applications (interference).

6   Conclusion

In this paper, we introduce a new feature on LIMITLESS, a lightweight monitoring and scheduling framework that was designed to monitor and schedule the execution of the applications on large-scale computing infrastructures. This feature consists of creating synthetic micro-benchmarks (proxies) from the applications executed in the cluster, based on the performance models that LIMITLESS already produces in an iterative fashion. One of the main characteristics of the framework is the performance prediction, which allows the scheduler to improve its tasks. It generates proxies based on the collected data and then uses those proxies to generate new execution data, which are included in the dataset to train the networks and the machine learning algorithms. With this proposal, LIMITLESS can predict the application performance with one execution and without user intervention. Besides, those application proxies can be shared to exhibit the performance of the real applications that have been running in the platforms because they do not contain proprietary information nor include any piece of code of the original application. Moreover, the system uses different application proxies to perform interference studies between applications, which allows the scheduler to share nodes between compatible applications. Note that, in case of performance degradation (interference) during the execution of real applications, the system will detect that situation, avoiding it by means of application migration or increasing or decreasing the processes using the malleability features.

As future work, we are studying the possibility of including a more precise application characterization to replicate, not only the performance metrics but the performance behaviour: FLOPs, IPC, syscalls, I/O phases, etc. Currently, it is not an option because we want to keep the overhead in the compute nodes as lower as possible.

References

1. Badr, M., Jerger, N.E.: SynFull: synthetic traffic models capturing cache coherent behaviour. ACM SIGARCH Comput. Architect. News **42**(3), 109–120 (2014)
2. Cascajo, A., Singh, D.E., Carretero, J.: Performance-aware scheduling of parallel applications on non-dedicated clusters. Electronics **8**(9), 982 (2019)

3. Cascajo, A., Singh, D.E., Carretero, J.: Limitless - light-weight monitoring tool for large scale systems. In: 2021 29th Euromicro International Conference on Parallel, Distributed and Network-Based Processing (PDP), pp. 220–227 (2021). https://doi.org/10.1109/PDP52278.2021.00042

4. Ganesan, K., Jo, J., John, L.K.: Synthesizing memory-level parallelism aware miniature clones for SPEC CPU2006 and implant bench workloads. In: ISPASS 2010 - IEEE International Symposium on Performance Analysis of Systems and Software, pp. 33–44 (2010)

5. Ganesan, K., John, L.K.: Automatic generation of miniaturized synthetic proxies for target applications to efficiently design multicore processors. IEEE Trans. Comput. **63**, 833–846 (2014)

6. Gormley, C., Tong, Z.: Elasticsearch: the Definitive Guide: a Distributed Real-Time Search and Analytics Engine. O'Reilly Media, Inc. (2015)

7. Joshi, A., Bell, J., Ibm, R.H., John, L.K.: Distilling the essence of proprietary workloads into miniature benchmarks. TACO - ACM Trans. Archit. Code Optim. **5**(2), 1–33 (2008). https://doi.org/10.1145/1400112.1400115

8. Joshi, A., Eeckhout, L., Bell, R.H., John, L.: Performance cloning: a technique for disseminating proprietary applications as benchmarks. In: Proceedings of the 2006 IEEE International Symposium on Workload Characterization, IISWC - 2006, pp. 105–115 (2006)

9. Luk, C.K, et al.: Pin: building customized program analysis tools with dynamic instrumentation. ACM SIGPLAN Not. **40**(6), 190–200 (2005)

10. Martín, G., Marinescu, M.-C., Singh, D.E., Carretero, J.: FLEX-MPI: an MPI extension for supporting dynamic load balancing on heterogeneous non-dedicated systems. In: Wolf, F., Mohr, B., an Mey, D. (eds.) Euro-Par 2013. LNCS, vol. 8097, pp. 138–149. Springer, Heidelberg (2013). https://doi.org/10.1007/978-3-642-40047-6_16

11. NASA Advanced Supercomputing (NAS) Division: NAS Parallel Benchmarks. https://www.nas.nasa.gov/software/npb.html

12. Panda, R., John, L.K.: Proxy benchmarks for emerging big-data workloads. In: Parallel Architectures and Compilation Techniques - Conference Proceedings, PACT 2017-September, pp. 105–116 (2017)

13. University, P.: PARSEC - CSWiki, http://wiki.cs.princeton.edu/index.php/PARSEC-Blackscholes

14. University, P.: The PARSEC Benchmark Suite. https://parsec.cs.princeton.edu/

15. Van Ertvelde, L., Eeckhout, L.: Benchmark synthesis for architecture and compiler exploration. In: IEEE International Symposium on Workload Characterization, IISWC 2010, pp. 1–11 (2010)

16. Van Ertvelde, L., Eeckhout, L.: Dispersing proprietary applications as benchmarks through code mutation. In: ACM SIGPLAN Notices, pp. 201–210 (2008)

17. Wang, Y., Awad, A., Solihin, Y.: Clone morphing: creating new workload behavior from existing applications. In: ISPASS 2017 - IEEE International Symposium on Performance Analysis of Systems and Software, pp. 97–108 (2017)

An Emulation Layer for Dynamic Resources with MPI Sessions

Jan Fecht[1]([✉])[iD], Martin Schreiber[1,2][iD], Martin Schulz[1][iD], Howard Pritchard[3], and Daniel J. Holmes[4][iD]

[1] Technical University of Munich, Garching bei München, Germany
{fecht,schulzm}@in.tum.de
[2] Université Grenoble Alpes, Saint-Martin-d'Hères, France
martin.schreiber@univ-grenoble-alpes.fr
[3] Los Alamos National Lab, Los Alamos, NM, USA
howardp@lanl.gov
[4] Collis Holmes Innovations Ltd, Scotland, UK
danholmes@chi.scot

Abstract. The current static job scheduling on supercomputers for MPI-based applications is well known to be a limiting factor for the exploitation of a system's top performance in terms of application throughput. Hence, allowing fully flexible and dynamically varying job sizes would provide multiple advantages compared to the current approach, e.g., by prioritizing jobs dynamically and optimizing resource usage by transferring resources economically.

A critical step in achieving dynamic resource management with MPI on supercomputers is the development of sound and robust interfaces between MPI applications and the runtime system. Our approach extends the concept of MPI Sessions, a new concept introduced with MPI 4.0, by adding new features to support varying computing resources via the MPI process set abstraction. We then show how these features can be used, as a proof of concept, to request (active) and cope with (passive) varying resources from an application's perspective. To validate of our approach, we develop *libmpidynres*, a C library providing an emulated MPI Sessions environment on top of existing MPI implementations without MPI Sessions support, which we then use to integrate our proposed extensions to the interface specification. Using this proof-of-concept environment, we show how an MPI Sessions enabled application can use process sets to handle dynamically varying resources.

Keywords: MPI · MPI Sessions · Dynamic resources · Resource management

1 Introduction

1.1 Motivation

Job scheduling systems for MPI-based applications allocate a fixed amount of resources (cores, nodes, GPUs, FPGAs, ...) for the job's runtime. This is a strong constraint on resource usage, leading to various inefficiencies, e.g., idling

© Springer Nature Switzerland AG 2022
H. Anzt et al. (Eds.): ISC High Performance 2022 Workshops, LNCS 13387, pp. 147–161, 2022.
https://doi.org/10.1007/978-3-031-23220-6_10

cores, lack of taking runtime-changing resource requirements into account, to name just a few.

To solve this issue, dynamic resources, meaning that the number of available resources can change during an application's execution, need to be introduced to and supported by applications as well as the runtime. For example, with dynamic resources, the job scheduler can withdraw resources from an application and transfer them to another application. This could potentially lead to a higher throughput of application on the entire system, hence an overall better parallel efficiency. Furthermore, this approach allows the job scheduler to prioritize certain jobs dynamically by having more flexibility and scheduling abilities than in the static resource allocation case.

To use dynamic resources in high-performance scenarios, the following components need to be carefully designed and realized:

1. **API**: a flexible, robust interface for dynamic resources that can be used by MPI applications.
2. **Runtime**: dynamic resource support in the runtime (MPI library, job scheduler, . . .).
3. **Applications**: MPI-based software using this interface to handle dynamic resource changes including all required changes in the software.

Having all three components working together in the right way is a very long lasting process and this work is on the first component.

Our contributions are a proposal of an API for robust and flexible dynamic resource changes based on the new MPI Sessions concept introduced with MPI 4 [16]. In addition to this, we evaluate our proposal based on a library called *libmpidynres* which emulates a dynamic resource environment on top of an existing MPI communicator.

1.2 Related Work

MPI 2's Dynamic Process Model: The MPI Forum already addressed the need for a more dynamic process management approach with the introduction of the MPI dynamic process model in the MPI 2 standard [17]. However, the number of running MPI processes is still limited to MPI_UNIVERSE_SIZE, which is typically equal to the number of resources reserved by the job scheduler.

Task-based Parallelization Models: Another set of applications are task-based parallel programs. E.g. *DucTeip* is a framework for creating task-based MPI programs [19]. That could be exploited rather in a straight-forward manner by, e.g., executing different applications using the same MPI context in parallel. In such a scenario, having a separate MPI context with dynamic resources could be used not only to avoid idling MPI processes, but also to avoid applications influencing each other, e.g., due to a bug.

Invasive Computing (IC): The IC paradigm suggests varying resource utilization for embedded systems [15] with certain progress to adopt this also in HPC. As a first step, the OpenMP and Threading Building Blocks parallelization models have been modified to allow for varying resources, see e.g. [13].

Here, the underlying idea has been to allow a resource manager to improve the system-wide efficiency for concurrently running applications and to start applications at arbitrary points in time where the present work also borrows this idea of a resource manager. Based on the aforementioned work, an extension for distributed-memory systems with MPI was developed [3]. However, this led to several drawbacks of this approach, such as that resource changes are solely based on MPI_COMM_WORLD (which is obviously a serious problem for, e.g., coupled simulations) and that only specialized cases have been taken into account.

MPI Fault Tolerance: Work on MPI fault tolerance approaches, including MPI *global restart* [9] and the Fenix project [5], share some of the features of *libmpidynres*. Both provide mechanisms for an application to recover from an initial loss of compute resources and utilize replacing resources when available, but their functionality is limited in scope to resilience. Our proposed approach, on the other hand, covers a much wider field, but can be used to implement the recovery models supported by these approaches to fault tolerance.

Malleability in MPI: Dynamic resource management in MPI has been studied intensively over the last years, usually under the umbrella term of "malleability". Since then, multiple frameworks have been created to support malleability in MPI applications [4,6,8,11,14]. These frameworks used different techniques and APIs to achieve malleability. For example, some authors propose process splitting and merging for expansion and shrinking of the application [4,8]. Other authors start new processes while keeping the old, existing processes running [14]. Another approach is to use checkpointing systems and restart the actual MPI application for resizing it [10,12].

Although there has been much research around malleability, there is still a lack of a highly flexible, efficient and future proof API. The work presented in this paper takes the attempt to propose such an API and further differs from previous approaches by its use of MPI Sessions for malleability.

2   MPI Sessions

We start with a brief introduction to MPI Sessions since this is at the core of our proposal.

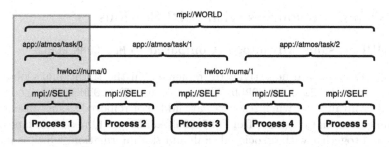

Fig. 1. The process sets of an application example. Process sets are represented as curly brackets. MPI Process 1's view on its process sets is highlighted in green. (Color figure online)

The concept of MPI Sessions was first introduced in 2016 [7] and was later included into the MPI standard with the release of MPI 4.0 in June 2021 [7,16]. It defines a new object, the *MPI Session*, which is a lightweight handle to the MPI runtime. Using a session, MPI can be initialized without the MPI_COMM_WORLD communicator. Further, an application and its libraries can allocate multiple independent sessions allowing for better isolation and a higher degree of composability compared to traditional global MPI intitialization. MPI Sessions also offer a tighter runtime integration by allowing the runtime to expose available resources via *process sets*. A process set groups together multiple potential MPI processes and is identified by a name in a URI-like format (e.g., "mpi://world", "mpi://self"). Using process sets, an application can create local MPI groups, which can be further used to create communicators that connect MPI processes contained in the respective process sets.

Process sets allow the runtime to expose available resources to the application. Figure 1 shows an example view of an application's process sets. A process set can represent something of a static nature (e.g., a NUMA node, "mpi://numa/0" in Fig. 1), but it can also represent more dynamic groups of resources (e.g., a specific task in an application: "app://atmos/task/1" in Fig. 1). There is still ongoing discussion about the exact nature of process sets, their lifetime, scope and dynamic behavior. Our approach takes a look at process sets from a more dynamic perspective, which leads to the following assumptions for the remainder of the paper:

Immutability: A process set identified by a unique name will always represent the same resources, even if resources are not actually available to an MPI application, e.g., because the job scheduler removed the resource during a resource change. This property avoids race conditions in cases where an MPI group is created from the process sets by different MPI processes.

Change of Process Sets: We expect the available process sets to change frequently during an application run. At the same time, the number of available process sets at any point in time is expected to remain small as process sets that become invalid (due to an MPI process exiting a process set) are removed in our model (compare with Sect. 4.2).

3   Dynamic Resources with MPI Sessions

3.1   MPI Sessions Advantages Compared to MPI_COMM_WORLD

Dynamic resources are non-trivial to implement in the traditional global MPI architecture with MPI_COMM_WORLD. This is because MPI_COMM_WORLD needs to be mutated or invalidated when resources are added or removed. As a consequence, communicators that originate from MPI_COMM_WORLD would need to adapt or get invalidated together with associated rank and size information, which is hard to do in a consistent fashion that is transparent to an application.

MPI Sessions provide one way to tackle the aforementioned problem by allow-ing `MPI_COMM_WORLD` to be avoided entirely. Besides various other benefits, we briefly discuss the main advantages in the context of varying resources.

In our work, process sets are used to globally express resource changes. Once an MPI object is invalidated, new MPI objects from process sets can be created without the need for complex application coordination. Also, there is no need to change the mechanism and semantics of MPI groups and communicators like we would may need to do in the mutable `MPI_COMM_WORLD` case. Another advantage of MPI Sessions is given by the current interfaces that already permit the dynamic modification of an applications point of view on available MPI processes by changing the process sets that are exposed to the application.

3.2 Resource Changes with Process Sets

Next, we discuss our strategy to realize dynamic resource changes. We would like to point out, though, that our approach focuses on loop-based applications similar to the application shown in Sect. 6.

Resource changes happen when the runtime removes or adds new resources from/to an application. For our dynamic resource model we assume that the runtime does not implicitly add new resources in the form of a new process set, but an explicit function call needs to be made by the application. From the application point of view, implicit adding of resources is problematic due to assumptions on a particular number of resources in a communicator, e.g. the number of ranks. This explicit approach is also useful as the application might need to do load balancing/process coordination work after each resource change. Once a resource change arrives, the application has a time window to do cleanup/load balancing and then accepts the resource change. This is especially important when MPI processes are being removed because the data from these MPI processes needs to be transmitted to avoid data loss.

A resource change consists of a *resource change type* and a *resource change process set*:

The *resource change type* indicates how the application's resources are mod-ified. In the present work, we only investigate two resource change types: *addition* and *removal* of processes. To migrate resources, both operations have to be applied sequentially. Obviously, a *replace* resource change type could be also implemented that both removes and adds processes, as well as a *split/join* change that (de-)partitions existing process sets. However, these type of changes are not the focus of this work.

The *resource change process set*, on the other hand, describes the difference between the current set of processes and the set of processes after the resource change. In the case of MPI process addition, the resource change process set will contain all to-be-started MPI processes and in the case of MPI process removal all to-be-removed MPI processes.

4   Interface Design

4.1   MPI Sessions Interface

libmipdynres's MPI Sessions interface was developed along the lines of the Sessions interface in the MPI 4.0 draft from November 2020 [18]. The draft's interface description matches the one that was finally published with the official MPI 4.0 standard in June 2021 [16].

The MPI 4.0 standard document defines multiple C signatures of MPI Sessions functions and explains the semantics of these functions. However, the document does not fully define all concepts of MPI Sessions. Many questions remain open in regard to process sets. Because of that, we have modified and extended the MPI Sessions interface to fit the way process sets are viewed in this work (see Sect. 2). The MPI Sessions interface that is included in our library, *libmpidynres*, contains the following functions:

- `MPI_Session_init` - initialize an MPI Session
- `MPI_Session_finalize` - finalize an MPI Session
- `MPI_Session_get_info` - query information about an MPI Session
- `MPI_Session_get_psets` - query for available process sets
- `MPI_Session_get_pset_info` - query information about a process set
- `MPI_Group_from_session_pset` - create an MPI group from a process set
- `MPI_Comm_create_from_group` - create an MPI communicator from an MPI group without a parent communicator

These functions match the functionality and semantics described in MPI 4.0 [16], except for `MPI_Session_get_psets`, which we discuss in the next section.

4.2   `MPI_Session_get_psets`

The signature of `MPI_Session_get_psets` is shown in Fig. 2.

The function replaces two functions in MPI 4.0: `MPI_Session_get_num_psets` and `MPI_Session_get_nth_pset`. These two functions assume a more static behavior of process sets, as they use a virtual array model for querying process sets. With the `MPI_Session_get_num_psets` function one can query the length of the virtual array and with the `MPI_Session_get_nth_pset` one can query a process set at a specific index. The runtime can only append new process sets to the array, an index can become invalid if the process set does not exist anymore. This approach has multiple disadvantages with our assumed process set properties (see Sect. 2):

1. The frequent change of process sets leads to an ever-growing array that will lead to increasing memory usage and increasing access times.
2. The frequent change will also lead to most indices being invalidated at some point in time. This in return increases the chance of invalid requests and creates an additional management overhead on the application side.

```
int MPI_Session_get_psets(MPI_Session session, MPI_Info info,
                          MPI_Info *psets);
IN   info  Info object containing runtime hints
OUT  psets Info object containing process set names as keys
           and process set sizes as decimal values
```

Fig. 2. *libmpidynres* API for querying available process sets.

```
int MPIDYNRES_pset_create_op(
        MPI_Session session, MPI_Info hints, const char pset1[],
        const char pset2[], MPIDYNRES_pset_op op, char pset_result[]);
IN   hints       Hints passed to runtime
IN   pset1       Name of first process set argument
IN   pset2       Name of second process set argument
IN   op          Operation type to apply
OUT  pset_result Name or resulting process set
```

Fig. 3. Proposed API for creating process sets by applying a set operation on existing process sets.

To adapt the API to our model, we replace the two function calls with one. Instead of querying each process set on its own, the application queries the names and sizes of available process sets at once. The result is returned in the psets argument of MPI_Session_get_psets. It consists of an MPI Info object with process set names as the keys and the respective process set size as the value, basically representing a snapshot of the current process set state. While this leads to more data being transferred, we expect the number of active process sets at any point in time to remain low. However, to make the API more future-proof and allow for more complex process set situations, an MPI Info object can be passed to the function. This object could be used to filter the results and only return a subset of available process sets.

4.3 Process Set Management Interface

When dealing with resource changes, an application must be able to establish communication with new resources. In our work, new resources are expressed via process sets. To establish communication, an application can create an MPI Group from the new process set and use MPI group operations to create a group that both contains the new processes and old application processes. However, this approach has to be made by each process in the new group. This can become quite complex with increasingly more resource changes and is hard to coordinate. This is especially a problem for the newly created processes as they need to know which process sets they need to use to create MPI groups containing old application processes. To avoid these problems, we allow the application to create new process sets.

In our design, only one MPI process, which we will refer to as "main process", is responsible for operations on process sets. Note that these operations could be executed by *all* involved MPI processes, but leave this to future work and here strictly follow the "main process" approach.

To create new process sets, the application must call the [4] `MPIDYNRES_pset_create_op` function, whose signature is shown in Fig. 3. The names of two existing process sets need to be given in the `pset1` and `pset2` arguments. Additionally, a set operation to be applied needs to be passed in the `op` argument. Calling the function has the effect that, if the arguments are valid, the runtime will create a new process set containing the result of the set operation on the process sets. Currently, three set operations are supported, see also Fig. 4:

- **Union**: The result contains all processes from both psets. This can be used to add new processes from a resource change set to the application's main process set.
- **Difference**: The result contains all processes from `pset1` that are not in `pset2`. This is useful to remove a resource change set (if the resource change takes away resources) from the application's main process set.
- **Intersection**: The result contains all processes that are both in `pset1` and `pset2`.

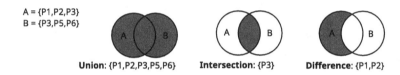

A = {P1,P2,P3}
B = {P3,P5,P6}

Union: {P1,P2,P3,P5,P6}   Intersection: {P3}   Difference: {P1,P2}

Fig. 4. Venn diagrams of the process set operations. Process set A contains the processes P1, P2, P3 and P4; Process set B contains the processes P3, P4, P5 and P6. The operation's result is written underneath each Venn diagram.

Allowing these fundamental set operations has multiple advantages which we like to summarize as follows:

- Process set changes do not rely on collective operations involving, e.g., processes which have not yet been started. Therefore, process sets including processes not yet available to the application (see Fig. 8) can be created.
- Since resource changes can be abstractly described as a directed acyclic graph as transitions on resource sets, designing an interface supporting such resource changes should also cover the typical requirements of such resource changes without taking application-specifics into account.
- A "main process" driven change of resources makes the process coordination easier since all management can happen in a single process. The only information that needs to be shared with other processes are process set names which are available globally. An extension to a consensus-based management should still be possible.
- Process set operations fit nicely into applications that rely on a single communicator during their runtime. There, the operations can be used to derive a new "main process set" from the previous "main process set" and the resource change process set (see Fig. 5).

Our main goal is the creation of rather generic interfaces to cover various requirements on resource change patterns. As usual, there are always optimizations possible by providing specialized interfaces or more feature-rich interfaces, however this is left for future work.

4.4 Resource Change Management Interface

To implement the mechanisms described in Sect. 3.2, the resource change API has to provide a way to a) query for pending resource changes and b) accept and apply these resource changes.

For a), *libmpidynres* offers the MPIDYNRES_RC_get function. Its signature is shown in Fig. 6. If there is a resource change, the type of resource change and the resource change process set are returned in the rc_type and delta_pset respectively. Furthermore, a handle to the resource change is returned in the tag argument.

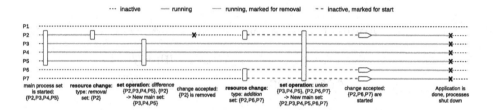

Fig. 5. Diagram showing how to use process set operations for resource changes.

```
int  MPIDYNRES_RC_get ( MPI_Session  session ,
        MPIDYNRES_RC_type  *rc_type ,  char  delta_pset [] ,
        MPIDYNRES_RC_tag  *tag ,  MPI_Info  *info );
OUT rc_type      Type of resource change
OUT delta_pset  Name of the new resource change process set
OUT tag          Identifier for the resource change
OUT info         Optional additional information about the resource change


int  MPIDYNRES_RC_accept ( MPI_Session  session ,
        MPIDYNRES_RC_tag  tag ,  MPI_Info  info );
IN tag  Identifier of the resource change to accept
IN info Runtime hints and hints for newly created processes
```

Fig. 6. Proposed API for managing resource changes.

For b), *libmpidynres* offers the MPIDYNRES_RC_accept function. Using this function, the application can tell the runtime to *apply* the resource change referenced by the tag argument. The info argument can be used to pass information new processes. Once this function is called with valid arguments, the runtime will start new processes in the case of resource addition. If the resource change removes resources, the application has to shutdown the relevant processes itself.

If possible, the runtime can try to enforce the shutdown by forcefully shutting down running processes after a specific amount of time. In the case of *libmpidynres*, due to its architecture, the shutdown cannot be enforced.

An example application execution with both resource changes and process set operations in shown in Fig. 5. The application shown constructs a new "main pset" after each resource change. Note that the "main process" main thread is not highlighted, as it is application dependent to choose a main rank. One possible way to choose a "main process" is to use rank 0 of the communicator based on the "main pset".

5   libmpidynres

In order to evaluate our proposal, we implement the runtime component in the form of a C library, called *libmpidynres*, that emulates a dynamic resource environment on top of an existing MPI communicator.

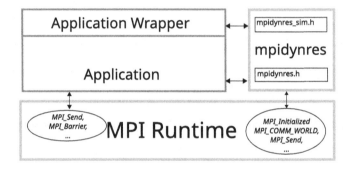

Fig. 7. The different components of an application using *libmpidynres*. Both the application and *libmpidynres* access the same MPI library. However, the application should derive most of its MPI objects from *libmpidynres*.

The library uses a communicator of fixed size to emulate an MPI Sessions environment with dynamic resources by using subsets of the fixed-size communicator. This is achieved by hiding and exposing the processes of the communicator to the application. Using this emulated environment, applications can use the MPI Sessions and dynamic resource management API described in Sect. 4, hence already explore and test these features even if the underlying MPI implementation and job scheduler do not support MPI Sessions and dynamic resource management. For sake of reproducibility and open science, the source code of libmpidynres is available on GitHub.[1]

---

[1] https://github.com/boi4/libmpidynres.

5.1   libmpidynres as an Emulation Layer on Top of MPI

libmpidynres is implemented as a C library that is used on top of an existing MPI library. This means that *libmpidynres* uses MPI calls internally for communication and management. From the application's point of view, it extends the available MPI API with additional functions.

Before the MPI Sessions environment becomes active, the application has to configure *libmpidynres* and initialize MPI. This part of the user application is called the *application wrapper*. The application wrapper then passes an entry point and a communicator for the emulated application to *libmpidynres*.

From there, *libmpidynres* manages the communicator's processes and runs the *emulated application* from the given entrypoint. The emulated application should only use MPI communicators and groups that are returned by *libmpidynres* or were derived from these. This ensures that *libmpidynres* has full control over the available processes. This architecture is illustrated in Fig. 7.

5.2   Emulated Process States

libmpidynres emulates dynamic resources on a communicator of fixed size (typically MPI_COMM_WORLD). This is achieved by selectively exposing a subset of the communicator's processes to the application as its world process set. Consequently, the maximum number of processes that can be scheduled is limited by the size of the communicator used for emulation. Inactive processes are idling (in an MPI_Recv operation) and are waiting to be requested and then made available to the MPI application. However, unlike a full implementation inside a runtime, such processes cannot be made available to other, separate applications. Therefore, it is again important to stress that *libmpidynres* is only a proof-of-concept library for testing the interface and real support for dynamic resources has to be included in the various software components of the MPI stack.

The process of starting and stopping resources is quite complex and involves multiple temporary states a process can be in. These states are illustrated in Fig. 8. Note that these are the states from the library's point of view.

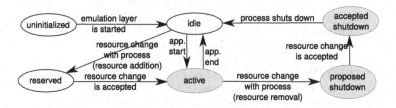

Fig. 8. The different states that an emulated process can be in, from *libmpidynres'* point of view. States where the application has control over the (OS-)process are highlighted in green. (Color figure online)

5.3   Resource Manager

libmpidynres uses a server-client model for managing process sets and resource change states. For that, the MPI process with rank zero of the libmpidynres MPI communicator acts as a dedicated *resource manager*.

This server-client approach avoids race conditions and assures a consistent state across all MPI ranks. However, the additional communication overhead leads to decreased performance especially with redundant requests from multiple ranks and to increased latency when doing API calls. However, the proof-of-concept, emulating nature of *libmpidynres* justifies this trade-off.

6   Case Study

To evaluate the proposed interface and *libmpidynres*, we implement an application example that is based on a loop where work is distributed among all processes in each iteration. In the following, we describe this example application.

Let us first look at the initialization part of the application given in lines 1–10 in Fig. 9. When an MPI process is started, it needs to set up and gain information

```
1     session = MPI_Session_init ()
2     psets = MPI_Session_get_psets ( session )
3     if "mpi://world" in psets:
4        main_pset = "mpi://world"; cur_iter = 0
5     else:
6        info = MPI_Session_get_info ( session )
7        main_pset = info.get ("main_pset")
8        cur_iter = info.get ("cur_iter")
9     group = MPI_Group_from_sessions_pset ( main_pset )
10    comm = MPI_Comm_create_from_group ( group )
11    for (; cur_iter < N; cur_iter++): /* MAIN LOOP */
12       rc_type , rc_set = MPIDYNRES_RC_get ()
13       if (rc_type != NONE):
14          if (rc_type == ADDITION):
15             main_pset = pset_create_op (UNION, main_pset , rc_set )
16          if (rc_type == REMOVAL):
17             main_pset = pset_create_op (DIFF, main_pset , rc_set )
18             psets = MPI_Session_get_psets ( session )
19             if main_pset not in psets: break
20          MPIDYNRES_RC_accept ({"cur_iter":  cur_iter ,
21             "main_pset":  main_pset })
22          group = MPI_Group_from_sessions_pset ( main_pset )
23          comm = MPI_Comm_create_from_group ( group )
24          ...
25       do_work ()
```

Fig. 9. Pseudo code showing using the proposed interface to successfully query and adapt to dynamic resources changes.

about its environment. For that, the application initializes an MPI Session using MPI_Session_init. Furthermore, the application queries its process sets using MPI_Session_get_psets. If the process is part of the "mpi://world" process set, the process was started together with the start of the application. If it is not part of the process set, the process was started because of a resource change and has to query some information to successfully join the application. In this example, it queries the current loop iteration and the process set that should be used for communication from its MPI session (the information was passed with an Info object when the resource change was accepted).

Once a communicator is created from the main_pset, the main loop is started. This is shown in lines 11–25 of Fig. 9. The application queries for resource changes at the beginning of each loop iteration. When dealing with resource changes, the application follows the strategy from Fig. 5. This means that the application tries to have all of its available resources grouped together in one process set, the "main process set". If a resource change adds new resources, the *union* process set operation is used to create a new "main process set". If a resource change removes existing resources, the *difference* process set operation is used instead. When the application accepts a resource change using MPIDYNRES_RC_accept, some information (the main process set name and the current loop iteration) are passed to newly started processes.

Using this system, the application is able to handle and adapt to resource changes while constantly having a valid MPI communicator. A concrete C implementation of this application was tested and evaluated using different scheduling algorithms and different communicator sizes. The application could successfully finish all of its loop iterations without any crashes or race conditions in the application or *libmpidynres*. More *libmpidynres* examples can be found on GitHub.[2].

7   Conclusion

In this work, we presented an interface that uses new MPI Sessions concepts to handle dynamically varying resources. The interface uses process sets to express resource differences that will be applied to the application. We implemented an emulation layer that allows applications to use the new interface. This makes prototyping of malleable applications with the proposed interface possible, even without MPI providing support for this, yet. Furthermore, using an example application built on top of this emulation layer, we have validated that using this interface, applications are capable of dealing with resource changes.

Regarding future work, one of the next steps is an extension of the prototype with the implementation of different parallel programming patterns (beside the *loop pattern*) and combine them with the interface proposed in this work. While the current interface is quite general and therefore may be useful for other programming patterns, it still provides some global changes that may affect all processes of the application. For more distributed programming patterns, a less

---

[2] https://github.com/boi4/libmpidynres/tree/master/examples.

global approach is needed where the application can group its own processes and tell the runtime that only certain groups should be affected by resource changes.

Another interesting area to apply this new interface to are existing tools for dynamic computing. For example, tools like *p4est* and *PETSc* can help with automating parts of the load balancing process in dynamic mesh refinement applications [1,2]. Integrating dynamic resources into these tools is currently work-in-progress and could abstract the dynamic resources away from the library user and ease the creation of scalable parallel applications.

Besides many other future research aspects, we like to finally point out the problem of scheduling, which will require disruptive algorithms to cope with runtime-varying resources.

Acknowledgments. This project has received funding from the Federal Ministry of Education and Research and the European HPC Joint Undertaking (JU) under grant agreement No 955701, Time-X and No 955606, DEEP-SEA. The JU receives support from the European Union's Horizon 2020 research and innovation programme and Belgium, France, Germany, Switzerland.

References

1. Balay, S., Abhyankar, S., Adams, M.F., Brown, J., Brune, P., et. al: PETSc Web page (2019). https://www.mcs.anl.gov/petsc
2. Burstedde, C., Wilcox, L.C., Ghattas, O.: p4est: scalable algorithm for parallel adaptive mesh Reference on forests of octrees. SIAM J. Sci. Comput. **33**(3), 1103–1133 (2011)
3. Compres, I., Mo-Hellenbrand, A., Gerndt, M., Bungartz, H.J.: Infrastructure and API extensions for elastic execution of MPI applications. In: Proceedings of 23rd EuroMPI (2016), pp. 82–97 (2016)
4. El Maghraoui, K., Desell, T.J., Szymanski, B.K., Varela, C.A.: Dynamic malleability in iterative MPI applications. In: Seventh IEEE International Symposium on Cluster Computing and the Grid (CCGrid 2007), pp. 591–598 (2007)
5. Gamell, M., Katz, D.S., Kolla, H., Chen, J., Klasky, S., Parashar, M.: Exploring automatic, online failure recovery for scientific applications at extreme scales. In: SC 2014: Proceedings of the International Conference for High Performance Computing, Networking, Storage and Analysis, pp. 895–906 (2014)
6. Gupta, A., Acun, B., Sarood, O., Kalé, L.V.: Towards realizing the potential of malleable jobs. In: 2014 21st International Conference on HPC (HiPC), pp. 1–10 (2014)
7. Holmes, D., et al.: MPI Sessions: leveraging runtime infrastructure to increase scalability of applications at exascale. In: ACM International Conference Proceeding Series 25–28-Sept, pp. 121–129 (2016)
8. Iserte, S., Mayo, R., Quintana-Ortí, E.S., Peña, A.J.: DMRlib: easy-coding and efficient resource management for job malleability. IEEE Trans. Comp. **70**(9), 1443–1457 (2021)
9. Laguna, I., et al.: Evaluating and extending user-level fault tolerance in MPI applications. Int. J. HPC Appl. **30**(3), 305–319 (2016)

10. Lemarinier, P., Hasanov, K., Venugopal, S., Katrinis, K.: Architecting malleable MPI applications for priority-driven adaptive scheduling. In: Proceedings of the 23rd European MPI Users' Group Meeting, pp. 74–81. EuroMPI 2016, Association for Computing Machinery, New York, NY, USA (2016)
11. Martín, G., Marinescu, M.-C., Singh, D.E., Carretero, J.: FLEX-MPI: an MPI extension for supporting dynamic load balancing on heterogeneous non-dedicated systems. In: Wolf, F., Mohr, B., an Mey, D. (eds.) Euro-Par 2013. LNCS, vol. 8097, pp. 138–149. Springer, Heidelberg (2013). https://doi.org/10.1007/978-3-642-40047-6_16
12. Prabhakaran, S., Neumann, M., Rinke, S., Wolf, F., Gupta, A., Kale, L.V.: A batch system with efficient adaptive scheduling for malleable and evolving applications. In: 2015 IEEE International Parallel and Distributed processing Symposium, pp. 429–438 (2015)
13. Schreiber, M., Riesinger, C., Neckel, T., Bungartz, H.J., Breuer, A.: Invasive compute balancing for applications with shared and hybrid parallelization. Int. J. Parallel Prog. **43**(6), 1004–1027 (2015)
14. Sudarsan, R., Ribbens, C.J.: ReSHAPE: a framework for dynamic resizing and scheduling of homogeneous applications in a parallel environment. In: 2007 International Conference on Parallel Processing (ICPP 2007), pp. 44–44 (2007)
15. Teich, J., Henkel, J., Herkersdorf, A., Schmitt-Landsiedel, D., Schröder-Preikschat, W., Snelting, G.: Invasive Computing: An Overview, pp. 241–268. Springer, New York, New York, NY (2011)
16. The MPI Forum: MPI: A Message-Passing Interface Standard Version 4.0
17. The MPI Forum: MPI: A Message-Passing Interface Standard Ver. 2.2 (2009)
18. The MPI Forum: MPI: A Message-Passing Interface Std. Ver. 4.0 (Draft) (2020)
19. Zafari, A.: Advances in task-based parallel programming for distributed memory architectures (PhD dissertation) (2018)

Exploiting OpenMP Malleability
with Free Agent Threads and DLB

Joel Criado[✉][iD], Victor Lopez[iD], Joan Vinyals-Ylla-Catala[iD],
Guillem Ramirez-Miranda[iD], Xavier Teruel[iD], and Marta Garcia-Gasulla[iD]

Barcelona Supercomputing Center, Barcelona, Spain
{jcriado,vlopez,jvinyals,gramire1,xteruel,martag}@bsc.es
http://www.bsc.es

Abstract. This paper presents the evolution of the free agent threads
for OpenMP to the new role-shifting threads model and their integration with the Dynamic Load Balance (DLB) library. We demonstrate
how DLB efficiently manages the malleability exposed by the role-shifting
threads to address load imbalance issues. We use two real-world scientific
applications, one of them with a coupling case, to illustrate the potential
of this approach. In addition, we also demonstrate that the new implementation is more usable than the former one, letting the runtime system
automatically make decisions that were to be made by the programmer
previously. All software is released open source.

Keywords: Dynamic load balancing · Free agents · OpenMP ·
Tasking · Malleability

1 Introduction

During the last years in the HPC community, both hardware and software are
getting ready for the exascale era. On the one hand, hardware boosts the computational power of nodes by increasing the number of cores per node and using
different accelerators as much as augmenting the number of nodes. On the other
hand, software needs to evolve to use this massive computational power efficiently.

One of the main characteristics of software that has proven necessary to
deal with the immense computational power is malleability. Malleability allows
dealing with heterogeneous hardware, noise at all levels, load imbalance, communication inefficiencies, and dynamic workloads, among other issues.

Moreover, with the growing variety in hardware architectures, portability
is another *must-have* characteristic for all the software components because it
is not a sustainable approach to port every software to each newly designed
platform.

In this challenging scenario, all the software stack layers must be malleable,
flexible, and portable. We have already seen this direction in using workloads

© Springer Nature Switzerland AG 2022
H. Anzt et al. (Eds.): ISC High Performance 2022 Workshops, LNCS 13387, pp. 162–175, 2022.
https://doi.org/10.1007/978-3-031-23220-6_11

instead of monolithic applications [6], job schedulers managing adaptable applications [7,17], the development of malleable codes [8], and parallel programming models offering dynamic malleability [10].

In this work, we focus on OpenMP; the OpenMP parallel programming model has embraced malleability since its appearance, instead of much more rigid parallel models such as MPI, which only recently has started to offer this feature. However, even the original malleability of the OpenMP model has proven not to be enough. For this reason, we extend our previous free agent threads proposal that expands the malleability of the programming model outside the parallel construct. This new feature allows the Dynamic Load Balancing (DLB) library to exploit the malleability of hybrid MPI+OpenMP applications further, achieving better efficiencies.

The main contributions of this paper are the following: a new implementation of the free agent threads; this new implementation aims to add a lower overhead, be more usable, and offer an extensible framework; the integration of the free agent threads with the DLB library, and the demonstration using two real HPC applications.

The remaining of this document is organized as follows. Section 2 reviews the related work that can be found in the literature. In Sect. 3, we explain the details of the proposed implementation and how it has been integrated with the DLB library. In Sect. 4, we present the performance evaluation, and finally, in Sect. 5, we summarize the paper's findings in the conclusions.

2   Related Work

This work relies on two main principles: a task-based programming model, where the parallel decomposition leverages the creation of unstructured work units (called tasks), and runtime malleability, in terms of resource allocation, of the associated task-based programming runtimes.

Among the set of task-based programming models currently used in HPC, we can find:

The *OmpSs* programming model [1,9] expresses parallelism using compiler directives. These directives are transformed at compile time into runtime services with well-defined semantics. Among others, programmers may create new tasks, wait for their execution, establish the proper order of task executions, atomic/-critical memory updates, etc. When ignoring directives, sequential behavior is expected.

The *Intel Threading Building Blocks* (TBB) [13] is a C++ template library that allows program parallelization through tasks. Programmers may use high-level or low-level interfaces to spawn tasks; with such information, the runtime creates a Task Dependency Graph and executes tasks in parallel when possible.

The *Intel Cilk++ SDK* [12] is a C++ language extension that includes a runtime library within the family of Intel compilers. It allows expressing the parallelism through a few language keywords (similar to compiler directives), which ease iteration space decomposition, stand-alone tasks creations, and the synchronization among these work units. The current version of this approach is the *OpenCilk project* [15], under the *Massachusetts Institute of Technology* (MIT) supervision.

The *OpenMP* programming model [16] includes a task-based approach (in addition to its traditional work-sharing model). The tasking sub-model allows creating new tasks, waiting for their execution, and adequately ordering tasks using data dependences. This tasking approach is similar to the aforementioned OmpSs programming model, although the execution model is still bound to the creation of parallel regions.

Resource usage malleability is the other pillar on which our implementation relies. Changing the number of assigned processing elements at runtime requires a parallel decomposition that does not depend on them. This requirement removes from the equation the traditional OpenMP work-sharing constructs. Once we start a parallel region, the number of threads participating in it must remain constant until the end of the construct. Otherwise, some fundamental definitions will be broken (e.g., the barrier directive or a static distribution of iterations among threads).

Task-based approaches, instead, will ease resource malleability. As the created tasks are not bound to a particular thread before starting their execution, the number of threads (and the number of cores, consequently) may change at runtime. Several existing implementations leverage such malleability:

The *OmpSs* programming model implements a Thread Manager module, which provides support to the number of threads and their bindings to the underlying CPUs. The OmpSs Thread Manager may also interact with the *Dynamic Load Balance* library [7,11]. This library gathers information about the system occupancy beyond the process level, having an overall picture of the whole node status. With this information, it can decide and change which should be instant resource ownership for each of the processes along with the program execution.

Some OpenMP implementations also include the idea to use additional threads, not directly included in the parallel region, to help execute tasks. The *Hidden Helper Threads* feature [18] implemented in the LLVM compiler presents a common use case in which the target construct may leverage the presence of these other threads to relieve the critical path. The main differences with our current implementation are: 1) the *Hidden Helper Threads* approach does not allow to change the number of threads; and 2) it is restricted to the use of target tasks, while our proposal intends to be more generic[1].

Our initial implementation of *free agent threads* [14] combines two previous approaches. On one hand, we implement the mechanism on top of an OpenMP runtime fully integrated as a standard programming model. On the other hand, we implement it in such a generic way that all the instantiated tasks could leverage the presence of these additional threads to be executed. The DLB component is responsible for increasing or reducing the number of threads participating in

---

[1] This is also the reason we are not comparing against this proposal; the study's use cases do not take any benefit from the *Hidden Helper Threads* implementation.

the process. This previous work demonstrated how free agent threads could address load imbalances problems inherent in some HPC applications.

The current version, presented in this work, generalizes and simplifies the implementation by allowing an existing thread to change its role during the execution. Taking advantage of existing threads that no longer participate in the parallel region reduces the cost of creating and managing such threads. In addition, the implementation is more consistent with the definitions of the model itself regarding the *limit of threads*. We also prepare the runtime to host other types of roles in the future. We believe it is interesting for OpenMP users and developers to increase the model's extensibility further. For instance, the standard could consider dedicating specific threads to execute communication tasks (i.e., the thread role will be *communicator*). Finally, it also simplifies the way programmers interact with the execution of the resulting programs by pushing the rationale of specific decision-making configurations as part of the OpenMP runtime (i.e., automatize parameters). The evaluation section will show that the runtime's automated decisions always improve the best configuration used in the previous implementation.

3   Implementation

Our previous free agent thread implementation used a mechanism of two pools of threads, one containing the *initial* plus the *worker threads* and the other pool containing the set of free agent threads. The idea behind was to have a representative thread per processor and enable either the *worker thread* or the free agent thread depending on whether the thread on that processor was needed for a *parallel region*.

After evaluating our first approach, we observed two undesirable situations. Firstly, a *worker thread* and a free agent thread both bound to the same processor could be active simultaneously. When the first was needed for a new *parallel region* while the second was still executing an *explicit task*, i.e., a task generated by a `task` construct, thus provoking a short time-lapse of processor oversubscription. Secondly, should the OpenMP model implement a new type of thread, its implementation may also be done using a third pool of threads overcomplicating the implementation. Our new implementation solves both problems by using the same thread running with different roles and adding extensibility to the model.

The new free agent thread and role-shifting implementation presented in this paper are based on the LLVM OpenMP runtime version 14.0.0.

3.1   The LLVM OpenMP Runtime

The LLVM OpenMP runtime implements *parallel regions* as follows. When a thread encounters a `parallel` construct, the thread creates the structure for the team of threads and assigns as many threads as needed to the team. Threads will be created the first time that the runtime needs such threads. Upon completion of the *parallel region*, threads are suspended and moved to a thread pool structure until another *parallel region* is encountered. If subsequent *parallel regions* do not need more threads than any other previous region, existing threads will be reused.

The LLVM OpenMP runtime implements the thread fork-join model using two different kinds of barriers. The first kind of barrier is called *fork-barrier*, and this is where all idle threads are waiting until they are needed for some team. When an idle thread is assigned to a team, the thread is *released* and executes an *implicit task*, which is the task assigned to each team member that includes all the *parallel region* code. One particularity of this barrier is that a thread is released as soon as it is ready; whether the other threads participating in the same *parallel region* have arrived at the barrier is irrelevant.

The second kind of barrier is called *join-barrier*, and it is used to join all threads at the end of a *parallel region*. It is a more traditional barrier where all threads must reach the barrier before the rest may proceed. After that, all threads again enter the *fork-barrier*.

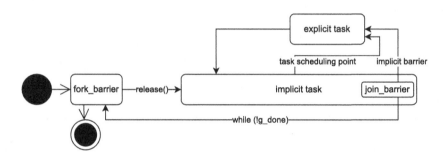

Fig. 1. OpenMP worker thread flowchart.

The described flowchart of a worker thread is shown in Fig. 1. A thread may reach task scheduling points while executing its *implicit task*, typically when encountering `taskgroup`, `taskwait`, `barrier` constructs, etc. The implementation may perform a task switch at this point, beginning or resuming the execution of an *explicit task* bound to the same team. Once it reaches the implicit barrier, a worker thread may also execute *explicit tasks*.

3.2   The Role-Shifting Threads

The role-shifting threads are an evolution of the current OpenMP threads. We can differentiate two types of OpenMP threads: the *initial* and *worker* threads. When a non-nested *parallel region* ends, all the *worker threads* become idle until the *initial thread* encounters another *parallel region*. The idea behind role-shifting threads is to use the already existing idle threads to perform different jobs based on their available roles.

Under the new model, all threads, including the *initial thread*, can have from 0 to n potential roles, but only one of them can be active at a time. The *initial thread* may not, and probably must not, use any role, but we do not enforce the restriction for simplicity in the specification. The *worker* role is implicit in all the threads since they may be able to participate in a *parallel region* at any time.

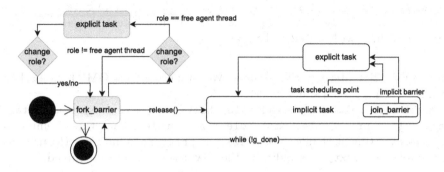

Fig. 2. OpenMP role-shifting thread flowchart.

A thread can shift its active role at different points. At the start of a *parallel region*, all the required threads must abandon their current role and execute their assigned *implicit task*; after finishing it, they may shift to one of their potential roles. Regarding the free agent role, these threads may change their role before and after executing an *explicit task*. These role-shifting points are depicted in Fig. 2. In the future, other roles may use the same shifting points and introduce new ones if required.

New API Routines. We have extended the OpenMP API to interact with the role-shifting threads model and introduced the concept of *global thread id* in the runtime to interact with the API. This thread id is a unique identifier assigned at thread creation and lasts for the entire execution. The global thread id must not be confused with the current OpenMP thread number, which identifies each thread participating within a parallel region.

- `int omp_get_thread_id(void)`: Obtains the global thread id of that thread.
- `int omp_get_thread_roles(int tid, omp_role_t *roles)`: Returns the number of potential roles for thread with *global id* `tid` and sets `roles` to the potential roles of the thread.
- `void omp_set_thread_roles(int tid, omp_role_t roles)`: Sets the potential roles of the thread with *global id* `tid` to `roles`. It will remove all previous potential roles from the thread. If `tid` is higher than the current number of threads, the runtime will create a new thread with the appropriate `roles`.

Environment Variables. We propose a unique environment variable to unify all the role-shifting threads model:

OMP_ROLES: Indicates the initial number of threads with the desired potential roles. Usage examples:

OMP_ROLES="{role1},{role2},{role1,role3}". Three different threads, one with role1, one with role2, and another with role1 and role3.

OMP_ROLES="{role1},{role2,role4}*3". Four different threads, one with role1 and three with role2 and role4.

New OMPT Callback Signature. We propose a new OMPT callback to identify when a thread shifts its active role.

void ompt_callback_thread_role_shift(ompt_data_t *thread_data, ompt_role_t prior_role, ompt_role_t next_role): Each thread emits the callback each time it changes the active role: prior_role indicates the previous active role, and next_role indicates the new active role of that thread.

3.3 Integration with DLB

We have integrated the free agent threads role from the role-shifting threads implementation with the *Lend When Idle* (LeWI) module of DLB. LeWI aims at optimizing the performance of hybrid applications (MPI+OpenMP) by improving their load balance. Figure 3 shows how LeWI operates for an unbalanced application. When an MPI process executes a blocking call, it lends all the CPUs it has at that moment, and other processes may acquire them for their use. After exiting the MPI call, the process reclaims all the CPUs it owns, and it can continue its execution transparently.

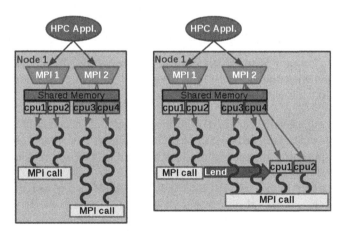

Fig. 3. Example of DLB and LeWI balancing algorithm. On the left is an unbalanced hybrid application. On the right, the application is balanced using LeWI.

Regarding the OpenMP integration, we capture specific OMPT callbacks and perform different actions with DLB:

- **Parallel_begin**: We must register when executing a parallel region and the number of threads associated with it. Those threads are required for the entire execution of the region and cannot shift their role at any moment.
- **Parallel_end**: The parallel region ends, and DLB may use the threads from the former parallel region for load balancing purposes.
- **Task_schedule**: When starting the execution of a task, DLB tries to acquire a CPU from any other process if there are more pending tasks. When a free agent thread ends the execution of a task, it returns the CPU if it has been reclaimed, or it lends the CPU if there are no more pending tasks, or it proceeds silently.
- **Thread_begin**: We extract the global thread id for each thread and set the affinity of the free agents to their correspondent CPU.
- **Thread_role_shift**: When a thread changes from worker to free agent, we deactivate it if the CPU has been reclaimed or there are no more pending tasks.

When an MPI process receives a CPU for the first time, it creates a new thread with the role of free agent, and it assigns that CPU for the rest of the execution to that thread. When it receives that same CPU in the future, instead of creating a new thread, it will change the role of that thread with the API. We also tried a different strategy where we rebind inactive threads to new CPUs when possible, but it had more overhead and was more sensitive to system noise (e.g., CPU preemptions by the OS), so it was discarded.

4   Evaluation

In this section, we present the performance evaluation of the proposed implementation. In this evaluation, we will compare three versions of each application:

- **Original**: The original application executed as in a production run.
- **Double-pool**: The original application using the DLB load balancing library with the LLVM free agent threads implementation based on the double pool of threads. For this implementation, the user must provide the maximum number of free agent threads used per MPI process. We will consider this variable in the evaluation as *Num. free agent threads*.
- **Role-shifting**: The original application using the DLB load balancing library with the LLVM free agent threads implementation based on the role-shifting. This version does not need additional parameters, and the runtime automatically decides the number of free agent threads.

4.1   HPC Environment

All the experiments presented in this work have been obtained using MareNostrum4. MareNostrum4 is a supercomputer based on Intel Xeon Platinum processors; each node comprises two sockets (Intel Xeon Platinum 8160 CPU) with

24 cores each at 2.10 GHz for a total of 48 cores per node and 96 GB of main memory. Its nodes are connected using a 100 Gbit/s Intel Omni-Path network. It houses 3456 nodes accounting for a total of 165888 cores.

The runtime, DLB, and all the applications have been compiled using the Intel 2017.4 suite, and the MPI library used to run is Intel MPI 2017.4 version. We use DLB version 3.0 [2] and the extended LLVM OpenMP runtime library [3] to support the free agent threads in all cases.

For the evaluation, we test 2 HPC applications used in production runs, a parallel remesher, ParMmg, and a simulation code for high-performance computational mechanics, Alya.

4.2   ParMmg

ParMmg [5] is a parallel remesher developed by INRIA, based on top of the sequential Mmg remesher. Mesh adaptation is widely used in computational solid mechanics (CSM) and computational fluid dynamics (CFD) domains to improve the quality of the solution. The application is written in C and parallelized with MPI. The input set used in the study is prepared to do a weak scaling using power of two MPI ranks from 2 to 256 processes.

We added an OpenMP taskification on the main loop iterations to implement a second level of parallelism in that region that allows us to exploit the load balancing capabilities of DLB.

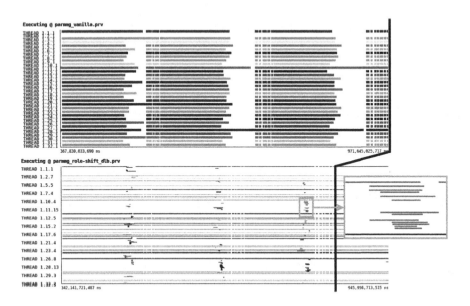

Fig. 4. Top: ParMmg Paraver trace execution of 3 iterations using 32 MPI ranks. Bottom: Same execution using role-shifting threads and DLB. Each color represents different MPI ranks, and both traces are at the same duration scale.

ParMmg presents an irregular load imbalance among the different iterations, as seen in the top trace of Fig. 4. In this figure, we show a Paraver trace of an execution of ParMmg using 32 MPI ranks; each horizontal line corresponds to one MPI process, and in the x axis is represented the time. White means that the MPI process is not doing useful computation, i.e., it is inside an MPI call, and any other color means computing. In this trace, we can identify three steps and observe that the load distribution changes from one iteration to another. For these two reasons, ParMmg can benefit from the load balancing capabilities of DLB because the load imbalance can not be predicted and changes dynamically during the execution.

We can see the same execution using DLB and role-shifting threads in the bottom trace of the same figure. We can observe that each MPI process can now have more than one OpenMP thread; these are the different lines below an MPI process. We can also observe how the additional threads are used to speed up the execution of the most loaded MPI ranks.

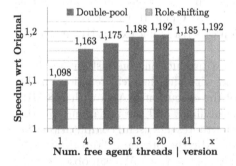

Fig. 5. ParMmg speedup with DLB and different free agents implementations.

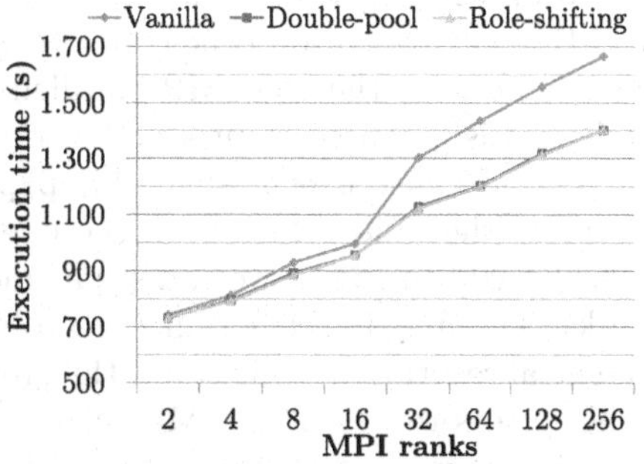

Fig. 6. ParMmg execution time.

In Fig. 5, we show the speedup obtained with the different versions with respect to the original execution of ParMmg without DLB add free agent threads. In the x-axis, we show the different versions of the free agent threads implementations and the different number of free agent threads used for the *Double-pool* implementation. There are two important outcomes from this plot. On the one hand, the role-shifting implementation obtains the same performance as the best configuration of the double-pool implementation. On the other hand, the performance of the double-pool implementation depends highly on the number of free agent threads that the user specifies.

Figure 6 displays the execution time of ParMmg using different number of MPI ranks (and cores) on the x-axis. The different versions are represented by different lines. The number of free agent threads allowed per MPI rank is set to the best configuration measured in the previous experiment for the Double-pool version. As ParMmg is a weak scaling application, the ideal execution would be a flat line. We can see that for all the cases, the execution using DLB and free agent threads improves the performance of the vanilla ParMmg code. For all the executions, the role-shifting implementation performs as well as the best configuration of the double-pool implementation.

4.3 Alya

Alya [19] is a high-performance computational mechanics code that can solve multiple physics, standalone or coupled. Most of the problems it can address come from the engineering realm. Among the different physics solved by Alya, we can mention incompressible and compressible flows, non-linear solid mechanics, chemistry, particle transport, heat transfer, turbulence modeling, electrical propagation, etc. Alya was specially designed for massively parallel supercomputers and is part of the *Unified European Application Benchmark Suite* (UEABS), a set of 13 highly scalable, relevant, and publicly available codes. Alya is written in Fortran and parallelized at different levels, including MPI, SIMD, OpenMP, and GPUs. This paper will use the MPI+OpenMP version, and the OpenMP parallelization will be used only for load balancing. The executions will be launched as an MPI-only execution (one core per MPI rank, 1 OpenMP thread per process). This is because the OpenMP parallelization of Alya is not exhaustive in all the code and is not used in production runs.

The use case executed in this paper is a production combustion problem, coupling the fluid solution on the one hand with the chemical reaction on the other [4,20]. In Fig. 7, we can see a trace of the execution of Alya with 768 MPI ranks. The first 96 MPI ranks are solving the fluid, and the remaining 672 the chemical reaction. In this trace, the grey color represents useful computation, the other colors represent the MPI calls executed by the program. We can identify two time steps and the two coupled problems in the trace. We can observe that the computing region before the *MPI_Barrier* (red) is the more time-consuming one, and at the same time, it presents a significant load imbalance.

We evaluate three different executions of Alya, the original code, using DLB and the double-pool implementation of the free agent threads, and using DLB with the role-shifting version. In Fig. 8a, we can see the speedup obtained when using DLB and free agents with the different versions with respect to the original execution of Alya, using 768 MPI ranks in 768 cores for all cases. In the x-axis, we show the different number of free agent threads enabled for the double-pool implementation. We can see that the role-shifting version achieves a better speedup than the best configuration of the double-pool implementation. We can also observe that the performance of the double-pool implementation depends on the number of free agent threads enabled by the user.

In Figs. 8b and 8c, we can see the same study running Alya with 1152 and 1536 MPI ranks. In both plots, we can see that the role-shifting implementation outperforms all the configurations of the double-pool one. Alya's tasks have finer grain than ParMmg (a few milliseconds per task), and the program benefits from the reduction in overhead in the runtime and DLB integration. It is also interesting to notice that the best configuration of the double-pool implementation is not consistent between the executions with the different number of MPI ranks.

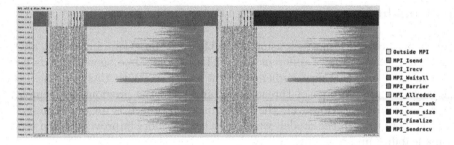

Fig. 7. Alya Paraver trace execution of 2 iterations coupling 96 MPI ranks for the fluid simulation and 672 MPI Ranks for the chemical simulation.

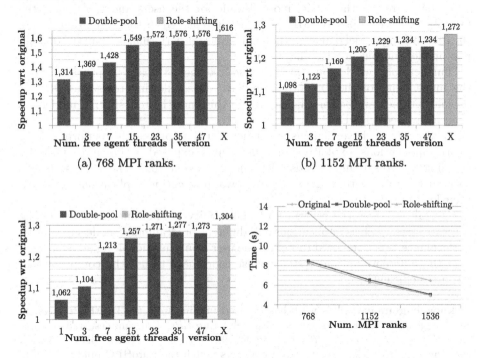

Fig. 8. Speedups obtained running Alya with different implementations of free agents and DLB, and execution time with different number of MPI ranks

Figure 8d shows the execution time achieved by the different versions when running Alya varying the number of MPI ranks. We show that the use of DLB and free agent threads improves the performance of the original Alya code in all the cases. In this plot, we use the best configuration achieved in the previous experiments for the double-pool implementation. However, the best option is to use the role-shifting version of the free agent treads implementation.

5   Conclusions

This paper presents a new extension of the OpenMP programming model, allowing their threads to have different roles. The previous free agent threads have been merged into this new implementation as a role. With this approach, the model has a unique pool of threads, in contrast to the previous one, employing fewer resources. Moreover, the role-shifting approach is an opportunity to include more roles in the model, which may lead to more improvements in terms of malleability and flexibility.

Previously, the user had to select the desired number of free agent threads at the start of the execution, but the role-shifting allows for changes at runtime. This change makes the model more flexible for the users and tools using the OMPT interface from OpenMP. This fact is reflected in the evaluation, where the role-shifting model delivered the same or better performance than the double-pool model without any tunning required.

Furthermore, we demonstrate how the free agent threads proposal increases the malleability of the OpenMP standard, thus, allowing tools like DLB to exploit it to achieve better efficiencies. To this end, the role-shifting model has been integrated with DLB.

In Sect. 4, we have demonstrated how DLB improves the performance of hybrid applications, exploiting the malleability exposed by OpenMP tasks by enabling and disabling threads with the free agent role. The results showed speedups from $1.2x$ to $1.62x$ in two real-world scientific applications, mending their load imbalances.

Overall we show the relevance of malleability at the different levels of the software stack, such as applications and different programming models to achieve performance. Also, the need to isolate the user from these low-level decisions and that the different runtime systems must coordinate to use the computational resources efficiently.

Acknowledgements. This work has received funding from the DEEP Projects, at the European Commission's FP7, H2020, and EuroHPC Programmes, under Grant Agreements 287530, 610476, 754304, and 955606. In the latter (DEEP-SEA), national contributions from the involved state members match the EuroHPC funding. It also has the support of the Spanish Ministry of Science and Innovation (Computacion de Altas Prestaciones VIII: PID2019-107255GB).

References

1. Barcelona Supercomputing Center: OmpSs Specification. https://pm.bsc.es/ompss, Accessed Mar 2022
2. DLB repository. https://github.com/bsc-pm/dlb/commit/7e91a80a, Accessed Mar 2022
3. LLVM repository. https://github.com/bsc-pm/llvm/commit/3c5352db, Accessed Mar 2022

4. Cavaliere, D.E., Kariuki, J., Mastorakos, E.: A comparison of the blow-off behaviour of swirl-stabilized premixed, non-premixed and spray flames. Flow Turbulence Combust. **91**(2), 347–372 (2013). https://doi.org/10.1007/s10494-013-9470-z

5. Cirrottola, L., Froehly, A.: Parallel unstructured mesh adaptation using iterative remeshing and repartitioning. Research Report RR-9307, INRIA Bordeaux, équipe CARDAMOM (2019). https://hal.inria.fr/hal-02386837

6. Conejero, J., Corella, S., Badia, R.M., Labarta, J.: Task-based programming in COMPSs to converge from HPC to big data. Int. J. High Perf. Comput. Appl. **32**(1), 45–60 (2018)

7. D'Amico, M., Garcia-Gasulla, M., López, V., Jokanovic, A., Sirvent, R., Corbalan, J.: DROM: enabling efficient and effortless malleability for resource managers. In: Proceedings of the 47th International Conference on Parallel Processing Companion, p. 41. ACM (2018)

8. Desell, T., Maghraoui, K.E., Varela, C.A.: Malleable applications for scalable high performance computing. Clust. Comput. **10**(3), 323–337 (2007)

9. Duran, A., et al.: OmpSs: a proposal for programming heterogeneous multi-core architectures. Parallel Process. Lett. **21**, 173–193 (2011)

10. El Maghraoui, K., Desell, T.J., Szymanski, B.K., Varela, C.A.: Dynamic malleability in iterative mpi applications. In: Seventh IEEE International Symposium on Cluster Computing and the Grid (CCGrid 2007), pp. 591–598. IEEE (2007)

11. Garcia, M., Labarta, J., Corbalan, J.: Hints to improve automatic load balancing with LeWI for hybrid applications. J. Parallel Distrib. Comput. **74**(9), 2781–2794 (2014)

12. Intel Corporation: Intel Cilk++ SDK Programmer's Guide (2009). https://www.clear.rice.edu/comp422/resources/Intel_Cilk++_Programmers_Guide.pdf

13. Intel Corporation: Intel Threading Building Blocks (2011). https://www.inf.ed.ac.uk/teaching/courses/ppls/TBBtutorial.pdf

14. Lopez, V., Criado, J., Peñacoba, R., Ferrer, R., Teruel, X., Garcia-Gasulla, M.: An OpenMP free agent threads implementation. In: McIntosh-Smith, S., de Supinski, B.R., Klinkenberg, J. (eds.) IWOMP 2021. LNCS, vol. 12870, pp. 211–225. Springer, Cham (2021). https://doi.org/10.1007/978-3-030-85262-7_15

15. Massachusetts Institute of Technology: OpenCilk Language Extension Specification Version 1.0 (2021). https://cilk.mit.edu/docs/OpenCilkLanguageExtensionSpecification.htm

16. OpenMP Architecture Review Board: OpenMP Application Programming Interface, Version 5.2 (2021). https://www.openmp.org/wp-content/uploads/OpenMP-API-Specification-5-2.pdf, Accessed 14 Mar 2022

17. Prabhakaran, S., Neumann, M., Rinke, S., Wolf, F., Gupta, A., Kale, L.V.: A batch system with efficient adaptive scheduling for malleable and evolving applications. In: 2015 IEEE International Parallel and Distributed Processing Symposium, pp. 429–438 (2015)

18. Tian, S., Doerfert, J., Chapman, B.: Concurrent execution of deferred openmp target tasks with hidden helper threads. In: Chapman, B., Moreira, J. (eds.) Languages and Compilers for Parallel Computing, pp. 41–56. Springer, Cham (2022). https://doi.org/10.1007/978-3-030-95953-1_4

19. Vázquez, M., Houzeaux, G., Koric, S., et al.: Alya: multiphysics engineering simulation toward exascale. J. Comput. Sci. **14**, 15–27 (2016)

20. Zhang, H., Garmory, A., Cavaliere, D.E., Mastorakos, E.: Large eddy simulation/conditional moment closure modeling of swirl-stabilized non-premixed flames with local extinction. Proc. Comb. Inst. **35**(2), 1167–1174 (2015)

QR Factorization Using Malleable BLAS on Multicore Processors

Adrián Castelló[1], Sandra Catalán[2], Francisco D. Igual[2],
Enrique S. Quintana-Ortí[1], and Rafael Rodríguez-Sánchez[2(✉)]

[1] Universitat Politècnica de València, Valencia, Spain
{adcastel,quintana}@disca.upv.es
[2] Universidad Complutense de Madrid, Madrid, Spain
{scatalan,figual,rafaelrs}@ucm.es

Abstract. We demonstrate that significant performance benefits can be obtained via the exploitation of malleability in a framework designed to implement portable and high-performance BLAS-like kernels. For this purpose, we integrate thread-level malleability within the BLIS library, providing an experimental evaluation for a representative dense linear algebra operation such as the QR factorization for dense matrices enhanced with look-ahead.

Keywords: Malleability · Basic Linear Algebra Subprograms (BLAS) · High performance · Multi-threading · Multicore processors

1 Introduction

Thread-level malleability aims at dynamically scaling up (or down) the degree of thread parallelism exploited by parallel applications, at runtime, possibly while parallel regions are already under execution. Unfortunately, as of today, the support for this type of malleability is scarce or non-existent in many fundamental libraries and parallel software infrastructures. For example, for portability and performance, many scientific applications rely on computational Linear Algebra (LA) kernels specified in the Basic Linear Algebra Subprograms (BLAS) interface [10], and implemented in the form of high performance instances of the BLAS specification such as those in Intel MKL, AMD AOCL, ARM PL, NVIDIA cuBLAS, OpenBLAS, BLIS, etc.; see, e.g., [14,17,21]. When mapped to parallel architectures, including multicore platforms and hardware accelerators, these threaded libraries (TLs) realizations of the BLAS are not thread-malleable at the kernel level in the sense that, when an application invokes one of their routines, its execution is configured to exploit a certain degree of parallelism, and this setting remains unchanged till the completion of the routine execution.

In an application (mainly) composed of LA kernels, parallelism can be exploited in three different ways:

1. From inside the LA kernels, that is, extracting only *intra-task parallelism* via a threaded instance of the BLAS, but avoiding the execution of different kernels in parallel. This is the conventional approach to exploit parallelism in the Linear Algebra PACKage (LAPACK) [1].

H. Anzt et al. (Eds.): ISC High Performance 2022 Workshops, LNCS 13387, pp. 176–189, 2022.
https://doi.org/10.1007/978-3-031-23220-6_12

2. From inside the application only, exposing independent kernels as tasks that can run in parallel but internally invoke sequential versions of the LA kernels (*inter-task parallelism*) [3,4,7,8].
3. Leveraging a combination of both (*hybrid parallelism*) [9].

In this paper, we revisit the third option, introducing and evaluating the benefits of introducing a few subtle yet important changes in the design of applications featuring *hybrid parallelism*. Concretely, in our case, we combine the Task-parallel Application approach (TA, second option) with a thread-level parallel *malleable* (MLB) BLAS (first option). For this purpose, similarly to previous efforts that follow a hybrid approach, we divide the existing threads into a number of teams, controlled by the application, with each team in charge of exploiting intra-task parallelism. However, the main difference of our work lies in that threads cannot only migrate between teams dynamically during the timespan of the application (as is the case in previous hybrid efforts), *but also during the execution of each individual linear algebra kernel (task).*

In [6] a prototype hybrid and malleable solution was reported to deliver considerable benefits for the execution of the (dense) LU factorization on current multicore processors in comparison with classical solutions that exploit parallelism only from within the BLAS as well as more modern realizations of this factorization that exploit parallelism only at the task/application level [4,18]. Later, we modified the BLIS application programming interface (API) to allow that the application specifies the maximum number of threads that are initially active when invoking a routine as well as the actual number of threads that will actually execute the code of that routine [19]. This in turn accommodates the malleability mechanism leveraged in our work at the application level. In this paper we conduct a significant step forward toward demonstrating the practical benefits of the TA+ MLB approach by making the following new contributions:

- For the particular case of the QR factorization, we propose a parallelization scheme that integrates look-ahead [20] to expose coarse-grain task-parallelism in the main loop, dividing the iteration workload into two large independent kernels.
- We combine the TA scheme with a multi-threaded implementation of *Basic Linear Algebra Instantiation Software* (BLIS) [21] that, in addition, accommodates thread malleability.
- We offer a full comparison between the new parallelization scheme against efficient realizations of the pure conventional loop-parallel (BLAS-level) approach and the task-parallel counterpart.

The rest of the paper is structured as follows. Section 2 provides a general overview of the mechanisms to exploit parallelism in task-parallel applications. Section 3 assesses the benefits gathered by the introduction of the malleability mechanism in a representative LA application: The QR factorization. Finally, Sect. 5 ends the paper with some concluding remarks and proposals for further application of malleability in BLIS.

2   Exploiting Parallelism in Task-Parallel Applications

We next elaborate in some detail the three approaches to exploit parallelism in scientific applications that employ LA kernels. For this purpose, we will consider a very simple workhorse application, divided into four tasks and with dependencies among them, as shown in the task dependency graph (TDG) in Fig. 1: The application consists of the tasks labelled as T0, T1, T2, T3 in the figure, and the arrows represent the data dependencies among them. Because of these dependencies, only T0 can run at the beginning of the application. Once T0 is completed, both T1 and T2 can run simultaneously because there are no dependencies between them. Finally, the execution of T3 must wait for the finalization of both T1 and T2. For the sake of simplicity, the figure is intended to specify the task dependencies, and the box sizes do not reflect execution time or task granularity, which will be in general heterogeneous across tasks. In addition, we consider that each task boils down to a LA kernel.

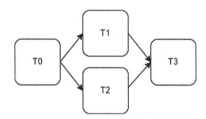

Fig. 1. A simple task dependency graph.

This type of application can be parallelized via one of the following four schemes, each presenting its own advantages and caveats [9]:

- **Sequential application invoking a sequential library (SA+SL).** This is the most basic scheme, in which only a single task is in execution at any given time, and no parallelism is extracted within each task/LA kernel (that is, the execution of a LA kernel is carried out by invoking a sequential BLAS/LAPACK library). Figure 2a illustrates this scenario, with the width of each task roughly matching the time expected for the sequential execution of the associated kernel.
- **Sequential application invoking a threaded library (SA+TL).** Here "sequential" means that only a single task is in execution at any given time, but parallelism is extracted, if possible, within the LA kernel corresponding to each task. Thus, at any given point in time, all running threads can only cooperate with the execution of the same single task. This scenario is illustrated in Fig. 2b. Again, the width of the tasks reflects the execution time after parallelization.

  Unfortunately, not all LA kernels (and to be more generic, not all tasks within the application) are "sufficiently" parallel and a performance pitfall can thus

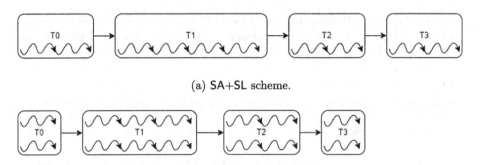

(a) SA+SL scheme.

(b) SA+TL scheme using two threads per task.

Fig. 2. Sequential application invoking a sequential library (SA+SL, 2a) and a threaded library (SA+TL, 2b) scheme.

appear. In the simple example in Fig. 2b this would occur, for example, if task T1 was mostly sequential, so that its execution using several threads would yield no reduction of its running time.

- **TA invoking a sequential library (TA+SL).** In this scheme parallelism is extracted at the application level only, usually by a *runtime* that orchestrates a dependency-aware execution of the tasks. Moreover, each task internally does not exploit parallelism but invokes sequential LA kernels. This is illustrated in Fig. 3. The width of each box is proportional to the time cost of each task, which is executed by a single thread, once the corresponding dependencies are fulfilled. Here, tasks T1 and T2 can proceed simultaneously, as they do no depend on each other.

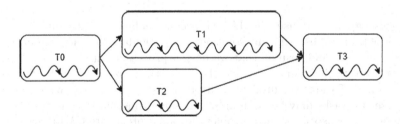

Fig. 3. TA invoking a sequential library (TA+SL) scheme.

A drawback of this scheme is that it requires decomposing the application into a "sufficient" number of tasks, of the "appropriate" granularity, exposing a delicate balance:
- First, some applications cannot be easily divided into tasks and/or those that can be obtained are too coarse constraining the application-level scalability.

- The opposite case results in the creation of too many fine-grain tasks, increasing the overhead of performing a dependency-aware schedule of those tasks. In addition, having fine-grain LA kernels can lead to a performance drop a sub-optimal exploitation of the memory hierarchy of the node [16].
- Finally, it is usual that for large compute-bound embarrassingly parallel kernels (such as the Level-3 BLAS kernels), the SA+TL scheme outperforms the TA+SL scheme. In general, these kernels can be divided easily into finer-grain sub-tasks, but this division usually leads to an overall performance drop [5,6].

- **TA invoking a threaded library (TA+TL).** This scheme is similar to the one depicted in Fig. 3, in the sense that parallelism is extracted at the application level (TA approach). However, additional (nested) parallelism is extracted from within the LA kernels by, for example, relying on a multi-threaded instance of the BLAS (TL approach). In this approach though, regardless of their degree of parallelism, all the tasks are executed with the same number of threads, for example using two threads as in Fig. 4.

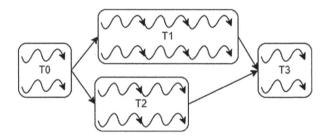

Fig. 4. TA invoking a threaded library (TA+TL) scheme.

In this paper we revisit the TA+TL scheme enhanced with malleability in order to obtain a more efficient solution. In particular, consider the execution depicted in Fig. 4 and assume that we have a processor with 4 cores. There we can identify two situations in which the resource utilization can be improved: First, T0 and T3 are executed by a fixed number of threads, which assumes that these two tasks may be running at the same time, but this is not the case. Fortunately, this aspect is not a problem for state-of-the-art LA libraries as the number of threads assigned to the execution of a task can be fixed at task level, as it is depicted in Fig. 5. In principle, it could seem good enough to vary these numbers of threads *at the beginning of the execution of the TA* (but not within the kernels). With this intermediate solution, prior to executing a LA kernel, the application team decides the number of threads that will produce an efficient execution, and invokes the kernel with that number of threads (or less, to avoid over-subscription.)

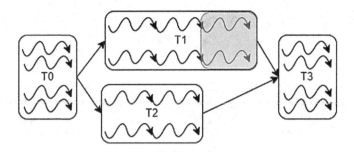

Fig. 5. TA invoking a threaded library (TA+TL) scheme enhanced with task-level specification.

However, the two threads that participate in the execution of task T2 now must remain idle till the execution of task T1 is completed, see the area colored in pink in the figure. Unlike the previous situation, this issue is not solved by recent LA libraries, which are not thread-malleable. In response to this issue, the approach proposed in this work goes one step further towards the complete integration of malleability in a scientific application *by allowing that the number of threads that participate in the execution of a given task/LA kernel dynamically varies at run time.* This solution is illustrated in Fig. 6, where as soon as the threads in charge of executing task T2 complete their job, they proceed to collaborate in the execution of task T1, which contributes to accelerating the execution of the final phase for the latter task by leveraging these (two) extra threads (area colored in green).

Our dynamic and kernel-level malleable solution tackles the two previously analyzed problems. To make this possible we use a task-parallel application executed by a *runtime* using a number of "application thread teams", with each application team in charge of executing a single task at any given moment. Furthermore, to avoid the aforementioned problems, we adopt a dynamic solution where the threads migrate between application teams on-the-fly, during the execution of the LA kernels, using a particular malleability mechanism built on top of BLIS [21]. The goal of this malleability mechanism is that, at any instant, there are no idle threads in the platform.

In the next section, we illustrate the benefits of this approach using a representative LA operation, such as the QR factorization enhanced with look-ahead, running on a multi-core processor.

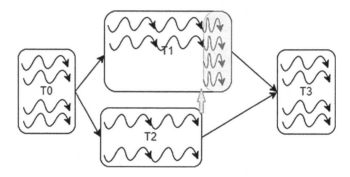

Fig. 6. TA invoking a threaded library (TA+TL) scheme enhanced with Malleability.

3   QR Factorization with Look-Ahead

Consider an $m \times n$ nonsingular matrix A, and its QR factorization given by $A = QR$, where Q is an $m \times m$ orthogonal matrix and R is an $m \times n$ upper triangular factor [12]. Assume for simplicity that n is an integer multiple of the "algorithmic block size" b, and consider a column partitioning scheme of A into $s = n/b$ blocks, each one comprising b columns. Hereafter, $A(:, c_1 : c_2)$ refers to the submatrix that spans the $c_1, c_1 + 1, \ldots, c_2$-th panels (or column blocks) of A, consisting of the matrix columns $c_1 \cdot b, c_1 \cdot b + 1, \ldots, c_2 \cdot b - 1$.[1]

Listing 1.1 displays the structure of a blocked algorithm for the QR factorization of A expressed with a high level of abstraction. The algorithm performs $s = n/b$ iterations, with the loop body first processing the "current" panel (that is, the k-th column block of the matrix) in routine PF (for panel factorization); to next update the panels to its right with respect to the corresponding orthogonal transforms via routine TU (for trailing update). From the performance point of view, PF is mostly a sequential operation while TU can be performed via highly parallel Level-3 BLAS.

The conventional approach to exploit parallelism for this LAPACK matrix factorization is to target loop-parallelism in the (Level-3) BLAS only, which corresponds to the SA+TL scheme discussed in Sect. 2. Alternatively, task-parallelism can be leveraged from the LAPACK routines themselves, yet combined with calls to a sequential version of the BLAS; see also Sect. 2. For the target factorization, this can be attained by 1) dividing both PF and TU into finer-grain tasks; 2) leveraging a runtime to orchestrate a dependency-aware parallel scheduling of these tasks; and 3) employing a sequential version of the BLAS to execute each individual task [4,18].

In this work, we exploit a hybrid TA+TL scheme that exploits task-parallelism at the factorization level and loop-parallelism from within the invoked routines of BLAS. For TAs composed of compute-intensive BLAS kernels, this approach offers competitive performance compared with the SA+TL and TA+SL

---

[1] Note that, in our notation, the indices for blocks and elements start at 0.

```
1  void QR( matrix A, int s )
2  {
3    for ( k = 0; k < s; k++ ) {
4      // Factorize panel k
5      PF( A(k : s − 1, k) );
6      // Update panels k + 1 : s − 1 w.r.t. panel k
7      TU( A(k : s − 1, k), A(k : s − 1, k + 1 : s − 1) );
8    }
9  }
```

Listing 1.1. Simplified routine for the QR factorization.

schemes [5,6]. Nevertheless, in order to expose nested parallelism for this TA+
TL scheme, we first need to reformulate the basic algorithm in Listing 1.1, in
order to eliminate the strict task dependency between the two operations in the
loop body. In order to attain this, we adopt a variant of this blocked algorithm
enhanced with *look-ahead* [20], where an iteration of the loop body comprises
the update of the trailing sub-matrix with respect to the current panel and the
factorization of the "next" panel ($k + 1$-th column block). Concretely, the loop
body of this variant then becomes:

```
1      // Update panel k + 1 w.r.t. panel k
2      TU( A(k : s − 1, k), A(k : s − 1, k + 1) );
3      // Factorize panel k + 1 (if k + 1 < s)
4      PF( A(k + 1 : s − 1, k + 1) );
5      // Update panels k + 2 : s − 1 w.r.t. panel k
6      TU( A(k : s − 1, k), A(k : s − 1, k + 2 : s − 1) );
```

For simplicity, in the following we compile the update of the trailing $(k + 1)$-th
panel and the subsequent factorization of the same panel in this code excerpt
into a single operation named panel update (PU). The (high-level) structure of
the resulting QR factorization with look-ahead is shown in Listing 1.2.

The variant with look-ahead consists of a loop body comprising two tasks: PU
and TU. The former is still mostly sequential while the latter can be performed via
highly parallel Level-3 BLAS. However, in contrast with the standard algorithm,
in Listing 1.1, the two tasks in the loop body are now independent and, therefore,
they can run simultaneously. This is relevant since, as the number of cores grows,
the panel update cannot take advantage of the increasing volume of hardware
resources, and eventually becomes a performance bottleneck.

In order to exploit the task independence in the look-ahead variant via nested
parallelism (TA+TL) we proceed as follows: We divide the threads into two
application thread teams so that, at each iteration of the loop, team T_P is in
charge of PU while team T_T tackles TU. In addition, to handle the different degrees
of parallelism of the two tasks, we naturally assign many more threads to team
T_T than to team T_P.

```
 1  void QR_LA( matrix A, int s )
 2  {
 3    // Factorize first panel
 4    PF( A(:,0) );
 5    for ( k = 0; k < s; k++ ) {
 6      // Update panel k + 1 w.r.t. panel k, and factorize
 7      // panel k + 1 (if k + 1 < s)
 8      PU( A(k : s − 1,k), A(k : s − 1,k + 1) );
 9      // Update panels k + 2 : s − 1 w.r.t. panel k
10      TU( A(k : s − 1,k), A(k : s − 1,k + 2 : s − 1) );
11    }
12  }
```

Listing 1.2. Simplified routine for the QR factorization with look-ahead.

In [5], we analyzed how to integrate task-parallelism with MLB, from the point of view of parallel programming. That work evaluated this solution for three matrix factorizations: LU (with partial pivoting), QR, and reduction to symmetric band form. However, the study performed there made several relevant simplifications: 1) the team in charge of the panel factorization comprised a single thread only; 2) the solution did not include an early termination safeguard [6]; and 3) the malleability mechanism was not integrated into BLIS but was manually inserted into the application code. In this paper we overcome these issues to offer a more complete experimental assessment of the benefits of the nested TA+TL scheme.

4   Performance Evaluation

The following experiments were carried out on a platform equipped with a 20-core Intel® Xeon® Gold 6138 processor [13] (Skylake micro-architecture). In addition, in order to analyze the impact of integrating malleability running on different core count configurations, we use the *taskset* tool to simulate a processor of the same Skylake family but containing a smaller number of cores. In order to avoid the performance distortions caused by the aggressive utilization of the power modes (and associated frequencies) featured by Linux governor of the processor, the operating frequency for all cores was set to 1.7 GHz.

In this work, the reference codes are linked with either BLIS v0.5.1 or MKL 2018.1.163. Malleability is integrated within an independent instance of the aforementioned version of the BLIS library [19]. All experiments were performed using IEEE double precision arithmetic.

Figure 7 reports the GFLOPS rates (billions of floating-point operations per second) of the following codes for the QR factorization of square ($m = n$) matrices:

- **MKL.** The multi-threaded implementation of this operation in Intel MKL. As this library offers a "black-box" solution, it is not possible to infer how parallelism is exploited from within the Intel realization.
- **SQR+MKL/BLIS.** C implementation of the LAPACK routine to calculate the QR factorization (routine `dgeqrf`) enhanced with some algorithmic optimizations (in particular, the Level-3 BLAS scheme to accumulate the orthogonal transforms described in [15]), and linked with multi-threaded (TL) instances of either Intel MKL or BLIS to execute the kernels invoked from within the LAPACK routine. The implementation exclusively relies on Level-3 BLAS kernels, that is, no Level-1 and Level-2 BLAS kernels are instantiated. Note that this corresponds to a SA+TL scheme as the algorithm for the QR factorization is "sequential" but invokes BLAS kernels from a multi-threaded LA library.
- **TQR+LA.** A variant of the SQR implementation modified to encode lookahead, linked with BLIS, and with task parallelism exploited using OpenMP. This is the baseline version to obtain a TA+TL scheme.
- **TQR+MLB.** Same variant as TQR+LA, but linked with our malleable version of BLIS and enhanced with the early termination mechanism.

TQR+LA and TQR+MLB are both realizations of the TA+TL scheme. At the beginning of each algorithm iteration, both options split the threads into two teams, $T_P + T_T$, with the team in charge of the panel update comprising one thread, and the remaining $t - 1$ threads dedicated to the trailing update (t equals the number of available cores on each tested configuration). The difference between both options is that the malleability mechanism allow us to "migrate" the thread in charge of the panel update to help with the update as soon as this task is completed. In all cases (except **MKL**, for which we have no control), the algorithmic block size was manually tuned to optimize performance.

The plots report the performance results of the execution of the routines for the QR factorization using 4, 12 and 20 cores (that is, the full socket in the latter case). Focusing on the SQR curves, the plots reveal that the version linked with Intel MKL outperforms that with BLIS by a large margin. The reason for this is that MKL is able to extract higher parallel performance than BLIS for certain GEMM shapes (in particular, those involving very narrow panels) that appear in the panel factorization. At this point, we would like to clarify that this feature is out of our control and that the SQR implementation linked with BLIS is the starting point of this work.

The introduction of look-ahead (TQR+LA lines) improves the performance results of the SQR + BLIS option and, for certain problem dimensions, it even improves the results obtained with the SQR version that is linke to MKL. By integrating the look-ahead mechanism, the cost of the mostly sequential panel factorization is (partially or totally) hidden with the embarrassingly parallel execution of the trailing update. An exception to this observation can be found in the 4-core configuration. There, for mid to large problem dimensions, the look-ahead-based implementation is inferior to the baseline SQR version. The reason for this behaviour is that, for this small core count and large problem

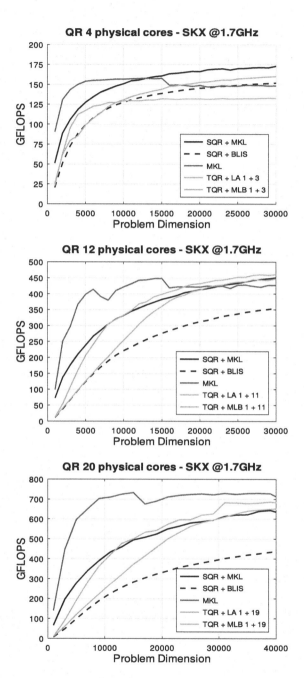

Fig. 7. Performance evaluation of different QR factorization implementations on the Skylake platform.

dimension, the panel factorization does not represent a performance bottleneck, and therefore it is more beneficial to use all cores from the beginning to perform the trailing update.

Focusing on the TQR+MLB results, the plots reveal that the integration of malleability largely outperforms its counterparts that only leverage look-ahead. By adding this technique there appear no idle threads during the execution of the entire QR factorization and, as a consequence, the resources are more efficiently utilized. Again, an exception to this positive scenario is found in the 4-core configuration, but in this case for small problem dimensions. In this case, the early termination mechanism is applied in most of the factorization iterations and, the fact of dedicating only 3 threads to the trailing update, makes the next block size to be used reasonably small. The reduced size of the new block size results in the execution of sub-optimal BLAS-3 operations during the panel update (due to the participation of narrow panels in GEMM) and, thus, in a performance reduction.

Finally, the approach proposed in this work outperforms the routine in MKL for the QR factorization for medium to large problems when 4 or 12 cores are employed. This benefit is not repeated for 20 cores as, with this configuration, the execution of the panel factorization becomes critical, and the baseline kernels in BLIS are not as efficient as those in MKL with the operand shapes that appear in this particular LA operation.

5 Conclusions

In this paper, we have demonstrated the performance benefits of integrating malleability into the BLIS framework to avoid the rigidity of current instances of BLAS, for which the number of threads used for the execution of a routine or kernel is fixed from the beginning to the end. In practice, this new functionality is exposed to the programmer via a minimal modification of the BLIS expert API. The programmer just needs to identify the code points where the distribution of the computation threads must be modified and the change is seamless.

The performance results expose that the benefits of this approach are widely appealing in scenarios where the parallelism is extracted at both application- and library-level. More specifically, when the workload is not equally balanced at application-level, the malleability allows us to modify, at runtime, the parallelism at the library-level with the net result of improving the overall core occupation.

Considering future work, we believe that malleability can also offer significant advantages in runtime-based task scheduling or popular task-based programming models such as StarPU [2] and OmpSs [11]. There, the scarce task-level parallelism in some parts of the application can be by-passed by means of dynamically increasing the parallelism within the tasks. Hence, a fully malleable underlying library becomes mandatory.

Acknowledgements. This work was supported by the research project PID2020-113656RB-C22 of MCIN/AEI/ 10.13039/501100011033, project RTI2018-093684-B-I00 of the *Ministerio de Ciencia, Innovación y Universidades*, project S2018/TCS-4423 of the *Comunidad Autónoma de Madrid* and project Prometeo/2019/109 of the *Generalitat Valenciana*. A. Castelló is a FJC2019-039222-I fellow supported by MCIN/AEI/10.13039/501100011033. We also acknowledge the support of EU (FEDER) and Spanish MINECO (RTI2018-093684-B-I00 and PID2021-126576NB-I00), and Comunidad de Madrid under the Multiannual Agreement with Complutense University in the line Program to Stimulate Research for Young Doctors in the context of the V PRICIT under projects PR65/19-22445 and CM S2018/TCS-4423

References

1. Anderson, E., et al.: LAPACK Users' guide, 3rd edn. Society for Industrial and Applied Mathematics, Philadelphia (1999)
2. Augonnet, C., Thibault, S., Namyst, R., Wacrenier, P.A.: StarPU: a unified platform for task scheduling on heterogeneous multicore architectures. Concurr. Comput. Pract. Expe. Spec. Issue: Euro-Par **2009**(23), 187–198 (2011)
3. Badia, R.M., Herrero, J.R., Labarta, J., Pérez, J.M., Quintana-Ortí, E.S., Quintana-Ortí, G.: Parallelizing dense and banded linear algebra libraries using SMPSs. Conc. Comp. Pract. Exper. **21**, 2438–2456 (2009)
4. Buttari, A., Langou, J., Kurzak, J., Dongarra, J.: A class of parallel tiled linear algebra algorithms for multicore architectures. Parallel Comput. **35**(1), 38–53 (2009)
5. Catalán, S., Castelló, A., Igual, F.D., Rodríguez-Sánchez, R., Quintana-Ortí, E.S.: Programming parallel dense matrix factorizations with look-ahead and OpenMP. Cluster Comput. **23**, 359–375 (2020)
6. Catalán, S., Herrero, J.R., Quintana-Ortí, E.S., Rodríguez-Sánchez, R., Van De Geijn, R.: A case for malleable thread-level linear algebra libraries: the LU factorization with partial pivoting. IEEE Access **7**, 17617–17633 (2019)
7. , Chan, E., Zee, F.G.V., Bientinesi, P., Quintana-Ortí, E.S., Quintana-Ortí, G., van de Geijn, R.A.: Supermatrix: a multithreaded runtime scheduling system for algorithms-by-blocks. In: Proceedings of the 13th ACM SIGPLAN Symposium on Principles and Practice of Parallel Programming, PPOPP 2008, Salt Lake City, UT, USA, 20–23 February 2008. pp. 123–132. ACM (2008). https://doi.org/10.1145/1345206.1345227
8. Chan, E., Zee, F.G.V., Quintana-Ortí, E.S., Quintana-Ortí, G., van de Geijn, R.A.: Satisfying your dependencies with supermatrix. In: Proceedings of the 2007 IEEE International Conference on Cluster Computing, Austin, Texas, USA, 17–20 September 2007, pp. 91–99. IEEE CS (2007). https://doi.org/10.1109/CLUSTR.2007.4629221
9. Dolz, M.F., Igual, F.D., Ludwig, T., Piñuel, L., Quintana-Ortí, E.S.: Balancing task- and data-level parallelism to improve performance and energy consumption of matrix computations on the intel xeon phi. Comput. Electr. Eng. **46**, 95–111 (2015). https://doi.org/10.1016/j.compeleceng.2015.06.009, http://www.sciencedirect.com/science/article/pii/S004579061500213X
10. Dongarra, J.J., Du Croz, J., Hammarling, S., Duff, I.: A set of level 3 basic linear algebra subprograms. ACM Trans. Math. Softw. **16**(1), 1–17 (1990)

11. Duran, A., Ayguadé, E., Badia, R.M., Labarta, J., Martinell, L., Martorell, X., Planas, J.: OmpSs: a proposal for programming heterogeneous multi-core architectures. Parallel Process. Lett. **21**(2), 173–193 (2011)
12. Golub, G.H., Loan, C.F.V.: Matrix Computations, 3rd edn. The Johns Hopkins University Press, Baltimore (1996)
13. Intel: Intel® Xeon® Processor Scalable Family. Specification udpate. Technical report (2019). https://www.intel.com/content/dam/www/public/us/en/documents/specification-updates/xeon-scalable-spec-update.pdf
14. Intel: Math Kernel Library (2022). https://software.intel.com/en-us/intel-mkl
15. Joffrain, T., Low, T.M., Quintana-Ortí, E.S., van de Geijn, R., Van Zee, F.G.: Accumulating Householder transformations, revisited. ACM Trans. Math. Softw. **32**(2), 169–179 (2006). https://doi.org/10.1145/1141885.1141886
16. Low, T.M., Igual, F.D., Smith, T.M., Quintana-Ortí, E.S.: Analytical modeling is enough for high performance BLIS. ACM Trans. Math. Soft. (2014). http://www.cs.utexas.edu/users/flame
17. OpenBLAS (2022). http://www.openblas.net
18. Quintana-Ortí, G., Quintana-Ortí, E.S., van de Geijn, R.A., Zee, F.G.V., Chan, E.: Programming matrix algorithms-by-blocks for thread-level parallelism. ACM Trans. Math. Softw. **36**(3), 14:1–14:26 (2009)
19. Rodríguez-Sánchez, R., Igual, F.D., Quintana-Ortí, E.S.: Integration and exploitation of *intra-routine malleability* in BLIS. J. Supercomput. **76**(4), 2860–2875 (2019). https://doi.org/10.1007/s11227-019-03078-z
20. Strazdins, P.: A comparison of lookahead and algorithmic blocking techniques for parallel matrix factorization. Technical Report. TR-CS-98-07, Department of Computer Science, The Australian National University, Canberra 0200 ACT, Australia (1998)
21. Van Zee, F.G., van de Geijn, R.A.: BLIS: A framework for rapidly instantiating BLAS functionality. ACM Trans. Math. Softw. **41**(3), 14:1–14:33 (2015)

IMSS: In-Memory Storage System for Data Intensive Applications

Javier Garcia-Blas$^{(\boxtimes)}$ ⓘ, David E. Singhⓘ, and Jesus Carreteroⓘ

University Carlos III of Madrid, Leganes, Spain
{fjblas,dexposit,jcarrete}@inf.uc3m.es

Abstract. Computer applications are growing in terms of data management requirements. In both scientific and engineering domains, high-performance computing clusters tend to experience bottlenecks in the I/O layer, limiting the scalability of data-intensive based applications. Thus, minimizing the number of cycles required by I/O operations constitutes a widely addressed challenge. In order to cope with that constraint, distributed in-memory store solutions provide a network-attached storage system using the compute nodes main memory as storage device. This solution provides a temporary but faster storage approach than those based on non-volatile memory like SSDs. This work presents a novel ad-hoc in-memory storage system focused on data management and data distribution, namely IMSS. Our solution accelerates both data and metadata management, taking advantage of ZeroMQ, a fast and flexible communication mechanism. One of the main contributions of IMSS is that it incorporates multiple distribution policies for both optimizing network performance and increasing load-balance. The experimental evaluation demonstrates that our proposal outperforms Redis, a well-known in-memory data structure store, outperforming Redis in both write and read data accesses.

Keywords: HPC · Data intensive · In-memory storage

1 Introduction

Current scientific and engineering applications running on today's large-scale supercomputers are usually characterized by a data-intensive nature. A single

This work was partially supported by the EU project "ASPIDE: Exascale Programming Models for Extreme Data Processing" under grant 801091. This work has been partially funded by the European Union's Horizon 2020 under the ADMIRE project, grant Agreement number 956748-ADMIRE-H2020-JTI-EuroHPC-2019-1. This research was partially supported by Madrid regional Government (Spain) under the grant "Convergencia Big Data-HPC: de los sensores a las Aplicaciones. (CABAHLA-CM)". Finally, this work was partially supported by the Spanish Ministry of Science and Innovation Project "New Data Intensive Computing Methods for High-End and Edge Computing Platforms (DECIDE)" Ref. PID2019-107858GB-I00.

H. Anzt et al. (Eds.): ISC High Performance 2022 Workshops, LNCS 13387, pp. 190–205, 2022.
https://doi.org/10.1007/978-3-031-23220-6_13

application's workflow easily generates tens of terabytes of data, mostly produced by on-line operations. As M. Radulovic et al. [14] stated, from the performance point of view, that a set of tested applications behave as data intensive ones when all of them, but two, spent a significant portion of time with a memory bandwidth utilization above 60% or even 80%. Due to the appearance of these data-demanding high-performance applications, multiple software solutions have been introduced in an attempt to cope with challenges along the entire I/O software stack [6], such as high-level I/O libraries, parallel file systems, and I/O middleware, with a final objective consisting on reducing the amount of file system calls and offloading I/O functionalities from compute nodes, respectively. Those optimizations are even more important for data-intensive workflows, consisting of interdependent data processing tasks often connected in a DAG-style sequence, which communicate through intermediate storage abstractions, typically files. While workflow management systems deployed on HPC systems (e.g., parallel machines) typically exploit a monolithic parallel file system that ensures a high efficiency in data access [18], workflow systems implemented on distributed infrastructures (most often, a public Cloud) must borrow techniques from the Big Data computing field [7].

For several years, I/O-intensive HPC-based applications have been primarily based on distributed object-based file systems, which separate data from metadata management and allow each client to communicate in parallel directly with multiple storage servers. Exascale I/O raises the throughput and storage capacity requirements by several orders of magnitude. Therefore, to develop methods that can manage the network and storage resources accordingly is a must [12]. It is assumed that the systems already developed for data analytics are not directly applicable to HPC due to the fine-granularity I/O involved in scientific applications. Another weakness of existing systems is the semantic gap between the application requests and the way they are managed by the storage back-end at the block level.

Addressing the challenge, different solutions have been implemented throughout the years. Alluxio [9] conforms a storage solution located between computation frameworks and persistent data stores that aims to reduce the complexity of storage APIs while taking advantage of memory speed I/O. However, the former does not provide an application-dedicated ad-hoc storage facility. Approaching another viewpoint, Hermes [11] focuses on the implementation of a MRAM-based storage system improving file system performance through the effective use of MRAM devices. Nevertheless, it does not provide locality policies. Also, solutions, such as WekaIO[1], that provide a high-performance storage architecture, do not consider locality within the implementation neither ad-hoc storage characteristics.

This work presents the design, implementation, and evaluation of a distributed ad-hoc in-memory storage system (IMSS), a proposal to enhance I/O in both traditional HPC and High-Performance Data Analytics (HPDA) systems. The architectural design follows a client-server design model where the

---

[1] https://www.weka.io.

client itself will be responsible of the server entities deployment. We propose an application-attached deployment constrained to application's nodes and an application-detached considering offshore nodes. The client layer is in charge of dealing with data locality exploitation alongside the implementation of multiple I/O patterns providing diverse data distribution policies.

Our approach offers the following benefits. First, the storage facility provides a flexible API tackling the storage servers' elastic deployment. It is possible to specify the number of servers to be deployed as well as the compute nodes where those servers will execute. Each server will have a storage buffer, whose size is specified at server creation. Second, IMSS makes use of main memory as the storage device so as to reduce as much as possible response time within requests, avoiding querying data from disk. IMSS provides multiple data distribution policies, which consider data scattering among storage processes and adapts the distribution behavior to each application's use case. Finally, IMSS exposes a non-POSIX interface so as to cope with the semantic gap existing in current high-performance I/O systems. The interface provided relies on *get-set* functions that enable non-contiguous data-related operations, unlike the traditional POSIX interface.

The rest of the paper is structured as follows. Section 2 presents related work to our research. Section 3 introduces the architectural design of the IMSS system. Section 4 introduces the deployment options of IMSS. In Sect. 5, we discuss the experimental evaluation results. Finally, Sect. 6 closes the paper with the main conclusions from our work.

2   Related Work

General-purpose parallel file systems such as GPFS [16] and Lustre [2] have been providing for a long time well-known solutions for long term persistent storage. However, they are very rigid and cannot be modified or suited to an application one they are deployed. To avoid this problem, new distributed storage architectures, like CEPH, have been proposed. CEPH storage system provides a distributed architecture that can be deployed on virtual systems, allowing block- and file-level storage, replication, and custom storage backends in Distributed Storage Systems [1]. However, current HPC systems and applications are not well suited to that kind of systems.

Moreover, increasing the complexity of the I/O stack with traditional I/O devices, generates an increasing in I/O operations latency that hampers applications' performance. Thus, nowadays use cases have empowered the proliferation of low-latency storage systems using local or remote in-memory storage devices as a feasible approach to the problem [10,23]. Such has been the impact of these storage systems [24] that multiple solutions, such as in-memory relational databases, in-memory NoSQL databases, in-memory cache systems, and in-memory data processing systems, have been implemented in the last years.

Considering the widespread spectrum of solutions, Redis [15] is a well-known key-value in-memory store that offers storage support for multiple data structures. Redis' implementation employs a single thread in charge of both, I/O communications and data storage/retrieval operations. Redis provides a distributed version called Redis Cluster, which provides an absolute decentralization through a hash slot partition strategy to find out which server within the deployment will store a certain record. Nevertheless, our tool has significant enhancements over Redis. First of all, the IMSS storage system follows a multi-threaded design architecture. Secondly, our IMSS provides to the applications a set of distribution policies that can be chosen at dataset level. As a result, IMSS will increase awareness in terms of data distribution at the client side, providing benefits such as a better data locality exploitation.

Another alternative that has been explored in order to approach the data challenge is ad-hoc file systems [3]. Ad-hoc file systems provide a custom data resource at application level, taking advantage of internal storage devices while acting as a middleware between persistent storage entities and the application itself. Major features are: (i) negligible deployment overhead, to be deployed either on a HPC cluster for lifetimes as small as the runtime of a single job; (ii) global name space for all nodes linked to the same ad-hoc file system; and (iii) interaction with the back-end storage system through data staging.

Within the current state-of-the-art ad-hoc file systems, GekkoFS [19] conforms an exemplary implementation of an ad-hoc file system which offers a user-space file system that combines application's node-local persistent storage devices in order to provide a global name space within the context of a particular use case, such as an HPC job, distribution of data and metadata as evenly as possible among the nodes conforming the file system instance by using hash indexing to discover which server will be storing each data element. GekkoFS relaxes the POSIX semantics and relies on the application in order to ensure that data overlapping conflicts do not arise. Therefore, the main differences considering GekkoFS and IMSS involves data distribution strategies and storage resources. On the one hand, IMSS enables multiple data distribution policies at dataset level increasing the application's awareness about the location of the data itself. On the other hand, IMSS uses main memory so as to store records and also the possibility of persistent storage.

BurstFS [20] constitutes a burst-oriented storage system that shares basic design considerations with GekkoFS. The main difference between them involves write operations: BurstFS clients always write to the corresponding local storage in a log-type manner. BurstFS instances are dynamically deployed along with the allocation of a job over a set of compute nodes. Then, the storage system will be using whatever node-local burst buffers are available, which may consist of SSDs or any other fast storage device. Moreover, BurstFS uses the key-value data model in order to handle metadata. In this case, the distribution policies enabled by our IMSS arise as an advantage against the BurstFS system. The IMSS client will be able to write to local/internal storage devices and to distribute the same workload among the set of servers conforming the storage entity by means of different data distribution strategies achieving improved load-balance strategies respect to BurstFS. BurstFS system makes use of persistent storage devices while IMSS store makes use primarily of main memory resources. As a result, the benefits of the data-locality exploitation will be achieved more easily using the IMSS tool.

In a previous work, we presented Hercules [4], a hierarchical parallel storage system based on distributed memory. IMMS differs in the following aspects. First, Hercules was based on Memcached [13] for both front and back-end layers. This approach suffers from the limitation of the Memchached protocol for data transferring modes, such as inter-process communication and inter-thread communication. IMSS employs its own communication protocol based on ZeroMQ, offering more flexible communication patterns. In contrast to Hercules, IMSS provides its own in-memory storage back-end. This alternative outperforms Memcached by eliminating the global cache lock system [22]. IMSS offers an ad-hoc oriented deployment, which facilitates the integration of IMSS in both applications and systems. Finally, IMSS offers a scalable metadata management layer that exploits data locality in large supercomputers.

3   IMSS Architecture Design

As, shown in Fig. 1, the architectural design of IMSS follows a client-server design model where the client itself will be responsible of the server entities deployment. We propose an application-attached deployment constrained to application's nodes and an application-detached considering offshore nodes.

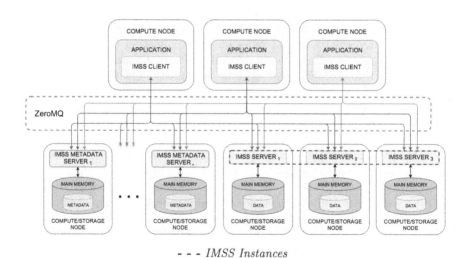

Fig. 1. Representation of an IMSS deployment.

The development of the present work was strictly conditioned by a set of well-defined objectives. Firstly, IMSS should provide flexibility in terms of deployment. To achieve this, the IMSS API provides a set of deployment methods where the number of servers conforming the instance, as well as their locations, buffer sizes, and their coupled or decoupled nature, can be specified. Second, parallelism should be maximized. To achieve this, IMSS follows a multi-threaded design architecture. Each server conforming an instance counts with a dispatcher thread and a pool of worker threads. The dispatcher thread distributes the incoming workload between the worker threads with the aim of balancing the workload in a multi-threaded scenario. Main entities conforming the architectural design are IMSS clients (front-end), IMSS server (back-end), and IMSS metadata server. Addressing the interaction between these components, the IMSS client will exclusively communicate with the IMSS metadata server whenever a metadata-related operation is performed, such as: *create_dataset* and *open_imss*. Data-related operations (*get_data* & *set_data*) will be handled directly by the corresponding storage server. Finally, IMSS offers to the application a set of distribution policies at dataset level increasing the application's awareness about the location of the data. As a result, the storage system will increase awareness in terms of data distribution at the client side, providing benefits such as data locality exploitation and load balancing.

Two of the most suitable network interfaces are sockets and Remote Procedure Calls (RPC). To choose the best one, we made a comparison between several communication mechanisms (sockets, gRPC, and we chose ZeroMQ [5] in order to handle communications between the different entities conforming an IMSS instance[2]. ZeroMQ has been qualified as one of the most efficient libraries for creating distributed applications [8]. ZeroMQ provides multiple communication patterns across various transport layers, such as inter-threaded, inter-process, TCP, UDP, and multicast. ZeroMQ provides a performance-friendly API with an asynchronous I/O model that promotes scalability. In addition, ZeroMQ library offers zero-copy messages, avoiding further overheads due to data displacements.

Furthermore, to deal with the IMSS dynamic nature, a distributed metadata server, resembling CEPH model [21], was included in the design step. The metadata server is in charge of storing the structures representing each IMSS and dataset instances. Consequently, clients are able to join an already created IMSS as well as accessing an existing dataset among other operations.

3.1   Front-End Layer

The client application will handle IMSS and dataset instances through an IMSS client library. The API provides a set of operations to *create*, *join*, *get*, *set*, and *release* data, datasets, and IMSS instances.

Along any session, clients create and join multiple *IMSS instances*. An IMSS instance is defined as an ephemeral dedicated storage entity conformed by multiple servers distributed along a set of user-defined machines that use main memory in order to store datasets. An IMSS instance is identified by a unique *Uniform Resource Identifier* (URI) and it is represented by a data structure

---

[2] (https://gitlab.arcos.inf.uc3m.es/mandres/imss/blob/master/
Middleware_Comparison.pdf).

storing parameters such as the number of servers conforming the instance and their respective location. Moreover, a dataset entity corresponds to a collection of data elements with a constant size that are distributed among the storage servers of a single IMSS instance following a certain data distribution policy. As IMSS instances, datasets are identified by a unique URI, which reflects the storing IMSS entity. A data structure representing the dataset abstraction is created per instance, gathering parameters such as the distribution policy assigned to the dataset, the number of data elements conforming the dataset, and the replication factor, among others.

3.2   Back-End Layer

Each IMSS instance is formed by multiple IMSS storage servers. Each one stores multiple data blocks of different datasets. Each IMSS server deploys a *dispatcher* thread that distributes and balances client connection requests among worker threads following a round-robin policy. In addition, worker threads belonging to the same server associate data blocks' identifiers to memory locations in a map-based memory container.

In order to handle *get* and *set* requests, each worker thread exclusively accesses the map container for the provided data block location. Afterwards, the requested data block is wrapped into a message and is sent back to the client in case of a *get* operation. If the requested data block is not found, an error code is returned. If the operation is a *set*, the worker thread overwrites the concerned block if it was already stored. Otherwise, the data block is written and a new key-value pair representing the previous block is added to the map.

Data persistency is provided through period dump operations that write all the buckets of an IMSS to SSD or hard disks. The period can be defined when the IMSS is created.

3.3   IMSS Metadata Server

Dataset and IMSS data structures appear whenever the client creates one of the previous instances. The metadata server was introduced in order to keep track of the aforementioned structures. In terms of internal design, IMSS metadata server aims to balance workload among a thread pool. The architecture consists of a single *dispatcher* thread and multiple *worker* threads. The dispatcher thread serves incoming connection requests distributing new clients between the worker threads following a round robin policy. A map container, which associates datasets' and IMSS instances' URIs to a memory location, is used to keep track of the stored structures.

The metadata server implements a persistence module. The server is able to write the structures associated to the dataset and IMSS entities handled along the session once it is over, as well as reading them during the deployment of a new session.

3.4   Data Distribution Policies

Dataset distribution policies included in IMSS define the distribution of each dataset in the instance deployed. The policy determines the back-end server in charge of storing data blocks. The IMSS front-end layer handles the policy assignment whenever a dataset is created. The IMSS metadata server maintains the dataset's data structure, annotating the distribution policies of each one. The following policies have been developed:

- **ROUND_ROBIN**: data blocks are distributed among the IMSS servers following a round-robin strategy.
- **BUCKETS**: each dataset is divided into the same number of chunks as number of servers. Each chunk is composed by a consecutive number of data blocks, equally distributed. Then, each chunk is assigned to a unique server.
- **HASHED**: a hash operation is applied over each data block key to discover the mapped server.
- **CRC16bits** & **CRC64bits**: similar to HASHED policy, but a sixteen/sixty four bits CRC operation is applied over the data block key.
- **LOCAL**: each data block is handled by the IMSS server running in the same node that the client. The data block key is not considered in this policy. If no IMSS server was deployed in the client node, every dataset's data-related operation will return an error.

With those policies, IMSS enables the possibility to tune the dataset distribution. These distribution policies aim to increase performance. As demonstrated in Sect. 5, the LOCAL policy experimentally obtains the greatest performance due to the exploitation of locality. In the current prototype, the distribution policy is established at creation time and it cannot be modified. In the future, we plan implement a dynamic distribution policy that enables to adapt the behavior in terms of system metrics (CPU, memory consumption, etc.). Within the previous possibilities, a *LOCAL* policy should be highlighted as it will have the objective of exploiting data locality as much as possible: data requests will be forwarded to the storage server running in the same machine where the request was made. Finally, a non-POSIX *get-set* interface will be provided in order to manage *datasets*, which conform a storage abstraction used by IMSS instances in order to manage data blocks (smallest data unit considered within the storage system).

4   Deployment Strategies

Two strategies were considered so as to adapt the storage system to the application's requirements. On the one hand, the *application-detached* strategy, consisting of deploying IMSS clients and servers as process entities on decoupled nodes. IMSS clients will be deployed in the same computing nodes as the application, using them to take advantage of all available computing resources within an HPC cluster, while IMSS servers will be in charge of storing the application datasets and enabling the storage's execution in application's offshore nodes. In this strategy, IMSS clients do not store data locally, as this deployment was thought to provide an application-detached possibility. In this way, persistent IMSS storage servers could be created by the system and would be executed longer than a specific application, so as to avoid additional storage initialization overheads in execution time. Figure 2 (left) illustrates the topology of an IMSS application-detached deployment over a set of compute and/or storage nodes where the IMSS instance does not belong to the application context nor its nodes.

On the other hand, the *application-attached* deployment strategy seeks empowering locality exploitation constraining deployment possibilities to the set of nodes where the application is running, so that each application node will also include an IMSS client and an IMSS server, deployed as a thread within the application. Consequently, data could be forced to be sent and retrieved from the same node, thus maximizing locality possibilities for data. In this approach each process conforming the application will invoke a method initializing certain in-memory store resources preparing for future deployments. However, as the attached deployment executes in the applications machine, the amount of memory used by the storage system turns into a matter of concern. Considering that unexpectedly bigger memory buffers may harm the applications performance, we took the decision of letting the application determine the memory space that a set of servers (storage and metadata) executing in the same machine shall use through a parameter in the previous method. This decision was made because the final user is the only one conscious about the execution environment as well as the applications memory requirements. Flexibility aside, as main memory will be used as storage device, an in-memory store will be implemented so as to achieve faster data-related request management. Figure 2(right) displays the topology of an IMSS application-attached deployment where the IMSS instance is contained within the application.

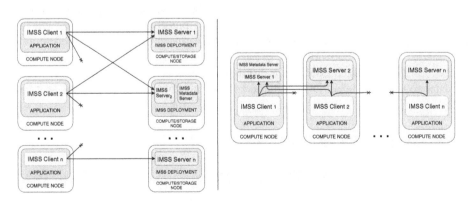

Fig. 2. IMSS application-detached deployment (left side) vs IMSS application-attached deployment (right side)

5   Experimental Evaluation

An IMSS prototype, as well as micro-benchmarks used for evaluation are available[3]. IMSS has been evaluated in different scenarios in order to ascertain the tool's appropriateness for the task addressed in the current work. First, we evaluated IMSS in a bare-metal cluster. Second, in order to evaluate the scalability of IMSS, we carried out experiments using the Google Cloud infrastructure. The former evaluations aimed to measure the system's scalability reaching up to 128 nodes. The workload was fixed to a single dataset of 8 GB that clients handle collectively: one client creates it and the remaining open it. Multiple distribution policies and block sizes were once again considered.

The Google Cloud Platform[4] was chosen as a feasible solution. The virtual instances are composed by nodes with 4 cores and 16 GB of RAM memory. We have employed up to 128 virtual nodes. The software layer is based on Ubuntu 18.10 LTS, GCC compiler 7.3.0, and MPICH 3.2.0. The results shown in the experiments correspond with the average value of five consecutive executions. In order to depict the performance of IMSS, we have compared our solution with four storage alternatives. First, IMSS was directly compared with the Redis object store. Second, IMSS was compared with maximum network bandwidth (in terms of MB/s), denoted in the plots with the label *network_limit*. The network throughput was obtained by using the *iperf* tool [17]. Within the results presented, Redis deployment time is not considered. However, it is important to note that the deployment step of IMSS is significantly smaller than Redis.

5.1   Block Size Variation

The first scenario presents the aggregated performance obtained from writing and further reading steps of an 8 GB dataset achieved by 128 clients. Figure 3 represents the aggregated throughput obtained from the previous experiments. In this case, the lack of variation of any kind is differentiated. In the first place, there is no performance increment with bigger block sizes. This takes place as the dataset's portion left to each client is so small (64 MB) that it does not leave possibility for improvement. There is no difference in writing such a small number of bytes with a block size of 4 KB (16384 blocks) or 16 MB (4 blocks) taking into account the asynchronous nature of the operation. Secondly, the previous condition plus the minimal number of write operations per compute node leaves no chance for any *LOCAL* policy improvement. Besides, another factor that locates the observed performance under the referenced corresponds to the reduction in the number of write operations per client and create dataset call.

Moreover, Fig. 4 shows the aggregated throughput obtained from the consequent reading step. In this case, a significant improvement paired to the block size is ascertained. The previous fact takes place as the read operations involve

---

[3] https://gitlab.arcos.inf.uc3m.es/mandres/IMSS.
[4] (https://cloud.google.com).

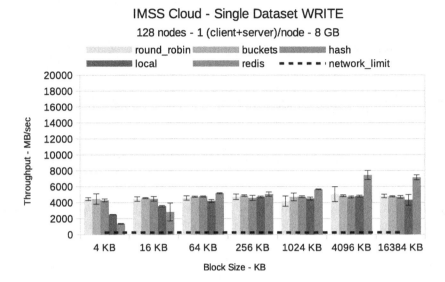

Fig. 3. Single dataset WRITE evaluation.   .

network overheads, which suffer from small blocks. In addition, a performance improvement could be noticed regarding the *LOCAL* distribution. The policy turns to be favored as each client's requests are handled by the server running in the same machine. As a whole, the *LOCAL* policy's effectiveness is once again justified through the results obtained in the reading step. In addition, the metadata influence is ascertained once more regarding the writing one.

5.2 Scalability

This scenario considers a scalability evaluation of the IMSS starting from 4 nodes up to 128 by writing and reading an 8 GB dataset collectivelly using a 16 MB block size. Figure 5 plots the performance obtained in the writing step. As it can be seen, the performance degradation detailed in the writing step explanation of Sect. 5.1 turns to be justified. The number of metadata operations also increases reaching a point where the number of clients is no longer an advantage, but a constraint. In case of IMSS, each execution involved both the initialization of the storage instances and the creation of datasets. We observe that as we increase the number of clients, IMSS suffers from a little metadata overhead due to the management of blocks and the distribution policies. In contrast, Redis does not suffer this constrains as it lacks those features. In addition, the asynchronous nature of the write operations is again considered as it justifies the lack of any *LOCAL* case improvement.

Reading results are shown in Fig. 6. In this case, the 4 and 8 clients cases stick out as the *BUCKETS* policy is able to reach the performance of the *LOCAL* policy. Consequently, considering the previous context and the *BUCKETS* distribution policy, the network limits the performance of the *LOCAL* policy's

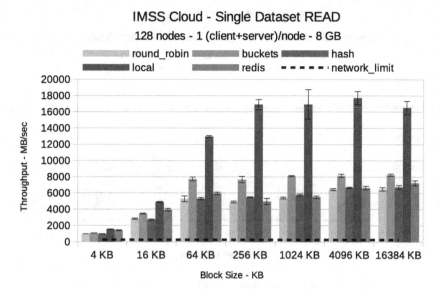

Fig. 4. Single dataset READ evaluation.

performance until the number of clients and the network topology constraint the case. Regarding the obtained results, the performance improvement of the *LOCAL* distribution policy through the exhaustive and aware exploitation of data locality are once again justified as well as the influence performed by the metadata operations.

5.3 Metadata Overhead

The last scenario evaluates the time required for invoking each API call of IMSS.

Figure 7 plots the mean time required in milliseconds to perform every metadata-related call. As shown in the figure, INIT operations are more computationally expensive as they have to create all IMSS environment. Thus, *stat_init* method produces an execution overhead as it initially creates the communication channel with the metadata server. Besides, this call involves the initialization of multiple internals required for an execution. We also observe that both *init_imss* and *open_imss* invocations constitute another couple of computationally expensive functions as they involve creating the corresponding communication channels with each server conforming the IMSS deployment. However, the *init_imss* execution time is above the *open_imss* one as the first function will initialize all server entities. It is important to highlight that the number of servers conforming the IMSS deployment significantly influences the execution time of the aforementioned functions as the number of servers to be awakened and the number of communications to be created increases with it. It is important to notice that those operations are executed only once at IMSS creation or opening.

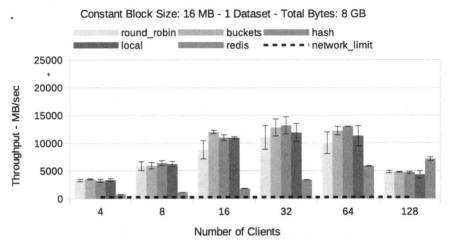

Fig. 5. Scalability evaluation. WRITE step of an 8 GB dataset.

However, status and operation calls creates a very low overhead. The *stat_release* and *release_imss* calls require a small execution time as they exclusively release the aforementioned communication resources and internals. Anyway, they are used only once, when the IMSS is destroyed. Moreover, *stat_imss* function, that requests an IMSS metadata structure to the metadata server, also creates a small execution overhead. Considering the set of metadata operations, *create_dataset*, *open_dataset* and *stat_dataset* methods, no significant execution overhead is created as they exclusively involve a request-reply dialogue with the metadata server, plus additional queries performed over the internal vectors storing datasets' metadata structures. Again, the *release_dataset* function will not suppose a significant overhead as it will just mark as free the position storing the involved metadata structure within the internal entity that keeps track of them.

As may be seen, the overhead of dataset operations is almost negligible. Those results are possible due to the usage of a metadata cluster, with a minimum of 3 nodes. The cluster could be enlarged, if needed, to ensure scalability and to keep performance.

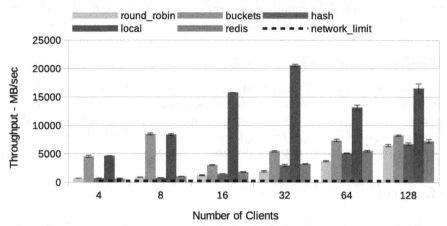

Fig. 6. Scalability evaluation. READ step of an 8 GB dataset.

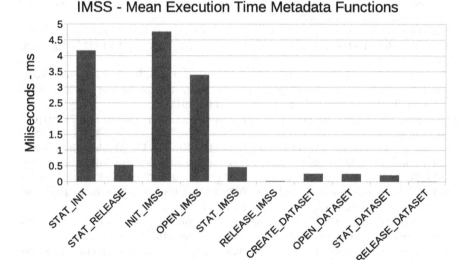

Fig. 7. Mean execution time of each IMSS API call.

6   Conclusions

In this work, we have introduced IMSS, an in-memory ad-hoc storage system for data intensive-based applications that provides a flexible API tackling the storage servers' elastic deployment, usage of main memory as the storage device so as to reduce as much as possible response time within requests, multiple data distribution policies at the dataset level to increased awareness at application level, and a non-POSIX interface that relies on *get-set* functions. Evaluation results presented in Sect. 5, comparing IMSS, Redis and a POSIX-compliant ext4 file system with caching techniques under different scenarios, show that our IMSS performs better in any operation involving distributed datasets, outperforming Redis and POSIX file systems. Moreover, we showed a low overhead for the execution of IMSS's API operations.

Future work guidelines involve the development of a more sophisticated persistence storage module. This new module will allow to provide more efficient operations to dump data from IMSS to the persistent storage back-end. We are currently working on a extended evaluation that covers an experimental evaluation under larger scenarios in terms of number of clients involved and workload in order to provide a more detailed performance analysis.

References

1. Aghayev, A., Weil, S., Kuchnik, M., Nelson, M., Ganger, G.R., Amvrosiadis, G.: The case for custom storage backends in distributed storage systems. ACM Trans. Storage (TOS) **16**(2), 1–31 (2020)
2. Braam, P.J., Schwan, P.: Lustre: the intergalactic file system. In: Ottawa Linux Symposium, vol. 8, pp. 3429–3441 (2002)
3. Brinkmann, A., et al.: Ad hoc file systems for high-performance computing. J. Comput. Sci. Technol. **35**(1), 4–26 (2020). https://doi.org/10.1007/s11390-020-9801-1
4. Duro, F.R., Blas, J.G., Carretero, J.: A hierarchical parallel storage system based on distributed memory for large scale systems. In: Proceedings of the 20th European MPI Users' Group Meeting, pp. 139–140 (2013)
5. Hintjens, P.: Zeromq: an open-source universal messaging library (2007). https://zeromq.org
6. Isaila, F., Garcia, J., Carretero, J., Ross, R., Kimpe, D.: Making the case for reforming the I/O software stack of extreme-scale systems. Adv. Eng. Softw. **111**, 26–31 (2017). https://doi.org/10.1016/j.advengsoft.2016.07.003, http://www.sciencedirect.com/science/article/pii/S0965997816301740, advances in High Performance Computing: on the path to Exascale software
7. Kune, R., Konugurthi, P.K., Agarwal, A., Chillarige, R.R., Buyya, R.: The anatomy of big data computing. Softw. Pract. Exp. **46**(1), 79–105 (2016)
8. Lauener, J., Sliwinski, W.: How to design & implement a modern communication middleware based on ZeroMQ. In: 16th International Conference on Accelerator and Large Experimental Physics Control Systems, p. MOBPL05 (2018). https://doi.org/10.18429/JACoW-ICALEPCS2017-MOBPL05
9. Li, H.: Alluxio: A virtual distributed file system. Ph.D. thesis, UC Berkeley (2018)
10. Lu, Y., Shu, J., Chen, Y., Li, T.: Octopus: an rdma-enabled distributed persistent memory file system. In: 2017 {USENIX} Annual Technical Conference ({USENIX}{ATC} 2017), pp. 773–785 (2017)
11. Miller, E.L., Brandt, S.A., Long, D.D.: Hermes: high-performance reliable mram-enabled storage. In: Proceedings Eighth Workshop on Hot Topics in Operating Systems, pp. 95–99. IEEE (2001)
12. Narasimhamurthy, S., et al.: Sage: percipient storage for exascale data centric computing. Parallel Comput. **83**, 22–33 (2019)

13. Nishtala, R., et al.: Scaling memcache at facebook. In: Presented as part of the 10th {USENIX} Symposium on Networked Systems Design and Implementation ({NSDI} 2013), pp. 385–398 (2013)
14. Radulovic, M., Asifuzzaman, K., Carpenter, P., Radojković, P., Ayguadé, E.: HPC benchmarking: scaling right and looking beyond the average. In: Aldinucci, M., Padovani, L., Torquati, M. (eds.) Euro-Par 2018. LNCS, vol. 11014, pp. 135–146. Springer, Cham (2018). https://doi.org/10.1007/978-3-319-96983-1_10
15. Sanfilippo, S., Noordhuis., P.: Redis (2009). https://redis.io
16. Schmuck, F.B., Haskin, R.L.: GPFS: a shared-disk file system for large computing clusters. In: FAST, vol. 2 (2002)
17. Tirumala, A.: Iperf: the TCP/UDP bandwidth measurement tool (1999). http://dast.nlanr.net/Projects/Iperf/
18. Vahi, K., Rynge, M., Juve, G., Mayani, R., Deelman, E.: Rethinking data management for big data scientific workflows. In: 2013 IEEE International Conference on Big Data, pp. 27–35. IEEE (2013)
19. Vef, M., et al.: Gekkofs - a temporary distributed file system for hpc applications. In: 2018 IEEE International Conference on Cluster Computing (CLUSTER), pp. 319–324 (2018)
20. Wang, T., Mohror, K., Moody, A., Sato, K., Yu, W.: An ephemeral burst-buffer file system for scientific applications. In: SC 2016: Proceedings of the International Conference for High Performance Computing, Networking, Storage and Analysis, pp. 807–818 (2016)
21. Weil, S.A., Brandt, S.A., Miller, E.L., Maltzahn, C.: Crush: controlled, scalable, decentralized placement of replicated data. In: SC 2006: Proceedings of the 2006 ACM/IEEE Conference on Supercomputing, pp. 31–31. IEEE (2006)
22. Wiggins, A., Langston, J.: Enhancing the scalability of memcached. Intel document, unpublished (2012). http://software.intel.com/en-us/articles/enhancing-the-scalability-of-memcached
23. Yang, J., Izraelevitz, J., Swanson, S.: Orion: a distributed file system for nonvolatile main memory and rdma-capable networks. In: 17th {USENIX} Conference on File and Storage Technologies ({FAST} 2019), pp. 221–234 (2019)
24. Zhang, H., Chen, G., Ooi, B.C., Tan, K.L., Zhang, M.: In-memory big data management and processing: a survey. IEEE Trans. Knowl. Data Eng. 27(7), 1920–1948 (2015)

On the Convergence of Malleability and the HPC PowerStack: Exploiting Dynamism in Over-Provisioned and Power-Constrained HPC Systems

Eishi Arima[1]([✉]), A. Isaías Comprés[1], and Martin Schulz[1,2]

[1] Technical University of Munich, Garching, Germany
{arima,compresu,schulzm}@in.tum.de
[2] Leibniz Supercomputing Centre, Garching, Germany

Abstract. Recent High-Performance Computing (HPC) systems are facing important challenges, such as massive power consumption, while at the same time significantly under-utilized system resources. Given the power consumption trends, future systems will be deployed in an over-provisioned manner where more resources are installed than they can afford to power simultaneously. In such a scenario, maximizing resource utilization and energy efficiency, while keeping a given power constraint, is pivotal. Driven by this observation, in this position paper we first highlight the recent trends of resource management techniques, with a particular focus on malleability support (i.e., dynamically scaling resource allocations/requirements for a job), co-scheduling (i.e., co-locating multiple jobs within a node), and power management. Second, we consider putting them together, assess their relationships/synergies, and discuss the functionality requirements in each software component for future over-provisioned and power-constrained HPC systems. Third, we briefly introduce our ongoing efforts on the integration of software tools, which will ultimately lead to the convergence of malleability and power management, as it is designed in the HPC PowerStack initiative.

Keywords: Malleability · Dynamic resource management · Power management · Over-provisioning · Co-scheduling · Heterogeneity

1 Introduction

The power consumption of top-class supercomputers or High-Performance Computing (HPC) systems have been increasing considerably over the past few decades. As a result, one of the most powerful supercomputers in the world now consumes an enormous amount of power, almost hitting 30MW [4]. Meanwhile, energy costs have been raising significantly in general, and thus setting a power constraint on the entire HPC system in order to keep within a budgetary upper limit is becoming more and more critical. As a consequence, future HPC

© Springer Nature Switzerland AG 2022
H. Anzt et al. (Eds.): ISC High Performance 2022 Workshops, LNCS 13387, pp. 206–217, 2022.
https://doi.org/10.1007/978-3-031-23220-6_14

systems will be deployed in an *over-provisioned* manner, i.e., installing more resources than the facility can (or wants to) afford in terms of supplied power at one time, and will be operated under a certain power constraint depending on the operation cost at the time, and using techniques like active power shifting to direct the limited resource power to the system components that require it most to optimize performance and/or throughput.

For this approach to work, though, we require significant flexibility in the entire system software stack. One promising solution for this is supporting dynamic malleability, i.e., dynamically scaling resource request/allocation to exploit the dynamism inside of an application. Because current standard resource schedulers in HPC employ static resource allocation policies, there is a significant room for system efficiency improvement by introducing dynamism at this level. Another promising solution is co-scheduling, i.e., co-locating multiple jobs that utilize complementary resources on the same node. As a compute node in an HPC system is becoming increasingly fat with heterogeneous processing elements, co-scheduling is indispensable to fully utilize the resources inside a node.

In this position paper, we explicitly target the near-future over-provisioned and power-constrained HPC systems and consider applying these novel approaches, which both boil down to sophisticated resource handling mechanisms, to these systems. More specifically, we first highlight the trends of HPC architectures, malleability support, co-scheduling, and power-aware HPC. We then discuss what would happen when these were combined together while providing some fundamental analyses on the convergence as well as clarifying the functionality requirements in each software component. We finally introduce our ongoing efforts on our software stack tool integration, which will ultimately lead to the convergence of malleability and power management, as e.g., targeted in the HPC PowerStack efforts [2].

2   Technology Trend

In this section, we first summarize the trend of hardware architecture in HPC systems. We second introduce several prior and ongoing efforts for the malleability support in HPC systems. We third highlight existing co-scheduling techniques for HPC systems. We finally present power management studies in HPC systems.

2.1   Hardware Architecture

Driven by the end of Dennard scaling in mid 2000s, the industry had to change their system designs toward multi-core and heterogeneous systems, instead of merely increasing the clock frequency [20,22]. As a consequence, CPU-GPU heterogeneous supercomputers have appeared around a decade ago, and now about 30% of the HPC systems ranked in the Top500 list are equipped with GPUs [4]. Nevertheless, we are now facing another serious issue, namely the slowing of Moore's law, and with that the end of the exponential growth that continued over the past 50 years is inevitable in the near future [22]. To keep the historical performance/energy-efficiency growth ratio, both hardware-/software-level system optimizations or even radical redesigns are essential. To this end, adopting extremely heterogeneous architectures that consist of multiple different specialized hardware components is a promising solution, in particular to maximize the performance or energy efficiency of various common HPC workloads [32]. *However, this hardware architecture trend, i.e., compute nodes will become fatter and more heterogeneous, will make it even harder to fully utilize the available resources, which will require more sophisticated resource management methodologies including co-scheduling, power management, and malleability support.*

2.2   Malleability Support

Malleability is the property of jobs or applications to remap themselves to varying numbers of compute resources at runtime [21]. When these resources are CPU cores in a shared memory environment, this kind of remapping requires less complicated data movements. In contrast, when whole nodes are added or removed from the resources available to a job or application, then network-based data re-distributions need to take place. In addition to this, communication software needs to be able to account for these changes, and update its internal data structures to represent the changes in resources. This is the case with MPI libraries or PGAS run-time systems. There has been active research in both shared-memory [30] and distributed-memory [17,19,23,24,33] malleable systems.

In distributed memory systems, as may be expected, the number of changes to support malleability is larger: Nearly the entire software stack needs to be updated to support malleability. The scheduler, node management, process managements, communication libraries, programming models, tools and applications, among other things, require changes to support malleability in distributed memory systems. Furthermore, existing elastic distributed memory systems, such as cloud software stacks, are incompatible with the bulk synchronous patterns that are common in scientific and engineering simulations. Therefore, systems like Kubernetes, that already support malleability for cloud computing workloads, cannot be reused without important changes. In spite of the larger scope and challenges, researchers have been exploring updates to systems such as schedulers [19,33], programming models [17,23] and applications [24] in the distributed-memory supercomputing field in recent years. Further, *as power is becoming more and more precious in supercomputers, in particular for over-provisioned systems, we should target power budgeting and compute resources at the same time.*

2.3   Co-scheduling

Ever since multi-core processors appeared on the market, a variety of co-scheduling techniques have been widely studied. In general, these techniques are useful in order to fully utilize the resources inside of a chip/node by mixing processes/applications/jobs which require complementary resources. R. Cochran et al. proposed Pack & Cap that co-locates multi-threaded applications on a multi/many-core processor while optimizing the number of threads for each of the applications [16]. M. Bhadauria et al. explored the feasibility of space-shared scheduling using a greedy-based co-run job selection and resource allocation policy [8]. J. Breitbart et al. created a resource monitoring tool useful for co-scheduling HPC applications [10] and provided a memory-intensity-aware co-scheduling policy [11]. Q. Zhu et al. targeted CPU-GPU heterogeneous processors and proposed a co-scheduling approach suitable for them [36]. Others examined the impact of hardware cache partitioning when co-running HPC jobs [6]. *In general, these seminal studies are not aware of malleable HPC applications.*

2.4 Power-Aware HPC

Since power consumption has become the first class design constraint when building supercomputers, there have been a variety of activities or studies on power-aware HPC. T. R. W. Scogland et al. developed a comparative power measurement methodology through the Energy Efficient HPC Working Group, which is used for the Green500 ranking today [31]. T Patki et al. firstly explored the feasibility of over-provisioning for HPC systems [26], and following this study, there have been various resource management and scheduling researches for over-provisioned and power-constrained HPC systems [27–29]. The PowerStack initiative community [2] was launched based on these studies, and *now we should extend the scope to cover malleability and co-scheduling to fully exploit the energy efficiency of HPC systems.*

3 Problem Statement

Our ultimate goal is to provide a software stack that is capable of handling malleable jobs while providing co-scheduling and power management features for near-future over-provisioned and power-constrained HPC systems. In this section, we cover the fundamental aspects such as job classification and the relationship between malleability, co-scheduling, and power management.

3.1 Job Classification

Before go into the details, we first classify jobs with respect to the applicability of the advanced resource management features in Table 1. The classification is based on the following two points: (1) whether or not the application supports the malleability; (2) whether or not the user accepts the slowdown caused by the power capping and/or node sharing (or co-scheduling). Even though introducing the malleability feature has various advantages by exploiting the dynamic behaviors of both systems and applications, as it requires code modifications, which can be significant depending on the complexity of the application, some

Table 1. Job classification

	Malleability	Accept slowdown	Power capping	Node sharing
Job Class1				
Job Class2		✓	✓	✓
Job Class3	✓			
Job Class4	✓	✓	✓	✓

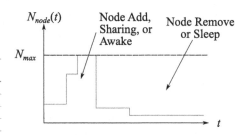

Fig. 1. Malleable job

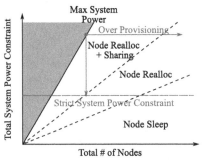

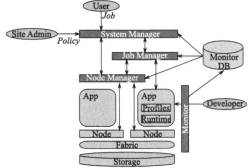

Fig. 2. Malleability handling policies and power constraint

Fig. 3. Our target strawman architecture

users may choose the traditional rigid option. Similarly, some users may prefer to exclusively utilize compute nodes without any power capping even if the administrators encourage the users to accept the slowdown (with an acceptable performance degradation rate) by offering them incentives, in terms of such as queuing priority and pricing. Therefore, these different classes of jobs will co-exist in future HPC systems with these advanced resource management features, and the entire software stack as well as the administrators must carefully handle them accordingly, in terms of resource allocations, queuing priority, token accounting, and so forth, which will be discussed later in this paper.

3.2 Malleable Jobs Under Power Constraint

Next we focus on malleable jobs and their dynamic behaviors (*Job Class 3/4*) as depicted in Fig. 1. The X-axis indicates time (t), while the Y-axis represents the number of requested nodes or the scale of MPI rank ($N_{node}(t)$). N_{max} is the maximum of $N_{node}(t)$ throughout the job execution.

We have several options to deal with the dynamic resource re-allocations to malleable jobs, and an optimal choice highly depends on the remaining resources in terms of both compute nodes and power. If available compute nodes are not very plentiful, dealing compute nodes across the job is a suitable choice. If no compute node is available (but power budget is still remaining), node sharing (or co-scheduling) should be considered. Note that the system must care about the job classes and the acceptable slowdown ratios designated by the users in this case. For an over-provisioned system with a very strict power constraint, allocating N_{max} nodes to a malleable job and sleeping/awaking them to deal compute nodes will be an option to be considered. As available compute nodes are very plentiful (but most of them must be in the low-power or sleep states) in such a system, the malleability can be handled by just turning them into the sleep/awake state.

Figure 2 intuitively summarizes the conditions mentioned above, and it is important for current/future HPC systems to analyze, model, and quantify the exact boundaries to determine the policy selection from these different resource management options. This exploration is a new research opportunity, and we need theoretical studies to demystify them by using such as job traces obtained from supercomputers and putting them into simulators with realistic setups. In this fundamental study, we will estimate or set some assumptions to classify the jobs in the trace into the categories shown in Table 1, in terms of number of jobs, job scale distributions, and execution time distributions, because the optimal policy setups and the effectiveness of these approaches will highly depend on these factors. To make the exploration more realistic, analyzing the scalability of representative applications at the granularity of application phase will help to assess the dynamic behavior. Further, quantifying the benefits of our approach from both the systems' and users' point of views will be essential, which includes the exploration on what incentives we should provide to users. Once a policy selection methodology established throughout this study, that will be deployed/implemented on the software stack.

4   Toward Convergence of Malleability and PowerStack

Driven by the problem statement and the basic assessment described in the last section, here we describe our high-level solution and ongoing efforts to realize it. First, we introduce our reference strawman software architecture. Second, we explain our high-level architectural solution and the detailed roles of components in the strawman architecture. We then finally highlight our ongoing efforts on the software integration to realize it.

4.1   Strawman Architecture

Figure 3 illustrates our high-level software architecture, consisting of several components and actors. The roles of the components are summarized as follows:

System Manager. The system manager receives a set of jobs to be scheduled within the system and indicatively decides upon when to schedule each job, to which specific compute nodes to map it, and under which power budget or setting. It also handles any dynamic resource/power requests from the job/node managers at runtime.

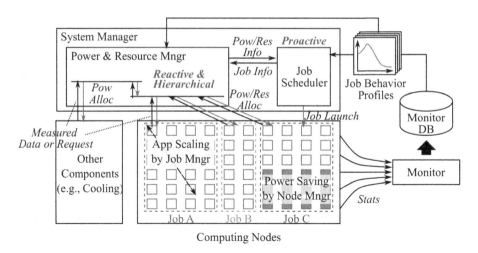

Fig. 4. Hierarchical and dynamic resource management

Job Manager. The job manager performs optimizations considering the performance behaviour of each application, its fine-grained resource footprint, its phases and any interactions/dependencies dictated by the entire workflow. It provides an option to users for a fine-tuned application-level hardware knob controlling and also provides the functionality to scaling up/down the job size.

Node Manager. The node manager provides access to node-level hardware controls and monitors. Moreover, the node manager implements processor level and node level power management or resource partitioning policies, and it mediate all the hardware control requests coming from the software stack.

Monitor. The monitor is responsible for collecting in-band and out-of-band data for performance, scheduling, resource management, and so forth. The monitor operates continuously without interfering with running jobs, and collects, aggregates, records, and analyses various metrics, and pushes necessary real-time or profiling data to the other components.

4.2 Solution Overview and Requirements

Figure 4 illustrates the high-level concept of our solution. Overall, we apply a hierarchical and feedback-driven resource management approach. The requirements for each software component and the administrators are as follows:

System Manager. The system manager mainly deals with two different tasks: (1) job scheduling, which is based on proactive decisions; and (2) dynamic and reactive resource adjustment across jobs/nodes. For the former, as the job scheduling decisions cannot be changed after job launches (unless we apply check-pointing and migrations that however can induce significant overheads), they are basically proactive relying on static information such as job profiles. Naive heuristics such as the FCFS with back-filling are widely used, however as we support malleable jobs, prediction-based approaches will be more important, e.g., those based on estimated dynamic behaviors of malleable jobs using such as profiling or any other information given by such as users. Further, as we apply co-scheduling and/or power capping to some classes of jobs, we need to revisit even the conventional back-filling strategy, e.g., choosing back-filling jobs based also on the remaining/requested power budget and the impact of node sharing. As for the dynamic resource management, we consider a hierarchical approach as shown in the figure: (1) jobs trade the power budgets and nodes by interacting with the system manager depending on their needs; (2) the system manager monitors the remaining nodes/power and governs the redistribution based on the requests; and (3) the node manager scales the power cap accordingly and optimizes the node resource partitioning (if co-scheduled). Note that if other components (e.g., I/O nodes or cooling facilities) support the power capping capability, the system manager should handle the power trading across compute nodes and them as well.

Job Manager. The major role of the job manager in this software stack is supporting the malleability functions and providing proper interfaces to the system manager, the node manager, and the developers. Beyond that, as the power budgeting should be supported for over-provisioned and power-constrained systems, the interface should also be able to handle the power budget requesting functionalities, not limited to removing/adding compute nodes. The power management should cover not only the sleeping/awaking decisions for the malleability behavior, but also should care about the per-phase/-loop characteristics (e.g., compute intensity, cache hit/miss, accelerator utilization, etc.) to determine the setups of hardware knobs during the active state. The characterizations should be based on such as profiling provided by the monitor tool, and the hardware knob setups are sent to the node manager and are handled by it.

Node Manager. The node manager mainly focuses on the hardware knob control, instructed by the job manager, or optimize the knobs by itself if the job manager (or the application) doesn't apply any application-oriented optimizations. It optimizes the power knob setup for each target hardware component inside a node while keeping the total node power constraint given by the system manager (or the job manager). In case the node becomes idle and unused for a malleable job, that should turn the node into the sleep state based on the instruction given by the system/job manager. Further, if multiple jobs are running the same node in a space sharing manner, it should handle the resource partitioning properly to meet the performance requirement for both of the co-running applications. For these decisions, the node manager can utilize statistics given by the monitor tool.

Monitor. The monitoring tool must be able to keep track of the power, resource usage information, and so forth, associated with each job/application, which will be ultimately utilized for various objectives. For instance, these collected information is useful for the other software components in their decisions, mainly the job profiling purpose as described before. In addition, the collected power/resource utilization information should be used for the human actors. One example is the job pricing purpose determined by the site administrators, which will be described later. Further, more advanced functionalities including modeling and analysis would help. One option is pointing out resource wastes or potential benefits of introducing malleability, power capping, or co-scheduling for users who submit jobs belong to *Job Class 1* (see Table 1). More specifically, notifying the estimated queuing time and cost reduction by applying/accepting these features would be a great encouragement for users to apply/accept these features.

Site Administrators. One of the major roles of the administrators is setting up the system configurations, including the total system power constraint or dividing the job queue per job class. Further, as introducing malleability into an application requires extra efforts to modify their codes, the administrators need to clarify the benefits to encourage their use. This is also the case for applying power capping and/or co-scheduling as they incur performance degradation even though the resource manager attempts to minimize the impact. One option is taking these advanced resource management features into account in the token consumption calculations, i.e., how much they charge for a job. The cost is usually calculated based on the number of occupied nodes multiplied by the job runtime. As the number of nodes dynamically changes during the execution of a malleable job, the cost should be significantly reduced. Further, if the power capping and/or co-scheduling is applied to the job as well, that should be also reflected on the cost, i.e., energy-based pricing or interference-aware pricing [12].

4.3   Our Ongoing Efforts on Software Tool Integration

To realize the high-level solution described above, several software integration projects are ongoing. One is DEEP-SEA project [1] that aims at providing a programming environment for European exascale systems, which includes the malleability support, and the other one is REGALE project [3] that focuses on realizing the HPC PowerStack [2], including both power management and co-scheduling aspects. In this subsection, we briefly introduce the current status of them, and our ambition is combining these two integration paths together in the near future.

Malleability Support. At the system management level, we are engaged in experimental development with resource managers like FLUX [5] and Slurm [35] as a part of DEEP-SEA project [1]. These are being extended with dynamic job allocation functionalities. In addition to this, new experimental scheduling heuristics are being developed. Currently, these are extensions to the well established FCFS with back-filling heuristic already available in these frameworks. We are also in collaboration with developers of monitoring and data-capture frameworks, such as DCDB [25], to identify metrics that are relevant to allocation size updates in jobs. These monitors are being updated to capture data of jobs with changing allocation sizes.

A set of application processes is created for workloads to run in our systems, in one or more nodes. These processes require relevant metadata and synchronization operations to establish communication, among other things. Between these system managers and the run-time systems of programming models, there are process management interfaces, that allow the exchange of such metadata. These interfaces have traditionally been vendor specific, and as a result has increased the challenge of developing run-time systems, especially in distributed memory systems. The PMIx [14] standard aims to remove these additional compatibility challenges. We are engaged in its standardization efforts, as well as in the development of its Open PMIx library. Both the standard and the library are being extended to better support the dynamic exchange of allocation metadata, required by malleable systems.

PowerStack Support. As an initial step, we are developing a software stack to realize the PowerStack [2] that enables a variety of power management functionalities from naive to a more sophisticated one in REGALE project [3]. We have already completed defining the initial software architecture, requirements, and supported use cases, and now we are working on the software tool integration based on the architectural definition. For the system manager, in particular the job scheduling, we are going to cover Slurm [35] and OAR [13], i.e., we are going to provide multiple different software stack instances to realize the architecture. For the job manager, EAR [18], Countdown [15], or BDPO [34] will be used. Note EAR has a variety of functionalities ranging from the system, job, and node manager, and thus is one of the key tools. Countdown tries to minimize the power consumption while waiting for the completion of an MPI communication, by scaling down the clock frequency or going into one of the CPU sleep states (C-state). BDPO is a job-oriented profile-based power-performance optimization tool, which optimizes clock frequency to trade-off performance and energy or to minimize energy while using its phase detection mechanism. As for the node manager, aside from EAR, BEO [34] and PULP Controller [7] are promising tools. BEO is an out-of-band power monitoring and controlling tool. PULP Controller is a low-level power controller, works transparently to the application, user, and system software, currently targeting EPI processors. As for the monitor, DCDB [25] and EXAMON [9] will be used, both of which support in-band/out-of-band monitoring properties as well as the functionalities to analyze/model the monitored data.

Some of the tools have been already integrated, and other integration is under construction. In addition to the tool integration, some sophistication paths are ongoing, one of which is the co-scheduling support. After completing the integration in this PowerStack implementation phase, we are planning to extend it to converge with the malleability software stack.

5   Conclusion

Near-future HPC systems will be over-provisioned and power-constrained. In this position paper, we explicitly target such systems and discussed the necessity/requirements of sophisticated resource handling mechanisms, i.e., the combination of malleability support, co-scheduling, and power management. More specifically, we first introduced the trends of HPC architectures and the prior studies on these resource management concepts. We second discussed what would happen when these were combined together while providing several prominent use cases as well as some fundamental analyses. We finally introduced our ongoing efforts on our software stack tool integration, which will ultimately lead to the convergence of malleability and PowerStack, leaving a significant impact on both of these communities.

Acknowledgements. We would like to express our sincere gratitude to the anonymous reviewers for their constructive suggestions. This work has received funding under the European Commission's EuroHPC and H2020 programmes under grant agreement no. 955606 and no. 956560.

References

1. Deep-sea: Programming environment for european exascale systems. https://www.deep-projects.eu/, Accessed 25 Apr 2022
2. The hpc powerstack. https://hpcpowerstack.github.io/index.html, LNCS Accessed 25 Apr 2022
3. Regale: Open architecture for exascale supercomputers. https://regale-project.eu/, Accessed 25 Apr 2022
4. Top 500. https://www.top500.org/statistics/list/, Accessed 28 Feb 2022
5. Ahn, D.H., et al.: Flux: overcoming scheduling challenges for exascale workflows. Future Gener. Comput. Syst. **110**, 202–213 (2020)
6. Aupy, G., et al.: Co-scheduling HPC workloads on cache-partitioned CMP platforms. In: CLUSTER, pp. 348–358 (2018)
7. Bartolini, A., et al.: A pulp-based parallel power controller for future exascale systems. In: ICECS, pp. 771–774 (2019)
8. Bhadauria, M., et al.: An approach to resource-aware co-scheduling for CMPs. In: ICS, pp. 189–199 (2010)
9. Borghesi, A., et al.: Examon-x: a predictive maintenance framework for automatic monitoring in industrial iot systems. IEEE Internet Things J. (2021)
10. Breitbart, J., et al.: Case study on co-scheduling for HPC applications. In: ICPPW, pp. 277–285 (2015)
11. Breitbart, J., et al.: Dynamic co-scheduling driven by main memory bandwidth utilization. In: CLUSTER, pp. 400–409 (2017)
12. Breslow, A.D., et al.: Enabling fair pricing on hpc systems with node sharing. In: SC (2013)

13. Capit, N., et al.: A batch scheduler with high level components. In: CCGrid, vol. 2, pp. 776–783 (2005)
14. Castain, R.H., et al.: Pmix: process management for exascale environments. Parallel Comput. **79**, 9–29 (2018)
15. Cesarini, D., et al.: Countdown slack: a run-time library to reduce energy footprint in large-scale mpi applications. IEEE TPDS **31**(11), 2696–2709 (2020)
16. Cochran, R., et al.: Pack & cap: adaptive dvfs and thread packing under power caps. In: MICRO, pp. 175–185 (2011)
17. Comprés, I., et al.: Infrastructure and api extensions for elastic execution of mpi applications, pp. 82–97. EuroMPI (2016)
18. Corbalan, J., et al.: EAR: energy management framework for supercomputers. In: Barcelona Supercomputing Center (BSC) Working paper (2019)
19. D'Amico, M., et al.: Holistic slowdown driven scheduling and resource management for malleable jobs. In: ICPP (2019)
20. Esmaeilzadeh, H., et al.: Dark silicon and the end of multicore scaling. In: ISCA, pp. 365–376 (2011)
21. Feitelson, D.G., et al.: Toward convergence in job schedulers for parallel supercomputers. In: JSSPP, pp. 1–26 (1996)
22. Hennessy, J., Patterson, D.: A new golden age for computer architecture: domain-specific hardware/software co-design, enhanced. In: ISCA (2018)
23. Kale, L.V., et al.: A malleable-job system for timeshared parallel machines. In: CCGRID, pp. 230–230 (2002)
24. Mo-Hellenbrand, A., et al.: A large-scale malleable tsunami simulation realized on an elastic mpi infrastructure. In: CF, pp. 271–274 (2017)
25. Netti, A., et al.: From facility to application sensor data: modular, continuous and holistic monitoring with dcdb. In: SC, pp. 1–27 (2019)
26. Patki, T., et al.: Exploring hardware overprovisioning in power-constrained, high performance computing. In: ICS, pp. 173–182 (2013)
27. Patki, T., et al.: Practical resource management in power-constrained, high performance computing. In: HPDC, pp. 121–132 (2015)
28. Sakamoto, R., et al.: Analyzing resource trade-offs in hardware overprovisioned supercomputers. In: IPDPS, pp. 526–535 (2018)
29. Sarood, O., et al.: Maximizing throughput of overprovisioned HPC data centers under a strict power budget. In: SC, pp. 807–818 (2014)
30. Schreiber, M., et al.: Invasive compute balancing for applications with hybrid parallelization. In: SBAC-PAD, pp. 136–143 (2013)
31. Scogland, T.R., et al.: A power-measurement methodology for large-scale, high-performance computing. In: ICPE, pp. 149–159 (2014)
32. Shalf, J.: The future of computing beyond moore's law. Phil. Trans. Roy. Soc. A **378**(2166), 20190061 (2020)
33. Utrera, G., et al.: A job scheduling approach for multi-core clusters based on virtual malleability. In: Euro-Par, pp. 191–203 (2012)
34. Vigouroux, X., et al.: Towards energy consumption application profiling with bull energy software. https://prace-ri.eu/wp-content/uploads/PRACE-at-SC17-Ludovic-Sauge.pdf, Accessed 14 Mar 2022
35. Yoo, A.B., et al.: Slurm: simple linux utility for resource management. In: JSSPP, pp. 44–60 (2003)
36. Zhu, Q., et al.: Co-run scheduling with power cap on integrated CPU-GPU systems. In: IPDPS, pp. 967–977 (2017)

The Fifth Workshop on Interactive High Performance Computing

Interactive, Cloud-Native Workflows on HPC Using KNoC

Evangelos Maliaroudakis[1,2]($\boxtimes$), Antony Chazapis[1], Alexandros Kanterakis[1], Manolis Marazakis[1], and Angelos Bilas[1,2]

[1] Institute of Computer Science, FORTH, Heraklion, Greece
{malvag,chazapis,kantale,maraz,bilas}@ics.forth.gr
[2] Computer Science Department, University of Crete, Heraklion, Greece

Abstract. Cloud and HPC platforms differentiate by many aspects, but both can run applications in identical contexts using containers. In this paper we present KNoC, an open-source virtual node (kubelet) for Kubernetes that transparently manages the container lifecycle on a remote HPC cluster using Slurm and Singularity. Our goal is on one hand to allow HPC users to leverage existing cloud-native tools, such as the popular Argo Workflows language to express complex data-processing pipelines, while on the other hand enabling Cloud setups to exploit computing resources available in HPC centers. KNoC bridges Cloud and HPC, transforming Argo to a cross-environment, portable solution, which allows the combination of Cloud-based tools and HPC steps into the same workflow, controlled and monitored through an interactive frontend. Deploying KNoC requires only a secure shell connection to the cluster's login node. We describe the design and implementation of KNoC, and evaluate the integration using several proof-of-concept workflows.

Keywords: Cloud-HPC convergence · Reproducible workflows · Kubernetes extensions · Virtual kubelet

1 Introduction

As we are gradually transitioning into the *exascale* era, there is no shortage of infrastructure to process large datasets: the Cloud provides an abundance of storage and computing resources, while High-Performance Computing (HPC) facilities around the globe are constantly powering on bigger and more powerful machines, each combining thousands of general-purpose and domain-specific processing units [16]. The increasing complexity of applications shifts the developers' focus to higher-level, more expressive languages, while the heterogeneous computing landscape places the emphasis on portability and integration issues. Large processing pipelines should ideally be synthesized as portable workflows that can move between setups, enabling deployment flexibility and reusability, while being able to combine existing data organization and processing components (i.e. libraries and computing frameworks) from different environments.

© Springer Nature Switzerland AG 2022
H. Anzt et al. (Eds.): ISC High Performance 2022 Workshops, LNCS 13387, pp. 221–232, 2022.
https://doi.org/10.1007/978-3-031-23220-6_15

HPC users typically integrate different stages of computation in custom scripts. In an effort to find a more expressive and portable language for defining application pipelines, we turned to existing work available in the "cloud-native" ecosystem. Bridging the two worlds is now possible as HPC installations increasingly support containers: reusable units of integrated, pre-packaged software that can run unmodified using different runtimes with minimal performance overheads. Singularity[1] [1] has become the *de facto* container runtime in HPC.

In Kubernetes [4] setups in the Cloud, Argo Workflows [2] is quickly gaining ground as the industry-standard workflow environment, providing a language and runtime to model and execute applications as directed acyclic graphs (DAGs). In Argo, every node of the graph is a container. The Argo controller processes each workflow by submitting respective containers for execution, monitoring their status, and collecting their outputs; all presented via a user-friendly, interactive, web-based frontend. The frontend also allows organizing workflows using templates, as well as planning repeated execution with a crontab-like syntax. Under the hood, Kubernetes delegates execution to available nodes. In this paper, we extend Kubernetes with a virtual node using *KNoC* (Kubernetes Node on HPC Cluster), which receives container management operations and forwards them to the cluster over ssh. KNoC consists of two main components: the virtual node at the Kubernetes side, which is implemented as a Virtual Kubelet [8] plug-in, and an executable (called *Door*) automatically installed at the HPC side, which provides a simple API for running the commands required to start and stop Singularity containers using Slurm [7]. KNoC is open-source [3].

In contrast to related works which bridge Cloud with HPC facilities through special "cluster job" objects in Kubernetes or other constructs, our approach allows us to transparently delegate execution to external compute clusters, while defining HPC-specific parameters directly in the workflow language. KNoC effectively elevates Argo workflows into a cross-platform standard, which can support open, reproducible science on heterogeneous computing facilities. With KNoC, Cloud users can easily tap on the vast amount of high-performance computing resources available in HPC centers, while HPC users can leverage the expressiveness and the interactivity of the Argo environment, while also exploiting the integration by mixing HPC workflow steps with other cloud-native utilities and runtimes. For instance, Argo Events enables triggering workflows on events coming from a variety of sources. The Kubernetes installation hosting the KNoC node may run locally to the user (in a simple virtual machine), or even in a "sidecar" environment offered by the HPC center.

2   Related Work

A tool for seamlessly combining jobs that run either in Kubernetes or in HPC environments is presented in [15]. *hpc-connector* acts as an HPC job proxy: users submit their jobs as hpc-connector instances with specific settings at the Kubernetes side, and hpc-connector forwards them to the HPC cluster, monitors their

---

[1] The Singularity project has recently been renamed to Apptainer.

execution, and collects their results. Docker and Singularity containers are also used to address portability issues. The authors identify five requirements for a system that allows running the same workloads on Cloud and HPC. Our work addresses all five, and extends the focus on workflow reproducibility and ease of use. We not only require the same *method* for job execution in both environments, but also the same *language* for defining workflows. With hpc-connector, users have to format their workloads to explicitly use it as a job-forwarding utility. Furthermore, since KNoC implements the functionality at the Kubernetes node level, it offers a generalized solution for forwarding container execution at the HPC side—not only for specific types of jobs. In [18], a Kubernetes installation is interfaced to a Torque-based HPC cluster, using a custom tool called Torque-Operator. Although this study offers the flexibility of running containerized Cloud and HPC jobs over the same front end interface through the WLM operator [9], it again uses a different language for describing jobs targeted for the HPC cluster.

Workflow reproducibility has recently been in the spotlight, especially in life sciences. Driven by the need to share both results and methods in a collaborative environment, as well as the need to verify the accuracy of computational results, a number of "infrastructure-agnostic" tools have been proposed. In the area of bioinformatics, examples include Nextflow [13], Snakemake [14] and Arvados [11]. These systems typically define their own DSLs (Domain Specific Languages) to construct workflows and most support containers for transparent job submission to either Cloud or HPC environments. As another example, the StreamFlow [12] runtime allows the execution of workflow steps onto multiple heterogeneous sites, automatically copying required data where needed. Groups of workflow steps may require specific environments to run, which are translated to runtime deployment dependencies. A proof-of-concept implementation uses the Common Workflow Language (CWL). In this paper we use the Argo language, however the hybrid Cloud-HPC platform offered by KNoC is language-independent and should be able to support other workflow runtimes as well. Also, it allows running workflows combining steps using other cloud-native frameworks, external to the workflow environment (within the limits described in Sect. 4.3).

3 Design

KNoC is implemented as a virtual node at the Kubernetes level—a virtual *kubelet*. The kubelet is the primary agent that runs on each node of a Kubernetes cluster. It is responsible for starting and stopping containers, reporting on their status, gathering their logs, etc. Each kubelet receives *PodSpecs*, which are Kubernetes objects that describe Pods and ensures that the containers comprising those Pods are running and healthy. Kubelets running on physical machines practically implement the interfacing between Kubernetes and the underlying container runtime; typically Docker or containerd. KNoC, on the other hand, directly manages containers that run on a remote HPC cluster. KNoC is implemented using Virtual Kubelet, an open source kubelet implementation featuring a pluggable architecture for extensions that connect Kubernetes to other container execution environments. Virtual Kubelet provides the necessary features to support the lifecycle management of Pods (as a collection of containers) and supporting resources in the context of Kubernetes, while exposing simpler APIs at the back-end for plug-ins.

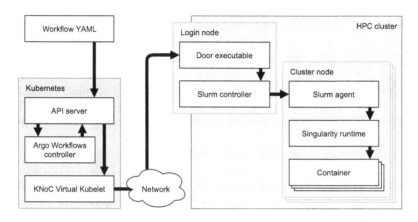

Fig. 1. Running a cloud-native workflow on an HPC cluster using KNoC

An overview of the main components involved in KNoC's deployment environment is shown in Fig. 1. The main goal is to run the container-based workflow provided by the user in Argo format (top-left) on the HPC cluster with Singularity containers (bottom-right). The Argo Workflows engine receives the workflow YAML and creates the corresponding Pods through the Kubernetes API. Then Kubernetes selects "KNoC" as the execution node to run the respective containers. If other, physical nodes also exist, this can be accomplished using node-selection constraints in the workflow language.

When KNoC receives a request to create a container as part of a Pod specification, it forwards the request to the remote HPC system supplied in the configuration. The assumption is that all interfacing with the remote environment can only happen by running commands through a secure shell (ssh) connection. To simplify the integration and add an abstraction layer at the remote end, the KNoC virtual kubelet installs and runs the Door agent remotely. Door receives simple requests from KNoC related to container creation and tear down, and produces the commands necessary to perform the respective actions. A temporary folder for each container at the HPC side keeps all runtime outputs and state, and is used by KNoC for monitoring the status of execution.

Door may implement different container execution plug-ins: it currently runs containers using Singularity, through Slurm, by creating sbatch scripts that form an execution environment for launching the containers. However, it can be easily reimplemented to use a different container runtime. Slurm is one of the most popular job schedulers used in HPC environments. It will distribute jobs—in our case

Singularity containers—across available resources. Singularity will automatically convert the Docker images used in the workflow to create Singularity-compatible image files that run with the same commands as their entrypoints. We use Singularity for container execution due to its wide-spread availability in HPC, thanks to its performance and security characteristics.

To access special hardware features of the HPC environment (such as GPUs), or specify other requirements or constraints at the level of the generated Slurm job (such as MPI parameters), the user can use specific labels in the workflow, which Door includes as flags in the respective Slurm command.

4   Implementation

4.1   The KNoC Virtual Kubelet Provider

KNoC is implemented as a Virtual Kubelet *provider*. Providers use Virtual Kubelet as a library which implements the core logic of a Kubernetes node agent (kubelet), and wire up their implementations for performing necessary actions. There are 3 main interfaces that a provider may offer:

- PodLifecycleHandler is consumed by the PodController which implements the core logic for managing Pods assigned to the node. Creating, updating, or deleting Pods in Kubernetes results in API calls for performing corresponding actions at the kubelet level.
- NodeProvider is responsible for notifying Virtual Kubelet about node status updates. Virtual Kubelet will periodically check the status of the node and update Kubernetes accordingly. The implementation of this interface is optional.
- PodNotifier is used by the provider to notify the Virtual Kubelet about Pod status changes. The implementation of this interface is optional.

The KNoC virtual kubelet implements the PodLifecycleHandler and Pod-Notifier interfaces. KNoC also introduces the RemoteExecutionHandler module that complements the PodLifecycleHandler, to handle the interaction with the remote execution environment. KNoC is written in Go, using approximately 1200 lines of code.

When a new Pod is created, KNoC's implementation of the PodLifecycle-Handler will first go through the description and isolate any *initContainers*. A Pod can have multiple initContainers that need to run to completion sequentially before any other containers are started. Once the ordering of container execution is decided, KNoC will submit the containers in phases: first the initContainers, wait for them to complete, then the rest of the Pod members.

KNoC connects via ssh to the remote HPC cluster. The network address, username, and ssh key necessary to perform the connection are stored in a Kubernetes Secret and passed as environment variables to the KNoC executable on initialization. Also, on deployment, KNoC should be configured to advertise the total CPU cores and memory that are available at the cluster side, as Kubernetes keeps track of what resources have been allocated on each node.

For each container to be created, KNoC will:

1. Check if the Door binary is available remotely; if not, transfer it over.
2. Create a temporary folder in the form ~/.KNoC/<namespace>/<pod_uuid> /<container_name>/ for keeping files related to the execution of the respective container.
3. Place any attached Kubernetes Secrets and container environment variables as files in the temporary folder in key-value form.
4. Create folders for any attached Kubernetes *emptyDir* volumes in the temporary folder.
5. Run Door submit in the background, handing it over a JSON with details about the container and its environment, including references to the files and folders created above.

When the PodNotifier API implementation is triggered, KNoC starts a timer to periodically check the status of all Pods. The container execution command generated by Door places the containers' output and error streams, along with their exit codes into different files inside their temporary folders. KNoC uses the exit code files to monitor changes of container states, which are then consolidated to devise the corresponding Pod states that must be reported back to Kubernetes. To delete a Pod, KNoC calls Door stop remotely for each container. After the containers are stopped, the monitoring function will note the changes in exit codes and update their Pod status in Kubernetes.

4.2   The Door Executable

Our initial KNoC implementation produced a full Singularity command with environmental variables, mount paths, container commands, and arguments to be submitted over ssh. However, we decided to abstract this interaction into a simple API and synthesize the command at the remote end, using different implementations supporting different execution environments. This also solved the potential problem of having to run several commands (or a complete script) to manage container execution at the HPC cluster side. The remote functionality is realized by the Door executable, written in Go, using approximately 200 lines of code. Door started by using "plain" Singularity, while it currently uses Slurm to submit Singularity commands. Other Door implementations may use different container runtimes.

When Door is called to create a container:

1. It converts the given JSON description to an sbatch script that runs the respective Singularity command, including environment variables, values from Secrets, volumes, etc.
2. It submits the job to Slurm.
3. It writes down the resulting job id into a file in the container's temporary folder, which is used in case it needs to stop or cancel the job.

```
1   kind: Workflow
2   metadata:
3     ...
4   spec:
5     podMetadata:
6       annotations:
7         slurm-job.knoc.io/flags: "--mem=32gb"
8         slurm-job.knoc.io/mpi-flags: "..."
9     ...
```

Listing 1.1. Adding Slurm-specific annotations to workflows

Through Slurm, jobs may request exclusive or non-exclusive resources for execution. Door will pass particular annotations in the container description (coming from the respective Pod) to the generated Slurm command, so that the corresponding container will run with the specified resources. A simple example is shown in Listing 1.1, where the annotations used in the Workflow will be copied over by Argo Workflows to the Pods submitted for each step, and Door will use the value --mem=32gb verbatim when invocating the sbatch executable. If mpi-flags are defined, Door will invoke MPI to run the container with the additional parameters given. Also, container names may refer to either Docker images (which will automatically be converted to Singularity upon execution), or Singularity .sif files.

4.3   Integration with Argo Workflows

To successfully run Argo workflows with KNoC, we had to overcome several issues related to the availability of the Kubernetes API, volumes and associated data at the remote side. KNoC implements general-purpose remote container execution—amid, however, practical limitations. Local and remote systems may not share the same storage facilities. Also, the Kubernetes volume abstractions and mechanics are not available in the HPC environment.

For each workflow step, the Argo Workflows controller runs a sidecar container, called *executor*, in parallel to the "main" container defined by the user. The controller communicates with the executor to perform control actions (like kill, suspend, abort, etc.), monitor the state of execution, and collect outputs. Several executor implementations are available; each for a different container runtimes. When running Argo Workflows in Kubernetes, we select the "k8sapi" executor that actually uses the Kubernetes API to retrieve information and submit commands.

Running the Argo executor container remotely did not initially work. First, the executor could not communicate with the Kubernetes API. For this reason, we require that a ~/.kube/config file is placed at the remote side, configured appropriately so that Kubernetes is accessible from the HPC cluster. This file is then available within containers, as Singularity automatically mounts the user's home folder in all containers. Most applications using Kubernetes API libraries will work without changes, as the libraries check for the file at predefined paths and use it. Future versions of KNoC will automatically create the Kubernetes configuration file inside the remote container's temporary folder, depending on the Namespace and ServiceAccount of the running Pod.

Second, the default Argo k8sapi executor (in version 3.0.2) uses the Kubernetes *Downward API* to examine the Pod's status. The Downward API is a method to provide Pod introspection in Kubernetes. When the Downward API is "mounted" within a Pod, all containers can access the Pod's status and annotations as files. Moreover, applications can monitor these files for changes to the Pod's state or configuration. In Argo Workflows 3.0.2, the controller mounts a Downward API volume at each executor instance, which is then used to get updates on the main container's execution status. Instead of implementing the Downward API functionality at the HPC cluster side, we changed the Argo controller and executor to not use it at all. This was already a request by the Argo Workflows community, as some Cloud providers do not support the Downward API in their Kubernetes nodes (i.e., in AKS virtual nodes). Our changes have been approved by the project's maintainers and the Downward API is no longer necessary.

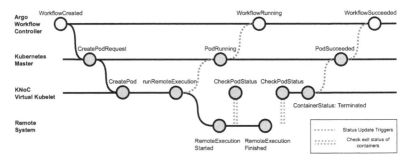

Fig. 2. Lifecycle of containers as part of an Argo workflow submitted to a remote system through KNoC

Figure 2 depicts the timeline of status updates, as workflow steps, corresponding Pods, and remote containers are created during the execution of an Argo workflow. A WorkflowCreated event happens when a workflow YAML is submitted to Kubernetes as a CRD instance. Then the Argo Workflows controller requests the creation of a number of Pods that relate to the workflow steps, by issuing respective CreatePodRequest calls at Kubernetes. Each call results in Kubernetes picking an appropriate Node to assign the Pod, and instructing that Node (through the kubelet API) to create the Pod including every container inside it. In the case of KNoC, once every container in the given Pod has been sent for remote execution, KNoC updates the Pod status to "Running". In turn, the workflow controller, which monitors Pod status changes, updates the workflow status to "Running". During this time, KNoC periodically polls for changes in remote container state. When the process running the container finishes, the exit code is written to a file. KNoC will pick up the change, and set the container status as "Terminated". If every container exits without errors, then the Pod status is updated to "Succeeded". As a result, the Argo controller marks the workflow step as "Succeeded" and moves on.

5   Evaluation

To evaluate KNoC, we deploy a minimal Kubernetes setup using minikube [5] in one machine, and configure KNoC to use the login node of our HPC cluster. As highlighted in Sect. 4.1, we instruct KNoC to report the sum of all cluster CPUs and memory to Kubernetes, so the latter will take full advantage of the available resources. We use Kubernetes version 1.19.10, Slurm 20.11.8, and Singularity 3.8.5. In our setup, we only use the KNoC node for scheduling pods, so all workflow steps will be sent to the cluster. In case KNoC runs alongside physical nodes, workflow specifications should be augmented with the appropriate NodeSelector, so their containers will be routed to the HPC side.

The KNoC source repository includes several workflow examples that we have used to evaluate the integration, including workflows defined as DAGs, loops, conditionals, etc. A simple example of an HPC workflow running the "embarassingly parallel" NAS benchmark [6] is shown in Listing 1.2. We use the language's withItems construct to spawn 4 parallel steps, each running another instance of the executable with different parameters. Also, note the use of the Slurm flag, defined as an annotation on the step template, to control the number of tasks used for each instance. This template showcases a method to run a parallel parameter sweep as part of a larger workflow. The "items" used may be explicitly set or be dynamically generated as the output of a previous step.

```
1   kind: Workflow
2   metadata:
3     ...
4   spec:
5     entrypoint: npb-with-mpi
6     templates:
7     - name: npb-with-mpi
8       dag:
9         tasks:
10        - name: A
11          template: npb
12          arguments:
13            parameters:
14            - {name: cpus, value: "{{item}}"}
15          withItems:
16          - 2
17          - 4
18          - 8
19          - 16
20    - name: npb
21      metadata:
22        annotations:
23          slurm-job.knoc.io/flags: "--ntasks={{inputs.parameters.cpus}}"
24          slurm-job.knoc.io/mpi-flags: "..."
25      inputs:
26        parameters:
27        - name: cpus
28      container:
29        image: mpi-npb:latest
30        command: ["ep.A.{{inputs.parameters.cpus}}"]
```

Listing 1.2. A simple workflow executing parallel MPI steps

On the other hand, to better understand the issues involved in compiling workflows that can easily migrate from a cloud-native to a KNoC-based setup, we use a real-life Argo workflow from the bioinformatics domain. This workflow performs genotype imputation [17], a computational method which is used to artificially increase the number of identified mutations in an input human DNA using a large dataset containing several thousand samples as a reference. The process, from a computational perspective, involves two basic steps: extracting the chromosomes from the input DNA and performing quality control/phasing, and then doing the actual imputation in batches of chromosomes, each measuring 5,000,000 base pairs long. The respective tools have been packaged into a container image, which is then used by the workflow. Each chromosome and each batch can be processed independently of each other, so each workflow phase deploys multiple containers in parallel, as shown in Fig. 3. The first phase processes 22 chromosomes and the second 589 ranges in parallel.

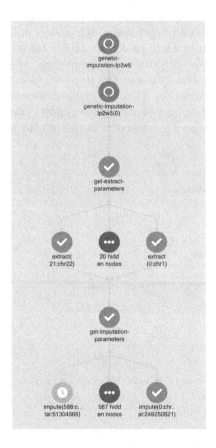

Fig. 3. The genotype imputation workflow as shown in Argo

A major point that should be considered when preparing cross-platform workflows (running on both Cloud and HPC sides) is *data availability*. Workflow stages may require shared datasets or a mechanism for communicating processed data from one stage to the next. This can be achieved by using an Argo *artifact repository*, as a common place to deposit files, or a *shared folder*, mounted across all containers at a known path. Argo supports many S3-compatible services for artifacts; the executor will copy in specific files so they are available to running containers before startup and copy out results after stage completion. On the other hand, a shared folder has the benefit of avoiding data copies. Currently, for simplicity, we use USL [10] at the Kubernetes side, to provide all containers with a common mountpoint, and allow Door to use the default Singularity behavior of mounting the user's home folder at the cluster side. Then we define a workflow *parameter* that determines the base path that the workflow will use at runtime for data. In the imputation workflow, one preparatory step downloads the reference dataset in the shared folder (which is about 11 GB in size), and subsequent steps use it for writting out intermediate files and results. We plan to address data availability across environments in more detail in future work.

By using KNoC, we are able to easily scale out the workflow using the resources available at the HPC side. Argo provides a "parallelism" parameter to specify the maximum number of parallel pods that can run at the same time during execution, which in turn allows controling the maximum number of Slurm jobs that are submitted in parallel to the cluster. At the cluster side, job scheduling is exclusively handled by Slurm.

6   Conclusion

The distributed computing landscape is continuously growing with new Cloud and HPC offerings. Applications, expressed as workflows, deal with increasingly large and diverse datasets, requiring more and more processing capacity, as well as the integration of a variety of tools from both domains. The Cloud heavily relies on container-based technologies to provide standardization across providers and portability of execution. With the same abstractions available at "traditional" HPC installations, we can now embrace the heterogeneity of available platforms under a common higher-level workflow language and enable workloads to exploit all available resources. KNoC is a step in the direction of bridging Cloud and HPC computing. It adds a virtual node at the Kubernetes layer, which acts as a proxy orchestrating container execution at the HPC cluster using Slurm and Singularity. KNoC allows *any* Kubernetes Pod to run remotely—not just workflow steps. In this paper, we present the design and implementation of KNoC, and focus on its applicability from both the HPC and Cloud perspectives, by examining the integration of Argo Workflows within the KNoC-based system and discussing on the issues that must be considered when constructing applications.

Acknowledgements. We thankfully acknowledge the support of the European Commission under the Horizon 2020 Programme through project HiPEAC (GA-871174), as well as the European Commission and the Greek General Secretariat for Research and Innovation under the EuroHPC Programme through projects EUROCC (GA-951732) and DEEP-SEA (GA-955606). National contributions from the involved state members (including the Greek General Secretariat for Research and Innovation) match the EuroHPC funding.

References

1. Apptainer. https://apptainer.org
2. Argo workflows. https://argoproj.github.io/projects/argo
3. Knoc: A kubernetes node to manage the container lifecycle on an hpc cluster. https://github.com/CARV-ICS-FORTH/KNoC
4. Kubernetes: Production-grade container orchestration. https://kubernetes.io
5. Minikube. https://minikube.sigs.k8s.io
6. Nas parallel benchmarks. https://www.nas.nasa.gov/software/npb.html
7. Slurm workload manager. https://slurm.schedmd.com/documentation.html
8. Virtual-kubelet. https://github.com/virtual-kubelet/virtual-kubelet
9. Wlm-operator. https://github.com/sylabs/wlm-operator
10. Chazapis, A., Pinto, C., Gkoufas, Y., Kozanitis, C., Bilas, A.: A unified storage layer for supporting distributed workflows in kubernetes. In: Proceedings of the Workshop on Challenges and Opportunities of Efficient and Performant Storage Systems. CHEOPS 2021 (2021)
11. Chojnacki, S., Cowley, A., Lee, J., Foix, A., Lopez, R.: Programmatic access to bioinformatics tools from embl-ebi update: 2017. Nucleic Acids Res. **45**(W1), W550–W553 (2017)
12. Colonnelli, I., Cantalupo, B., Merelli, I., Aldinucci, M.: Streamflow: cross-breeding cloud with hpc. IEEE Trans. Emerg. Topics Comput. **9**(04), 1723–1737 (2021)
13. Di Tommaso, P., Chatzou, M., Floden, E.W., Barja, P.P., Palumbo, E., Notredame, C.: Nextflow enables reproducible computational workflows. Nat. Biotechnol. **35**(4), 316–319 (2017)
14. Köster, J., Rahmann, S.: Snakemake-a scalable bioinformatics workflow engine. Bioinformatics **28**(19), 2520–2522 (2012)
15. López-Huguet, S., Segrelles, J.D., Kasztelnik, M., Bubak, M., Blanquer, I.: Seamlessly managing HPC workloads through kubernetes. In: Jagode, H., Anzt, H., Juckeland, G., Ltaief, H. (eds.) ISC High Performance 2020. LNCS, vol. 12321, pp. 310–320. Springer, Cham (2020). https://doi.org/10.1007/978-3-030-59851-8_20
16. Ungerer, T., Carpenter, P., et al.: Eurolab4HPC Long-Term Vision on High-Performance Computing, 2nd edn. (2020). https://www.eurolab4hpc.eu/media/public/vision/vision_final.pdf
17. Van Leeuwen, E.M., et al.: Population-specific genotype imputations using minimac or impute2. Nat. Prot. **10**(9), 1285–1296 (2015)
18. Zhou, N., Georgiou, Y., Zhong, L., Zhou, H., Pospieszny, M.: Container orchestration on hpc systems. In: 2020 IEEE 13th International Conference on Cloud Computing (CLOUD), pp. 34–36 (2020)

Workflows to Driving High-Performance Interactive Supercomputing for Urgent Decision Making

Nick Brown[1]([✉]), Rupert Nash[1], Gordon Gibb[1], Evgenij Belikov[1],
Artur Podobas[2], Wei Der Chien[2], Stefano Markidis[2], Markus Flatken[3],
and Andreas Gerndt[3]

[1] EPCC, The University of Edinburgh, Edinburgh, UK
`n.brown@epcc.ed.ac.uk`
[2] KTH Royal Institute of Technology, Stockholm, Sweden
[3] German Aerospace Center (DLR), Braunschweig, Germany

Abstract. Interactive urgent computing is a small but growing user of supercomputing resources. However there are numerous technical challenges that must be overcome to make supercomputers fully suited to the wide range of urgent workloads which could benefit from the computational power delivered by such instruments. An important question is how to connect the different components of an urgent workload; namely the users, the simulation codes, and external data sources, together in a structured and accessible manner.

In this paper we explore the role of workflows from both the perspective of marshalling and control of urgent workloads, and at the individual HPC machine level. Ultimately requiring two workflow systems, by using a space weather prediction urgent use-cases, we explore the benefit that these two workflow systems provide especially when one exploits the flexibility enabled by them interoperating.

Keywords: Workflows · Interactive HPC · Urgent computing

1 Introduction

From human health emergencies to natural disasters, the global pandemic and the recent bouts of extreme climate events have demonstrated the need to make urgent, accurate, decisions for complex problems. The use of near real time detection of unfolding disasters and computational modelling of such situations is a powerful tool in aiding urgent responders to tackle such disasters and disease outbreaks. Combining HPC computational models with real-time data and interactive user interaction can significantly aid in such urgent decision-making for disaster response and other societal issues, which ultimately saves lives and reduces economic loss.

However the major challenge is that whilst HPC machines have a long tradition of simulating disasters in retrospect, they have not been commonly used

© Springer Nature Switzerland AG 2022
H. Anzt et al. (Eds.): ISC High Performance 2022 Workshops, LNCS 13387, pp. 233–244, 2022.
https://doi.org/10.1007/978-3-031-23220-6_16

in-the-loop whilst a disaster is unfolding in real-time. There are numerous reasons for this including limits imposed based upon the classical way in which users interact with HPC machines via the batch queue system. Recent years have seen numerous advances in technologies and machine access policies that open up the possibility of using such HPC machines in a more interactive fashion for urgent workloads, and a major question is how we should best develop our codes to most effectively exploit these technologies.

In this paper we explore the role of workflows in high-performance interactive supercomputing for supporting urgent decision making. The paper is structured as follows, after briefly describing the background to this work in Sect. 2 we then explore the use of our workflows in Sect. 3. Section 4 uses a space weather prediction urgent workload to explore key facets of our approach on ARCHER2, the UK national supercomputer, before drawing conclusions and discussing further work in Sect. 5.

2   Background

There are numerous examples of emergency situations that we face as society including COVID, wildfires, hurricanes, extreme flooding, earthquakes, tsunamis, winter weather conditions, public unrest, food and energy resource management, and traffic accidents. Numerical modelling has already demonstrated [3–5] that it can contribute to insights which will then benefit these areas. However this alone is not enough, as in order to drive these codes for such workloads then the ability to consume real-time input data [6], and enable interaction with emergency responders in the field using rich visualisation technologies such as ParaView [7] is required.

However a key challenge is that there are numerous facets at play, often comprising multiple simulation codes that might need to be coupled in non-trivial ways, numerous data sources which might publish new data at unpredictable times when it becomes available (and which might then require the creation of new simulation instances), and the end-users who need to interact with running simulations or view processed results. An important question is how to connect all of these together in the most efficient manner which is complicated by the fact that we aim to support a general solution that can be applied to many different urgent workloads. We have found that the answer to this is the use of workflows however there is not a simple *one size fits all approach*, but instead different workflow technologies suit different parts of the technology stack.

Workflows are highly popular in other fields such as bioinformatics [2], and are becoming steadily more popular in HPC especially as the community continues to embrace data workloads. There are numerous workflow technologies and choices, with the most popular including the Common Workflow Language (CWL) [1]. Nevertheless, there is still work to be done in successfully exploiting many of these in the field of supercomputing.

3   The Anatomy of Our Workflows

In our approach we deploy workflows in two major areas, and these are illustrated in Fig. 1. The first is in our marshalling and control system which is a standalone system, represented by *VESTEC* in Fig. 1, and drives the execution of workloads across the HPC machines. The second is on the HPC machines themselves where the simulation codes and supporting functionality will actually execute.

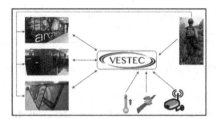

Fig. 1. Overview of VESTEC system and interaction with users, data sources, and HPC machines.

3.1   Marshalling and Control System Workflows

The VESTEC marshalling and control system drives the execution of workloads across HPC machines. It is not installed on a supercomputer, as the system is not intended to undertake any computationally intensive tasks. Instead, this middleware technology resides on a server, most likely enterprise class, and will manage the life span of urgent workloads when responding to specific disasters.

Figure 2 illustrates the technology stack view of our marshalling and control system, where the two black boxes on the bottom layers represent support required by the hosting server that the system is running on, namely Linux OS and Python. In green are a subset of the major Python packages that are in use by the system. The blue boxes above represent constituent components of the VESTEC system, where at the top the *external services* presents a publicly accessible API for clients to integrate with the system for the management of incidents, users, and the system itself. The *external data interface* enables the system to both poll for new data from sources such as sensors, and for external sources, such as client GUIs, to push data into the system.

However the major way in which urgent workload owners integrate with the system is by developing their own workflows definitions and plugging these into the system which is represented by *workflows* in Fig. 2. Our view is for lower layers of the system stack to provide a series of services and managers that undertake specific activities required by the workflows and can be called using a well documented API. Put simply, we provide a separation of concerns where lower layers of the stack provide the mechanism that urgent workload owners can leverage by developing their bespoke workflows which constitute the policy side of what such workloads require.

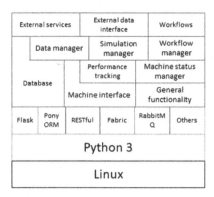

Fig. 2. Illustration of technology stack of the marshalling and control system

Moreover, we have found that it is effective to present the marshalling and control system to users as primarily a workflow system, where each workflow stage represents progression through a disaster's lifetime and these stages are triggered by some combination of external stimulus and/or preceding workflow stages. Consequently, to integrate a disaster scenario with the system then one must develop a workflow description. Individual stages can undertake a wide range of functionality including data transformation, preparation and submission of job to an HPC machine, and data clean-up activities. At any point during execution, stages can send messages to corresponding queues which will activate other stages. We provide in our *workflow manager* the building blocks required for users to express workflows, and Listing 1.1 illustrates a sketch of workflow code where programmers are interacting with the *simulation manager* to submit a job to an HPC machine. There are two phases required for job submission, firstly the creation of the job which determines which machine to allocate to [3] and creates the necessary folders, and secondly the submission of the job to the batch queue system. The reason for this multi-phase approach is that in the middle the workflow code can then create, copy, or move data to this location before submission, for example in Listing 1.1 the *data manager* is called to put some configuration onto the HPC machine between lines 10 and 15.

```
1   try:
2     callbacks = { 'COMPLETED': callback }
3     sim_id = createSimulation(incidentID, 120, "00:15:00", "Example
4                 simulation", "submit.sh", callbacks,
5                 template_dir="templates/mysimulation")
6
7     simulation=Simulation[sim_id]
8     machine_name=simulation.machine.machine_name
9
10    try:
11      putByteDataViaDM("myconfig", machine_name, "Simulation
```

```
12                          configuration", "text/plain", configuration_data,
13                          path=simulation.directory)
14    except DataManagerException as err:
15      print("Can not write simulation configuration "+err.message)
16
17      submitSimulation(sim_id)
18    except SimulationManagerException as err:
19      print("Error creating or submitting simulation "+err.message)
```

Listing 1.1. Sketch of workflow code required for creating and submitting a simulation on an HPC machine

The overarching flow and interaction with underlying services for this example is illustrated in Fig. 3, where it can be seen that the user's workflow code (on the left in yellow) calls into the *simulation manager* which itself will then issue calls to other parts of the technology stack into order to undertake the required activities. This call is non-blocking, where once job submission has completed and the job is waiting in the queue then control flow will return to the workflow, and once the job reaches a successful completion stage then the callback workflow stage will be executed. This is provided via the *callbacks* dictionary in Listing 1.1, again leveraging the workflows concept, to execute a workflow stage provided by the user once a job has reached a specific state of execution (in this case completion, but it can also be when the job has started to run or an error has occurred).

The purpose of this paper is not to describe the underlying services or activities in detail, as there are many such processes involved in the system but instead to illustrate how our approach provides overarching infrastructure for the development and management of workflows via the *workflow manager*, which then call into a set of internal services via their APIs in order to undertake specific actions on the HPC machines.

3.2 HPC Machine Side Workflows

In Sect. 3.1 we described the role of workflows from the VESTEC middleware perspective which provide marshalling and control functionality. Additionally, workflows are also useful on the HPC machines themselves to support interactive urgent workloads. The initial reason for this was to enable coupling of applications on an HPC machine, where the results from one application feed in as input to a subsequent code which is run when the former terminates. This requirement for coupling is commonplace, for instance undertaking pre-processing before execution of the main simulation code or post-processing of results. In this work we have adopted the Common Workflow Language (CWL) [1] which is a specification for workflows common in fields such as bioinformatics. There is a CWL reference runner tool, which is used in this work, to drive these workflows and in previous work this was extended to increase compatibility with expressing MPI workloads [8]. The intention of using CWL has been to describe the simulation steps on the HPC machine as workflow stages in CWL, with the

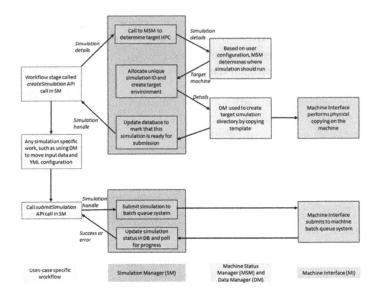

Fig. 3. Illustration of how the workflow creates and submits jobs on the HPC machines by calling into the simulation manager which itself will call other appropriate internal services

reference runner tool then submitted to the batch queue system and executing the workflow on the allocated nodes. We found that the benefits of driving the HPC simulation jobs via CWL include:

- Being able to inject configuration options that are specific to a disaster, scenario, or HPC machine via YAML configuration file(s). The overarching CWL workflow, that has been provided as a skeleton, is then concretised, or fleshed out, based upon this information.
- The ability to write a generic workflow description for a disaster only once which is independent across HPC machines. Whilst some machine configuration specifics might need to be provided, these can sometimes be shared across use-cases and/or represent a small number of machine specific tuning parameters injected via YAML.
- A structured way in which simulation codes can be coupled together, with the outputs of one fed into another based upon the workflow logic.
- Usage of a standardised technology which is well documented and supported. Therefore use-case owners can enjoy a wealth of documentation and tutorials when developing their own CWL workflows.

The interplay between CWL and configurations is illustrated in Fig. 4, where a generic CWL configuration file is provided to the reference runner tool which defines the inputs and outputs for the file, along with the coupling of stages, but does not contain the concrete values. These are defined once for a simulation code and do not change between different scenarios or from machine to

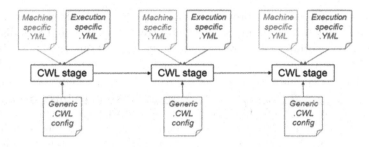

Fig. 4. Illustration of CWL workflow on HPC machine coupling execution with configurations injected

machine because, furthermore, a machine and execution specific YAML file is injected in. The idea is that not only can configuration options required from one execution of the code to the next be specialised, but furthermore configurations for different HPC machines exist which enable specialisation of the code between supercomputers in a portable manner. It can be thought of as the generic CWL configuration providing a skeleton which is then *fleshed out* by the YAML files. Listing 1.1 provided an example of placing configuration data on the HPC machine before simulation execution, and commonly this configuration is in the form of YAML file(s) which concrete the generic CWL configuration.

4 Case-Study: Interactive Urgent Space Weather Ensembles

The study of space weather [9] involves modelling magnetic reconnection under several different condition. This involves a study of the configuration of the Earth's magnetotail, can be applied for studying magnetic reconnection under different conditions, and is important because it is the magnetotail which protects the Earth and orbiting bodies from solar emissions. Phenomena in this magnetotail results in expensive satellite electrical failures and can also lead to electrical storms that short out earth-bound power networks.

The magnetic reconnection simulation code works on the basis of ensemble modelling, where many distinct permutations are executed and the results integrated. However HPC machines are often not suited for scheduling large numbers of individual jobs, for instance in our case when interactively simulating space weather, as the batch schedulers often tend to work in units of nodes. Consequently if the simulation is executing a low number of cores per ensemble then, on a machine with large numbers of cores per node such as ARCHER2 the UK national supercomputer, this can result in significant wasted resource.

CWL provides two benefits which can ameliorate this problem; firstly a scatter mode which creates a number of concurrent workflow stages across a node and waits for these to complete. In the case of ensembles, these stages will be running the same executable, but with different parameters spread across the cores of a node. Secondly it provides a choice around granularity between the HPC machine and VESTEC marshalling and control system that was discussed in Sect. 3.1. For example, if there are numerous simulations that must be coupled together then there is a choice of the marshalling and control system driving each of individually, submitting the next job when the previous one completes, and this is the finest grained approach. At the other extreme there is the coarse-grained view, where a single CWL workflow can be written which itself couples the jobs and is submitted to the HPC machine. As the execution of each CWL workflow is atomic, as far as the marshalling and control system is concerned, then the entire workflow will run through to completion before the marshalling and control system is notified it has finished.

To explore the performance benefits of CWL scatter against batch queuing all ensembles separately, a synthetic benchmark has been developed. This provides a configurable number of ensemble members, each with a single-core job and we ran an experiment on ARCHER2 which imposes a maximum of 64 jobs queued at any one time and 16 jobs running concurrently. Due to this limitation, as the number of ensembles was increased, using the batch queue-only approach the marshalling and control system was forced to queue up submissions for the HPC machine and submit these only when an existing job had completed and left the queue. Otherwise the 64 limit would be reached and job rejected by ARCHER2. Each individual job in this benchmark is effectively a no-operation, completing immediately. By comparison, the CWL scatter mode will schedule ensemble members across the cores of nodes, enabling sharing of a node between many ensembles. Even though there is still a separate submission for each node, the overall number of nodes is greatly reduced as all the cores of a node are utilised running a member.

Figure 5 illustrates the time to the last job being queued on the HPC system for this synthetic benchmark, where the Y axis is log scale. This metric was adopted as it measures the time to interact with the HPC system rather than for jobs to run on the machine which depends upon a simulation code by simulation code basis. The major limitation of the batch queue only approach is that as each ensemble can only exploit one individual core, there are therefore very many queue submissions required, which equals the number of ensembles. Conversely, for the CWL scatter approach as CWL can scatter ensembles over the cores of a single node, there are 128 ensembles per node. Therefore, whilst there is still an individual submission required for each node, now the number of nodes needed is the number of ensembles divided by 128. It can be seen from Fig. 5 that, as the number of ensembles is scaled, the completion time of the batch queue only approach is very significantly higher than that of the CWL scatter approach, most importantly because at 2048 ensembles batch queue only approach must submit 2048 separate jobs with the marshalling and control system having to queue up and track the completion of each and each progress through the queue, whereas the CWL scatter approach only needs to submit 16. It can be seen with the batch queue only approach how there is a sharp jump at 128 ensembles, this is because there is a maximum of 64 jobs in the batch queue and-so beyond that

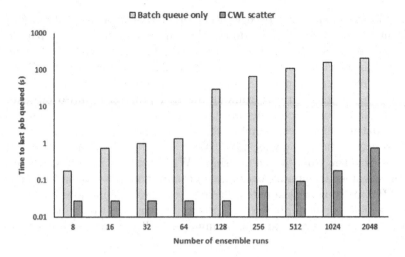

Fig. 5. Time to last job being queued on HPC machine (ARCHER2) based on total number of ensembles and whether this is driven by the marshalling and control system (fine grained) or CWL workflow (coarse grained)

number of jobs the marshalling and control system must wait for existing jobs to complete before subsequent ensemble jobs can be submitted.

The experiment presented in Fig. 5 is rather extreme, and the synthetic benchmark is a little artificial. Many, but not all, HPC systems provide job launching capabilities that enable the ability to run different executables across the cores of nodes. However, the downside is that often these can be fairly complex to interact with, driven by multiple issues of the launch command in a loop, and require support from the batch queue system. Such approaches can add complexity when preparing the job and limit the ability to target many different HPC machines irrespective of exactly what their batch queue system supports. From the marshalling and control system's perspective it is desirable for the workflow to be machine agnostic and not have to be concerned with such specific details. By contrast, the settings for the CWL scatter approach can be provided via machine specific YAML which is created when the use-case was installed on the machine, and/or by higher level parameters sent from the marshalling and control system. Nevertheless, this experiment illustrates one of the challenges faced when designing our general approach, namely the diversity of the urgent applications that we aim to support. This means that there are many different possible usage modes, ranging from large numbers of ensembles illustrated in Fig. 5, to single distributed memory applications that run over large numbers of cores. Consequently, one single approach to all these possibilities is not appropriate and instead selecting technologies that enable flexibility was required, and this has been demonstrated with the use-case implementations. Thus, giving the use-case developer a choice around key aspects by designing flexibility and generality into the approach is highly beneficial.

Considering interactive space weather prediction as a motivation, there is significant flexibility around scheduling the required ensembles and parallelism (i.e. number of cores) allocated to each individual member. We therefore undertook an experiment across space weather simulation ensembles on ARCHER2 where each member comprises 8 cores (which is optimal for the problem size being studied), with each core running an MPI process. Figure 6 presents the results of this performance experiment where three configurations were tested; **MPI+Scatter** which uses a combination of MPI parallelism for each ensemble (8 MPI processes per ensemble) and CWL scatter to run 16 of these ensembles per node. **Scatter only** which is using CWL scatter in isolation, where each ensemble member is running over one core only and 128 ensembles per node. Lastly **MPI only** using the batch-queue system to schedule jobs only so there is one ensemble per node, but with MPI parallelism enabled for each ensemble member and hence each member is running over all 128 cores of a node.

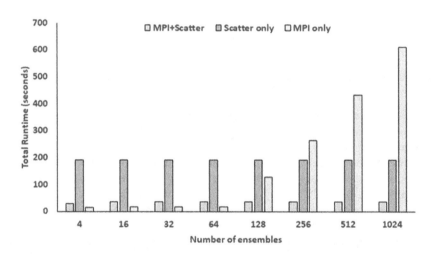

Fig. 6. Total runtime of multiple B0z0.0 ensembles from space weather simulation on ARCHER2 as the number of ensembles is scaled and different approaches to scheduling these adopted.

It can be seen from Fig. 6 that the approach we have adopted is generally most efficient, especially for larger ensemble sizes. The Scatter only approach is uniformly consistent and always slower than the MPI+Scatter approach. This is because it only allocates one core per ensemble and-so is dominated by the runtime that this configuration results in. The MPI only approach is fastest for smaller numbers of ensembles because all 128 cores of the node are allocated to each ensemble member rather than the 8 cores as used by the MPI+Scatter approach. However, there is a trade-off, namely that with 8 cores per ensemble it is possible to run 16 ensembles per node compared with one ensemble member per node when allocating all 128 cores per ensemble. Consequently, for the MPI only case as the number of ensembles increases, especially after 64 ensembles where the marshalling and control system must queue these up and wait for others to complete due to limits imposed by the batch queue system, then the overhead of queuing up ensembles jobs and tracking them outweighs the benefits gained by running each member over 128 cores compared with 8 cores. This behaviour drives the very significant increase in overall runtime for the MPI only approach beyond 64 members, as the marshalling and control system must wait for ensemble jobs to complete before queuing up new ones. In consequence, for 1024 ensembles the MPI+Scatter approach requires the allocation of 64 nodes in total which can all fit as a single submission into the queue system, whereas the MPI only approach requires the allocation of 1024 nodes and this must be undertaken in segments.

The purpose of the experiments described in this section have been to illustrate the flexibility provided by workflows for urgent, interactive, use-cases. Whilst it has been highlighted that some batch queue systems provide their own functionality to achieve similar scheduling flexibility, the benefit of exploiting this via CWL is that such decisions are undertaken in a standard manner across machines, irrespective of exactly what the batch queue system supports or not, with the marshalling and control system only needing to provide numeric settings via YAML files in combination with any pre-defined machine specific configurations also in YAML.

5   Conclusions

In this paper we have explored the role of workflows for expressing and running interactive urgent workloads on HPC machines. With two separate workflow systems, one in the VESTEC middleware system which provides marshalling and control functionality, and the other on the individual HPC machines, not only do these provide complimentary support for different facets but furthermore can work together to provide additional flexibility and most effectively suit the codes being run.

Using the space weather prediction urgent workload we then explored the challenges around ensemble scheduling on modern HPC machines, where we demonstrated that the flexibility provided by the two workflow systems working in combination is a powerful enabler for such situations. For future work we believe that it would be worthwhile to integrate the CWL and marshalling and control workflows, not necessarily at the underlying technology level but instead exploiting some of the safety provided by CWL definitions to ensure that those workflows expressed in the marshalling and control system are suitable.

Acknowledgements. The research leading to these results has received funding from the Horizon 2020 Programme under grant agreement No. 800904. This work used the ARCHER2 UK National Supercomputing Service (https://www.archer2.ac.uk). For the purpose of open access, the author has applied a Creative Commons Attribution (CC BY) licence to any Author Accepted Manuscript version arising from this submission.

References

1. Amstutz, P., et al.: Common workflow language, v1.0. Online. https://w3id.org/cwl/v1.0/
2. Korhonen, P.K., Hall, R.S., Young, N.D., Gasser, R.B.: Common workflow language (CWL)-based software pipeline for de novo genome assembly from long-and short-read data. GigaScience **8**(4), giz014 (2019)
3. Brown, N., et al.: Utilising urgent computing to tackle the spread of mosquito-borne diseases. In: 2021 IEEE/ACM HPC for Urgent Decision Making (UrgentHPC), pp. 36–44. IEEE Computer Society, November 2021
4. Ramirez, J., Monedero, S., Silva, C.A., Cardil, A.: Stochastic decision trigger modelling to assess the probability of wildland fire impact. Sci. Total Environ. **694**, 133505 (2019)
5. Krenz, L., et al.: 3D acoustic-elastic coupling with gravity: the dynamics of the 2018 Palu, Sulawesi earthquake and tsunami. In: Proceedings of the International Conference for High Performance Computing, Networking, Storage and Analysis, pp. 1–14, November 2021
6. Brown, N., et al.: The role of interactive super-computing in using HPC for urgent decision making. In: Weiland, M., Juckeland, G., Alam, S., Jagode, H. (eds.) ISC High Performance 2019. LNCS, vol. 11887, pp. 528–540. Springer, Cham (2019). https://doi.org/10.1007/978-3-030-34356-9_40
7. Ahrens, J., Geveci, B., Law, C.: ParaView: an end-user tool for large data visualization In: The Visualization Handbook, vol. 717(8) (2005)
8. Nash, R.W., Crusoe, M.R., Kontak, M., Brown, N.: Supercomputing with MPI meets the Common Workflow Language standards: an experience report. In: 2020 IEEE/ACM Workflows in Support of Large-Scale Science (WORKS), pp. 17–24. IEEE, November 2020
9. Chien, S.W., Nylund, J., Bengtsson, G., Peng, I.B., Podobas, A., Markidis, S.: sputniPIC: an implicit particle-in-cell code for multi-GPU systems. In: 2020 IEEE 32nd International Symposium on Computer Architecture and High Performance Computing (SBAC-PAD), pp. 149–156. IEEE, September 2020

The 3rd ISC HPC International Workshop on Monitoring and Operational Data Analytics

The 3rd International Workshop on Monitoring and Data Analytics (MODA22)

Florina Ciorba[1], Utz-Uwe Haus[2], Nicolas Lachiche[3],
and Martin Schulz[4]

[1] University of Basel, Switzerland
[2] HPE HPC/AI EMEA Research Lab, Switzerland
[3] University of Strasbourg, France
[4] Technische Universität Munich, Germany

1 Introduction

Computing at the Exascale poses significant challenges for the collection and analysis of the vast amount of data that current and future Exascale HPC systems will produce, in terms of increasing complexity of the machines, scalability of the adopted monitoring solution, minimizing monitoring intrusiveness, maximizing the interpretability and effective response, driven by inference from the acquired data.

After two very successful installments of the International Workshop on Monitoring and Operational Data Analytics in 2020 and 2021, we were excited to organize the 3nd ISC-HPC International Workshop on Monitoring and Operational Data Analytics (MODA22).

The goal of the MODA workshop series is to provide a venue for sharing insights into current trends in MODA for HPC systems and data centres, identify potential gaps, and offer an outlook into the future of the involved fields of high performance computing, databases, machine learning, and possible solutions that can contribute to the co-design and procurement of future computing and data processing systems. To this end, we solicited contributions related to:

- Challenges and currently envisioned solutions and best practices for monitoring systems at data and computing centers. Of particular focus are operational data collection mechanisms i) covering different system levels, from building infrastructure sensor data to CPU-core performance metrics, and ii) targeting different end-users, from system administrators to application developers and computational scientists.
- Effective strategies for analyzing and interpreting the collected operational data. Of particular focus are visualization approaches and machine learning-based techniques, potentially inferring knowledge of the system behavior and allowing for the realization of a proactive control loop.

Topics that fall outside the scope of the MODA workshop series include: new solutions proposed in the context of application performance modeling and/or application performance analysis tools; and novel contributions in the area of compiler analysis, debugging, programming models, and/or sustainability of scientific software.

While MODA is already common practice at various data and computing centers, each site adopts a different, insular approach, rarely adopted in production environments and mostly limited to the visualization of the system and building infrastructure metrics for health check purposes. In this regard, we observe a gap between the collection of operational data and its meaningful and effective analysis and exploitation, which prevents the closing of the feedback loop between the monitored HPC system, its operation, and its end-users.

Under these premises, the **goals of the MODA22 workshop** are summarized as:

1. Gather and share knowledge and establish a common ground within the international community with respect to best practices in monitoring and operational data analytics.
2. Discuss future strategies and alternatives for MODA, potentially improving existing solutions and envisioning a common baseline approach in data and computing centers.
3. Establish a debate on the usefulness and applicability of AI/ML techniques on collected operational data for optimizing the operation of production systems (e.g. for practices such as predictive maintenance, runtime optimization, optimal and adaptive resource allocation and scheduling).

MODA22 offered a forum for invited presentations, technical contributions, and discussions on:

- Monitoring and operational data analysis challenges and approaches (data collection, storage, visualization, integration into system software, adoption).
- State-of-the-practice methods, tools, techniques in monitoring at various HPC sites.
- Solutions for monitoring and analysis of operational data that work very well on large- to extreme-scale systems with a large number of users.
- Solutions that have proven limitations in terms of efficiency of operational data collection in real-time or in terms of the quality of the collected data.
- Opportunities and challenges of using machine learning methods for efficient monitoring and analysis of operational data.
- Integration of monitoring and analysis practices into production system software (energy and resource management) and runtime systems (scheduling and resource allocation).
- Explicit gaps between operational data collection, processing, effective analysis, highly useful exploitation, and propose new approaches to closing these gaps for the benefit of improving HPC and data centres planning, operations, and research.
- Means to identify (intentional or unintentional) misuse of resources, and methods to mitigate its effects: taking automatic steps to contain the effects of one application/job/user allocation on others, supporting users to identify causes for the misbehavior of their application, linking to intrusion detection and safe multitenancy.
- Concepts to integrate MODA into the system design at all levels, including dedicated hardware components, middleware features, and tool support that make `monitoring and analysis by default' a viable option without sacrificing performance.

- FAIR data practices, including sharing of monitoring workflows and tools across sites while ensuring compliance with GDPR regulations and user access agreements.

2 Workshop Organisation

The workshop organising and program committees consist of academics and researchers at leading HPC sites and in industry. The workshop is unique to the European HPC arena being the among the few to address the topic of monitoring and operational data analytics for improving HPC operations and research.

2.1 Organising Committee

Workshop Chairs

- Florina Ciorba – University of Basel, Switzerland
- Utz-Uwe Haus – HPE HPC/AI EMEA Research Lab, Switzerland
- Nicolas Lachiche – niversity of Strasbourg, France
- Martin Schulz – Technische Universität Munich, Germany

Publicity Chairs

- Thomas Jakobsche – University of Basel, Switzerland

Program Committee

- Norm Bourassa – NERSC Lawrence Berkeley National Laboratory, USA
- Jim Brandt – Sandia National Labs, USA
- Daniele Cesarini – CINECA, Italy
- Ann Gentile – Sandia National Laboratories, USA
- Victor Holanda – Swiss National Supercomputing Centre, Switzerland
- Thomas Ilsche – Technische Universität Dresden, Germany
- Terry Jones – Oak Ridge National Laboratory, USA
- Jacques-Charles Lafoucriere – CEA, France
- Erwin Laure – Max Planck Computing and Data Facility, Germany
- Filippo Mantovani – Barcelona Supercomputing Center, Spain
- Diana Moise – Cray/HPE, Switzerland
- Dirk Pleiter – KTH, Sweden
- Melissa Romanus – NERSC Lawrence Berkeley National Laboratory, USA
- Dominik Strassel – Fraunhofer ITWM Kaiserslautern, Germany
- Keiji Yamamoto – RIKEN, Japan
- Aleš Zamuda – University of Maribor, Slovenia

Technical Program The reviewing of the submitted papers was balanced among the program committee members, and each paper received three or more high quality reviews. The following papers were accepted and presented at MODA22:

- Wholistic and Physics-Based Data Center Monitoring, by Hilary Egan, Avi Purkayastha, and David Sickinger
- Rule-based Thermal Anomaly Detection for Tier-0 HPC systems, by Mohsen Seyedkazemi Ardebili, Andrea Bartolini, Andrea Acquaviva, and Luca Benini

MODA22 was held as an in-person (with ad-hoc solution for camera and microphone to support presenters that could not travel in-person present online) half-day workshop with a balanced mix between technical paper presentations, keynote and invited talks, and a discussion panel. The full live program is available on the MODA22 website[1].

The workshop debuted with the live keynote address

- **[Keynote presentation]** Deploying and Managing the LUMI Supercomputer, Sustainably by Dr. Pekka Manninen (LUMI Leadership Computing Facility, Finland)

followed by a lively questions and answers (Q&A) session.

The workshop continued with the presentation of one of the accepted papers followed by an invited talk:

- **[Accepted paper]** Wholistic and Physics-Based Data Center Monitoring, by Hilary Egan, Avi Purkayastha, and David Sickinger,
- **[Invited talk]** A Conceptual Framework for HPC Operational Data Analytics, by Torsten Wilde (HPE),

which led to engaging discussions that also continued in the coffee breaks.

The second part of the MODA22 workshop consisted of the presentation of the other accepted paper followed by another invited talk:

- **[Accepted paper]** Wholistic and Physics-Based Data Center Monitoring, by Hilary Egan, Avi Purkayastha, and David Sickinger,
- **[Invited talk]** Opportunities & Challenges with Quantitative Codesign, by Terry Jones (Oak Ridge National Laboratory, USA).

MODA22 was concluded with a **panel discussion** on *Recent Developments in MODA* including speakers at the workshop as well as the organizers (in the role of moderators). This panel ended up being very interactive and turned into a direct discussion with the audience. The panel focused on the following questions, mostly targeted on majority interest and implementable techniques for production systems, which the panelists were able to make short intro statements before turning to a wider discussion.

- Multitenancy monitoring: How to deal with the fact that monitoring data is a perfect side-channel even in trusted execution systems?
- Bridging user-side and system-side monitoring: How much system-side monitoring data can and should be exposed to users.

---

[1] https://moda.dmi.unibas.ch/program/.

– Where are we regarding cross-vendor data schemata?
– How do you deal with the ETL-process?

Overall, this resulted in nice and quick paced discussion, despite the hybrid setup of the workshop using ad-hoc solution for camera and microphone.

3 Conclusion

The MODA22 paper presentations, keynote and invited talks and discussions showed the broad scope of topics addressed, as well as the continued growth in importance of this topic for the HPC and data analysis communities. At the same time, they documented to progress that has been made since MODA21, but also showed the current state-of-the-art and the missing breadth of solutions as well as their reliability and stability. It further also showed that the key challenges still remain. In particular, to name just a few:

– To understand how different data sources or different data formats influence the analytics that can be performed.
– To interpret and annotate the collected data to increase their likelihood of being identified with analytic methods.
– The availability of open-source datasets and traces to allow open, reproducible research on MODA and associated topics.

We hope that these and other aspects will figure prominently in submissions to the next edition(s) of the MODA workshop.

Data Center Facility Monitoring with Physics Aware Approach

Hilary Egan$^{(\boxtimes)}$ (ID), Avi Purkayastha, and David Sickinger

National Renewable Energy Laboratory,
15013 Denver W Pkwy, Golden, CO 80401, USA
`hilary.egan@nrel.gov`

Abstract. U.S. Department of Energy's National Renewable Energy Laboratory (NREL) hosts one of the world's most energy-efficient HPC data centers; this system uses component-level warm-water liquid cooling to efficiently remove heat from the data center and capture it for reuse in the building or rejection to the atmosphere. Given the complexity of this system, building data-driven tools for holistically monitoring and operating the entire data center is a priority for ensuring maximal efficiency and resiliency. In this advanced smart facility, over one million metrics are recorded per minute using state-of-the-art streaming data architecture and software to capture and process the state of the system in real time. Here we detail two efforts to effectively analyze, visualize, and interpret this large volume streaming data. We have developed a novel, flexible system for identifying and visualizing individual metric anomalies and component performance across the data center through automatic metadata extraction and physically-motivated visualization for quick interpretation. Additionally, to directly connect system maintenance to data stream processing we explore a physics informed multimetric drift and anomaly detection application to detect scale-build up in heat exchangers.

Keywords: Anomaly detection · Visualization · Data center monitoring

1 Introduction

The Energy Systems Integration Facility (ESIF) at the U.S. Department of Energy's National Renewable Energy Laboratory (NREL) currently hosts one of the world's most energy efficient HPC data centers [2], maintaining a trailing 12-month average PUE of 1.06 or better since opening in 2013. The data center was designed to both capture waste heat and to facilitate the efficient use of energy resources. Where traditional data center designs rely on rows of air-cooled components, the NREL ESIF data center relies on component-level warm-water liquid cooling. Furthermore, the waste heat is captured for reuse within ESIF or rejected to the atmosphere without any mechanical compression cooling.

© Springer Nature Switzerland AG 2022
H. Anzt et al. (Eds.): ISC High Performance 2022 Workshops, LNCS 13387, pp. 251–261, 2022.
https://doi.org/10.1007/978-3-031-23220-6_17

This facility represents a unique opportunity to design and demonstrate next-generation methods for optimizing facility operations and maximizing energy efficiency through data center monitoring and control.

Given the complexity of this system and continual growth of HPC scales, building data-driven tools for holistically monitoring and operating the entire data center is a priority for ensuring maximal efficiency and resiliency. Here we detail two efforts to effectively analyze, visualize, and interpret this large volume streaming data. In Sect. 2 we describe our data collection infrastructure and methodology for the large volume streaming data. Section 3 we illustrate the novel, flexible system for identifying and visualizing individual metric anomalies and component performance across the data center. This effort includes automatic metadata extraction and physically-motivated visualization for quick interpretation. In Sect. 4 we demonstrate our work on directly connecting system maintenance to data stream processing through an exploration of physics informed multi-metric drift and anomaly detection applications. Finally, in Sect. 5 we summarize our conclusions and directions for future investigation.

2   Data Collection Infrastructure

Over 1 million metrics are collected per minute related to NREL's flagship supercomputer Eagle [1], and more than 4,000 metrics are collected per minute related to the ESIF data center and facilities. The full facility heat rejection hierarchy and energy flow is depicted in Fig. 1. The facility metrics are tracked for data center components including data center cooling towers and thermosyphon [7] (advanced dry cooler), pumps, fan walls, heat exchangers, hydronic loops, as well as environmental conditions (e.g., outdoor air temperatures and humidity). For individual devices, metrics include power, temperature, flow rate, pressure, and other states (e.g., alarm, position, speed). Eagle hardware metrics include both rack level hardware data such as air temperature, fan speeds, rack hardware, water temperatures, and inverter data. Data from the cooling distribution units (CDUs) and HPE Adaptive Rack Cooling System (ARCS) includes temperatures, flow rates, and pressures. Node metrics such as memory, disk, network, processor, and GPU utilization, InfiniBand, Lustre, and application metrics are also collected and correlated to integrated eagle job logs. Many of these metrics are collected every few seconds, while some are collected at 1-minute intervals.

The data architecture was implemented with a focus on open-source platforms and highly scalable systems. The data sources either push data to a single-node Influx database running at the network interface to enable meter collection (device historian) or push data directly to a five-node Apache Kafka streaming data cluster. Data collected into the device historian is periodically queried and pushed to the streaming data cluster. This architecture is depicted in Fig. 2.

The data streams are then accessible from a number of clients for either real-time visualizations and analytics or are collected into a time-series cluster for storage. The time-series cluster is an Apache Druid installation: an open-source, distributed data store that is designed to quickly ingest massive quantities of

Method of Heat Rejection

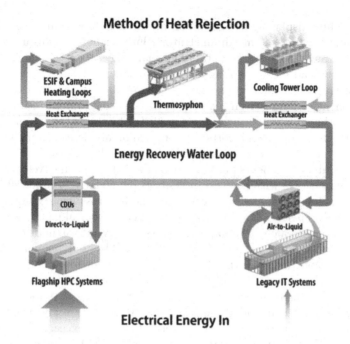

Fig. 1. System components and associated heat flow.

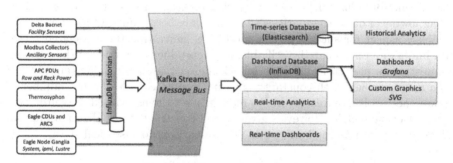

Fig. 2. Data collection architecture.

event data and allows for real-time analytics on top of the data. The data is persistent in the time-series cluster for historical analysis and interactive dashboards over the entire dataset.

3   Data Center Anomaly Detection and Visualization

A major task in data center monitoring and operations is identifying anomalies in data streams that are indicative of larger system issues. Given the number complexity of these data streams, it is critical to automate this process as much as possible while displaying the results in an immediately intuitive and quickly digestible manner for system administrators. Furthermore, to ensure tools stay relevant they must be easily adaptable to changing system configurations and have a low overhead for re-training and re-deployment.

Monitoring and diagnostic techniques like anomaly detection are an important component of data-driven techniques for ensuring system resiliency. Runtime data at the node level (including e.g. CPU utilization, node temperatures, memory efficiency) has been incorporated into anomaly detection modules using statistical feature extraction and supervised learning [8,9], principal component analysis [6], and autoencoders [3]. Further methods have been developed to associate detected outliers with root cause analysis [5]. Relatively fewer efforts have been made to develop anomaly detection methods across facility infrastructure beyond node level performance, though supervised statistical methods have been used to isolate component level failures across facility infrastructure [4].

While there a large variety of sophisticated AI-based anomaly detection methods, the deployment overhead for implementing such methods is substantial, especially for constantly changing systems. We have therefore implemented a baseline, low-maintenance method for implementing simple statistical tests combined with automated metadata generation methods. For a given data stream (e.g., a single pump speed) we generate alerts if the data exceeds either a soft or hard upper (or lower) limit. A soft alert is indicative of behaviour slightly outside of typical parameterization, while a hard alert indicates extreme behaviour. This distinction is useful for both a quick indication of severity and the ability to flag low level data irregularities that may only be meaningful in sum.

A key aspect for success in this method is generating the associated metadata limits in an automated, verifiable, and reproducible manner. While system administrators may have intuitive knowledge on reasonable value ranges for a given measurement, with constantly growing system complexity and number of tracked metrics it is unreasonable to manually set the associated measurements limits for every metric. However, given a well constructed visualization one can quickly verify the learned metadata in comparison to historical data; this is demonstrated in Fig. 3.

To automatically generate limits for each metric we use historical data to calculate the 0.02 and 99.8 percentiles (soft limits) and the absolute max and minimum plus/minus 0.5* the standard deviation (hard limits). Any time periods that are deemed irregular, e.g., system time, are masked out. The results of the metadata generation are then stored in a database for use in the anomaly detection summary visualization. The complete pipeline can then be re-run for either individual metrics or the system as a whole over different time periods in the event of a configuration change. In the event of a metric where this parameterization does not work, the pipeline can also accept manual overrides for limits of individual metrics.

Figure 4 shows an example of the summary dashboard for the anomaly detection system. On the left are a selection of data center subsystems from the Energy Recovery Water (ERW) loop to the Eagle supercomputer nodes. Each subsystem

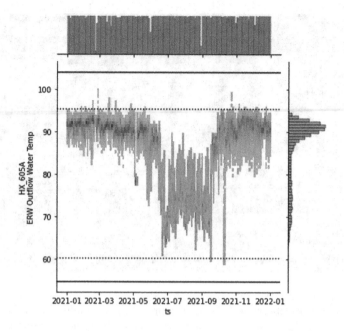

Fig. 3. Automated metadata generation verification figure example; the figure shows data from the corresponding metric (ERW outflow water temperature from heat exchanger 605A) binned by time (x-axis) and value (y-axis). The histograms on the sides show the same distribution collapsed over time/value for the y and x axis accordingly. The dashed (solid) lines indicate the soft (hard) limits identified by the automated metadata generation procedure.

is coupled with a status indicator for a simple overview of the entire system as a glance. The right panel shows a schematic figure of the components that make up the selected subsystem (in this case the ERW loop) with status indicators for each component. The schematic figure for each subsystem were designed in collaboration with data center experts to facilitate interpretation and are tied to the physical subsystem layout. Each component has another corresponding status indicator that indicates alert status, if the component is off, or if the component is missing data. When hovering over the status indicator additional metadata describing the component and current status is displayed.

Below the schematic figure is a list of associated metrics either for the entire subsystem or an individual component if selected via the schematic figure, this lower panel is depicted in Fig. 5. Each row of the table indicates the device, metric, mean value, and anomaly score. If a metric is selected in the table, the associated data is shown in the time series figure below for the past 6 h, along with the associated hard and soft metadata limits. Any points that exceed the limits are highlighted in red.

All together, this dashboard creates the opportunity for both high-level, at a glance understanding, as well as increasingly fine resolution via data drill-

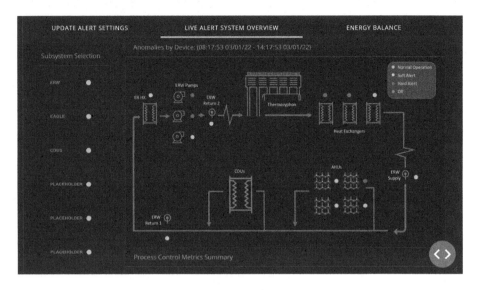

Fig. 4. Upper panels of the data center anomaly detection dashboard. The left panel shows a selection of subsystems and corresponding status indicators while the right panel shows a physical layout of devices for a subsystem and corresponding status indicators.

down. This workflow was developed in conjunction with system administrators to reflect the manner in which problems are typically investigated. Additionally, tying the visualization to the physical layout has been a well received improvement over simple metric lists. Finally, the entire dashboard and underlying metadata generation system was designed to be flexible and easily re-configurable via database infrastructure and templated software development paradigms. As the system is continually updated and devices gain or lose function this allows the anomaly detection infrastructure to be similarly flexible with a minimal amount of overhead. Furthermore, this will also allow the easy inclusion on multi-metric anomalies in the future.

4   Physics-Informed Anomaly Monitoring

In Sect. 3 we described our data stream monitoring and visualization infrastructure. While useful for identifying potential issues, it is limited by design in not being able to associate an anomaly with an underlying maintenance issue. To address this short-coming, we have begun to explore physically motivated metrics and associated anomaly and drift models; here we describe a case study in connecting heat exchanger data streams with scale build-up detection.

Heat exchangers remove heat from a system by flowing two separate streams of water through a series of baffles. Scaling is a type of fouling caused by inorganic salts in the water circuit; a build-up of these inorganic salts will insulate the heat transfer surface, preventing efficient heat transfer. While the build-up will

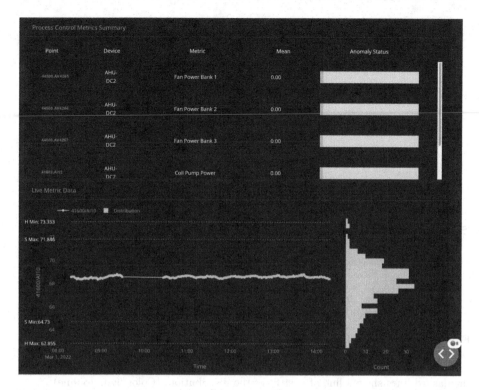

Fig. 5. Lower panels of the data center anomaly detection dashboard. The upper panel shows a table of metrics associated with a selected device, with columns indicating the label of the point in the streaming database, the name of the associated device, a short description of the metric, the mean value over the past six hours, and the current anomaly status shown as a bar progressing from green (OK) to red (high alert). The lower panel shows a time-series of the selected point over the past six hours with points exceeding the anomaly thresholds highlighted in red. The soft and hard anomaly shown as red dashed and solid lines. (Color figure online)

increase the pressure drop across the water circuit, this change is both gradual and easily masked by the varying conditions of the heat exchanger over the course of operation.

We address this by calculating the effective K-value of the flow through the heat exchanger over time. Flow rate through a constriction (Q) is related to the pressure drop (ΔP) via constants K and C as

$$Q = K\sqrt{\Delta P} + C \tag{1}$$

where K and C depend on properties of the physical system. A significant scale build up will slowly decrease the corresponding value of K over time.

Figure 6 shows a series of histograms of hourly averaged flow rate Q vs the square root of the differential pressure $\sqrt{\Delta P}$ for each heat exchanger device indicated by the panel labels. Over each histogram we plot a line of best fit

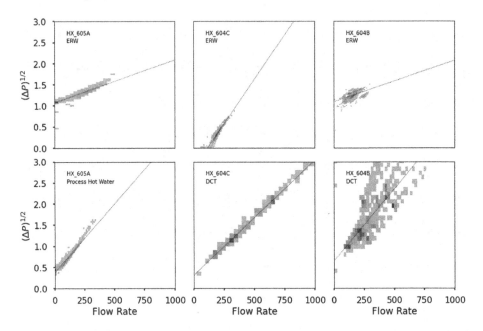

Fig. 6. Relationship of the square root of differential pressure and flow rate for a variety of heat exchanger devices (indicated by text labels). The blue points indicate a histogram of previously measured data with darker blue indicating more points, while the dashed lines show a line of best fit of the distribution. (Color figure online)

for the entire data set. While some devices show reasonably tight and linear correlations (HX 605A, HX 604C) the data for the HX 604B in the rightmost panels does not show a well fitting relationship, indicating a systematic problem.

A straightforward visualization of this effect over time is shown in Fig. 7, where the residual from applying the fits shown in Fig. 6 to each data point is averaged by day and plotted over time. Heat exchanger 604B Direct Cooling Tower water (DCT) has continually had performance issues that have been traced to scale build-up. The bottom most panel showing the DCT portion of HX 604B shows a smooth yet steady increase in residual values after May 2019, this is a clear signature of scale build up that can be monitored for intervention prior to cooling tower failure. The sharp transition at May 2019 is due to a chemical cleaning in order to resolve previous scale build-up issues.

This combination of identifying physically motivated meta-metrics and visualization over long time periods can both give proactive warnings that may be obfuscated by looking at individual metric anomalies and connect these warnings to physical issues and maintenance solutions.

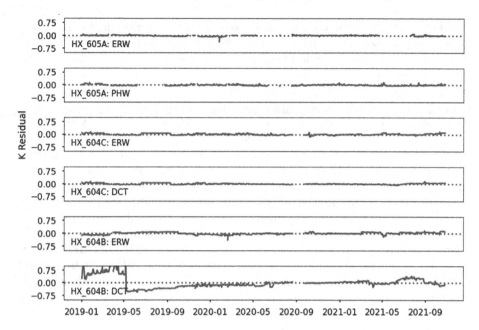

Fig. 7. Residuals from data points to the best fit relationship shown in Fig. 6 for each heat exchanger plotted over time. Data is averaged by day. HX-604B DCT shows signs of scale build up from the gradual increase of residual values from May 2019 on; the sharp drop at May 2019 is due to device maintenance at that time.

5   Conclusions

In this paper we have described two efforts to effectively analyze, visualize, and interpret the large volume streaming data associated with the ESIF data center. We have developed a novel, flexible system for identifying and visualizing individual metric anomalies and component performance across the data center, which includes work on automatic metadata extraction and physically-motivated visualization for quick interpretation. We also prototyped an example on using physically motivated meta-metrics to directly connect data stream processing to system maintenance with a specific focus on scale build-up in heat exchangers.

Through discussion with system experts we have determined that key priorities for monitoring infrastructure and visualization include low maintenance and setup overhead, ease of interpretability, and providing useful feedback without an overburden of extraneous information; our dashboards have been developed with these needs in mind. In particular our templated approach to device level metadata generation and anomaly detection can drastically reduce maintenance overhead, particularly as new devices come on and off line, and the system undergoes standard operating procedure changes. Without developing a systematic templated approach we have found that custom dashboards can quickly become out of date and fall to disuse or require an undue burden to retrain and redeploy.

These considerations are also important when considering deploy more ML based anomaly detection methods rather than simple statistical tests we have shown here. Often we have found that the amount of tuning required for ML techniques to properly alert based on a given data stream without over alerting (and causing user alert fatigue and subsequent disregard) can be quite large, particularly when taking into account retraining overhead. While we will continue to investigate these more sophisticated methods in parallel to the work shown here, we will continue to put a particular focus on minimizing overhead and automating as much of the retraining and redeployment as possible. Regardless, we have designed our dashboard in such a way to seamlessly incorporate the results of these more sophisticated models using Kafka streams into the same easily interpretable framework, allowing maximum flexibility for future efforts.

Additional future work will involve developing more physically motivated meta-metrics and directly integrating these into our anomaly detection dashboard. Furthermore, we will also continue development on a historic trends dashboard for better understanding and identifying long term behaviour trends and drift. In conjunction these efforts will allow us to establish and evaluate next-generation methods for optimizing facility operations and maximizing energy efficiency through data center monitoring and control.

Acknowledgements. This work was authored in part by the National Renewable Energy Laboratory, operated by Alliance for Sustainable Energy, LLC, for the U.S. Department of Energy (DOE) under Contract No. DE-AC36-08GO28308. Funding provided by U.S. Department of Energy Office of Energy Efficiency and Renewable Energy and Hewlett-Packard Enterprise.

References

1. Eagle system configuration. https://www.nrel.gov/hpc/eagle-system-configuration. html
2. NREL, 2018: NREL garners top sustainability honor at data center dynamics awards. Technical report, National Renewable Energy Laboratory (2018)
3. Borghesi, A., Bartolini, A., Lombardi, M., Milano, M., Benini, L.: A semisupervised autoencoder-based approach for anomaly detection in high performance computing systems. Eng. Appl. Artif. Intell. **85**, 634–644 (2019). https://doi.org/10.1016/j.engappai.2019.07.008, https://www.sciencedirect.com/science/article/pii/S0952197619301721
4. Bortot, L., Nardelli, W., Seto, P.: Data centers are a software development challenge. In: 48th Annual International Conference on Parallel Processing, pp. 1–5 (2019)
5. Demirbaga, U., et al.: AutoDiagn: an automated real-time diagnosis framework for big data systems. IEEE Trans. Comput. **71**(5), 1035–1048 (2022). https://doi.org/10.1109/TC.2021.3070639
6. Guan, Q., Fu, S.: Adaptive anomaly identification by exploring metric subspace in cloud computing infrastructures. In: 2013 IEEE 32nd International Symposium on Reliable Distributed Systems, pp. 205–214. IEEE (2013)

7. Sickinger, D., Geet, O.V., Belmont, S., Carter, T., Martinez, D.: Thermosyphon cooler hybrid system for water savings in an energy-efficient HPC data center: results from 24 months and impact on water usage effectiveness. Technical report NREL/TP-2C00-72196, National Renewable Energy Laboratory, September 2018
8. Tuncer, O., et al.: Diagnosing performance variations in HPC applications using machine learning. In: Kunkel, J.M., Yokota, R., Balaji, P., Keyes, D. (eds.) ISC High Performance 2017. LNCS, vol. 10266, pp. 355–373. Springer, Cham (2017). https://doi.org/10.1007/978-3-319-58667-0_19
9. Tuncer, O., et al.: Online diagnosis of performance variation in HPC systems using machine learning. IEEE Trans. Parallel Distrib. Syst. **30**(4), 883–896 (2018)

Rule-Based Thermal Anomaly Detection for Tier-0 HPC Systems

Mohsen Seyedkazemi Ardebili[1]([☒]) [iD], Andrea Bartolini[1] [iD],
Andrea Acquaviva[1] [iD], and Luca Benini[1,2] [iD]

[1] Universitá degli Studi di Bologna, Viale Risorgimento, 2, 40136 Bologna, Italy
{mohsen.seyedkazemi,a.bartolini,andrea.acquaviva,luca.benini}@unibo.it
[2] Eidgenössische Technische Hochschule Zürich,
Gloriastrasse 35, 8092 Zürich, Switzerland
lbenini@iis.ee.ethz.ch
http://www.dei.unibo.it/, http://ee.ethz.ch/

Abstract. Today, significant advances in science and technology can not be envisioned without high computing capacity. To solve large problems in science, engineering, and business, data centers provide High-Performance Computing (HPC) systems with aggregation of the computing capacity of thousand of computing nodes with the cost of millions of euros per year [12]. In the datacenter, an anomaly is a suspicious/abnormal pattern in the monitoring signals. The severity of the anomaly can be different, and in extreme conditions, it can yield the outage of the datacenter. By defining complex statistical rules-based anomaly detection methods, this paper investigates the thermal anomaly detection task in one of the most powerful HPC systems in the world, namely Marconi100 hosted at CINECA. The suggested anomaly detection method is successfully validated against real thermal hazard events reported for the studied HPC cluster while in production.

Keywords: HPC · Anomaly detection · HPC Monitoring Systems

1 Introduction

High-performance computing (HPC) most generally refers to the practice of aggregating computing power in a way that delivers much higher performance than one could get out of a typical desktop computer or workstation in order to solve large problems in science, engineering, or business [2]. HPC rooms are composed of thousands of computing nodes and may consume megawatts of electrical power, which is entirely converted into heat; to achieve efficient heat dissipation requires to (i) leverage sophisticated cooling system, design the cooling system targeting the typical workload power consumption and not worse-case one [15], and account for the dependency of the cooling cost with absolute ambient temperature which may change during seasons [16]. When an unbalance between the cooling capacity and the computational demand happens we are in presence of a thermal anomaly. This can be the result of: *(i)* an abnormal working

© Springer Nature Switzerland AG 2022
H. Anzt et al. (Eds.): ISC High Performance 2022 Workshops, LNCS 13387, pp. 262–276, 2022.
https://doi.org/10.1007/978-3-031-23220-6_18

condition of the cooling system, *(ii)* abnormal power fluctuation as well as a computing demand above the typical case, *(iii)* cooling capacity reduction due to an abnormal ambient temperature, *(iv)* different response latency of computing and cooling elements to workload variations. The severity of the thermal anomaly can be different - ranging from a mechanical fault in the cooling system to node's temperature fluctuation.

Anomaly detection is an important research topic and is applied in a wide range of fields. A common problem in anomaly detection is the fact that anomalies are rare events. Solutions in the state of art overcome this issue by employing test suites or other software which simulates the anomaly condition. In contrast in this study, we used the real monitoring data of an in-production HPC cluster and cooling infrastructure. The data was collected for 4 months of 2021 (2021-04-08 to 2021-08-18) from one the HPC room which hosts the Marconi100 HPC cluster in the CINECA data center. To collect the monitoring data, we used a holistic monitoring system, namely ExaMon [7]. During the monitored period the system experienced a real/physical thermal failure on the day of the 28-07-2021. We introduced a rule-based statistical method for anomaly detection, which uses statistical characteristics of data to define a set of simple rules for detecting anomalies. The main advantages of this method are that it is fast and easy to implement, which makes it a practical approach for implementation as online anomaly detection on large-scale HPC systems. We focus our approach to the central rack of Marconi100 and its cooling infrastructure. Based on that we defined 281 rules that we refer to as flags. Each flag checks a rule in the monitoring signals for anomaly detection. We validated the performance of the introduced method in anomaly detection by a detailed study of monitoring signals around the real/physical failure on 28-07-2021.

1.1 Background

CINECA is a non-profit consortium of 69 Italian universities, 27 national public research centers, the Italian Ministry of Universities and Research (MUR), and the Italian Ministry of Education (MI). Marconi100 HPC cluster of CINECA is a Tier-0 cluster, with about 32 PFlop/s, is ranked 9th (list of June 2020) and 18th (list of November 2021) in the list of the most powerful supercomputers worldwide [1].

Cooling Systems: CINECA datacenter has three HPC rooms. This study mainly focused on the room that hosts the Marconi100 HPC cluster, the most powerful HPC cluster of CINECA. Marconi100 HPC rooms are cooled with Computer Room Air Conditioning (CRAC) units by the Direct Expansion (DX) Air-conditioning system. In DX Air-conditioning, the air used for cooling the room is directly passed over the cooling coil. There are six CRAC units in the room, and four of these CRAC units support the Direct Free Cooling (DFC) system, which is referred to by the CRAC+DFC in this study. The DFC system is designed to reduce energy dissipation and improve the carbon footprint by utilizing the external cold air for cooling the room. In this case, the DFC system starts to work when the outdoor temperature is lower than 18 °C. Without the DFC system, the CRAC units work in standard air recirculation mode with refrigeration-based cooling. Empowering the CRAC units with a DFC system can reduce the compressor's operation.

Also, there is a water cooling system for Rear Door Heat Exchangers (RDHX), with the chiller loop (cold loop) temperature around 12 °C to 17 °C, and RDHX loop (hot loop) temperature around 23 °C to 30 °C. The RDHX device is placed in front of the hot outlet airflow of the compute node. During operation, the compute node's hot airflow is forced through the RDHX device by the compute node fans and exchanges heat from the hot air to circulating water from a chiller. Thus, the compute node outlet air temperature reduces before its discharge into the datacenter. RDHX is used to augment the computing density in air-cooled computing rooms.

The hot/cold aisle approach is employed to cool the room. Six computer room air conditioning (CRAC) units support two cold aisles. The cold airflow moves under the raised floor and gets to the loaded areas; then, the hot air returns to the CRAC units above the raised floor. All racks are equipped with RDHX, and RDHX of racks are in the hot aisle.

HPC Cluster: The Marconi100 HPC cluster started production in April 2020. Figure 1a depicts the racks and cooling facilities arrangement in the room. Marconi100 is an accelerated cluster based on IBM Power9 architecture and Volta NVIDIA GPUs with a computing capacity of about 32 PFlops. The HPC room (Fig. 1a) hosts 55 racks (49 computing racks), and each rack has 20 chassis, and each chassis host one computing node. Marconi100 comprises 980 nodes; each node has 2×16 cores IBM POWER9 (@3.1 GHz) processors and is empowered with 4 x NVIDIA Volta V100 GPU accelerators (16 GB), RAM: 256 GB/node.

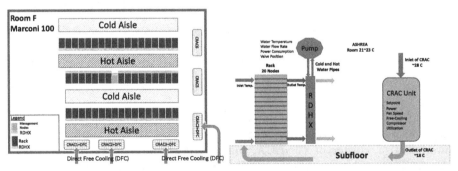

(a) Racks Arrangements of Marconi100 HPC Room in CINECA Datacenter.   (b) Schematic of the HPC Room's Facilities and a Rack.

Fig. 1. Schematic of Marconi100 HPC room in CINECA datacenter.

Monitoring System: The CINECA datacenter features a holistic monitoring framework, namely ExaMon, which aggregates a wide set of telemetry data [7]. ExaMon is one of the state-of-the-art datacenter monitoring systems [25]. For each node and its associated components, such as voltage regulators and fans, the Intelligent Platform Management Interface (IPMI) provides remote telemetry access to the built-in sensors [21]. The ExaMon monitoring system collects sensor data with the IPMI interface with 20 s sampling rate [7]. From April 2021, ExaMon, in addition to nodes metrics, starts to collect important metrics of CRAC room facilities (CRAC units, RDHX, and Modbus). ExaMon monitored data is stored in its internal KairosDB database as time traces and remotely accessible through RESTfull APIs [7]. These are the low-level components having the task of reading the data from several sensors scattered across the system and deliver them, in a standardized format, to the upper layer of the stack. These software components are composed of two main objects, the MQTT API and the Sensor API object. The former implements the MQTT protocol functions, and it is the same among all the collectors, while the latter implements the custom sensor functions related to the data sampling and is unique for each kind of collector. Considering the specific sensor API object, we can distinguish collectors that have direct access to hardware resources like PMU, IPMI, accelerators, sensor nodes, and collectors that sample data from other applications as switchboards Modbus collectors.

2   Related Work

By approaching exascale computing systems [20], the importance of anomaly detection research topics in HPC systems increases [5]. In the HPC system, anomalies reduce the performance and increase the cost by affecting the computing capacity and energy of HPC systems. Anomalies are reported due to network contention [9], shared resources contention [8,19], hardware-level problems [23], memory [3], CPU [14], and cooling system failure [26,27]. Some researchers used the rule-based analysis to define the anomalies; researchers manually, or based on the statistical analysis or recommendations, set thresholds for system metrics [4,22]. The monitoring data of the system and component is investigated to find the correlation between the different problems (like detecting I/O congestion and out-of-memory) and causes by other studies [3,14]. ML-based approaches are used by researchers for anomaly detection [5,5,6,10,11,13,17,18,24,28].

Most studies investigate the anomalies employing one of the statistical rule-based or ML-based methods for anomaly detection at the application or node levels without considering the room level facilities, which can create severer anomalies than the application and node levels. This study employed a comprehensive statistical rule-based method on a big dataset composed of node-level metrics as well as room-level facilities metrics (like two different sophisticated cooling systems metrics, total power consumption metrics of different parts of HPC room collected from Modbus, etc.) to anomaly detection at room-level, node-level, system-level, and subsystem-level. Anomalies are infrequent, so some studies employed synthetic anomalies at the test state and out of production HPC. In this study, all the data is collected from the in-production HPC cluster (one of the most powerful computing systems worldwide). Moreover, the study and approach are validated against the real physical failure of the in-production HPC cluster. So, to the best of our knowledge, this is the first time that a study employed rule-based statistical tools on different levels of monitoring signals of an in-production HPC cluster to anomaly study at different levels of node, system, subsystem, and HPC room. This study included a detailed study of the real thermal failure, which caused the outage of half of the computing nodes of the HPC cluster.

The rest of the paper is organized as follows: First in methodology section, we introduce the rule-based statistical anomaly method and severity level of anomaly. We then discuss the experimental results, and as proof of the performance of the proposed method in anomaly detection, we validated the method with real thermal failure of the HPC cluster. Finally, we provide a summary of the study along with ideas about future work regarding this framework.

3   Methodology

3.1   Dataset

This study is done on the monitoring signals (data collected in ExaMon) of the Marconi100 cluster. In Fig. 1b, the schematic of the HPC room's facilities and a rack is depicted. For the computing nodes, we studied different metrics like inlet, PCIe, CPU [0,1], and GPU [0,1,2,3] temperatures, fan speed, and power supply. The racks are equipped with RDHX, and for this cooling system, we studied different essential metrics, such as water flow rate, inlet, and outlet water temperature, the position of the three-way valve, and delta temperature of the water. Moreover, there are six CRAC units in the room; for CRAC units, we studied metrics like compressor utilization, free cooling, free cooling valve open position, fan speed, return, and supply air temperature. From the main electrical power distributions system (from Modbus), we extracted the metrics: total power consumption of ICT, total power consumption of RDHX pumps, total power consumption of chillers, and total power consumption of CRAC units. In total, for one rack with 20 nodes and room facilities, 242 metrics are collected. The data collection period starts on 2021-04-08 and ends on 2021-08-21.

3.2   Rule-Based Statistical Method (Flags)

We find two main groups of abnormal patterns with the study of the monitoring signals in normal and abnormal conditions. Figure 2 shows the two monitoring signals blue line on the right y-axis shows the total power consumption of the chillers, while the red line on the left y-axis shows one random node's inlet temperature. The green zone demonstrates part of the signal that we know the cluster is in normal production; in contrast, the red zone is the failure zone (reported by the experts of CINECA). The inlet temperature of a node (red line) in the abnormal zone (red zone) reaches a very high value compared to the normal zone (green zone); we name this pattern (1) **Constraint Violations** condition for this signal. Moreover, the total power consumption of chillers (blue line) has a high variation in a small time interval in the abnormal zone (red zone); we name this pattern (2) **High Derivative** condition for this signal. Considering these two abnormal patterns of the monitoring signal, we used High Derivative and Constraint Violations in the definitions of the flags to find the anomalous and suspicious patterns. A set of flags is defined for all the critical metrics of computing nodes and room facilities (CRAC Units, RDHX, Modbus, etc.).

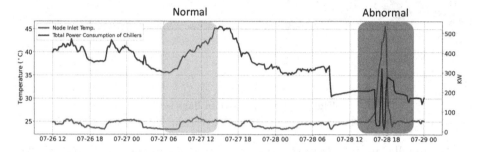

Fig. 2. Comparison of normal and abnormal signals. (Color figure online)

3.3   Mathematical Definition of the Flags

In this section, the mathematical formula of the flags is presented. Each rack of Marconi-100 has 20 chassis, and each chassis host one node. From chassis 1 to 20 from bottom to top. So for Marconi100, we can interchangeably use the chassis temperature, and node temperature since each chassis hosts one node. Chart 3 shows the different parts of the set of flags. In the top, chart 3 shows two main groups of flags: (1) **Constraints violation**; $\mathcal{M}(t) > threshold$ or $\mathcal{M}(t) < threshold$, $\mathcal{M}(t)$ is a metric, and t shows time, and (2) **High derivative**; $\mathcal{M}(t) - \mathcal{M}(t-1) > threshold$ or $\mathcal{M}(t) - \mathcal{M}(t-1) < threshold$.

Group (1) Constraints violation has three subgroups: *(a)* Cooling Shortage, indicating a part of the cooling system reached its maximum capacity ($\mathcal{M}(t) > threshold$), or the failure of one part ($\mathcal{M}(t) < threshold$). *(b)* Thermal/ASHRAE, which shows CPU/GPU or inlet temperature of the node, violated the ASHRAE recommendations. *(c)* The Computing Load shows that the Rack/Room consumes more power than typical and reaches its maximum computing capacity based on the history. In group (2) high derivative, there are flags due to the high variation of the signals, for example, a high derivative of the power consumption or temperature. In total, we defined 281 flags for 242 metrics.

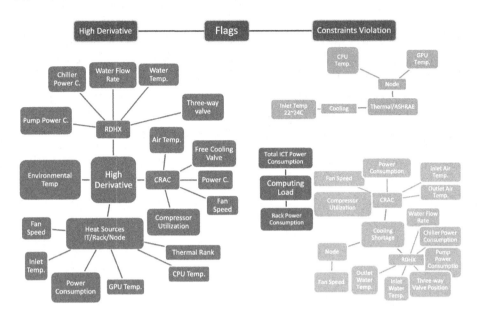

Fig. 3. Different parts of flags set.

In the following, the **thresholds** are different individually for each formula, and we set them based on the recommendations like ASHRAE or historical data analysis for metrics with no recommendation. For example, for historical data analysis, for inequality like $\mathcal{M} > threshold$ with no recommendation, we can use a quantile of 0.99 of the parameter as a threshold, or for inequality like $\mathcal{M} < threshold$ quantile of 0.01, this is a straightforward approach. In the equations, $\mathcal{M}(t)$ is a metric, and t shows time. $\mathcal{M}(t)$ can be power consumption of node, chiller, CRAC unit, pumps or temperature of GPU, CPU, PCIe, Inlet, water of RDHX, Air of CRAC, or the fan speed of node, CRAC units or compressor utilization of CRAC units, the position of the valve of RDHX, CRAC units, water flow rate, etc. Each rack has 20 nodes/chassis; each node experiences a different inlet, CPU core, and GPU temperatures. $_{rack}\mathcal{M}_{max}(t)$ and $_{rack}\mathcal{M}_{min}(t)$ show the maximum and minimum value measured for a metric by these 20 nodes of the rack at time t. Flag 1 and 2 check if a metric experience is higher and lower than a threshold. This is a constraint violation check flag.

$$_{rack}\mathcal{M}_{max}(t) > {}_{major}threshold \tag{1}$$

$$_{rack}\mathcal{M}_{min}(t) < {}_{minor}threshold \tag{2}$$

The Flag 3 checks the maximum heterogeneity of measured value by a metric at one timestamp for the nodes of a rack.

$$_{rack}\mathcal{M}_{max}(t) - {}_{rack}\mathcal{M}_{min}(t) > threshold \tag{3}$$

Flag 4 and 5 examine the rack's maximum and minimum value variation for a metric, respectively.

$$|_{rack}\mathcal{M}_{max}(t) - {}_{rack}\mathcal{M}_{max}(t-1)| > threshold \tag{4}$$

$$|_{rack}\mathcal{M}_{min}(t) - {}_{rack}\mathcal{M}_{min}(t-1)| > threshold \tag{5}$$

Flag 6 controls the number of items of a metric that violate the threshold. For example how many GPUs experience high temperature in the rack.

$$\sum_{i=1}^{20*C} ({}_{rack}\mathcal{M}_i(t) > threshold) \tag{6}$$

Flag 7, 8, and 9 how many items of a metric experience abnormal variation and C for CPU, GPU, inlet, and PCIe temperature is 2, 4, 1, and 1, respectively.

$$\sum_{i=1}^{20*C} (|_{rack}\mathcal{M}_i(t) - {}_{rack}\mathcal{M}_i(t-1)| > threshold) \tag{7}$$

$$\sum_{i=1}^{20*C} ({}_{rack}\mathcal{M}_i(t) - {}_{rack}\mathcal{M}_i(t-1) > {}_+threshold) \tag{8}$$

$$\sum_{i=1}^{20*C} ({}_{rack}\mathcal{M}_i(t) - {}_{rack}\mathcal{M}_i(t-1) < {}_-threshold) \tag{9}$$

Flags 10, 11, 12, and 13 check the metrics' constraint violation and abnormal variation (except the node metrics).

$$_{major}\mathcal{M}(t) > threshold \tag{10}$$

$$_{minor}\mathcal{M}(t) < threshold \tag{11}$$

$$\mathcal{M}(t) - \mathcal{M}(t-1) > {}_+threshold \tag{12}$$

$$\mathcal{M}(t) - \mathcal{M}(t-1) < {}_-threshold \tag{13}$$

Flags 14 check the number of metric items that experience abnormal value based on their own history. There is a difference between this flag 14 and flag 6 which checks the number of the items of metric which violate a defined threshold for all of the items, i.e., in flag 14, GPU-1 has a threshold based on the history of just GPU-1. However, flag 6 has a fixed value as a threshold for all GPUs of the rack, which can be based on the ASHRAE recommendation or history of all the GPUs in the rack.

$$\sum_{i=1}^{20*C} ({}_{rack}\mathcal{M}_i(t) > {}_c thresholds) \tag{14}$$

Flag 15 checks the number of nodes that are in an odd situation due to the abnormal value of a metric, while the flag 16 controls the number of nodes that have strange variations in a metric.

$$\sum_{i=1}^{20} (\sum_{c=1}^{C} (_{rack}\mathcal{M}_{i,c}(t) > _c thresholds) \geq 1) \tag{15}$$

$$\sum_{i=1}^{20} (\sum_{c=1}^{C} (|_{rack}\mathcal{M}_c(t) - _{rack}\mathcal{M}_c(t-1)| > _c thresholds) \geq 1) \tag{16}$$

Variation of Coldest Chassis at a Rack: Subscript i shows chassis/node number. $\mathcal{C}^{inlet}(t)$ shows chassis-number of coldest chassis at time t, based on the inlet temperature.

$$|_{rack}\mathcal{C}^{inlet}(t) - _{rack}\mathcal{C}^{inlet}(t-1)| > threshold \tag{17}$$

Thermal Rank of Chassis $_{node}\mathcal{R}_i^{inlet}(t)$**:** Index of the chassis/node in a sorted list of chassis/node based on its inlet temperature at time t. For example, in Marconi 100 $chassis-7$ of rack-5 at 2021-02-05 15:50:00 is the coldest chassis, so its thermal rank is one at that time $_{node}\mathcal{R}_7^{inlet}(2021/02/01 - 15:10:00) = 1$.

$$\sum_{i=1}^{20} |_{node}\mathcal{R}_i^{inlet}(t) - _{node}\mathcal{R}_i^{inlet}(t-1)| > threshold \tag{18}$$

In general, this flag can detect a situation that there is switching in the thermal rank of most of the chassis of the one rack, which mostly appears when chassis temperatures of a rack quickly change from compact/dense to widespread pattern or vice versa.

4   Experimental Results

4.1   Severity Level of Anomaly ($\sum Flags$)

We have access to the dataset of monitoring signals of the HPC cluster is, but it does not contain any normal or abnormal labels to distinguish between the normal or abnormal samples. There are some reports related to the anomaly/failure that the experts of CINECA provided. However, these reports are very rare and just for situations where the bad side effects of the anomaly are evident, and it caused a reduction of computing capacity or even an outage of the cluster. Some abnormalities restrict the effective utilization of resources in HPC systems. Although these anomalies degrade the performance of HPC clusters, they are not effortlessly noticeable to human experts. These anomalies can generally affect energy-to-solution, time-to-solution, again of the nodes, etc. In this study, the flags are introduced with accuracy to find the suspicious patterns (especially related to the thermal and power characteristic of the HPC cluster) in the monitoring signals of the Marconi100 HPC room and cluster. Therefore, the sum of the raised flags at each timestamp shows the severity level of the anomaly. The first row of Fig. 4b shows the severity level of anomaly (sum of flags) with the blue line on the left y-axis and the moving average (with a time window of 3 h) of the sum of flags with the red line on the right y-axis. A moving average is a widely used statistical indicator that smooths out signals by filtering out short-term fluctuations. There is a peak in the moving average of the sum of flags in the yellow zone in Fig. 4b, which is related to the real physical failure on 2021-07-28. The second row of Fig. 4b illustrates the zoom-in version of the first row around the real thermal failure of the HPC room. By expert reports, we know point C is a real failure and as it is the evident severity level of anomaly (sum of flags) and its moving average reached its peak at this point. As we can see in Fig. 4b, before the failure, which caused an outage of half of the capacity of the HPC cluster, there were two signs of future failure (zones A and B) in the severity level of abnormality graph. The sign of a future disaster was unclear to human experts without tools like the suggested one. So the suggested method of definition of the flags and then severity level of anomaly and its moving average (which cancels fast fluctuations of signals) provides applicable metrics to indicate anomalous patterns in the signals for anomaly detection and preventing future disasters. In the following in the anomaly location section, we will show a heatmap, which provides to the sysadmin the anomaly's location and sources.

4.2 Detailed Study of Real Physical Failure

In this section, the method's performance for anomaly detection is evaluated by a detailed study of the monitoring signals at three critical points around the physical failure 28-07-2021. To understand the reasons behind the high severity level of anomaly (i.e., a high number of raised flags) of these points, we did a detailed study by generating the line plots of all sensors' signals, which are summarized in the two Figs. 4c and 4a, and finally, heatmap Fig. 5 summarized the location of the issues. In these two Figs. 4c, 4a, the colored lines show the value of each sensor, and the black dashed line shows the average value of parameters in each row. Figure 4c shows the monitoring signals of different metrics of the computing nodes of one rack in the HPC room. It illustrates the CPU, GPU, PCIe, Inlet temperature and fans speed, and finally, power consumption in rows 1 to 6. While Fig. 4c shows the node level metrics of the HPC room, Fig. 4a shows room level metrics, especially the cooling system metrics. Figure 4a from the first row to last row respectively shows: (i) total power consumption of the ICT devices, (ii) CRAC units: total power consumption of the CRAC units, fans speed of the CRAC units, compressors utilization of the CRAC units, Free cooling valve open position of CRAC units, outlet and inlet temperature of the CRAC units, (iii) RDHX: total power consumption of the chillers, total pumps power consumption, inlet, outlet temperature of the water, the position of three-ways valve, delta temperature of outlet and inlet water temperature, (iv) ambient temperature (temperature of outside).

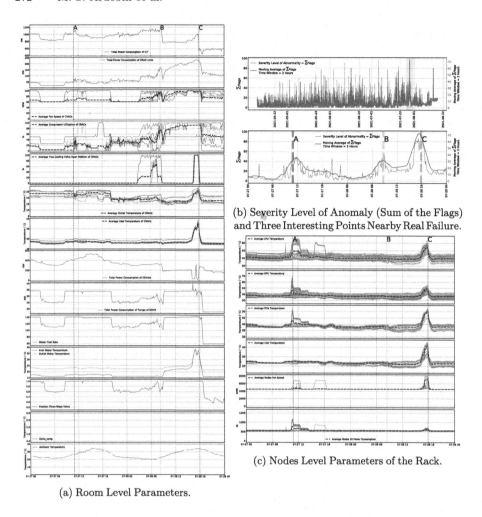

(a) Room Level Parameters.

(b) Severity Level of Anomaly (Sum of the Flags) and Three Interesting Points Nearby Real Failure.

(c) Nodes Level Parameters of the Rack.

Fig. 4. Experimental results (Color figure online)

Considering Point A: While nodes experience the normal inlet temperature, the inside temperature (CPU, GPU, and PCIe) is high. So the room temperature is normal, and the cooling system operates correctly. Before point A the power consumptions of the nodes start to increase due to the computing demands, which turns into the high temperature inside the nodes, and then quickly, the computing loads are reduced. Meanwhile, the fans of nodes increase the speed, and it seems that after point A the high power consumption of nodes is due to the fans rather than the computing load. Although there is some fluctuation in the compression utilization, and it reduces the outlet temperature of the CRAC units, this is not enough to change the inlet temperature of the nodes. The anomaly of point A was related more to some nodes' computing load, and the cooling system's reaction was not fast enough to support this quick increase in the computing demand or power consumption, which turned into the nodes as a high temperature of nodes. *So, while nodes' inlet temperatures are normal, computing loads are high, and the reaction of the cooling systems are not fast enough to support computing load, which turns into high temperature at nodes level.*

Considering Point B: The node-level parameters of this point, like temperature, fan speed, and power consumption of nodes, are completely normal. In room-level parameters before this point, the free cooling activated (first two CRAC units out of four units, then three out of four), and this is the primary source of signal fluctuations of the other parts of the two cooling systems. Activating the free cooling has caused (i) an increase in the power consumption of the RDHX, which means the water cooling system works more, and also (ii) an increase in power consumption (fans speed and compressors utilization) of CRAC units. This situation is controlled by deactivating the free cooling as well as a reduction in computing load of the room, and as it is explicit, it is successful, and there is no rise in the node level temperature. *So node level parameters are normal, and activation of free cooling is the primary source of signals' fluctuations of cooling systems, and flags identify these signals' fluctuations as a suspicious condition.*

Considering Point C: All the node level parameters like temperature and fans speed of the nodes are high, and nodes experience high inlet temperature, so the cooling systems are in trouble. After a reduction of point B (some parameters like total power consumption of the ICT and CRAC units), continuously the power consumption of the CRAC units is increased, and it reached its peak at C. Before C, the free cooling activated for four out of four CRAC units meanwhile by activating of free cooling the power consumptions of the chillers of the RDHX reduced, and in the same time, the computing load increased these three action 1- increasing the computing load 2- activation of free cooling and 3- reduction in chillers cooling capacity, create thermal emergency which cause an increase in the temperature of the room and temperature of the inlet and outlet water of the RDHX and inlet and outlet temperature of the CRAC units which turn into thermal emergency in the cores of nodes and it creates out of control situation in node level and room level. *So three actions create a thermal emergency; 1- increasing the computing load, 2- activation of free cooling, and 3- reduction in RDHX cooling capacity. Which increase: 1- room temperature, 2-inlet and outlet water temperature of RDHX, and 3- inlet and outlet temperature of CRAC units, which leads to out-of-control conditions in node level and room level.*

4.3 Locations of Anomalies

Heatmap in Fig. 5 shows the severity and zone of anomalies that flags identified in three points around failure. The figure is composed of two heatmaps; the first heatmap from the left in the x-axis shows different parts of the HPC room: room level facilities metrics and node-level metrics, so it shows the zone of detected anomalies, but the second heatmap shows total severity of anomalies in three points. The annotation of the first heatmap is a normalized number, while the annotation of the second one is the sum of the metrics identified as anomalies. As reported in the second heatmap in point A, suggested methods identified 37 out of the 281 sub anomalies (37 raised flags) in different zones of the HPC room; meanwhile, for point B, there are 46 sub anomalies, and finally, for point C, which is the physical thermal failure, the system experienced maximum sub anomalies (raised flags) of 92 out of 281. As reported in Fig. 5, at point A, the temperature of node level for a few hours is high, and the suggested method identified some anomalies in node level temperatures like CPU, GPU, and PCIe and also the power consumption of nodes, and in the room level facilities, it discovers some minor anomalies mostly on water cooling system (RDHX). In point B, it recognizes the node level metrics as almost normal, but it sees some anomalies in the cooling system and total power consumption (as is also evident in the first two rows of Fig. 4a). There are raised flags in almost all parts of systems for point C.

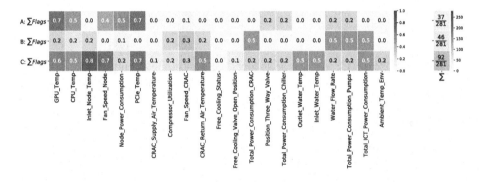

Fig. 5. Severity and zone of the anomaly in the HPC room.

5   Summary and Future Work

We employed monitoring signals of the in-production HPC cluster and HPC room facilities for thermal anomaly detection in HPC room. We proposed a set of rule-based statistical methods (flags) that explore different metrics at the HPC room, system, sub-system, and node level to find abnormal patterns. Moreover, we defined the sum of raised flags at each timestamp as metrics for the severity level of abnormality in the HPC room. We show that this method successfully could identify the thermal anomalies utilizing the telemetry system in the Exa-Mon database. This approach generates a heatmap report which provides details of locations and source of the anomaly in the HPC room. This report has high potential in maintenance and troubleshooting.

This study mainly focused on thermal anomaly detection, which can extend to other kinds of anomalies (like application-level anomaly detection, etc.) in future work. We are working to remedy flags' weakness in analyzing the complicated correlation of the signals in finding the anomalies or suspicious patterns by employing a semi-supervised ML-based approach to improve anomaly detection performance.

Acknowledgments. The study has been conducted in the context of EU H2020-JTI-EuroHPC-2019-1 project REGALE (g.n. 956560), EuroHPC EU PILOT project (g.a. 101034126), EU Pilot for exascale EuroHPC EUPEX (g.a. 101033975), European Processor Initiative (EPI) SGA2 (g.a. 101036168), and CINECA.

References

1. The 53th, 55th, 58th editions of the top500 list, June 2022. https://www.top500.org/
2. ACM: Getting started with HPC (2021). https://selects.acm.org/selections/getting-started-with-hpc
3. Agelastos, A., et al.: Toward rapid understanding of production HPC applications and systems. In: 2015 IEEE International Conference on Cluster Computing, pp. 464–473. IEEE (2015)
4. Ahad, R., Chan, E., Santos, A.: Toward autonomic cloud: Automatic anomaly detection and resolution. In: 2015 International Conference on Cloud and Autonomic Computing, pp. 200–203. IEEE (2015)
5. Aksar, B., et al.: E2EWatch: an end-to-end anomaly diagnosis framework for production HPC systems. In: Sousa, L., Roma, N., Tomás, P. (eds.) Euro-Par 2021. LNCS, vol. 12820, pp. 70–85. Springer, Cham (2021). https://doi.org/10.1007/978-3-030-85665-6_5
6. Arzani, B., Ciraci, S., Loo, B.T., Schuster, A., Outhred, G.: Taking the blame game out of data centers operations with Net Poirot. In: Proceedings of the 2016 ACM SIGCOMM Conference, pp. 440–453. SIGCOMM 2016. Association for Computing Machinery, New York, NY, USA (2016). https://doi.org/10.1145/2934872.2934884
7. Bartolini, A., et al.: Paving the way toward energy-aware and automated datacentre. In: Proceedings of the 48th International Conference on Parallel Processing: Workshops, pp. 8:1–8:8. ICPP 2019. ACM, New York, NY, USA (2019). https://doi.org/10.1145/3339186.3339215, http://doi.acm.org/10.1145/3339186.3339215
8. Bhatele, A., Mohror, K., Langer, S.H., Isaacs, K.E.: There goes the neighborhood: performance degradation due to nearby jobs. In: SC 2013: Proceedings of the International Conference on High Performance Computing, Networking, Storage and Analysis, pp. 1–12. IEEE (2013)
9. Bhatele, A., et al.: The case of performance variability on dragonfly-based systems. In: 2020 IEEE International Parallel and Distributed Processing Symposium (IPDPS), pp. 896–905. IEEE (2020)
10. Borghesi, A., Bartolini, A., Lombardi, M., Milano, M., Benini, L.: Anomaly detection using autoencoders in high performance computing systems. In: Proceedings of the AAAI Conference on Artificial Intelligence, vol. 33, pp. 9428–9433 (2019)
11. Borghesi, A., Bartolini, A., Lombardi, M., Milano, M., Benini, L.: A semisupervised autoencoder-based approach for anomaly detection in high performance computing systems. Eng. Appl. Artif. Intell. **85**, 634–644 (2019)

12. Borghesi, A., Bartolini, A., Milano, M., Benini, L.: Pricing schemes for energy-efficient HPC systems: design and exploration. Int. J. High Perform. Comput. Appl. **33**(4), 716–734 (2019). https://doi.org/10.1177/1094342018814593
13. Borghesi, A., Molan, M., Milano, M., Bartolini, A.: Anomaly detection and anticipation in high performance computing systems. IEEE Trans. Parallel Distrib. Syst. **33**(4), 739–750 (2021)
14. Brandt, J.M., et al.: Enabling advanced operational analysis through multi-subsystem data integration on trinity. Technical report, Sandia National Lab. (SNL-CA), Livermore, CA (United States); Sandia National (2015)
15. Conficoni, C., Bartolini, A., Tilli, A., Cavazzoni, C., Benini, L.: Integrated energy-aware management of supercomputer hybrid cooling systems. IEEE Trans. Industr. Inf. **12**(4), 1299–1311 (2016)
16. Conficoni, C., Bartolini, A., Tilli, A., Cavazzoni, C., Benini, L.: HPC cooling: a flexible modeling tool for effective design and management. IEEE Trans. Sustain. Comput. **6**(3), 441–455 (2018). https://doi.org/10.1109/TSUSC.2018.2809574
17. Dalmazo, B.L., Vilela, J.P., Simoes, P., Curado, M.: Expedite feature extraction for enhanced cloud anomaly detection. In: NOMS 2016–2016 IEEE/IFIP Network Operations and Management Symposium, pp. 1215–1220. IEEE (2016)
18. Das, A., Mueller, F., Rountree, B.: Aarohi: making real-time node failure prediction feasible. In: 2020 IEEE International Parallel and Distributed Processing Symposium (IPDPS), pp. 1092–1101. IEEE (2020)
19. Dorier, M., Antoniu, G., Ross, R., Kimpe, D., Ibrahim, S.: CALCioM: mitigating I/O interference in HPC systems through cross-application coordination. In: 2014 IEEE 28th International Parallel and Distributed Processing Symposium, pp. 155–164. IEEE (2014)
20. ECP: Exascale computing project. https://www.exascaleproject.org/what-is-exascale/
21. Intel server board S2600IP and workstation board W2600CR technical product specification, October 2013
22. Jayathilaka, H., Krintz, C., Wolski, R.: Performance monitoring and root cause analysis for cloud-hosted web applications. In: Proceedings of the 26th International Conference on World Wide Web, pp. 469–478 (2017)
23. Marathe, A., Zhang, Y., Blanks, G., Kumbhare, N., Abdulla, G., Rountree, B.: An empirical survey of performance and energy efficiency variation on intel processors. In: Proceedings of the 5th International Workshop on Energy Efficient Supercomputing, pp. 1–8 (2017)
24. Netti, A., Kiziltan, Z., Babaoglu, O., Sîrbu, A., Bartolini, A., Borghesi, A.: A machine learning approach to online fault classification in HPC systems. Future Gener. Comput. Syst. **110**, 1009–1022 (2020)
25. Netti, A., Ott, M., Guillen, C., Tafani, D., Schulz, M.: Operational data analytics in practice: experiences from design to deployment in production HPC environments. arXiv preprint arXiv:2106.14423 (2021)
26. Seyedkazemi Ardebili, M., Cavazzoni, C., Benini, L., Bartolini, A.: Thermal characterization of a Tier0 datacenter room in normal and thermal emergency conditions. In: Proceedings of High Performance Computing in Science and Engineering 2019 (2019)
27. Seyedkazemi Ardebili, M., et al.: Prediction of thermal hazards in a real datacenter room using temporal convolutional networks. In: 2021 Design, Automation & Test in Europe Conference & Exhibition (DATE), pp. 1256–1259. IEEE (2021)
28. Shaykhislamov, D., Voevodin, V.: An approach for dynamic detection of inefficient supercomputer applications. Procedia Comput. Sci. **136**, 35–43 (2018)

The 6th International Workshop on In Situ Visualization

The 6th International Workshop on In Situ Visualization (WOIV'21)

Peter Messmer[1] and Tom Vierjahn[2]

[1] NVIDIA, Switzerland
[2] Westphalian University of Applied Sciences, Muensterstr, Germany
tom.vierjahn@acm.org

1 Background and Description

Large-scale HPC simulations with their inherent I/O bottleneck have made in situ an essential approach for data analysis. In situ coupling of analysis and visualization to a live simulation circumvents writing raw data to disk. Instead, data abstracts are generated that capture much more information than otherwise possible.

The "Workshop on In Situ Visualization" series provides a venue for speakers to share practical expertise and experience with in situ visualization approaches. This 6th edition of the workshop, WOIV'22, took place as an on-site half-day workshop on June 3rd, 2022, co-located with ISC High Performance, after half-day workshops in 2016, 2017, and 2021, and two full-day workshops in 2018 and 2019. In 2020 we had to cancel the workshop due to the COVID-19 crisis. The goal of the workshop, in general, is to appeal to a wide-ranging audience of visualization scientists, computational scientists, and simulation developers, who have to collaborate to develop, deploy, and maintain in situ visualization approaches on HPC infrastructures.

For WOIV'22, we again also encouraged submissions on approaches that did not live up to their expectations. With this, we expected to get first-hand reports on lessons learned. Speakers should detail if and how the application drove abstractions or other kinds of data reductions and how these interacted with the expressiveness and flexibility of the visualization for exploratory analysis or why the approach failed.

As in the previous year, WOIV'22 encouraged submissions describing new developments for in situ software. These include both the creation of new in situ software as well as additions to existing in situ software. These submissions with a greater focus of "development" over "research" encourage the primary goal of WOIV to connect in situ techniques with science practitioners.

In addition to two invited talks, presentations at WOIV'22 were selected from submitted papers. These were reviewed by an international program committee comprising diverse members from academia, government, and industry and many nationalities. Each submitted paper received at least two reviews. Accepted papers were invited to present at WOIV and are published in this LNCS volume.

2   Workshop Summary

2.1   Keynote

Tim Gerrits gave the keynote speech. He presented insights gained during the ongoing project NHR4CES (National High Performance Computing Center for Computational Engineering Sciences) which is part of the German association for National High Performance Computing (NHR). NHR aims to provide scientists at German universities with the computing capacity they need for their research, and strengthen their skills for the efficient use of this resource.

Tim Gerrits leads the Crossectional Group Visualization at the National High Performance Computing Center for Computational Engineering Sciences (NHR4CES) as well as the Visualization Group at RWTH Aachen University, Germany. He and his team provide and develop visualization solutions for scientific data including interactive and immersive analysis tools. Tim holds a Bachelor and Master degree in Computervisualistics from the University of Magdeburg, Germany, where he also received his PhD in Visualization, working on the visualization of second-order tensor data and vector field ensembles.

2.2   Capstone

Chris R. Johnson gave the capstone speech. He presented an in depth view on the history and motivation of in situ visualization. He also outlined in situ visualization challenges and opportunities, ranging from reproducibility over adaptive meshes, topological data analysis, and uncertainty all the way to computational steering.

Chris R. Johnson is a Distinguished Professor of Computer Science and founding director of the Scientific Computing & Imaging (SCI) Institute at the University of Utah. He also holds faculty appointments in the Departments of Physics and Bioengineering. His research interests are in the areas of scientific computing and scientific visualization. In 1992, with Professor Rob MacLeod, Professor Johnson founded the SCI research group, now the SCI Institute, which has grown to employ over 150 faculty, staff and students. Professor Johnson serves on a number of international journal editorial and advisory boards to national and international research centers. He is a Fellow of AIMBE (2004), AAAS (2005), SIAM (2009), and IEEE (2014) and was inducted into the IEEE Visualization Academy (2019). He has received a number of awards including the NSF Presidential Faculty Fellow (PFF) award from President Clinton, a DOE Computational Science Award, the Governor's Medal for Science and Technology, the Utah Cyber Pioneer Award, the IEEE Visualization Career Award, IEEE CS Charles Babbage Award, the IEEE Sidney Fernbach Award, Rosenblatt Prize and most recently, the 2020 Leonardo Award.

2.3   Papers

Soumya Dutta et al., in their paper "In Situ Analysis and Visualization of Extreme-Scale Particle Simulations", presented a new in situ visual analysis pipeline for the extreme-scale multiphase flow simulation MFiX-Exa. They demonstrated how the pipeline can be used to process large particle fields in situ and produce informative visualizations of the data features. Having deployed their analysis pipeline on Oak Ridge's Summit supercomputer they studied its in situ applicability and usefulness.

Isaac Nealey et al., in their paper "Cinema Transfer: a Containerized Visualization Workflow", presented a containerized workflow demonstrating in situ analysis of simulation data rendered by a ParaView/Catalyst adapter for the generic SENSEI in situ interface which was then streamed to a remote site for visualization. They developed a web socket tool, cinema_transfer, for transferring the generated cinema databases to a remote machine while the simulation is running. They evaluated the performance of this containerized workflow and identified bottlenecks for large scale runs.

David Pugmire et al., in their short paper "The Need for Pervasive In Situ Analysis and Visualization (P-ISAV)", presented their thoughts and key properties on a fundamental requirement of future solutions: pervasive in situ visualization (P-ISAV). They addressed the fact that coupling HPC, experimental and observational facilities into computing ecosystems would lead to complex, distributed and heterogeneous systems. These would pose a significant challenge for current visualization tools, yet would provide unprecedented tools for scientific inquiry.

Marcel Krüger et al., in their paper "Insite: A Pipeline Enabling In-Transit Visualization and Analysis for Neuronal Network Simulations", presented a pipeline for in-transit analysis and visualization of data produced by neuronal network simulators. The pipeline enabled querying, filtering, and merging data from multiple simulation instances, and it applied traditional REST API paradigms and utilized data formats such as JSON to provide easy access to the generated data. The authors assessed the proposed architecture in the context of neuronal network simulations generated by the NEST simulator.

Pavel Novikov et al., in their short paper "Interactive Visualization of Large-Scale Oil and Gas Reservoir Simulation Models", presented the parallel implementation of a slicing algorithm for MPI CPU and multi-GPU computational systems in a form of a ParaView plugin. They compared the performance of their algorithm, an existing commercial oil and gas reservoir simulation software, and the built-in ParaView tool for model slicing. Their approach provided almost interactive visualization of a reservoir model with 1.9 billion cells of unstructured mesh.

3   Organising Committee

3.1   Workshop Chairs

Peter Messmer   NVIDIA, Switzerland
Tom Vierjahn   Westphalian University of Applied Sciences, Germany

3.2   Workshop Co-organizers

Steffen Frey   University of Groningen, The Netherlands
Kenneth Moreland   Oak Ridge National Laboratory, USA

Guido Reina   University of Stuttgart, Germany
Thomas Theussl   Visualization Core Lab, KAUST, Saudi Arabia

3.3   Program Committee

Andy Bauer   US Army Corps Of Engineers, USA
E. Wes Bethel   Lawrence Berkeley National Lab, USA
Jose Camata   Federal University of Juiz de Fora, Brazil
Berk Geveci   Kitware Inc., USA
Patrick Gralka   University of Stuttgart, Germany
Kevin Griffin   NVIDIA, USA
Ingrid Hotz   Linköping University, Sweden
James Kress   University of Oregon, USA
Joanna Leng   University of Leeds, UK
Shaomeng Li   National Center for Atmospheric Research, USA
Kwan-Liu Ma   University of California, Davis, USA
Nicole Marsaglia   University of Oregon, USA
Andrey Ovsyannikov   Intel, USA
Silvio Rizzi   Argonne National Laboratory, USA
Gunther Weber   Lawrence Berkeley National Lab, USA

In Situ Analysis and Visualization of Extreme-Scale Particle Simulations

Soumya Dutta[1]([⊠]), Dan Lipsa[2], Terece L. Turton[1], Berk Geveci[2], and James Ahrens[1]

[1] Los Alamos National Laboratory, Los Alamos, USA
soumyad@cse.iitk.ac.in, {tlturton,ahrens}@lanl.gov
[2] Kitware Inc., Clifton Park, USA
{berk.geveci,dan.lipsa}@kitware.com

Abstract. In situ analysis has emerged as a dominant paradigm for performing scalable visual analysis of extreme-scale computational simulation data. Compared to the traditional post hoc analysis pipeline where data is first stored into disks and then analyzed offline, in situ analysis processes data at the time its generation in the supercomputers so that the slow and expensive disk I/O is minimized. In this work, we present a new in situ visual analysis pipeline for the extreme-scale multi-phase flow simulation MFiX-Exa and demonstrate how the pipeline can be used to process large particle fields in situ and produce informative visualizations of the data features. We deploy our analysis pipeline on Oak Ridge's Summit supercomputer to study its in situ applicability and usefulness.

Keywords: In situ analysis · Visualization · Feature detection · High performance computing · Computational science · Particle data

1 Introduction

With increasing computing capabilities, scientific simulations are now producing very large-scale spatio-temporal data sets, containing intricate features that need to be analyzed and visualized efficiently to further scientific discoveries. While domain scientists focus on making their simulations more accurate and efficient, they need flexible and scalable analysis capabilities to study their data. Many research studies have shown that the traditional post hoc analysis paradigm is no longer scalable as handling, managing, and analysis of extreme-scale data sets will be prohibitive [2,3,9]. This is primarily due to slow disk I/O speed compared to the rate at which data is produced coupled with the post hoc processing needs of extreme-scale data [6,11,28]. As a result, only a sparse set of time steps of the simulation can typically be stored to disk for future analysis.

In situ analysis addresses this problem by deploying visualization algorithms directly with the simulation, i.e., while the data is produced. This powerful strategy has been shown very effective in producing high-quality visualization artifacts of the simulation data that otherwise would be significantly time-consuming

H. Anzt et al. (Eds.): ISC High Performance 2022 Workshops, LNCS 13387, pp. 283–294, 2022.
https://doi.org/10.1007/978-3-031-23220-6_19

to generate [3,16,19,25]. However, due to the complexity of the scientific data sets and the domain-specific features within them, it is often less effective if only the raw simulation data is visualized. An alternative approach is to first apply an appropriate data analysis algorithm in situ and then produce visual artifacts of the derived data that highlight the complex data features more clearly compared to the raw data. The informative visual artifacts generated from the derived data can be used to explore the evolution of the data features during the simulation run and application scientists can verify and/or validate various scientific hypotheses.

In this work, we present the first ParaView Catalyst-based [14] in situ analysis pipeline for the very large-scale multiphase simulation MFiX-Exa [20,21]. MFiX-Exa is currently being developed at the National Energy Technology Laboratory (NETL) and is on its way to harness the upcoming exascale supercomputers to further scientific discoveries [12] as part of the Exascale Computing Project (ECP) [13].

The primary focus of the MFiX-Exa simulation is to study the working principles of complex and large-scale chemical looping reactors. To comprehend the physics behind such rectors, MFiX-Exa developers study simulation cases where millions of particles interact with each other inside a fluidized bed. The formation of bubbles (void regions that are characterized by low particle density) in these fluidized beds is a prime phenomenon of interest for domain scientists as the evolution and characteristics of these bubbles can indicate the overall stability of the reactor. To study the bubble dynamics, the simulation needs to run for a sufficiently long duration, resulting in an extreme-scale spatio-temporal particle data set with tens of thousands of time steps. Post hoc analysis of such time-varying data is significantly time-consuming and so the experts typically run small-scale test cases as they currently lack the capability to explore full-fledged three-dimensional bubble dynamics.

Our in situ analysis pipeline addresses this issue and enables the domain experts to perform in situ analysis and visualization of their simulation data without needing to store the large-scale particle fields. We show that the Catalyst-based in situ pipeline can generate informative visualizations of the particle data and also can be used to apply data analysis algorithms so that the final visual artifacts show the bubble features clearly. Since for these large-scale particle simulations, it is impossible to see the bubbles clearly from the raw particle data, we first compute the particle density fields in situ and then produce volume-rendered images of the particle density field that clearly show the bubbles in the simulation data. We contribute a new VTK-based particle density estimation filter that users can use in their analysis pipeline to compute scalar particle density fields from particle data. Our in situ pipeline also allows storing of the in situ generated particle density fields which are significantly smaller compared to the original raw particles fields. These particle density fields can be used post hoc for further in-depth study of bubble dynamics.

2   Related Works

The need for in situ data analysis and visualization has grown significantly in recent years to address the problems arising from slow disk I/O. The visualization community has developed several high-quality libraries to enable in situ analysis and rendering of data. One of the early attempts of in situ visualization was made by Haimes [15] to visualize large unsteady data sets. For performing *in situ* analysis and visualization, Fabian et al. developed the Catalyst library [14], which uses functionalities of ParaView during in situ run. Catalyst-based in situ analysis has been widely adopted in the scientific visualization community [5, 8,29]. Similarly, run-time visualization with LibSim using VisIt was proposed by Whitlock et al. [27]. In another work, Lofstead et al. added ADIOS as an in situ visualization framework [18]. Vishwanath et al. enriched simulation time data analysis by proposing GLEAN [26]. A more recent flyweight in situ analysis infrastructure has been developed by Larsen et al. [17]. An open-source in situ visualization infrastructure called SENSEI is also being developed that allows interfacing between different in situ infrastructures with the simulation code [24]. For a more comprehensive guide of the various types of existing infrastructures, readers are referred to the following state-of-the-art report [6]. To gain detailed knowledge about the in situ relevant terminologies and standards, developed by the visualization community, please refer to [10].

3   ParaView Catalyst-based in Situ Visual Analysis Workflow

This section describes the analysis pipeline that we have developed to enable in situ analysis and visualization for the MFiX-Exa simulation. Starting with an overview of the Catalyst adapter, we describe its access of MFiX-Exa data in the in situ environment and then discuss the visualization methods and algorithms that are used to generate effective visual artifacts for MFiX-Exa data.

3.1   In Situ Catalyst Adapter Design

The first step to build an in situ analysis environment for a simulation code is to design an efficient in situ adapter that can tap into the simulation memory while the data is being generated. Making the data accessible in situ is necessary to move post hoc analyses into the simulation while it is running. Since different simulation codes have different data layouts in memory, designing a general in situ adapter can be a challenging task.

The MFiX-Exa simulation uses the AMReX [4,30] library as its internal software framework to store and process the simulated particle data. AMReX is a software framework that facilitates the development of scalable, block-based, massively parallel, and adaptive mesh refinement (AMR) applications. In this work, we have developed a ParaView (version 5.9.1) Catalyst-based (version 1) in situ adapter program that can read the particle data structures of AMReX (more

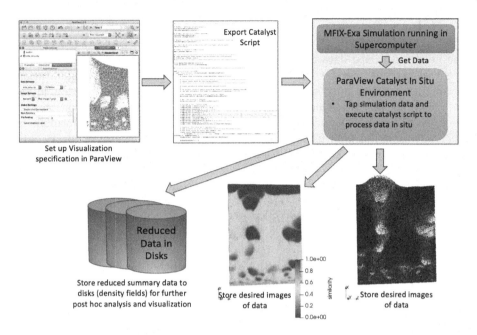

Fig. 1. Schematic of the in situ analysis and visualization pipeline showing different types of visualization and data artifact outputs.

specifically access the particle data from AMReX's ParticleContainer Class) and then convert it into a VTK-based [23] data structure and provide a handle to the user in the in situ environment. To convert AMReX -based particle data into a VTK-based data structure, currently the data is copied out. In the future, we will move to VTK's zero-copy capabilities to pass the pointers directly. Algorithm developers can directly use this VTK data in their program to analyze or produce visualizations of the data in situ. Since MFiX-Exa produces particle data, the simulation data is represented as VTK Polydata in the in situ environment. The in situ adapter also makes the simulation's MPI communicator accessible in the in situ environment so that users can deploy data processing and visualization algorithms that require distributed communication.

One of the advantages of the Catalyst adapter is that since this adapter is developed for the AMReX's particle container, it can be generalized and reused for performing in situ analysis for other simulations that use AMReX with minimal modification. Hence, even though the focus in this work is on the MFiX-Exa simulation, the in situ adapter and visualization techniques can be easily extendable to other particle-based simulations that use AMReX for data representation.

Figure 1 shows a schematic of the in situ analysis pipeline. Users can generate a Catalyst script that contains the visual analysis pipeline to be executed during the in situ run. This Python script is generated from the ParaView application as shown. The script is deployed in situ using Catalyst's in situ infrastructure. During the in situ run, the in situ adapter makes the data available in this Python

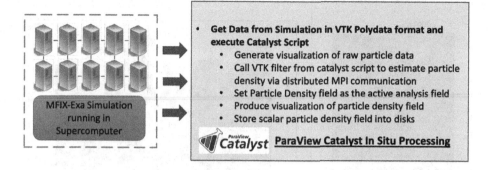

Fig. 2. Steps of in situ processing of the particle data for the proposed work.

script as a VTK Polydata at each MPI process, and the user can process and analyze the data further. The pipeline uses MFiX-Exa's MPI communicator and using Catalyst's built in fault tolerance capabilities, we ensure that even if our script is unable to process the data, the simulation does not crash. At each time step MFiX-Exa calls a Catalyst routine and passes it data. The Catalyst routine calls the Python script that the user provides to do the analysis and visualization. So on the cluster node, we run the MFiX-Exa simulation, which periodically calls Catalyst. So the Python script is periodically called to do the visualization. In Fig. 2, we present the in situ analysis and visualization tasks that we have used in this work to explore the MFiX-Exa data set. We generate visualization outputs of the raw particle data where each particle is rendered as a sphere and colored by their velocity magnitude. The velocity magnitude is computed in situ using ParaView's Calculator function. Since one of the primary focuses of the application developers is to study the bubble features in the simulation, we also compute the particle density field and generate visualizations of this field that can show the bubbles more clearly compared to the raw particle visualization. To further analyze the particle density field and the bubble features, we also allow storing the particle density fields onto disk. Note that, compared to the raw particle data, the size of this particle density scalar fields are significantly smaller and hence our method is also able to achieve sufficient data reduction. Using these reduced density fields, flexible bubble dynamics analysis can be done during post hoc analysis.

3.2 In Situ Particle Density Estimation for Effective Visualization of Data Features

Since the raw data format for MFiX-Exa is particle-based, we first add the capability to generate particle renderings at each time step. We also color each particle using its velocity magnitude so that the domain experts can glean additional information about the particle dynamics. In Fig. 3(a), we show the particle rendering of an MFiX-Exa simulation test case (MFiX-Exa Case 1), which contains around 4 million particles. The low-density particle regions, *bubbles*, can be

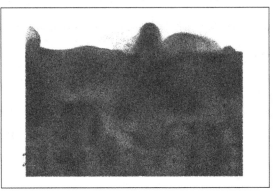

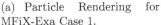

(a) Particle   Rendering   for   (b) Particle Rendering for MFiX-Exa Case 2.
MFiX-Exa Case 1.

Fig. 3. In situ generated visualization of raw particle fields for two different MFiX-Exa simulation test cases where the particles are colored by their velocity magnitude. Red particles indicate particles having higher velocity. (Color figure online)

seen in this figure. We also observe that particles underneath a bubble have high velocity. This visualization is similar to a post hoc visualization workflow. Potential issues with this visualization include that the actual bubble features are not seen and that smaller bubbles are difficult to visualize. These issues become much more severe as the number of particles is increased in the simulation domain. In Fig. 3(b), we present particle rendering of a much larger MFiX-Exa simulation test case (MFiX-Exa Case 2), containing around 54 million particles. As can be seen, even when the size of each particle radius is quite small, we barely see any bubble feature in the data. It appears that this simulation does not have any bubbles produced. Thus, the raw particle visualizations are not suitable when the experts want to study the bubbles in their data.

To address the shortcomings of the raw particle-based in situ visualizations, we use a particle density field-based visualization that clearly shows the bubble features in the data set. The resultant visualizations are much more informative and can be used to study bubble dynamics. Density estimation is often regarded as a fundamental step necessary for sampling particle fields into a structured continuous representation [22].

We have used a spatial histogram-based technique to group particles into non-overlapping bins and then a density field is finally constructed. As the particles are distributed across multiple compute nodes, we compute the histogram in the same distributed setting. A local histogram is first constructed at each processing unit by binning the 3D locations of all particles available to each processor. A 3D histogram is required since we are binning particle locations to estimate spatial particle density. The number of bins and bin widths on each local processing unit is the same and is estimated from the global bounds of the

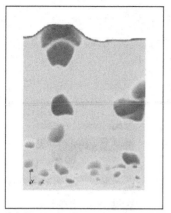
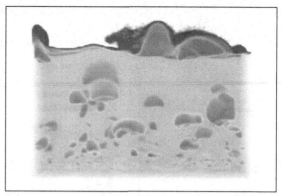

(a) Particle density rendering for MFiX-Exa Case 1.   (b) Particle density rendering for MFiX-Exa Case 2.

Fig. 4. In situ generated visualization of particle density fields for two different MFiX-Exa simulation test cases where the bubble features (blue regions with low density), are clearly seen. Note the clear delineation of bubble features and the ability to see the small bubbles, even for the large number of particles in MFiX-Exa Case 2. (Color figure online)

particles. Finally, the partial histograms are combined to construct the global density histogram by using a parallel reduction operation over all processing units. Each bin in this global spatial histogram represents particle counts in a local spatial region. The global 3D histogram is mapped into a 3D regular grid-based scalar field where each 3D bin center is mapped to a voxel in the regular grid data and the particle count for that bin is assigned as the particle density value at that voxel. Specific details about this histogram-based density estimation can be found in [7] where this technique was evaluated offline. Using a spatial histogram-based approach to convert the particle data into a density field can be efficiently performed in situ, keeping the computational cost low during in situ processing. Note that other density estimation methods can be used here to estimate the particle density field. However, we believe that the histogram-based technique is generally suitable for distributed environments as the histograms can be computed via parallel reduction operation efficiently and gives good results for MFiX-Exa data.

We have implemented the density estimation function in a VTK filter form so that it can be easily deployed from the Catalyst in situ script. The original code is implemented in C++ and is first integrated into VTK as an MPI-enabled parallel filter. Then we call the density estimation VTK filter from the Catalyst script. The input to the filter is the particle data and the output is a scalar field in the form of VTK ImageData. Once this field is produced, we generate visualizations of this density field and also store the raw density field for further post hoc analysis.

Fig. 5. Post hoc visual analysis of bubbles using in situ generated particle density fields. The left rendering window shows the density field and in the right rendering window, the bubbles are extracted using a low-density threshold value and then the connected component algorithm is applied to identify individual bubbles.

In Fig. 4(a), we show the in situ rendering of the particle density field for a time step of MFiX-Exa simulation Case 1. The corresponding particle field is shown previously in Fig. 3(a). We can observe that the low-density regions in the density field, the blue regions, correspond to the bubbles in the data. The effectiveness of the density field-based visualization can be compared to the visualization of the raw particles as seen in Fig. 4(b) which shows the density field visualization for the MFiX-Exa Case 2. The corresponding particle field is depicted in Fig. 3(b). Comparing Fig. 3(b) and Fig. 4(b), one can observe that the density field shows the bubbles in the data that are hard to see from the particle-based visualization when the number of particles is large.

The in situ generated particle density fields can also be used to perform flexible post hoc bubble analysis. Since the size of the density fields is significantly smaller compared to the raw particle fields, they can be loaded into ParaView and analyzed and visualized interactively. In Fig. 5, we show one such demonstration where on the left rendering window, the density field is visualized using volume rendering. On the right window, the segmented bubble features are shown.

Here, we first use a low-density value to threshold the density field and then apply the connectivity filter so that each connected segment is identified as an individual bubble feature.

4   Evaluation

We have tested the in situ pipeline on the Summit supercomputer [1], an IBM system located at the Oak Ridge Leadership Computing Facility (OLCF). Each compute node of Summit contains two IBM POWER9 processors, 512 GB of DDR4 memory, 1.6 TB of non-volatile memory, and six NVIDIA Tesla V100 GPUs. We performed an initial evaluation of our in situ pipeline by running the pipeline with two different test cases of MFiX-Exa. The first test case contains around 4 million particles, which we call MFiX-Exa Case 1, and the second case is a larger test case containing around 54 million particles. We denote the second test case as MFiX-Exa Case 2. For each of these cases, we performed particle rendering where the particles are colored with velocity magnitudes computed in situ and also volume rendering of the particle density field. The density field is first computed using a spatial histogram-based method as discussed before. In Table 1, we provide the computational timings taken by the simulation and the in situ methods. The renderings were done on GPUs and each MPI process were assigned with 1 GPU. As this timings reflect the total time for the catalyst script, they include the overhead due to data copying from AMReX to VTK data structure, the communication time, and the relevant I/O times. Since the simulation data evolves slowly over consecutive time steps and successive time steps are typically very similar, we performed in situ analysis at every 5th time step. Note that, we are reporting the initial performance of our in situ pipeline and we plan to run our workflow on a much bigger case of MFiX-Exa, containing hundreds of millions of particles, to conduct a full fledged performance study in the future and further optimize our code. We also plan to implement our density estimation filter as a VTKm filter so that we can execute the code with GPU acceleration in the upcoming exascale machines.

Table 1. In situ timings compared to the simulation timings for two different MFiX-Exa simulation test cases.

	Configuration	Avg. simulation time per time step (secs)	Avg. particle rendering time per time step (secs)	Avg. density estimation and rendering time per time step (secs)
MFiX-Exa Case 1 (~4M particles)	256 MPI processes with 1 GPU per process	2.240	0.179	1.057
MFiX-Exa Case 2 (~54M particles)	3072 MPI processes with 1 GPU per process	5.678	1.160	1.649

5   Conclusions

We have presented a ParaView Catalyst-based in situ analysis pipeline infrastructure for the ECP application MFiX-Exa. We demonstrate how the users can use our in situ pipeline to perform in situ analysis and produce various types of visualization artifacts. We believe that our in situ interface, which is able to read AMReX particle data structure, is an important capability for the domain scientists who can analyze and produce visualization of their data for extreme-scale simulation test cases with minimal effort to verify and validate their simulation and further improve it. In the future, we plan to deploy this in situ analysis pipeline in the upcoming exascale supercomputers to analyze and visualize extreme-scale MFiX-Exa simulation data and also develop more sophisticated in situ bubble detection algorithms.

Acknowledgements. The authors would like to thank the Department of Energy and Los Alamos National Laboratory for the funding and support in carrying out this research. This research was supported by the Exascale Computing Project (17-SC-20-SC), a collaborative effort of the U.S. Department of Energy Office of Science and the National Nuclear Security Administration. This research used resources of the Oak Ridge Leadership Computing Facility at the Oak Ridge National Laboratory, which is supported by the Office of Science of the U.S. Department of Energy under Contract No. DE-AC05-00OR22725. We thank our many ECP collaborators especially Jordan Musser, Ann Almgren, and Patrick O'Leary. This research is released under LA-UR-22-21278.

References

1. Summit supercomputer. https://docs.olcf.ornl.gov/systems/summit_user_guide.html. Accessed 24 May 2022
2. Ahern, S., Shoshani, A., Ma, K., Choudhary, A.: Scientific discovery at the exascale. Report from the DOE ASCR 2011 Workshop on Exascale Data Management. Analysis, and Visualization, February 2011
3. Ahrens, J., Jourdain, S., OLeary, P., Patchett, J., Rogers, D.H., Petersen, M.: An image-based approach to extreme scale in situ visualization and analysis. In: SC14: International Conference for High Performance Computing, Networking, Storage and Analysis, pp. 424–434 (2014). https://doi.org/10.1109/SC.2014.40
4. AMReX: A software framework for massively parallel, block-structured adaptive mesh refinement (AMR) applications (2021). https://amrex-codes.github.io/amrex/index.html. Accessed 7 Apr 2021
5. Atzori, M., et al.: In-situ visualization of large-scale turbulence simulations in nek5000 with paraview catalyst . https://doi.org/10.1007/s11227-021-03990-3
6. Bauer, A.C., et al.: In situ methods, infrastructures, and applications on high performance computing platforms. Comput. Graph. Forum **35**(3), 577–597 (2016). https://doi.org/10.1111/cgf.12930
7. Biswas, A., Ahrens, J.P., Dutta, S., Musser, J.M., Almgren, A.S., Turton, T.L.: Feature analysis, tracking, and data reduction: an application to multiphase reactor simulation MFiX-Exa for In-Situ use case. Comput. Sci. Eng. **23**(01), 75–82 (2021). https://doi.org/10.1109/MCSE.2020.3016927

8. Camata, J.J., Silva, V., Valduriez, P., Mattoso, M., Coutinho, A.L.: In situ visualization and data analysis for turbidity currents simulation. Comput. Geosci. **110**, 23–31 (2018). https://doi.org/10.1016/j.cageo.2017.09.013

9. Childs, H.: Data exploration at the exascale. Supercomput. Front. Innov. **2**(3) (2015). http://superfri.org/superfri/article/view/78

10. Childs, H., et al.: A terminology for in situ visualization and analysis systems. Int. J. High Perform. Comput. Appl. **34**(6), 676–691 (2020). https://doi.org/10.1177/1094342020935991

11. Dutta, S., Chen, C., Heinlein, G., Shen, H.W., Chen, J.: In situ distribution guided analysis and visualization of transonic jet engine simulations. IEEE Trans. Vis. Comput. Graph. **23**(1), 811–820 (2017)

12. Optimizing a new technology to reduce power plant carbon dioxide emissions (2022). https://www.exascaleproject.org/optimizing-a-new-technology-to-reduce-power-plant-carbon-dioxide-emissions/. Accessed 3 Feb 2022

13. Exascale Computing Project (2022). https://www.exascaleproject.org/. Accessed 12 Feb 2022

14. Fabian, N., et al.: The ParaView coprocessing library: a scalable, general purpose in situ visualization library. In: 2011 IEEE Symposium on Large Data Analysis and Visualization (LDAV), pp. 89–96 (2011). https://doi.org/10.1109/LDAV.2011.6092322

15. Haimes, R.: pv3: a distributed system for large-scale unsteady cfd visualization. In: AIAA paper, pp. 94–0321 (1994)

16. He, W., et al.: Insitunet: deep image synthesis for parameter space exploration of ensemble simulations. IEEE Trans. Vis. Comput. Graph. **26**(1), 23–33 (2020). https://doi.org/10.1109/TVCG.2019.2934312

17. Larsen, M., et al.: The alpine in situ infrastructure: ascending from the ashes of strawman. In: Proceedings of the In Situ Infrastructures on Enabling Extreme-Scale Analysis and Visualization, pp. 42–46. ISAV 2017, Association for Computing Machinery, New York, NY, USA (2017). https://doi.org/10.1145/3144769.3144778

18. Lofstead, J.F., Klasky, S., Schwan, K., Podhorszki, N., Jin, C.: Flexible IO and integration for scientific codes through the adaptable IO system (ADIOS). In: Proceedings of the 6th International Workshop on Challenges of Large Applications in Distributed Environments, pp. 15–24. CLADE 2008, ACM (2008). https://doi.org/10.1145/1383529.1383533

19. Lukasczyk, J., et al.: Cinema darkroom: a deferred rendering framework for large-scale datasets. In: 2020 IEEE 10th Symposium on Large Data Analysis and Visualization (LDAV), pp. 37–41 (2020). https://doi.org/10.1109/LDAV51489.2020.00011

20. MFIX-Exa   (2022).   https://amrex-codes.github.io/MFIX-Exa/docs_html/. Accessed 3 Feb 2022

21. Musser, J., et al.: MFIX-Exa: a path toward exascale CFD-DEM simulations. Int. J. High Perform. Comput. Appl. (2021). https://doi.org/10.1177/10943420211009293

22. Peterka, T., Croubois, H., Li, N., Rangel, S., Cappello, F.: Self-Adaptive Density Estimation of Particle Data. SIAM J. Sci. Comput. **38**(5), S646–S666 (2016). SISC Special Edition on CSE'15: Software and Big Data

23. Schroeder, W., Martin, K., Lorensen, B.: The Visualization Toolkit: An Object Oriented Approach to 3D Graphics, fourth edn. Kitware Inc. (2004). iSBN 1-930934-19-X

24. SENSEI: Scalable in situ analysis and visualization (2021). https://sensei-insitu.org/. Accessed 12 Feb 2022

25. Tikhonova, A., Correa, C., Ma, K.L.: Explorable images for visualizing volume data. In: 2010 IEEE Pacific Visualization Symposium (PacificVis), pp. 177–184 (2010). https://doi.org/10.1109/PACIFICVIS.2010.5429595

26. Vishwanath, V., Hereld, M., Papka, M.E.: Toward simulation-time data analysis and i/o acceleration on leadership-class systems. In: 2011 IEEE Symposium on Large Data Analysis and Visualization (LDAV), pp. 9–14 (2011). https://doi.org/10.1109/LDAV.2011.6092178

27. Whitlock, B., Favre, J.M., Meredith, J.S.: Parallel in situ coupling of simulation with a fully featured visualization system. In: Proceedings of the 11th Eurographics Conference on Parallel Graphics and Visualization, pp. 101–109. EGPGV 2011, Eurographics Association (2011). https://doi.org/10.2312/EGPGV/EGPGV11/101-109

28. Woodring, J., Petersen, M., Schmeißer, A., Patchett, J., Ahrens, J., Hagen, H.: In situ eddy analysis in a high-resolution ocean climate model. IEEE Trans. Vis. Comput. Graph. 22(1), 857–866 (2016). https://doi.org/10.1109/TVCG.2015.2467411

29. Yi, H., Rasquin, M., Fang, J., Bolotnov, I.A.: In-situ visualization and computational steering for large-scale simulation of turbulent flows in complex geometries. In: 2014 IEEE International Conference on Big Data (Big Data), pp. 567–572 (2014). https://doi.org/10.1109/BigData.2014.7004275

30. Zhang, W., Myers, A., Gott, K., Almgren, A., Bell, J.: Amrex: block-structured adaptive mesh refinement for multiphysics applications. Int. J. High Perform. Comput. Appl. 35(6), 508–526 (2021). https://doi.org/10.1177/10943420211022811

Insite: A Pipeline Enabling In-Transit Visualization and Analysis for Neuronal Network Simulations

Marcel Krüger[1]([✉])[iD], Simon Oehrl[1][iD], Ali C. Demiralp[1][iD],
Sebastian Spreizer[2][iD], Jens Bruchertseifer[2][iD], Torsten W. Kuhlen[1][iD],
Tim Gerrits[1][iD], and Benjamin Weyers[2][iD]

[1] Visual Computing Institute, RWTH Aachen University, Aachen, Germany
`krueger@vis.rwth-aachen.de`
[2] Human-Computer Interaction, University of Trier, Trier, Germany

Abstract. Neuronal network simulators are central to computational neuroscience, enabling the study of the nervous system through in-silico experiments. Through the utilization of high-performance computing resources, these simulators are capable of simulating increasingly complex and large networks of neurons today. Yet, the increased capabilities introduce a challenge to the analysis and visualization of the simulation results. In this work, we propose a pipeline for in-transit analysis and visualization of data produced by neuronal network simulators. The pipeline is able to couple with simulators, enabling querying, filtering, and merging data from multiple simulation instances. Additionally, the architecture allows user-defined plugins that perform analysis tasks in the pipeline. The pipeline applies traditional REST API paradigms and utilizes data formats such as JSON to provide easy access to the generated data for visualization and further processing. We present and assess the proposed architecture in the context of neuronal network simulations generated by the NEST simulator.

Keywords: In-transit visualization · In-transit processing · Neuronal networks · Simulation tools

1 Introduction

Activity within the nervous system occurs in and across groups of neurons assembled into networks. Studying the operation principles of these neuronal networks is important to our understanding of nervous system function [15]. Neuronal network simulators take a computational approach to this study, in which the components of the network are programmatically modeled and assembled to simulate biological and artificial behavior. Through utilization of high-performance computing resources, these simulators are capable of simulating increasingly complex and large networks of neurons.

M. Krüger and S. Oehrl—Equal contribution.

© Springer Nature Switzerland AG 2022
H. Anzt et al. (Eds.): ISC High Performance 2022 Workshops, LNCS 13387, pp. 295–305, 2022.
https://doi.org/10.1007/978-3-031-23220-6_20

The standard approach to the investigation of simulator outputs has been post-hoc analysis and visualization, where data is persisted to disk throughout the simulation and processed offline afterwards [10,17]. Yet, the increasing size of data generated by simulators, as well as the necessity to adjust simulation parameters interactively have led to the development of in-situ methods [12,13], which perform visualization in conjunction with the simulation. These approaches enable the users to get early feedback on their simulation which allows for quicker turnaround times and lets experts discuss the preliminary results shortly after the simulation has started. In this work we present the *Insite* pipeline. Insite is an in-transit analysis and visualization system for neuronal network simulations. Compared to existing in-transit/in-situ methods, Insite focuses on ease-of-use and accessibility. Users who would like to use in-transit capabilities are not required to change the simulator's code or interact with low-level programming APIs.

The pipeline integrates with neuronal network simulators in the form of extensions, writing data to in-memory ring buffers as well as providing means for front-end applications to query the data through a REST interface. Additionally, the architecture allows user-defined plugins that perform analysis tasks in the pipeline. To make the pipeline accessible to a broad audience of users, it uses traditional REST API paradigms and the JSON data format to provide easy access to in-transit data.

2   Related Work

In the context of computational neuroscience, a variety of approaches exist for simulation of neuronal activity. A major difference between simulators is the abstraction level that is used. Simulators that are capable of simulating morphology [1,4] require more complex computations than simulators that focus on abstract brain regions [16]. The proposed pipeline is designed to work with any simulator, however, this work particularly focuses on the Neural Simulation Tool (NEST) [11]. NEST is an actively developed simulator, providing modeling capabilities for biological and point neurons, and is capable of simulating large scale spiking neural networks of point neurons in a distributed manner.

Insite is the successor of the modular pipeline design presented in [14] consisting of a set of C++ libraries with corresponding Python wrappers. The earlier approach suffers from limitations regarding applicability; for example, web applications based on JavaScript are not natively supported. Building the libraries also requires a set of dependencies making the integration into potential clients an involved process. These two factors lead to the re-design of the pipeline with a strong focus on ease-of-use.

Post-processing of the simulation data is typically done using Python scripts using general statistical analysis packages or specialized ones such as the Electrophysiology Analysis Toolkit [8]. The results are then often visualized using general plotting packages as the final step of this process. However, there is also a variety of specialized visualization tools in the field of computational neuroscience. ViSimpl is a tool that allows visualization of simulation data in a spatial and temporal context utilizing multiple linked views [10]. VIOLA is a web-based application utilizing a similar method of multiple linked views [17]. Its main focus is the visualization of temporally and spatially binned spike data in 2D views along with a 3D visualization that combines the temporal and spatial aspects of the spiking behavior. The approach presented in [13] applies in-situ visualization and steering paradigms to the NEST simulator, focusing on connectivity generation. Spreizer et al. [19] present a graphical user interface that is not only able to visualize NEST simulations but also provides an easy-to-use interface for constructing and executing them.

Aside from domain-specific solutions [5, 7, 9] there is a wide variety of frameworks and tools that aim to provide generalized solutions for in-situ visualizations. Childs et al. [6] as well as Bauer et al. [3] presented an overview of the general challenges and considerations of in-situ data processing. ParaView Catalyst [2] provides a solution for generic in-situ visualization settings. The library couples with arbitrary simulations, converting and streaming output in the form of VTK primitives. Once received by a ParaView instance, the data may be further processed using the filtering and mapping capabilities of VTK. A similar alternative is VisIt LibSim [20], which enables interactive connections between a live simulation and VisIt instances. However, potential users, such as neuroscientists, often lack the knowledge of standard visualization libraries and data formats. The pipeline presented in this work eliminates this requirement by providing easy to use and widely supported data formats and protocols.

3   Method

The proposed pipeline enables the user to access data from neuronal network simulations with a focus on easy integration rather than performance or scalability. This is achieved by abstracting the internal representation and data acquisition of the simulator. The abstraction allows the user to avoid implementation details and instead interact with an HTTP REST API. While this may add more overhead than low-level transport protocols, the convenience aspect drastically outweighs the drawbacks. The endpoints return the requested data in a widespread and easy to handle JSON format. This way, front-end applications are not forced into a specific development environment as nearly all programming languages provide means to connect to such an API and parse the data. Providing simplified access to the data makes it possible for experts in fields other than computer science, such as neuroscientists, who might have limited programming knowledge to use the pipeline for analysis of in-silico experiments. Allowing the domain experts to access the data in a simplified manner eliminates the necessity for computer science experts in order to benefit from the advantages of in-situ processing. This is also in line with the development efforts of the simulators, which increasingly hide programming complexity and give neuroscientists easy-to-use simulator APIs, thus, allowing a simple way to describe simulations.

On the other hand the impact of the pipeline on the simulation performance is quite important, as a significant slow down in computation time would not be justified by the advantages gained through the use of the pipeline.

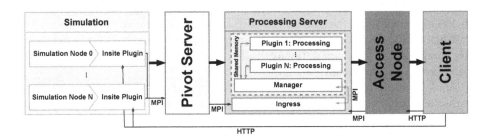

Fig. 1. Block Diagram showing all components of the pipeline and a client. Thick arrows indicate the direction of the data flow while thin arrows indicate who initiates the communication.

The pipeline consists of four different main components: the simulator module, the pivot server, the processing server, and the access node which are shown in Fig. 1. The following sections describe these components and their interaction in more detail.

Access Node. The access node serves as the single point of contact (SPOC) for any client interested in the data accessible through Insite. The role of the SPOC is two-fold: The access node is the SPOC for requests originating from various simulators but also for requests that require querying data from multiple nodes of a distributed simulation. Using the access node, clients can query data via an HTTP REST API that provides a corresponding response in JSON format. The data can be either *metadata* such as the simulation's neuron ids, neuron models, or plugin properties, *raw data* such as spike data or voltages, or *processed data* that are the result of in-transit processing. Additionally, each endpoint provides optional parameters that let the user filter the requested data. Data can be filtered by various properties, such as time, neurons, and properties that are specific to neuronal networks.

One key property is that the access node does not store data itself and is stateless towards clients. It gathers the data from either the simulation nodes or the processing server and returns it as a single response to the client. Clients are not notified but are responsible for querying the data regularly to avoid skipping data. There are three distinct mechanisms to gather data. The mechanism that is used depends on the type of the requested data:

Metadata such as the number of connected simulation nodes is known in prior by the access node, hence requests querying such data may be responded to by the access node without additional communication. For other requests, the access node has to query the processing server or the simulation node(s). *Raw data* is distributed across multiple simulator nodes and requests to the access node are forwarded to all simulation nodes. The responses are then aggregated by the access node and passed to the client. All requests for *processed data* are resolved through queries from the access node to the processing server. The response of the processing server is then returned to the client in an HTTP response.

The biggest architectural benefit of this approach is the fact that the access node hides any simulation-specific details such as how many simulation nodes are used. The clients can be oblivious to, and perform the queries independent of the existence or size of a distributed simulation.

Additionally, it is easy to provide different endpoints that add functionality to improve the convenience of accessing data such as various filters mapping to one or multiple endpoints in the simulator.

Simulator Module. For the collection of metadata and simulation data, the architecture uses modules or helper libraries that are developed as part of Insite. These modules are simulator specific and hook into the simulation to gain access to the required data. The integration of these modules should be easy for users that want to leverage in-transit properties in new as well as existing simulation description files. Users are only required to define which neurons' data should be made accessible in their network/simulation description. This can either be a subset or all neurons that are part of the simulation.

In the proposed architecture, the simulator module is split into two parts. The first part is responsible for raw simulation data, such as spike data or membrane voltages, as well as metadata. Both, the metadata and simulation data are stored locally in the module. The latter is stored in ring buffers which allows defining an upper bound for the memory requirements when using the module. The data is made available via an HTTP REST API that returns JSON allowing easy retrieval of the data by either the access node or clients directly. In the case of distributed simulations, each simulation module only holds an incomplete set of the data due to its local-only storage. Therefore, the use of the aforementioned access node is preferred for automatic data aggregation.

The second part of the module is responsible for data that is to be processed in-transit. Spikes are collected and are proactively pushed via the pivot server to the processing server using MPI as soon as a predefined amount is reached. Compared to the reactive pull approach used for raw data, the advantage is that the workload of processing the data can be distributed over time.

Pivot Server. Spike data is represented as a list of pairs consisting of spike times and neuron IDs. However, it is preferable to have a representation as a spike train for further processing. Generally, a spike train is represented such that each neuron ID is mapped to a list of spike times. The Pivot Server[1] developed by Sontheimer et al. [18] transforms spike tuples into a spike train representation. All of Insite's simulator modules connect to the pivot server which sends the aggregated spike trains to connected consumers.

---

[1] https://gitlab.jsc.fz-juelich.de/eni/thesis-and-implementation.

Processing Server. The processing server is responsible for in-transit processing of the raw data for further consumption by clients. This processing can be data transformations as well as domain-specific analyses. We decided not to include fixed processing functionality in the server. Instead, an architecture that allows the end-users to provide custom-written plugins that perform the processing in-transit was chosen. Plugins are written in Python through implementing an abstract class interface. Python was chosen as it is a well-established language in the field of computational neuroscience and offers libraries for domain-specific analysis. The interface consists of functions that are called on initialization, when new raw data is available or when data is explicitly requested by the end-user. Users have the ability to include any kind of library that provides Python bindings but can also choose to implement functionality on their own. This empowers many kinds of users to provide domain-specific processing and analysis plugins without prior knowledge regarding in-transit architectures or simulator specifics. The processing function has access to two different data buffers. The first buffer only contains spikes that were generated between the current call and the last call. However, there are scenarios where this information is not sufficient; for example, when temporal dynamics should be analyzed, the temporal analysis might need a time window that is larger than the update rate. Therefore, a second data buffer is accessible that stores spike data in a per-neuron ring buffer. Spikes are only overwritten when the neurons' ring buffer is full.

Data is received by an ingress process that places the received data in the shared memory buffers. A manager process is responsible for detecting plugins, returning processed data to the access node and managing the plugins' state. Every time new data arrives, it spawns a new process for each plugin to execute all computations in parallel.

Data processing happens asynchronously to the simulation, in a way that prevents the processing to slow down the simulation. On the other hand, this requires plugins to be fast enough to finish computation between the arrival of two data frames. In case plugins take too long, spike data will be overwritten in the ring buffer and data is lost. This is due to the current realization of the Pivot Server. Currently, no visualization task experienced this issue when efficient plugin implementations were used. A future rework of the server, however, could alleviate this issue.

The data generated by the processing is stored locally in the plugin and the plugin author defines the return format by overriding one of the interface functions. This architecture allows for maximum flexibility regarding the data format of the processed results. This is especially important because processing can reduce the data or alter its dimensionality which makes finding a general common representation challenging. The processed data of all plugins can be accessed by the access node through the manager process.

4 Application

In this section, we describe two use cases that benefit from using the functionality provided by Insite. The first application makes use of Insite's raw data interface while the second use case leverages its capabilities to pre-process the data for in-transit visualization.

Use Case 1: NEST Desktop[2] is a classroom learning tool that enables students and teachers to create, run and visualize neuronal network simulations in NEST from the browser. It provides functionality to create network layouts graphically and generates the corresponding simulation control code automatically. The simulation can then be run in the backend on a NEST instance that is controlled by NEST Server. It is possible to visualize the results in various views that display spike or voltage data, in 2D or 3D. Starting with version 3.1, NEST Desktop is able to utilize Insite to provide in-transit enabled visualizations (Fig. 2).

Use Case 2: We present a prototype implementation that shows the use case for in-transit processing. The prototype consists of an in-transit enabled re-implementation of VIOLA's 3D space-time view [17] which requires the mean firing rate (MFR) of temporally and spatially binned neurons.

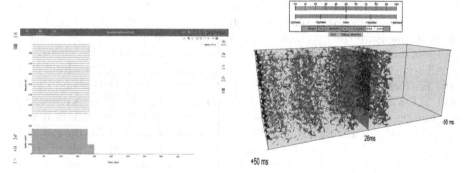

(a) NEST Desktop [19] running a simple simulation with spikes extracted during run-time using Insite.

(b) The adapted 3D space-time view of the VIOLA framework [17] with the added timeline.

Fig. 2. Example use cases.

In the original version, the binning process and MFR calculation must be manually performed by the user by running a Python script once the simulation has finished. The processed data is then uploaded to a web application where it is shown to the user. The in-transit enabled prototype moves the binning process and the MFR calculation to a processing plugin. Additionally, the visualization

---

[2] https://github.com/nest-desktop/nest-desktop.

was re-implemented to be in-transit compatible. The mean firing rates of the binned spikes are periodically requested from the access node via HTTP. A timeline showing the available time steps as well as the progress of the simulation in green was added to the visualization.

5   Performance

This section discusses the performance characteristics of the Insite pipeline. The performance evaluation is done by integrating with the NEST simulator based on a new pipeline implementation that is in active development. Results should be seen as preliminary, as not all components of the pipeline are currently optimized.

One of the key metrics is the overhead in simulation time produced by using the pipeline. Several simulation repetitions with different settings are used for evaluation. To establish a baseline, the simulation was first run without the ability to record spike data. Additionally, we measure the simulation time overhead of storing spike data in memory and writing the data in ASCII format to disk using the built-in functionality of NEST. The next runs were performed with Insite's raw data interface enabled. With respect to the raw data access, the frequency of requests and the amount of queried data might have an impact on the performance of the simulation. To evaluate this, we benchmarked the run-time of the simulation while querying spikes in intervals of 250 ms and 1000 ms. To represent a realistic workload, we assume that a potential client wants to access all spikes once, thus, every query requests all spikes that occurred since the last query. To measure the overhead of the Insite module itself, e.g., the writes to the spike buffers, we performed an additional run without any data queries.

All tests were executed on a single machine equipped with two Intel Xeon CPU E5-2680 v3 processors resulting in a total of 24 cores/48 threads, 128 GB 2133 MT/s Hynix DDR4 RAM and a 1TB Samsung 980 PRO NVMe SSD. Benchmarks for the baseline, memory, disk, and Insite's raw interface were repeated 40 times. Figure 3 shows the results of the benchmark for the raw data interface. It can be seen that a small overhead is introduced for all recording methods. On average the storage in memory has the lowest overhead of 1.41%. However, these settings do not scale well with long simulations as the spike data will grow linearly with the simulation time and is potentially uncapped. Persisting the data to disk in ASCII format adds on average an overhead of 2.22% compared to the baseline. This is still a minor impact and would not affect real-world use cases. However, it is important to state that our test machine was equipped with modern NVMe storage and results may change when writing to hard disks or remote storage solutions.

Figure 3 shows that the overhead of using Insite was comparable between the settings with no queries, 250 ms and 1000 ms. This suggests that the queries and their intervals do not have a strong impact on the overhead. The overhead for the three were around 4.61%, 4.60% and 3.72%, respectively. It is important to note that in the case where Insite was enabled, the Access Node as described in Sect. 3 was ran on the same machine but on resources that were not used for the simulation. One has to keep in mind that in a cluster setting our solution would impose an additional architectural performance overhead by reserving one cluster node for the access node, thus, removing one node from the simulation. However, with larger numbers of simulation nodes, this overhead diminishes so that it should not have a great impact on today's large scale simulations.

The overhead of the processing interface was evaluated in a separate test on the same machine. Its design of actively pushing all spikes to the pivot server and the decoupled design of the processing server makes the overhead independent of any incoming requests or time spent in the processing plugins. A simulation was ran using two settings; storing spikes in memory and with Insite's processing interface enabled. The run for each setting was repeated five times. On average the processing pipeline of Insite resulted in a 2% overhead compared to storing the spikes in memory.

Additional benchmarks need to be performed in the future that can give further insight into the performance of the single components and can be used to optimize the existing implementation.

The results show that enabling Insite has a low impact on the simulation time of under 5% compared to not storing spike data at all. Users can benefit from in-transit enabled simulations and the easy to use architecture of Insite without a serious impact on the simulation time and without modifications to the simulators code.

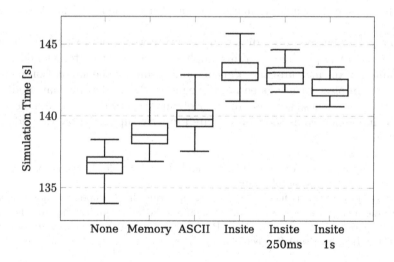

Fig. 3. Box plots indicating the measured total simulation times for the different methods of recording spike data. The time below Insite denotes the query interval of the connected client. No number means that no queries were performed.

6   Conclusion and Future Work

We have presented a novel pipeline for in-transit analysis and visualization of neuronal network simulations. Its focus lies on the usability aspect and low impact on simulation time. In addition, it provides a flexible, plugin-based processing pipeline enabling in-transit processing and analysis for domain experts. We introduced two example use-cases for the pipeline and showed that it is feasible for live inspection of a running NEST simulation. The overhead of the pipeline on NEST simulations has been evaluated.

Future work will focus on improving the capabilities of the pipeline: While JSON is a flexible and easy-to-use format with good tooling support, it also comes at the cost of converting the data to and from a text-based representation. This could become a bottleneck for large-scale simulations and large amounts of recorded neurons. It could hence be beneficial to provide mechanisms to query the data in binary formats such as FlatBuffers[3]. REST API paradigms allow this without breaking backward compatibility with earlier implementations by adding new endpoints or adding new parameters to existing ones.

While this work focused on the integration with the NEST simulator, another goal is to integrate Arbor [1] and TVB [16] into the Insite pipeline. Integration of additional simulators would allow development of multi-scale visualizations. These could be driven by co-simulation where multiple simulators are coupled and cooperatively work on one simulation. Each simulator could be used to simulate parts of the whole simulation on the abstraction level that it is designed for.

Finally, another potential direction for future work could be adding steering capabilities to the pipeline. Steering implies the ability to interact and change the simulation during run-time. Pausing and resuming the simulation could be seen as the simplest forms of steering while more advanced forms may modify the simulation itself. These actions can be nicely mapped to HTTP terminology and could be implemented as soon as they are properly supported by the underlying simulators.

Acknowledgements. We would like to thank Jan Müller for his contribution to the design and implementation of Insite.

This project/research has received funding from the European Union's Horizon 2020 Framework Programme for Research and Innovation under the Specific Grant Agreement No. 945539 (Human Brain Project SGA3) and Specific Grant Agreement No. 785907 (Human Brain Project SGA2).

References

1. Akar, N.A., et al.: Arbor – a morphologically-detailed neural network simulation library for contemporary high-performance computing architectures. In: 2019 27th Euromicro International Conference on Parallel, Distributed and Network-Based Processing (PDP), pp. 274–282, February 2019

---

[3] https://google.github.io/flatbuffers/.

2. Ayachit, U., et al.: Paraview catalyst: enabling in situ data analysis and visualization. In: Proceedings of the First Workshop on In Situ Infrastructures for Enabling Extreme-Scale Analysis and Visualization, pp. 25–29 (2015)
3. Bauer, A.C., et al.: In situ methods, infrastructures, and applications on high performance computing platforms. In: Computer Graphics Forum, vol. 35, pp. 577–597. Wiley Online Library (2016)
4. Carnevale, N.T., Hines, M.L.: The NEURON Book. Cambridge University Press, Cambridge (2006)
5. Chen, X., et al.: In situ tensorview: in situ visualization of convolutional neural networks. In: 2018 IEEE International Conference on Big Data (Big Data), pp. 1899–1904. IEEE (2018)
6. Childs, H.: Architectural challenges and solutions for petascale postprocessing. J. Phys. Conf. Ser. **78**, 012012. IOP Publishing (2007)
7. Crivelli, S., Kreylos, O., Hamann, B., Max, N., Bethel, W.: ProteinShop: a tool for interactive protein manipulation and steering. J. Comput. Aided Mol. Des. **18**(4), 271–285 (2004)
8. Denker, M., Yegenoglu, A., Grün, S.: Collaborative HPC-enabled workflows on the HBP Collaboratory using the elephant framework. In: Neuroinformatics 2018, p. P19 (2018)
9. Friesen, B., et al.: In situ and in-transit analysis of cosmological simulations. Comput. Astrophys. Cosmol. **3**(1), 4 (2016)
10. Galindo, S.E., Toharia, P., Robles, O.D., Pastor, L.: ViSimpl: multi-view visual analysis of brain simulation data. Front. Neuroinform. **10**, 44 (2016)
11. Gewaltig, M.O., Diesmann, M.: Nest (neural simulation tool). Scholarpedia **2**(4), 1430 (2007)
12. Klijn, W., Diaz-Pier, S., Morrison, A., Peyser, A.: Staged deployment of interactive multi-application HPC workflows. arXiv preprint arXiv:1907.12275 (2019)
13. Nowke, C., et al.: Toward rigorous parameterization of underconstrained neural network models through interactive visualization and steering of connectivity generation. Front. Neuroinform. **12**, 32 (2018)
14. Oehrl, S., et al.: Streaming live neuronal simulation data into visualization and analysis. In: Yokota, R., Weiland, M., Shalf, J., Alam, S. (eds.) ISC High Performance 2018. LNCS, vol. 11203, pp. 258–272. Springer, Cham (2018). https://doi.org/10.1007/978-3-030-02465-9_18
15. Parker, D.: Complexities and uncertainties of neuronal network function. Philos. Trans. R. Soc. B Biol. Sci. **361**(1465), 81–99 (2006)
16. Sanz Leon, P., et al.: The virtual brain: a simulator of primate brain network dynamics. Front. Neuroinform. **7**, 10 (2013)
17. Senk, J., Carde, C., Hagen, E., Kuhlen, T.W., Diesmann, M., Weyers, B.: Viola-a multi-purpose and web-based visualization tool for neuronal-network simulation output. Front. Neuroinform. **12**, 75 (2018)
18. Sontheimer, K.: In transit coupling of neuroscientific simulation and analysis on high performance computing systems. Master's thesis, Aachen University of Applied Sciences (2019)
19. Spreizer, S., Senk, J., Rotter, S., Diesmann, M., Weyers, B.: Nest desktop, an educational application for neuroscience. eNeuro **8**(6) (2021)
20. Whitlock, B., Favre, J.M., Meredith, J.S.: Parallel in situ coupling of simulation with a fully featured visualization system. In: Proceedings of the 11th Eurographics Conference on Parallel Graphics and Visualization, pp. 101–109. EGPGV 2011, Eurographics Association, Goslar, DEU (2011)

The Need for Pervasive In Situ Analysis and Visualization (P-ISAV)

David Pugmire[1]([✉]), Jian Huang[2], Kenneth Moreland[1], and Scott Klasky[1]

[1] Oak Ridge National Laboratory, Oak Ridge, TN 37831, USA
{pugmire,morelandkd,klasky}@ornl.gov
[2] University of Tennessee, Knoxville, TN 37996, USA
huangj@utk.edu

Abstract. A major direction for *big science* is the coupling of HPC, experimental and observational facilities into computing ecosystems. These ecosystems will provide unprecedented tools for scientific inquiry. At the same time, these systems, which are complex, distributed and heterogeneous, will be a significant challenge for the visualization tools of today. In this position paper, we present our thoughts and key properties on a fundamental requirement of future solutions: pervasive in situ visualization (P-ISAV).

Keywords: Scientific visualization · In situ visualization

1 Introduction

In situ analysis and visualization (ISAV) emerged as a core research area since the advent of petascale and exascale computing. Over the past decade, in situ visualization has become a vibrant area with considerable progress that challenges previous assumptions of system design in many ways. Building upon such a foundation, we believe it is time to consider pervasive in situ analysis and visualization (P-ISAV) as a logical and pressing next step due to the following trends.

Sensor and computing technology innovations are only accelerating. There is a pervasive need for experimental, observational and computational facilities to provide more powerful tools to support groundbreaking scientific inquiry. To this end, efforts to combine these scientific facilities into an efficient ecosystem will greatly expand the capabilities for scientific inquiry and discovery.

Simultaneously, this direction will also continue the trend for increasing volume, velocity and variety of data. In such a world, analysis and visualization will become an even more important tool for scientists to extract understanding. The illustration in Fig. 1 describes the complexity of a distributed computing ecosystem for fusion scientists. Teams and resources are distributed around the world. HPC simulations are used to prepare for and to steer experiments. Edge computing is used to process data generated from experiment. In all places, in situ processing is required to meet hard time constraints.

© Springer Nature Switzerland AG 2022
H. Anzt et al. (Eds.): ISC High Performance 2022 Workshops, LNCS 13387, pp. 306–316, 2022.
https://doi.org/10.1007/978-3-031-23220-6_21

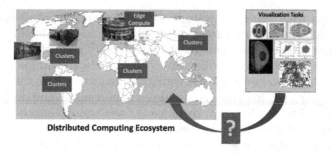

Fig. 1. An illustration on the complexity of efficient visualization in a distributed computing ecosystem. Teams of scientists need a variety of visualizations in order to understand and steer scientific campaigns. Efficiently running these tasks is a challenge and requires a balance among algorithms, concurrency, resource allocations as well as compute and network capabilities.

Specifically, computing resources across the world are used for analysis and visualization of the generated data. These teams can be very large and distributed throughout the world. Individual team members are interested in particular areas, while the lead scientists need to understand the overall state. Ensuring that the right analysis and visualizations of this streaming data are available to scientists in a timely manner is critical for successful science at this scale.

A new class of opportunities, such as this example from fusion science, are becoming common in all areas of science. But the complexity of these environments will bring significant challenges to gaining understanding from the data, and making timely decisions during these scientific campaigns is critical. Simulations need to be monitored to ensure they are running as planned and to do steering. During and between experiments, simulations and digital twins, simulated counterparts to real processes, will be run to help understand the data and to plan adjustments to experimental settings. Timely decision making in such a complex environment will require new modes of collaboration and increased efficiency among scientists. The scientific community needs tools that foster increased collaboration and sharing of analyses of data and that provide efficient ways to handle a wider variety of data, at higher velocity and in larger volumes.

In such a setting, in situ processing will have to become pervasive, especially to grow beyond the current confines of HPC, where in situ processing will exist on HPC, on the edge, and all points in between.

From this respect, even though in situ visualization has been an active area of research, production tools that are efficient and easily deployed across such complex environments are lacking. At present, most in situ visualizations tend to be problem specific, difficult to generalize and require collaborations between application and computer scientists with at least some bespoke software (such as adapters). Over the years there has been research that addresses some of these issues, but issues still remain. One of the primary findings identified in recent DOE workshop reports [21] is the need to overcome challenges that block in situ processing from being pervasive. For visualization, the challenge is driven by the cost differences between algorithm selection, in situ placement strategy, data complexity, timeliness requirements, adaptability and heterogeneous architectures (from HPC to edge). Wrong choices for in situ algorithms or placement can have dramatic consequences. Allocating too many resources will be wasteful, whereas allocating too few can lead to missed opportunities and delayed results. Scientific campaigns can be highly dynamic — few resources may be needed until something interesting begins to happen and then a large amount of resources are needed for visualization. Scientific teams are distributed and need visualizations at different times and places. At times, a human in the loop is needed, which may have unique resource requirements. Depending on timeliness and accuracy requirements, some tasks must be computed close to the data source, while others can be performed at different points along the data lifecycle. Analyses and visualizations need to be shared in real time so that teams can understand what is going on and communicate with the lead scientists. During the course of a scientific campaign, priorities may change requiring visualizations to be activated, deactivated, or become a lower priority.

P-ISAV solutions to this changing landscape will require visualization and analysis tools to be much more collaborative and shareable. A high degree of composability is needed so that scientists can easily construct visualization tasks and pipelines for *their* tool chains and workflows. Elasticity is critical, so that tasks can efficiently scale up or down to meet the timeliness requirements on the given data on available resources.

In this position paper, we advocate the importance of pervasive in situ by providing visualization tools that are equipped for the future needs of scientific inquiry. In Sect. 2 we provide a brief overview of related works. In Sect. 3 we describe the details and properties that next generation tools should have and offer suggested research directions. Finally, in Sect. 4 we discuss future directions for our position.

2   Related Work

In situ visualization has been an active and fruitful area of research. In situ processing is a rich space comprising numerous variations [5], but techniques are often grouped into three broad catagories: in-line (synchronous), in-transit (asynchronous), and hybrid. A major focus of in-line in situ has been on instrumenting a simulation code so that visualization tools can process data as they are produced. Libsim [30] and Catalyst [1] can be used to instrument a code so that VisIt and Paraview, respectively, can used for synchronous in situ visualization. Tools such as EPIC [8], Freeprocessing [9] and ICARUS [26] support an in transit model where the data producer and visualization run on separate resources. SENSEI [2] and Ascent [16] use instrumentation to support both in-line and in-transit models. The in-transit functionality in both of these is provided using the ADIOS [10] middle-ware library. Bauer et al. [3] provide a more detailed overview of contemporary in situ solutions.

The rapid growth of heterogeneous compute nodes, coupled with in situ processing, highlighted the need for portability across different architectures. VTK-m [20] provides a portability layer for visualization algorithms. These efforts have demonstrated the benefits of portable algorithm performance across a wide variety of architectures [19].

Methods for interpretation of data streams are required for data producers and data consumers to communicate, which has led to investigation of data models and schemas. Ascent and recent versions of ParaView Catalyst use the capabilities of BluePrint [17], whereas SENSEI and VisIt LibSim rely on the Visualization Toolkit (VTK) data model. VizSchema [28] and later Fides [23] provides an interpretation layer on top of ADIOS for streaming and file-based data.

3   Our Position

Large scale science will continue to challenge current capabilities for the foreseeable future. The data problem will persist as the volumes and velocities will continue to grow. The challenges of data variety will increase as simulations, experiments and observational facilities are coupled together as computational ecosystems. These ecosystems will be distributed, heterogeneous and require complex workflows and large teams of scientists to successfully operate. In such environments, significant challenges exist in minimizing the time required to make important decisions, making significantly more collaboration and efficiency paramount.

This new frontier requires cross cutting collaboration from experimental, observational, computational, computer and data scientists. In terms of complexity, the variety of high-value and high volume data sources is exploding. Be it simulation, experiment or observation, these data come with distinctive characteristics. The need to make high consequence decisions based on co-analyses of many disparate sources of data presents a unique challenge. The complexity of this challenge has significantly increased because of the rapidly growing problem space.

The use of simulations and digital twins often requires expensive and limited resources to make collaborative discoveries. However, the currently available tool chains are often too brittle to quickly adapt to rapidly changing needs, especially when data comes in different forms and from many sources. Typically, adaptation of available tool chains requires deep collaborations with visualization scientists. Due to resource constraints, these deep collaborations are often not possible. As a result, domain scientists do not feel empowered to customize their visualization tools, and even visualization researchers feel that it is cumbersome to keep up with spontaneous domain needs.

Solutions to these challenges are dependent on P-ISAV. Post hoc analysis and visualization will always be an important component in scientific discovery, but it can be viewed as a solved problem. Solutions to these coming challenges will require scientists to perform analysis and visualization on complex, remote streaming data and share their results without worrying about the data sources. Data access must be as easy, transparent and pervasive as post hoc methods. In other words, in situ visualization must become pervasive.

Key properties of P-ISAV are the following: agility, elasticity and intelligence, which are discussed below.

Agility. Next-generation tools for scientific insight will be composed from a large variety of production grade, highly scalable building blocks, many of which already exist. These tools need to be easily assembled and used by people with a wide range of specialties, including the lead scientist, domain scientists, post-docs, graduate students and visualization experts. These tools need to be able to leverage the range of distributed resources, from edge to HPC, in a scalable and shareable manner. These tools must be portable and easily integrated into a wide range of platforms (e.g., digital notebooks, web, etc.), and be easily modified and rerun during project meetings and conference calls. Central to this is the need for schemas and data models to provide the semantics of the underlying data and to allow connectivity between tasks. It should be easy to discover, use, integrate and share analysis and visualization tools. Most important, these tools must be built upon the foundation of P-ISAV. That is, there cannot be restrictions on where and when tools are run, on the source of input data, or the destination of the output data. Using these highly specific and individually composed tools, teams of scientists can make faster discoveries and more confident decisions in any projects that depend on precious facility resources.

Elasticity. While elasticity and portability started as a cloud computing method, the concepts are fundamental to meeting the time, complexity and adaptability challenges to scientific discovery. Resources will always be shared, and visualization tasks must provide on-demand or near real-time availability. Visualization tasks need to be able to appropriately scale across the amount, type and connectivity of resources, as well as consider the type and amount of data, the requirements for accuracy, interactivity and timeliness so that decisions can be made. Simply making visualization algorithms run on a different amount of computing resources is far from enough. P-ISAV algorithms need to be cost-aware and adaptive to optimally use computing resources with different levels of availability. Cost models can guide users to optimize resource configurations and data requirements that meet their time requirements with minimum resources. Finally, to be pervasive in these environments, resilience to network speeds and availability is required. When needed, tasks should be able to seamlessly handle variability in network availability and speeds.

Intelligence. When the amount, speed and variety of data are greater than the available computing and cognitive resources, it is natural for scientists to rely on their experience and intuition. However, in a complex computing ecosystem, which requires larger teams, more diverse expertise and greater financial costs, intuition is far from sufficient. The P-ISAV paradigm of composable applications enables each scientist to focus on their particular part of the problem and tailor visualization and analysis to their personal needs and requirements. These composed applications can be further composed into summary views that can help lead scientists to make timely decisions. In so doing, instead of relying on general purpose tools provided by the visualization community, scientists can easily compose tools that are more lightweight and customized for their particular needs. Additionally, by collecting and studying these composable apps, there is immense opportunity to leverage AI to better understand how scientists use analysis and visualization. The composition of visualization tasks, the data they consume, when and how they are used and who is using them can help the visualization community understand how to provide better tools and assist scientists in composing applications that fit their exact needs. AI can help make decisions on *which variables* to visualize, *how* they can be visualized most efficiently, and *which resource* is available and appropriate for the task.

In our view, a powerful paradigm that can be used as a foundation to addressing these P-ISAV challenges is the service-oriented architectures (SOA) [18]. At a high level, SOA is characterized by a self-contained black box that provides a well-defined set of features for users. SOA takes several forms, including infrastructure as a service (IaaS) [4], software as a service (SaaS) [11], and microservices [7]. Cloud computing is the most common example of IaaS in which costs are controlled by dynamically allocating resources in response to changing user requirements. SaaS is characterized by delivering a capability using a thin client or ergonomic application programming interface. Scalability for SaaS is provided by different types of back-end implementations that are appropriately sized. Microservices are small, independently deployable executables with a distinct goal. Groups of microservices can be orchestrated to perform more complex tasks.

The "as a Service (aaS)" paradigm has been explored in the context of scientific visualization already. A set of abstractions for using this paradigm for visualization has recently been published [22]. Tapestry is a system that can deliver interactive volume renderings of large-scale scientific simulation into the web browser on any device, including laptops, smart phones, and Microsoft Hololens [24,25]. It uses Amazon AWS where the costs for usage are very small. For another example, a group of small AWS instances can be organized into a swarm to provide interactive comparative visualization of terabyte scale turbulent flows [12] from NOAA/NCEP's modeled vs. actual observation data repository [27], where the total cost of the AWS instances are also very low. In both cases, the system can elastically scale up to support 20–100 concurrent users.

Using traditional approaches, these sophisticated visualization functionalities can be expensive to integrate into domain science codes, both in terms of man hours and runtime computing overheads. However, in the model of visualization as a service (VaaS), these costs are minuscule, thereby making P-ISAV possible.

Overall, VaaS would be an application of the principles from the SOA paradigm to provide flexible analysis and visualization for simulation, experimental and observational science. One key principle in the SOA paradigm is the separation between functionality and implementation. This principle is key to supporting both agility and elasticity properties discussed above, and underlies the ability to compose building blocks into intelligent visualization workflows.

3.1   Suggested Research Directions

In this subsection we identify four significant challenges (**CH1-4**) to pervasive in situ visualization and suggest research questions (**RQ1-4**) to provide solutions. The illustration of how each of the research questions addresses each challenge is shown in Fig. 2 and described below.

Research Challenges. In our view, there are four fundamental challenges that must be overcome to provide the type of P-ISAV we envision, which are listed below:

CH1: Difficulty in data ingestion across heterogeneous sources
CH2: Integration, use, and support costs of in-situ frameworks
CH3: Timely execution of visualization and efficient use of resources
CH4: Monolithic systems that are difficult to generalize, adapt and repurpose

First, **CH1**, getting data into the in-situ visualization tools can be a significant challenge. Interfacing with the many data sources, for which the data layouts, data types, and methods for data access can vary dramatically, can be a show stopper for in-situ visualization. This makes the creation of general-purpose, in-situ visualization tools challenging. Second, **CH2**, the cost for adopting an in-situ framework can be high, can have steep learning curves, and can often require direct collaboration with visualization experts. Current solutions require instrumentation that results in a tight coupling of simulation and visualization codes and limits the tools that can be used by scientists for in-situ visualization. Because of these problems, in-situ visualization *is not even possible* on pieces of a scientific workflow (both producers and consumers) that have not been instrumented beforehand. This limits the flexibility for scientists to investigate and probe unanticipated events during a simulation and imposes a requirement that scientists foresee every situation that may require in-situ visualization and then instrument, maintain, and support all of the code. Third,

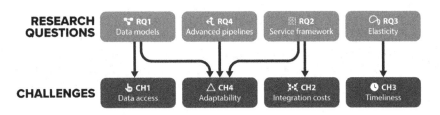

Fig. 2. Illustration of how the four research questions will address each of the challenges.

CH3, timely in-situ visualization results are imperative for scientists to obtain results within an actionable time frame. Inefficiencies can cause the simulation to block, thereby wasting costly resources or causing a loss of required results. In a post-hoc use case, if a visualization is taking too long, then the task can be killed and restarted with additional resources, or modified parameters can be used to reduce the time required to complete. Finally, **CH4**, visualization tools must be easy to generalize, adapt, and repurpose. Visualization tools must be interoperable with other visualization tools, workflow systems, and modes of interaction. Tools with specific capabilities should be combinable in different ways to solve different problems, be controllable by different workflow systems, be adaptable at both setup and run time, and operate on data from a spectrum of data sources.

Research Questions. To address these challenges, we advocate for fundamental research to address the following questions.

RQ1: What are the right modes of access and data models for in situ visualization?

RQ2: What are the required properties for a visualization service?

RQ3: How can services elastically scale at runtime?

RQ4: What are the required types of visualization pipelines needed for interoperability?

Our first question (**RQ1**) is to address the data access challenge described in **CH1**. In order to be pervasive, in situ data access needs to be as easy and straightforward as the post-hoc paradigm. The post-hoc paradigm is ubiquitous because it is simple and uses a standard API. With post-hoc, the producer and consumer are de-coupled and rely on files on disk to communicate. Similarly, in situ visualization must be de-coupled from data producers in order to be pervasive, and the I/O approach of post-hoc tools is a good metaphor to follow. Key to this will be identifying the right data models that can provide the semantics to map (ideally using zero-copy) the underlying diversity of data layout, the type, and the access mode onto structures that can be used by visualization algorithms. Additionally, these models can also be used to determine if services can be chained together to form more complex operations. In addition to addressing the data access challenge, data models will also enable service connectivity that will increase the adaptability of in-situ visualization (**CH4**).

A second research question (**RQ2**) will be to understand the properties required for a visualization task to have the interoperability and ease of use needed for deployment in an SOA environment (**CH4**). Services need to be discover-able, easy to create and deploy. Services also need to provide portability across a variety of platforms, including HPC centers, edge computing and clouds. An additional property, that is key, is that the service must not rely on integration with other codes (**CH2**).

Third (**RQ3**), visualization services needs to elastically scale in response to dynamic changes in data and resource availability (**CH3**). Elastic scaling enables a visualization service to make efficient use of resources as the visualization workload will often vary during the course of its use [6,29]. Cost models are needed that can accurately predict the time and cost to perform a visualization task on a given type of data [13–15]. Cost models and elasticity also allows workflow systems to schedule, allocate and run visualizations in the course of a scientific campaign. And finally, and most important, elasticity allows in situ visualization to provide timely results needed by scientists, and in a manner that does not throttle the simulation.

Finally, advanced hybrid visualization pipelines (**RQ4**) are needed to provide services with the flexibility needed for different modes of execution. In situ visualization will require both data- and demand-driven pipelines, also known as push and pull pipelines respectively. Support for both demand- and data-driven pipelines will reduce the development costs for using in-situ visualization (**CH2**) and provide significant increases to the generality and flexibility of in-situ visualization (**CH4**).

4   Conclusion and Future Directions

Things are radically changing. The research in in situ has been important, but it must be pervasive — that is, people shouldn't have to think about it.

The landscape for scientific inquiry is quickly and radically changing. Computing ecosystems that couple HPC, experiment and observational facilities will become powerful tools for scientific inquiry. While the factors that challenge HPC in situ visualization will continue, the complexity, heterogeneity and distributed nature of these environments, together with new types, greater volumes and velocities of data are new and daunting challenges. This will require P-ISAV, in situ visualization that can seamlessly span the diversity and locations of computing environments, data types, workflows and tool chains. The same rigid, customized, and closely collaborative model of in situ visualization is unlikely to be sustainable in a pervasive data world.

However, the need for in situ visualization is the same. After all, in situ literally means "in the original place". When the producer of big data is the HPC platforms, in situ needs to be on leadership class platforms. When the producer of big data is distributed on experimental or observational platforms, in situ needs to include and accommodate those scenarios as well.

Thankfully, many of the past successes have produced building blocks that can be leveraged by future research towards P-ISAV. In this context, agility, elasticity, and intelligence are new but key tenets of future in situ visualization. To this end, in situ visualization research will become even more exciting and inclusive than ever before.

References

1. Ayachit, U., et al.: Paraview catalyst: enabling in situ data analysis and visualization. In: Proceedings of the First Workshop on In Situ Infrastructures for Enabling Extreme-Scale Analysis and Visualization, pp. 25–29. ACM (2015)
2. Ayachit, U., et al.: Performance analysis, design considerations, and applications of extreme-scale in situ infrastructures. In: ACM/IEEE International Conference for High Performance Computing, Networking, Storage and Analysis (SC16). Salt Lake City, UT, USA, November 2016. https://doi.org/10.1109/SC.2016.78, LBNL-1007264
3. Bauer, A., et al.: In situ methods, infrastructures, and applications on high performance computing platforms. In: Computer Graphics Forum, vol. 35, pp. 577–597. Wiley Online Library (2016)
4. CDW: Infrastructure as a service, November 2018. https://webobjects.cdw.com/webobjects/media/pdf/Solutions/cloud-computing/Cloud-IaaS.pdf
5. Childs, H., et al.: A terminology for in situ visualization and analysis systems. Int. J. High Perform. Comput. Appl. **34**(6), 676–691 (2020)
6. Dorier, M., Yildiz, O., Peterka, T., Ross, R.: The challenges of elastic in situ analysis and visualization. In: Proceedings of the Workshop on In Situ Infrastructures for Enabling Extreme-Scale Analysis and Visualization, pp. 23–28 (2019)
7. Dragoni, N., et al.: Microservices: yesterday, today, and tomorrow. CoRR abs/1606.04036 (2016). https://arxiv.org/abs/1606.04036
8. Duque, E.P., et al.: Epic-an extract plug-in components toolkit for in situ data extracts architecture. In: 22nd AIAA Computational Fluid Dynamics Conference, p. 3410 (2015)
9. Fogal, T., et al.: Freeprocessing: transparent in situ visualization via data interception. In: Eurographics Symposium on Parallel Graphics and Visualization: EG PGV, vol. 2014, p. 49. NIH Public Access (2014)
10. Godoy, W., et al.: ADIOS 2: the adaptable input output system. a framework for high-performance data management. SoftwareX **12**, 100561 (2020). https://doi.org/10.1016/j.softx.2020.100561
11. Hang, H., Dibie, O.: Software as a service. https://www.cs.colorado.edu/~kena/classes/5828/s12/presentation-materials/dibieogheneovohanghaojie.pdf
12. Hobson, T., et al.: Interactive visualization of large turbulent flow as a cloud service. IEEE Trans. Cloud Comput. 1 (2021)
13. Kress, J., et al.: Comparing the efficiency of in situ visualization paradigms at scale. In: Weiland, M., Juckeland, G., Trinitis, C., Sadayappan, P. (eds.) ISC High Performance 2019. LNCS, vol. 11501, pp. 99–117. Springer, Cham (2019). https://doi.org/10.1007/978-3-030-20656-7_6
14. Kress, J., et al.: Opportunities for cost savings with in-transit visualization. In: ISC High Performance 2020. ISC (2020)
15. Larsen, M., et al.: Performance modeling of in situ rendering. In: SC 2016: Proceedings of the International Conference for High Performance Computing, Networking, Storage and Analysis, pp. 276–287. IEEE (2016)
16. Larsen, M., et al.: The ALPINE in situ infrastructure: ascending from the ashes of strawman. In: Proceedings of the In Situ Infrastructures on Enabling Extreme-Scale Analysis and Visualization, pp. 42–46. ACM (2017)
17. Lawrence Livermore National Laboratory: Blueprint. https://llnl-conduit.readthedocs.io/en/latest/blueprint.html. Accessed 6 Sep 2020

18. Lian, M.: Introduction to service oriented architecture, March 2012. https://www.cs.colorado.edu/~kena/classes/5828/s12/presentation-materials/lianming.pdf

19. Moreland, K., et al.: Minimizing development costs for efficient many-core visualization using MCD^3. Parallel Comput. **108**, 102834 (2021)

20. Moreland, K., et al.: VTK-m: accelerating the visualization toolkit for massively threaded architectures. IEEE Comput. Graph. Appl. **36**(3), 48–58 (2016)

21. Peterka, T., et al.: ASCR workshop on in situ data management: enabling scientific discovery from diverse data sources. Technical report, U.S. DOE ASCR, February 2019. https://doi.org/10.2172/1493245

22. Pugmire, D., et al.: Visualization as a service for scientific data. In: Smoky Mountains Computational Sciences and Engineering Conference, pp. 157–174. Kingsport, TN, August 2020

23. Pugmire, D., et al.: Fides: a general purpose data model library for streaming data. In: Jagode, H., Anzt, H., Ltaief, H., Luszczek, P. (eds.) ISC High Performance 2021. LNCS, vol. 12761, pp. 495–507. Springer, Cham (2021). https://doi.org/10.1007/978-3-030-90539-2_34

24. Raji, M., et al.: Scalable web-embedded volume rendering. In: Proceedings of the IEEE Symposium on Large Data Analysis and Visualization (LDAV), pp. 45–54, October 2017. https://doi.org/10.1109/LDAV.2017.8231850

25. Raji, M., et al.: Scientific visualization as a microservice. IEEE Trans. Vis. Comput. Graph. **26**(4), 1760–1774 (2020)

26. Rivi, M., et al.: In-situ visualization: State-of-the-art and some use cases. PRACE White Paper; PRACE: Brussels, Belgium (2012)

27. Saha, S., et al.: NCEP Climate Forecast System Version 2 (CFSv2) 6-Hourly Products (2011). https://doi.org/10.5065/D61C1TXF

28. Tchoua, R., et al.: Adios visualization schema: a first step towards improving interdisciplinary collaboration in high performance computing. In: eScience (eScience), 2013 IEEE 9th International Conference on eScience, pp. 27–34. IEEE (2013)

29. Wang, Z., Dorier, M., Subedi, P., Davis, P.E., Parashar, M.: An adaptive elasticity policy for staging based in-situ processing. In: 2021 IEEE Workshop on Workflows in Support of Large-Scale Science (WORKS), pp. 33–41. IEEE (2021)

30. Whitlock, B., et al.: Parallel in situ coupling of simulation with a fully featured visualization system. In: Eurographics Symposium on Parallel Graphics and Visualization. The Eurographics Association (2011). https://doi.org/10.2312/EGPGV/EGPGV11/101-109

Interactive Visualization of Large-Scale Oil and Gas Reservoir Simulation Models

Pavel Novikov[1]([✉]) [iD], Denis Sabitov[1] [iD], Nikita Bukhanov[1] [iD], Marwan Charara[1] [iD], Michel Cancelliere[2] [iD], Fahad Rashed[2] [iD], and Abdulaziz Baiz[2] [iD]

[1] Aramco Research Center - Moscow, Aramco Innovations LLC, Leninskiye Gory 1, bld 75-B, 119234 Moscow, Russia
pavel.novikov@aramcoinnovations.com
[2] Saudi Aramco, Dhahran, Saudi Arabia

Abstract. Accurate simulation of the processes in oil and gas reservoirs requires a detailed description of the geological and physical structure of the reservoir that leads to models containing billions of cells. Conventional approaches to the visualization of such large models are slow-going during the interactive processing of the data. This study is dedicated to the development of parallel algorithms suitable for interactive visualization of large-scale reservoir 3D models based on the preselection of data needed for constructing the model representation from the unstructured mesh. The key component of this workflow is the efficient slicing algorithm of the large mesh. We present the parallel implementation of a slicing algorithm for MPI CPU and multi-GPU computational systems in a form of a plugin program extension for an open-source software ParaView. We tested the performance of (1) our algorithm, (2) an existing commercial reservoir simulation software, and (3) the built-in tool for model slicing of ParaView. Our approach demonstrates an almost interactive visualization of the reservoir model with 1.9 billion cells of unstructured mesh with a slice viewing delay of 1.8 s using the GPU algorithm implementation.

Keywords: High performance visualization · Reservoir modeling · Unstructured mesh · 3D model slicing · GPU

1 Introduction

Optimization of the oil and gas fields development includes accumulating and processing a large amount of static and dynamic data. Together with the long history of measurements, it leads to a more accurate and detailed description of a reservoir's geological and physical structure. From a modeling perspective, this process produces large grid models that may contain billions and even trillions of cells. Designing efficient algorithms to tackle such large-scale models is a challenge in the recent decade [1]. The needs of the end-user include the ability to simulate the models in practical times together with the conventional methods of processing the results, including the visualization of the fields obtained as a solution during/after simulating the processes inside the reservoir. To

H. Anzt et al. (Eds.): ISC High Performance 2022 Workshops, LNCS 13387, pp. 317–323, 2022.
https://doi.org/10.1007/978-3-031-23220-6_22

achieve the interactive visualization speed, it is necessary to use both the advanced processing algorithms for large data sets and the low-level architecture features of modern HPC systems.

The current work is dedicated to the development of parallel algorithms for the loading and visualization of a large reservoir 3D model based on fast preselection of data subset that is needed to visualize at the current moment from the whole dataset. The visible part of a spatial object is a surface, and the fast and efficient construction of the surfaces from the meshed reservoir is the fundamental operation in the visualization of the objects. Slicing of reservoir models is a valuable operation in the visual analysis of simulated fields. Detailed reservoir models use a lot of local grid refinements that lead to unstructured meshes. For the latter, slicing with an arbitrarily oriented plane is the most reasonable operation. The recent developments in fast slicing algorithms for large meshes are connected to additive manufacturing [2, 3], where the interest is mainly focused on the efficient slicing process of STL files or complicated CAD models by a large set of parallel planes. The performance of such slicing operations implemented in conventional visualization software is not sufficient to provide an interactive user interface that controls the position and orientation of slicing planes in the large-scale reservoir models. We present the parallel implementation of the slicing algorithm for MPI-multi-GPU computation systems. We also provide performance testing results for our algorithm, the existing commercial reservoir simulation software, and the built-in slicing tool of the specialized open-source visualization package ParaView. The fast slicing algorithm is one of the key components in the development not of only the interactive user interface but also the in situ visualization, allowing researchers to analyze the fluid flow through porous media during the computation process and make modifications to the model without restarting the whole simulation.

2   Visualization Workflow

Conventional algorithms for visualization utilize the entire information of the mesh and data fields to construct the image. The typical manipulation of the image such as rotation and zooming can be implemented effectively. However, the change of the timestep for time-dependent data series or investigation of the inner structure of the model by slicing the data in spatial dimensions becomes a more resource-consuming task. The situation gets worse when the size of the mesh grows from millions of cells (Mcell) to billions of cells (Bcell) coming in pieces from remote distributed machines. Each part of the visualization procedure should be optimized both in memory usage and computation demands to aim for the interactive analysis of collected data.

The visualization workflow for a large-scale reservoir model can be split into three steps. First, we need to load the data containing vertex coordinates, 3D cells, and the fields connected to the cells into RAM from the physical medium used for data storage. Second, we need to preprocess the loaded mesh and remove the cells not required to form the image. In the case of time-series data visualization, it makes sense to load only field values for selected cells. The last step is to render the prepared model representation to the screen.

During the second step, we need to choose potentially visible cells in the current geometric configuration selected by the user. For the simple case, it can be just the cells that form the external surface of the model. In the case of reservoir modeling, the exterior surface of the model is constant, and we can preselect corresponding cells once on the initial stage of mesh loading. We should be able to construct the slice of the model representing the inner reservoir structure at a user's request. The slice position can change many times during dynamic properties analysis. Therefore, the key part of the visualization workflow is efficient mesh slicing. We demonstrate the process of visible surface selection in Fig. 1.

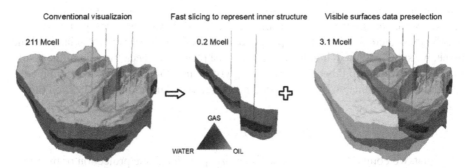

Fig. 1. The processing workflow of a large-scale reservoir model for efficient visualization. The initial 211 Mcell model (based on synthetic data) is used to construct a 2D slice (0.2 Mcell) and exterior surfaces. The final lightweight mesh used for rendering consists of only 3.1 Mcell.

We used the open-source ParaView visualization software [4] as a platform for implementing our visualization workflow. This platform offers the opportunity to extend its functionality by developing plugin programs. The flexible API interface allows the plugins to access the internal ParaView structures describing the mesh geometry and the information stored on the drive. The native parallel structure of ParaView provides the conventional MPI functions to control the process invocation and execution. The current implementation of our plugin codes written in Python programming language uses the MPI functions to load the data into ParaView in parallel and processes it to prepare the mesh of the slice. The rendering procedures are provided by internal ParaView functionality.

The first plugin extension for parallel loading and data preparation utilizes MPI functionality to split the job into several parts. Each MPI process analyzes the structure of the mesh and provides the grid partitioning procedure which divides the mesh into the number of parts equal to the requested number of MPI processes and loads into the memory only the data that is connected to its part. This procedure can be efficiently run in parallel owing to the availability of several disk drive read channels in modern computer hardware, and the speed of loading benefits from the number of drives in the system. The parallel loading procedure is important for interactive user experience as it allows to reduce the amount of time needed for loading the mesh and properties from tens of minutes to tens of seconds for reservoir models with Bcell-sized unstructured meshes. After the parallel loading procedure, each MPI process stores in memory the independent piece of the initial grid and the field data which do not intersect with the neighbor processes, jointly representing the full reservoir model. These model parts feed into another plugin program for parallel slicing procedures.

The second plugin extension program applies to the prepared data the vectorized version of a slicing algorithm. It uses the description of a slicing plane as a unit normal vector $\vec{n}_{3\times1}$ and a point on a plane $\vec{c}_{1\times3}$, which are controlled in a graphical user interface. As an input, each MPI instance of the slicing algorithm has an array of the coordinates of N mesh vertices $P_{N\times3}$, the information of the cell topology which describes the unstructured 3D grid, and corresponding field data. Each plane in three-dimensional space splits the space into two subspaces [5]. To construct the slice, we need to select the cells which are intersected by the plane. These cells have at least one pair of vertices which are located at different subspaces. To find the location of vertices relative to the plane, we substitute them into the equation of the plane and check the sign of the result. In the vectorized form this operation can be written in two steps. First, we compute the projection of coordinates $P_{N\times3}$ on a unit normal to the plane as a multiplication of two matrices:

$$\vec{v}_{N\times1} = P_{N\times3} \cdot \vec{n}_{3\times1} \tag{1}$$

After that, we compute the scalar $a = \vec{c}_{1\times3} \cdot \vec{n}_{3\times1}$, which is the projection of the given point $\vec{c}_{1\times3}$ on a slicing plane to the unit normal, and get the sign of the expression $(v_i - a)$ for each i, which shows us the position of a vertex in one of two subspaces. After that, we can obtain the sum of the vertex signs for each cell in the array and select the cells where the absolute value of this sum differs from the number of vertices. This set of cells is the sought for the goal. At the last step, a selected subset of cells can be sliced by the same plane using existing algorithms (e.g., built-in ParaView's filter "Slice with plane"). Because of the small cell amount connected to the slice, the duration of this last step is negligible compared with the previous operation.

All the operations for the construction of the slice can be performed in vectorized form. We use the Python package Numpy to manipulate vectorized functions for the CPU version of the slicing algorithm, and the Cupy package to address the GPU computations in the accelerated implementation of the slicer.

3 Performance Testing

We provide the comparison of the efficiency of in-house CPU and GPU-based codes for visualization with the original ParaView 5.9.1 slicing algorithm "Slice with Plane" (PV-swp) and the commercially available software for reservoir modeling (CS). A range of realistic data models with an unstructured 2.5D geometry grid was prepared in binary format for testing purposes. The size of the testing grids varied from 101 Mcell to 1.9 Bcell. The grid geometry together with the scalar field properties was copied from the open Johansen dataset [6]. The original size of the grid was $149 \times 189 \times 16$ cells. We applied several global grid refinement steps to obtain the range of models with different grid sizes and changed the grid storage format to an unstructured one. The porosity property from the data set was used to perform the visualization and slicing procedures. An overview of one of the refined Johansen models obtained by our slicing algorithm is shown in Fig. 2.

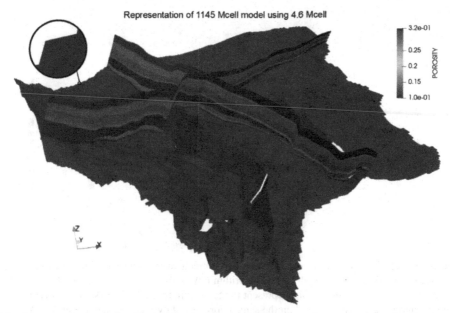

Fig. 2. An example of visualization for the large-scaled Johansen data set is represented by three slices. The grid size is 1145 million cells in total. The slices produced by the in-house algorithm are located above the underlying surface and represent the values of porosity in the input model. The size of the slices with the underlying surface is 4.6 million cells.

The tests were provided in two stages. In the first stage, we measured the performance of our in-house CPU code, PV-swp slicer, and the CS visualization algorithms on a set of models with increasing mesh size. The metric of performance was the time from the start of the slicing procedure to the rendered picture appearing on the screen normalized by the same parameter for PV-swp slicer applied to the testing model with 211 Mcell. Due to the limitations of the commercial package, these tests were provided on OS Windows-based workstation. It has two 16-core 3.6 GHz CPUs, 128 GB DDR4 RAM, 256 GB NVME solid-state drive, and one GPU card with 16 GB onboard memory which was used only for rendering purposes. The CS visualization algorithm successfully loaded and processed the meshes with sizes from 101 to 309 Mcells. To load and process the large-scale models, we switched to OS Linux-based workstation with one 64-core CPU, 512 GB DDR4 RAM, 1.92 TB NVME solid-state drive, and 4 GPUs with 80 GB onboard memory each. We used this system to measure the performance of CPU and GPU versions of our in-house code and PV-swp slicer on models with the size of up to 1.9 Bcells. We compute two models with the size of 211 and 309 Mcells both on the first and the second machine to show the performance ratio of two hardware platforms for the same codes. We combine the results from two test stages in Fig. 3.

The memory usage of the original ParaView slicing algorithm and our in-house codes is illustrated in Fig. 4. The ParaView slicer used only the CPU to provide the computations, and the excessive memory usage of this algorithm allowed to process the models up to 620 Mcells in size.

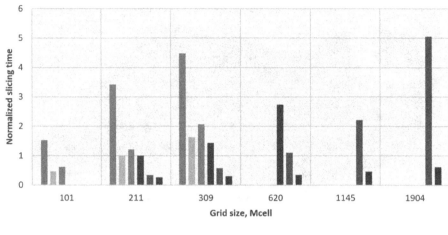

■ CS (win) ■ PV-swp (win) ■ In-house CPU (win) ■ PV-swp (lin) ■ In-house CPU (lin) ■ In-house GPU (lin)

Fig. 3. The results of the performance testing for commercial reservoir modeling software (CS), the original ParaView "Slice with Plane" algorithm (PV-swp), and our in-house CPU and GPU slicing algorithms. Bars on the plot represent the time from the start of the slicing procedure to the rendered picture that appeared on the screen normalized by the same parameter for PV-swp for 211 Mcell model. The hardware platforms are marked here as (win) and (lin) for the Windows and Linux-based systems respectively and described in the text.

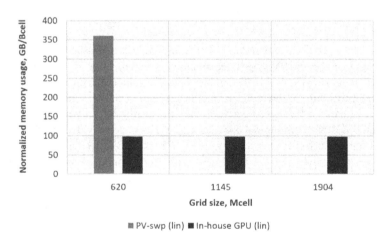

■ PV-swp (lin) ■ In-house GPU (lin)

Fig. 4. The memory usage for the original ParaView slice algorithm (PV-swp) and our in-house GPU code on a Linux machine for large-scale models normalized by the mesh size. The ParaView slicing algorithm successfully works only with the model up to 620 Mcells on the Linux-based workstation described in the text.

4 Discussion

The tested algorithms show almost linear scalability of slicing speed versus the model size but utilize the hardware resources with different efficiency. The self-implemented simple slicing algorithm allows us to control both the organization of computations and memory usage, making the performance comparable with an HPC application. The time to get a slice from the 1.9 Bcell unstructured mesh is 15.1 s for the CPU version of the algorithm. The GPU implementation reduces this delay to 1.8 s. Future work in this direction lies in the development and implementation of more sophisticated geometric algorithms, thus making the slicing faster for a user on a large-scale model.

Based on demonstrated performance, the presented approach for required data preselection before generating an unstructured mesh slice can be considered in the development of advanced visualization software.

5 Conclusions

We presented the algorithm for unstructured mesh slicing with an arbitrary plane and its implementation for MPI CPU and multi-GPU platforms. This algorithm is a key component of our visualization workflow for reservoir models. The efficiency of the algorithm was demonstrated based on a comparison with commercially available software and built-in tools of specialized open-source visualization software. The scalability of our algorithm implementation allows reaching the interactive speed of visualization for large-scale reservoir models. Performance tests showed a delay in construction and view of a new slice of 1.8 s for a 1.9 billion cell reservoir model based on unstructured mesh for the GPU version of the algorithm.

Acknowledgements. We are very grateful to our colleagues Tareq Shaalan, Tariq Qasim, Oleg Kovalevskiy, and Mustafa AlAli for productive discussions.

References

1. Dogru, A.H., et al.: New frontiers in large scale reservoir simulation. In: Society of Petroleum Engineers - SPE Reservoir Simulation Symposium 2011, vol. 2, pp. 1440–1451. (2011)
2. Ma, X., Lin, F., Yao, B.: Fast parallel algorithm for slicing STL based on pipeline. Chin. J. Mech. Eng. **29**(3), 549–555 (2016). https://doi.org/10.3901/CJME.2016.0309.028
3. Minetto, R., Volpato, N., Stolfi, J., Gregori, R.M.M.H., da Silva, M.V.G.: An optimal algorithm for 3D triangle mesh slicing. Comput. Aided Des. **92**, 1–10 (2017)
4. Ayachit, U.: The Paraview Guide: A Parallel Visualization Application. Kitware, Clifton Park (2015)
5. Ilyin, V.A., Poznyak, E.G.: Analytic Geometry [Russian]. 8th edn. Physmatlit (2017)
6. Eigestad, G.T., Dahle, H.K., Hellevang, B., Riis, F., Johansen, W.T.: The Johansen Data Set (2009). http://www.sintef.no/Projectweb/MatMoRA/Downloads/Johansen/. Accessed 25 Oct 2021

Cinema Transfer: A Containerized Visualization Workflow

Isaac Nealey[1]($\boxtimes$), Nicola Ferrier[2], Joseph Insley[2], Victor A. Mateevitsi[2], Michael E. Papka[2], and Silvio Rizzi[2]

[1] University of California-San Diego, La Jolla, CA, USA
`inealey@ucsd.edu`
[2] Argonne National Laboratory, Lemont, IL, USA

Abstract. We present a containerized workflow demonstrating in situ analysis of simulation data rendered by a ParaView/Catalyst adapter for the generic SENSEI in situ interface, then streamed to a remote site for visualization. We use Cinema, a database approach for navigating the metadata produced in situ. We developed a web socket tool, *cinema_transfer*, for transferring the generated cinema databases to a remote machine while the simulation is running. We evaluate the performance of this containerized workflow and identify bottlenecks for large scale runs, in addition to testing identical containers at different sites with differing hardware and Message Passing Interface (MPI) implementations.

Keywords: In situ visualization · Large-scale visualization · High performance computing

1 Introduction

In recent years, there has been an increasing gap between the floating point operations per second (FLOPs) and input/output (I/O) capabilities of state-of-the-art supercomputers. This has led to increased adoption of in situ analysis, circumventing traditional post-hoc methods which become prohibitively expensive as the quantity of data produced by an algorithm grows beyond the means of full-scale data transfer and analysis. As a result of this widening gap, tools have been developed to orchestrate the analysis of simulation data while the algorithm is still running. Our work focuses on the development of containers with ParaView/Catalyst [5] and SENSEI [4]. Catalyst is a library for in situ visualization which provides an application programming interface (API) to the backend of ParaView, allowing for the scripting of visualization and analysis tasks. SENSEI is a framework designed to provide a standard interface to several existing in situ infrastructures, including Catalyst, with the goal of providing a portable, unified approach to various in situ analysis routines.

Concurrent with the rise of novel analysis frameworks for performing operations on a live simulation, a database approach to navigating the data produced in situ was developed, known as Cinema [1]. Cinema databases consist of a mapping between a set of parameters and metadata, which can consist of any type

© Springer Nature Switzerland AG 2022
H. Anzt et al. (Eds.): ISC High Performance 2022 Workshops, LNCS 13387, pp. 324–343, 2022.
https://doi.org/10.1007/978-3-031-23220-6_23

of information extracted from the simulation. We focus on images rendered by Catalyst.

A Cinema viewer is a web application for navigating Cinema databases. In short, a viewer consists of a set of widgets associated with the parameters extracted from the data, which load the appropriate metadata dynamically. As we extract only images at this time, our cinema viewer will load images corresponding to the correct time step and viewing angle specified by the user. As several images are generated at each time step, it is possible to emulate interaction with three dimensional objects. As a user navigates using widgets, the corresponding image is loaded and displayed. Our goal was to combine these tools into one cohesive containerized workflow, demonstrating in situ analysis of simulation data rendered by a Catalyst adapter for SENSEI, then streamed to a remote site for visualization. Some use cases we have in mind are simulation configuration (a researcher may wish to run a small job and visually inspect the results before starting a large run), checking up on long-running jobs, and visualizing results on a multi-tiled display during and after a compute job in cases where moving an entire dataset is expensive or infeasible.

In this paper we present in situ/in transit workflows based on containers, where the simulation and analysis codes are bundled in producer and consumer containers that are executed concurrently. We demonstrate these workflows on a Kubernetes cluster and on a combination of leadership supercomputers and visualization clusters. We leverage Docker [7] and Singularity [18] container technologies. Our contributions include an open source repository of container recipes, configuration files, and scripts that other visualization researchers and students can use in their own research.

2   Related Work

Containerized workflows for HPC applications is an open area of research, with ongoing work towards end-to-end solutions [11,21]. These solutions and ours place a large emphasis on the portability of complex software configurations and reproducibility of experimental results. These container images, often shared through public repositories such as Docker Hub [7], are host-agnostic, yielding similar performance across systems regardless of the underlying operating system or libraries installed on the host. Indeed, the distribution and deployment of host-agnostic software is often the goal behind these efforts. A feature we wish to highlight with our solution is the ability to dynamically link vendor-optimized libraries if they are present on the host. We will discuss native MPI instances, however the same concept will extend to any tools optimized for a specific vendor's hardware. By using prior knowledge about the native MPI on systems we plan to run experiments on, we can enable the performance expected from bare-metal HPC applications running on machines with vendor optimized MPI libraries without sacrificing the portability afforded by using containers. We will demonstrate this by running the same containers on hosts with no native MPI and hosts with vendor-optimized MPI.

3   Workflow Description

In order to illustrate in situ and in transit concepts, we designed a pipeline that includes simulation, analysis, and remote visualization. Our workflow can be understood as three separate phases which work in concert. First, a data "producer" job runs, which consists of the containerized simulation code and a SENSEI adapter which can either write the simulation data from each time step to a shared filesystem or stream it over the network to a different compute resource. Second, a data "consumer" job runs containerized SENSEI endpoints and Catalyst instances, which read the simulation data and generate the analysis specified by a user-defined script. Finally, a lightweight websocket application reads the files generated by the Catalyst analysis and sends the metadata to a remote site for the user to see and interact with. This application may reside in its own containers, or run within a data consumer container, as its function is closely tied to Catalyst.

Figure 1 shows a block diagram of the LAMMPS producer block instrumented with SENSEI (top left), the consumer with SENSEI and Catalyst which perform in situ or in transit rendering (top right), and the remote visualization on tiled displays component (bottom right).

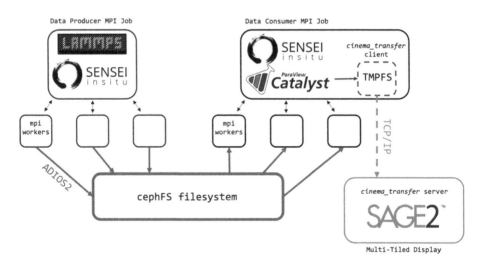

Fig. 1. A block diagram demonstrating data movement between simulation, in situ/in transit analysis, and remote visualization

4 System Configuration

4.1 Host Configuration

We conducted experiments on the Nautilus Cluster managed by the Pacific Research Platform (PRP) [17], and at the Argonne Leadership Computing Facility (ALCF) [3]. We used Kubernetes [9] to orchestrate deployment and scaling of Docker [7] containers across the PRP cluster, as well as the Cobalt HPC scheduler [6] to launch Singularity [18] containers at ALCF. The same container images are used with either Docker or Singularity, demonstrating the portability of this approach.

4.2 Message Passing Interface in Containers

There are three primary approaches to executing Message Passing Interface (MPI) applications in containers: embedded, host-based, and a hybrid approach. The host-based and hybrid paradigms rely on the configuration of the nodes upon which the containerized application executes. In the host-only approach, the host's MPI implementation is used to start the application, and all necessary libraries are mounted into the container. For a hybrid approach, the host's MPI is still used, but the corresponding implementation is also present inside the container, generally to build the MPI application. For a host-only and hybrid approach, the MPI implementations inside and outside the container must match, resulting in a less portable workflow. We tried both fully embedded and hybrid approaches.

4.3 Embedded MPI with Kubernetes

To enable an embedded MPI environment, we build MPICH [12] from source during one of our build stages and install openSSH [16] inside the containers. At runtime, a bash script is invoked from a machine where `kubectl` [9] can schedule the containers. This script creates and copies SSH keys into each container in the deployment, then starts the SSH servers and writes an MPI host configuration file. We use Kubernetes "statefulset" and "service" API objects to ensure consistent object names and name resolution between containers. As a result, we achieve an extremely portable MPI environment for our applications that requires no configuration, MPI implementation, or access to the bare metal hosts. In addition to preventing version and implementation clashes, an embedded approach also means that multiple containers may run concurrently on the same host while participating in different MPI environments. This promotes host sharing and reduction of idle resources, while also enabling in situ workflows like ours in which some resources are producing data while others are analyzing the data produced. The configuration scripts can be found in our Zenodo archive [15]. While these are written for Kubernetes, they could be easily adapted for other containerized ecosystems.

4.4 Hybrid MPI with Singularity

Some environments may have a vendor-optimized MPI build, such as the Cray implementation on Argonne's Theta supercomputer. While it would be possible to run a containerized application with a built-in MPI instance, vendor-intended performance can be achieved by leveraging the optimized build from within the containers. In order to do this, the corresponding MPI version is installed during container build time, and the desired application is compiled. At runtime, the host's MPI is linked instead of the embedded copy.

This is an important distinction from existing containerized in situ visualization pipelines [21] available on Docker Hub, which sacrifice performance for portability. As containers are so simple to build, it makes sense to use prior information about possible environments where the application may run and generate containers with corresponding MPI versions. In this way, the application is still portable, yet can leverage native MPI implementations for better performance.

The build process is automated by exposing arguments at container build time. If a hybrid configuration is desired, the user can input their host's MPI information as build flags, and the container will install the corresponding version. Otherwise, a known working version will be used by default.

4.5 Tmpfs Filesystems

Many container runtime environments provide some kind of temporary filesystem to be used for caching, sensitive files, etc. These filesystems, known as tmpfs mounts [20], can reside in memory, resulting in a very fast but ephemeral place to store data. We leverage a tmpfs filesystem to store the images generated by Catalyst before they are sent to be visualized by a Cinema viewer. We measured the performance difference between a volume on a local solid state drive (SSD) and a tmpfs filesystem, and found that using a tmpfs volume can result in a nearly 5x speedup [8,19,20].

4.6 Transferring Cinema Databases

Cinema_transfer. We developed a web socket tool for transferring the generated cinema databases to a remote machine while the simulation is running [13]. While still a prototype written in Python, it has worked as a proof of concept in our experiments and does not bottleneck performance. We will refer to this tool as *cinema_transfer* for ease of understanding. *cinema_transfer* consists of a websocket server and client. The client runs alongside Catalyst, with read access to the images stored in the memory filesystem. The server runs where visualization will take place, be it a workstation or multi-tiled display. As each simulation time step is completed, the client starts a connection to the server and sends all the image data collected during that step to the remote site. Once the images are received, the client closes the connection and waits for the next step to be completed. In future iterations, *cinema_transfer* can be easily extended to support connections from multiple simultaneous Catalyst instances, and could be optimized for faster transfer speeds. As we will show, however, rendering the images which make up a Cinema database consumes the majority of the time for a single step through the entire pipeline.

Algorithm 1. *cinema_transfer* Client

---
while time steps < total time steps **do**
    if new time step present **then**
        open connection
        send images
        close connection
    end if
end while

Leveraging the Cinema Viewer Design. A Cinema Viewer consists of a web application which is used for navigating Cinema Databases. A set of widgets associated with the parameters of the extracted metadata dynamically load the appropriate files, in our case images, using HTTP GET requests. This means that if the current file is present in cache it will load from there, else it will load from the path specified. We use this design to prepare the Cinema Viewer to load images extracted from simulation time steps which have not yet completed.

A spec D Cinema database is made up of the extracted metadata and a descriptor file in comma separated value (.csv) format which defines the mapping between parameters and metadata. In our experiments, we render 36 images per time step via the Catalyst PNG extractor pipeline object, capturing 36 different viewing angles of the simulation data. As Catalyst uses phi-theta angle pairs to represent the camera position at each of these angles, the parameters for our Cinema database in this case are time step, phi angle, and theta angle. The Catalyst extractor object will generate an appropriate .csv descriptor file after the last time step has finished rendering. However, if we wish to visualize the database prior to simulation completion, we must generate this mapping ourselves. Because these angles and the number of time steps are user-specified, we pass them to the *cinema_transfer* server and generate the proper descriptor file before the run has even begun. As such, when new metadata is generated and sent to the visualization server, the Cinema Viewer can load new images without the need to refresh the web page and lose widget states.

Figure 2 shows a Cinema viewer running on a browser and visualizing atoms of our LAMMPS simulations generated with the data "producer" container.

5   Evaluation

We evaluate the functionality and scalability of our workflow using the LAMMPS Lennard-Jones benchmark [10] instrumented with SENSEI. The simulation can be scaled along the three coordinate axes to create large datasets for testing

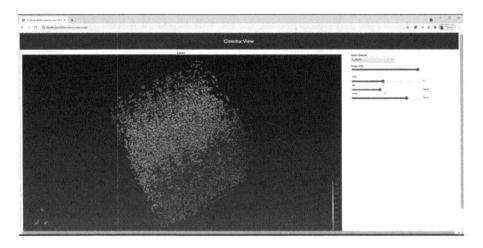

Fig. 2. A cinema viewer instance running in the browser

performance. For our experiments, we ran a simulation of 131,072,000 $(32,000 * 16^3)$ atoms for 50 time steps and measured the wall time each time step took to complete. We report the median loop time from these jobs. A producer time step consists of the time needed to compute the Lennard-Jones potentials and write the simulation results, which consume 12–14 GB of space per time step depending on the data format used. A consumer time step consists of the time needed to read the simulation data and render 36 images via Catalyst. Last, a *cinema_transfer* time step is simply the time needed to read and send the images to a remote server, and ends when the client has sent the images and closes the connection.

Table 1 presents a comparison between the disk space needed to save a time step in VTK format, ADIOS BP4, and rendered images as part of a Cinema database. Assuming that the Cinema database captures all the relevant information needed for analysis, this comparison shows that we could achieve a decrease of a few orders of magnitude in storage requirements by saving time step data as rendered images. This agrees with observations from Ahrens et. al in the original Cinema publication [2].

Table 1. Time step size

File format	Size/Time step
VTK PolyData	14 GB
ADIOS2 Binary-Pack v4	12 GB
36 * 3840×2160 PNG Images, level 5 compression	105 MB

5.1   Embedded MPI with Kubernetes, SENSEI In Situ

As demonstrated by Fig. 3, we observed strong scaling of the data producer when increasing from 32 to 128 MPI ranks, yet saw no improvement by scaling to 256 ranks. This is most likely because we had saturated I/O to the CephFS shared filesystem, as CPU and memory limits for the job were not breached.

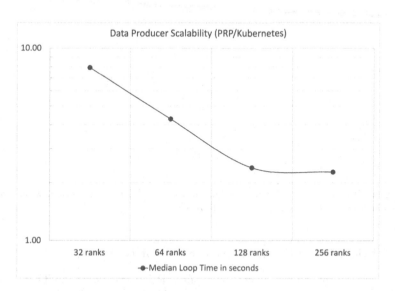

Fig. 3. Producer loop time for increasing numbers of MPI ranks. Strong scaling was observed up to 128 ranks but not for 256 ranks.

The data consumer job, Fig. 4, scaled weakly and is the clear bottleneck in this pipeline. Note that the minimum number of MPI ranks was 32, as any fewer would not meet the memory requirements for Catalyst to render each timestep on the PRP hosts. As we later learned, the VTK distributed rendering and compositing routines do not scale in our configuration. In future experiments, we plan to isolate the cause of this issue, explore other scheduling configurations such as a higher CPU and memory allocation per node, and test other shared containerized filesystem solutions.

5.2   Hybrid MPI with Singularity, SENSEI In Situ

Having already observed strong scaling for the data producer job, we ran the simulation on ALCF's Theta across 8192 ranks on 128 compute nodes equipped with Intel KNL processors, observing a median loop time of 0.369 s. The data is saved to a shared Lustre filesystem in ADIOS BP4 format. The consumer container runs on the Cooley visualization cluster, which also has access to the shared file system. We scaled the consumer job on Cooley from 1 to 64 ranks and observed the same rendering bottleneck as before, with minimal improvement after 16 ranks, Fig. 5.

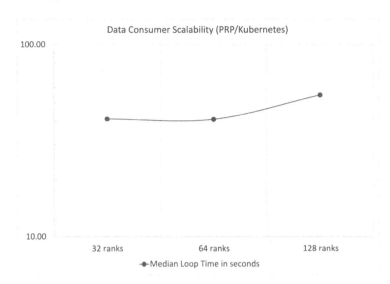

Fig. 4. Consumer loop time for increasing numbers of MPI ranks showed weak scaling and is clearly the bottleneck for this configuration.

5.3 Hybrid MPI with Singularity, SENSEI In Transit

For this experiment we use ThetaGPU, the GPU partition of the Theta super-computer at ALCF, coupled with the Cooley GPU visualization cluster via network. We run the producer with the LAMMPS simulation and SENSEI data adapter on ThetaGPU compute nodes. Similarly, we run the consumer container on Cooley and leverage its GPUs for rendering with Catalyst. ADIOS2 is configured to use its Sustainable Staging Transport (SST) with WAN for its DataTransport parameter. We demonstrate MxN in transit communication, with M=16 MPI producer ranks on ThetaGPU, and N = 2 MPI consumer ranks on Cooley.

Please refer to the Appendix for a description of our artifacts containing a video demonstration of this experiment.

5.4 Cinema_transfer Loop Time

As transfer time is subjective to connection speeds, we measured a transfer between containers running on two lab workstations connected at 1 GB/s, emulating a scenario where a high speed network between rendering machine and visualization machine is not available. The median loop time across 10 trials for transferring 36 4K images with *cinema_transfer* was 0.8826 s. Note that *cinema_transfer* is single threaded in its current state. It is unlikely that transferring the images will bottleneck the pipeline performance, however, as in a case where massive amounts of images are rendered in situ, the consumer (rendering) workload would also increase.

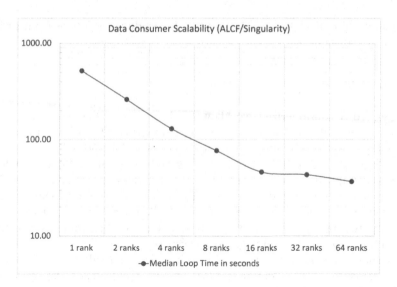

Fig. 5. Rendering on ALCF's Cooley machine showed strong scaling until 16 ranks, where it plateaued with the same loop time observed during the consumer job scheduled on PRP machines.

6 Discussion

When it comes to complex software stacks such as the simulation and in situ visualization use case we have demonstrated, containers can greatly simplify the process of deployment, especially to new systems which may have varying host configurations. We have shown a reproducible workflow in which the same software can be ported between drastically differing machines in terms of hardware, architecture, operating system, file system, container runtime engine, MPI implementation, and number of nodes.

In addition to the in situ visualization use case evaluated above, we also demonstrated how the same workflow can be used for in transit visualization, where the producer job runs on one machine and the consumer runs on another [15]. This configuration is useful for cases like ours where a simulation can scale dramatically across many compute nodes, but a rendering job requires machines with graphics cards and abundant memory.

From our experiments, we can deduce that the bottleneck in our workflow is not a result of a slow underlying file system or network, but is in fact a result of the parallel rendering algorithms. If we are to use this software stack to render simulation data in situ (and subsequently stream the results with *cinema_transfer*) at line rate, we first need to address the bottleneck at the rendering step in this pipeline.

It would also be illuminating to experiment with passing and consuming the simulation data using an in-memory solution, such as LibSim. This approach would confront the file system I/O saturation issue as the simulation is scaled, but would require blocking logic to prevent the producer processes from rushing ahead of the consumers.

7 Conclusion

We presented a containerized workflow for in situ visualization. To show its efficacy, we demonstrated a use case using LAMMPS, SENSEI, Catalyst, and a web socket tool for streaming rendered metadata. We showed how the same containerized MPI application can run fully embedded in containers, or leverage a host's implementation in the presence of vendor-specific optimized MPI libraries. We moved containers between a Docker/Kubernetes deployment on the PRP's cloud infrastructure and a Singularity/Cobalt deployment on three ALCF supercomputers by changing relevant environment variables and the directories mounted for MPI libraries and shared filesystems.

To visualize results, we developed a web socket tool called *cinema_transfer* which streams images to a remote site (in our case, a multi-tiled display) as they are rendered.

We have assessed the rendering step as a clear bottleneck in this pipeline, as we observed similar rendering times on three different machines with varying host configurations.

To conclude, we would like to emphasize that this work is absolutely reproducible, and indeed needs attention from the in situ visualization community to find solutions to the current rendering bottleneck. The entire software stack is open source, and all configuration files and scripts specific to our experiments are made available through public Github repositories [13,14] and our Zenodo archive [15] which we prepared specifically as a supplement to this manuscript.

Acknowledgments. This work was supported by and used resources of the Argonne Leadership Computing Facility, which is a U.S. Department of Energy Office of Science User Facility supported under Contract DE-AC02-06CH11357. This work was supported in part by the Director, Office of Science, Office of Advanced Scientific Computing Research, of the U.S. Department of Energy under Contract DE-AC02-06CH11357, through the grant "Scalable Analysis Methods and In Situ Infrastructure for Extreme Scale Knowledge Discovery". This project also used resources at the California Institute for Telecommunications and Information Technology (Calit2) at UCSD. These facilities are supported by the following National Science Foundation awards: CC*DNI DIBBs: The Pacific Research Platform- NSF Award Number:1541349; CC* NPEO: Toward the National Research Platform- NSF Award Number:1826967; CI-New: Cognitive Hardware and Software Ecosystem Community Infrastructure (CHASE-CI)- NSF Award Number:1730158; MRI: Development of Advanced Visualization Instrumentation for the Collaborative Exploration of Big Data- NSF Award Number:1338192; and Development of the Sensor Environment Imaging (SENSEI) Instrument- NSF Award Number:1456638.

Appendix: Reproducibility

We have aimed at making this work completely reproducible. For this purpose, a Zenodo repository of artifacts is available [15].

The repository contains our producer and consumer container recipes as Dockerfiles. These Docker images can be easily converted to Singularity images. In addition, we also include LAMMPS, SENSEI, and Catalyst configuration files to reproduce our experiments. The results of our experiments are also presented in log files and spreadsheets. Finally, we present videos that illustrate our runs with the producer and consumer running concurrently.

In addition to our Zenodo archive, we will present our container recipes below in an effort to make this workflow as reproducible and as transparent as possible. It may be informative to compare these with the block diagram above [Fig. 1] to ascertain how the containers are built to support this portable workflow.

GCC Base Container:

```
ARG BASE_IMAGE
FROM $BASE_IMAGE

## set gcc version in .gitlab-ci.yml ##
ARG GCC_VERSION
ENV GCC_VERSION=$GCC_VERSION

## set cmake version in .gitlab-ci.yml ##
ARG CMAKE_VERSION
ENV CMAKE_VERSION=$CMAKE_VERSION

## environment for build paths ##
ENV SRCDIR=/src
ENV BUILDDIR=/build
ENV INSTALLDIR=/install

WORKDIR $SRCDIR

## gcc dependencies ##
RUN yum -y install wget \
  bzip2 \
  gmp-devel \
  mpfr-devel \
  libmpc-devel

## install cmake ##
RUN wget "https://github.com/Kitware/CMake/releases/download/
    v$CMAKE_VERSION/cmake-$CMAKE_VERSION-linux-x86_64.sh" --
    no-check-certificate && \
  chmod +x cmake-$CMAKE_VERSION-linux-x86_64.sh && \
  ./cmake-$CMAKE_VERSION-linux-x86_64.sh --skip-license --
    prefix=/usr
```

```
## install new GCC ##
## see https://bipulkkuri.medium.com/
## install-latest-gcc-on-centos-linux-release-7-6-
   a704a11d943d ##
RUN wget https://ftp.gnu.org/gnu/gcc/gcc-$GCC_VERSION/gcc-
   $GCC_VERSION.tar.gz --no-check-certificate && \
  tar xzvf gcc-$GCC_VERSION.tar.gz && \
  rm gcc-$GCC_VERSION.tar.gz && \
  mkdir -p $BUILDDIR/gcc && \
  cd $BUILDDIR/gcc && \
  $SRCDIR/gcc-$GCC_VERSION/configure --disable-multilib \
    --enable-languages=c,c++ --prefix=$INSTALLDIR/gcc && \
  make -j8 && \
  make install

## remove default gcc ##
RUN yum -y remove gcc gcc-c++

## update environment ##
ENV PATH=$INSTALLDIR/gcc/bin:$PATH
ENV LD_LIBRARY_PATH=$INSTALLDIR/gcc/lib64:$LD_LIBRARY_PATH

WORKDIR /
```

Producer Build Container:

```
FROM gitlab-registry.nrp-nautilus.io/inealey/cudagl-build:
   centos-gcc-9.2.0

ENV SRCDIR=/src
ENV BUILDDIR=/build
ENV INSTALLDIR=/install
ENV MPICH_VERSION=3.2.1

WORKDIR $SRCDIR

## yum dependencies
RUN yum install -y git

#############################################

## install mpich ##
## disabling rpath to compiled executable allows use of host
   mpich ##
RUN echo $MPICH_VERSION && \
  wget -q https://www.mpich.org/static/downloads/
     $MPICH_VERSION/mpich-$MPICH_VERSION.tar.gz --no-check-
     certificate && \
```

```
    tar xzvf mpich-$MPICH_VERSION.tar.gz && \
    rm mpich-$MPICH_VERSION.tar.gz && \
    mkdir -p $BUILDDIR/mpich && \
    cd $BUILDDIR/mpich && \
    $SRCDIR/mpich-$MPICH_VERSION/configure --prefix=$INSTALLDIR
        /mpich \
      --disable-wrapper-rpath --disable-fortran && \
      make -j8 && \
      make install

## update environment ##
ENV PATH=$PATH:$INSTALLDIR/mpich/bin/
ENV LD_LIBRARY_PATH=$LD_LIBRARY_PATH:$INSTALLDIR/mpich/lib/

#############################################

## build LAMMPS ##
RUN git clone https://github.com/lammps/lammps && \
  cd lammps/src && \
  git checkout stable_29Sep2021 && \
  sed -i '0,/mpicxx/{s/mpicxx/gcc/}' MAKE/Makefile.mpi && \
  sed -i '0,/-g␣-O3/{s@-g␣-O3@-g␣-O3␣-std=c++11␣-I␣ /install/
      mpich/include/@}' \
  MAKE/Makefile.mpi && \
  make yes-KSPACE && \
  make yes-MOLECULE && \
  make yes-RIGID && \
  make mpi mode=lib -j8

#############################################

## install ADIOS2 v2.7.1 ##
RUN git clone https://github.com/ornladios/ADIOS2.git adios2
    && \
  cd adios2 && \
  git checkout v2.7.1 && \
  cmake -S $SRCDIR/adios2 -B $BUILDDIR/adios \
          -D CMAKE_INSTALL_PREFIX=$INSTALLDIR/adios \
          -D ADIOS2_USE_Fortran=OFF \
          -D ADIOS2_BUILD_EXAMPLES=OFF \
          -D CMAKE_BUILD_TYPE=Release \
          -D DHDF5_DIR=$INSTALLDIR/hdf5 && \
  cd $BUILDDIR/adios && \
  make -j8 && \
  make install

#############################################

## install VTK 8.2 ##
RUN git clone https://gitlab.kitware.com/vtk/vtk.git && \
```

```
   cd vtk && \
   git checkout v8.2.0 && \
   cmake -S $SRCDIR/vtk -B $BUILDDIR/vtk \
            -D VTK_Group_Imaging=OFF \
            -D VTK_Group_MPI=OFF \
            -D VTK_Group_Qt=OFF \
            -D VTK_Group_Rendering=OFF \
            -D VTK_Group_StandAlone=ON \
            -D VTK_Group_Tk=OFF \
            -D VTK_Group_Views=OFF \
            -D VTK_Group_Web=OFF \
            -D VTK_RENDERING_BACKEND=None \
            -D CMAKE_BUILD_TYPE=Debug \
            -D BUILD_TESTING=OFF \
            -D CMAKE_INSTALL_PREFIX=$INSTALLDIR/vtk && \
   cd $BUILDDIR/vtk && \
   make -j8 && \
   make install


###############################################

## install silvio's lammps fork of sensei ##
RUN git clone -b lammps https://github.com/srizzi88/SENSEI.
   git sensei && \
   cd sensei && \
   git checkout lammps && \
   cmake -S $SRCDIR/sensei -B $BUILDDIR/sensei \
            -D CMAKE_INSTALL_PREFIX=$INSTALLDIR/sensei \
            -D VTK_DIR=$INSTALLDIR/vtk/lib64/cmake/vtk-8.2 \
            -D ENABLE_VTK_IO=ON \
            -D ENABLE_PROFILER=ON \
            -D LAMMPS_DIR=$SRCDIR/lammps \
            -D ENABLE_LAMMPS=ON \
            -D ENABLE_MANDELBROT=OFF \
            -D ENABLE_OSCILLATORS=OFF \
            -D ENABLE_ADIOS2=ON \
            -D ADIOS2_DIR=$INSTALLDIR/adios/lib64/cmake/adios2
              \
            -D ENABLE_HDF5=OFF && \
   cd $BUILDDIR/sensei && \
   make -j8 && \
   make install
```

Consumer Build Container:

```
FROM gitlab-registry.nrp-nautilus.io/inealey/cudagl-build:
   centos-gcc-9.2.0

ENV SRCDIR=/src
```

```
ENV BUILDDIR=/build
ENV INSTALLDIR=/install
ENV MPICH_VERSION=3.2.1

WORKDIR $SRCDIR

## paraview yum packages ##
RUN yum install -y git \
  python3-devel \
  mesa-libGL-devel \
  java-11-openjdk-devel \
  libX11-devel \
  tbb-devel \
  epel-release

## epel packages ##
RUN yum -y install ninja-build


##########################################

## install mpich ##
## disabling rpath to compiled executable allows use of host
   mpich ##
RUN wget -q https://www.mpich.org/static/downloads/
    $MPICH_VERSION/mpich-$MPICH_VERSION.tar.gz --no-check-
    certificate && \
  tar xzvf mpich-$MPICH_VERSION.tar.gz && \
  rm mpich-$MPICH_VERSION.tar.gz && \
  mkdir -p $BUILDDIR/mpich && \
  cd $BUILDDIR/mpich && \
  $SRCDIR/mpich-$MPICH_VERSION/configure --prefix=$INSTALLDIR
     /mpich \
    --disable-wrapper-rpath --disable-fortran && \
    make -j8 && \
    make install


## update environment ##
ENV PATH=$PATH:$INSTALLDIR/mpich/bin/
ENV LD_LIBRARY_PATH=$LD_LIBRARY_PATH:$INSTALLDIR/mpich/lib

##########################################


## install ADIOS2 v2.7.1 ##
RUN git clone https://github.com/ornladios/ADIOS2.git adios2
    && \
  cd adios2 && \
  git checkout v2.7.1 && \
  cmake -S $SRCDIR/adios2 -B $BUILDDIR/adios \
```

```
              -D CMAKE_INSTALL_PREFIX=$INSTALLDIR/adios \
              -D ADIOS2_USE_Fortran=OFF \
              -D ADIOS2_BUILD_EXAMPLES=OFF \
              -D CMAKE_BUILD_TYPE=Release \
              -D DHDF5_DIR=$INSTALLDIR/hdf5 && \
     cd $BUILDDIR/adios && \
     make -j8 && \
     make install


##############################################

## install paraview ##
RUN git clone https://gitlab.kitware.com/paraview/paraview.
   git && \
        cd paraview && \
        git checkout v5.9.1 && \
        git submodule update --init --recursive && \
   cmake -G Ninja -S $SRCDIR/paraview -B $BUILDDIR/paraview \
     -D CMAKE_BUILD_TYPE=Release \
     -D CMAKE_INSTALL_PREFIX=$INSTALLDIR/paraview \
     -D PARAVIEW_USE_CUDA=OFF \
     -D PARAVIEW_ENABLE_ADIOS2=ON \
     -D ADIOS2_DIR=$BUILDDIR/adios \
     -D PARAVIEW_USE_MPI=ON \
     -D PARAVIEW_USE_QT=OFF \
     -D PARAVIEW_USE_PYTHON=ON \
     -D VTK_OPENGL_HAS_EGL=ON \
     -D VTK_USE_X=OFF && \
     cd $BUILDDIR/paraview && \
     ninja -j8 && \
     ninja install


##############################################

## install forked sensei repo ##
RUN git clone -b lammps https://github.com/srizzi88/SENSEI.
   git sensei && \
   cd sensei && \
   git checkout lammps && \
   cmake -S $SRCDIR/sensei -B $BUILDDIR/sensei \
       -D CMAKE_INSTALL_PREFIX=$INSTALLDIR/sensei \
       -D ENABLE_SENSEI=ON \
       -D ENABLE_VTK_IO=ON \
       -D ENABLE_MANDELBROT=OFF \
       -D ENABLE_OSCILLATORS=OFF \
       -D ENABLE_PROFILER=ON \
       -D ENABLE_CATALYST=ON \
       -D ParaView_DIR=$INSTALLDIR/paraview/lib64/cmake/
          paraview-5.9 \
       -D ENABLE_ADIOS2=ON \
```

```
    -D ADIOS2_DIR=$INSTALLDIR/adios/lib64/cmake/adios2 \
    -D ENABLE_HDF5=OFF && \
cd $BUILDDIR/sensei && \
make -j8 && \
make install


#############################################
```

Producer Runtime Container:

```
FROM nvidia/cudagl:11.4.1-runtime-centos7

## yum installs ##
#RUN yum install -y openssh-server openssh-clients

## environment ##
ENV LD_LIBRARY_PATH=$LD_LIBRARY_PATH:/install/gcc/lib64/:/
    install/vtk/lib64/:/install/adios/lib64/

## copy built files ##
COPY --from=srizzi/woiv22producer:latest /install /install

## copy config files ##
#COPY utils /config

## allow exection for setup scripts ##
#RUN chmod +x /config/setup.sh && \
#     chmod +x /config/updatepubkeys.sh

WORKDIR /install/sensei
```

Consumer Runtime Container:

```
FROM nvidia/cudagl:11.4.1-runtime-centos7

## yum installs ##
#RUN yum install -y openssh-server openssh-clients

## environment ##
#ENV PATH=$PATH:/install/mpich/bin/
ENV LD_LIBRARY_PATH=$LD_LIBRARY_PATH:/install/gcc/lib64/:/
    install/vtk/lib64/:/install/adios/lib64

## copy built files ##
COPY --from=srizzi/woiv22consumer:latest /install /install

## copy config files ##
#COPY utils /config

## allow exection for setup scripts ##
```

```
#RUN  chmod  +x  /config/setup.sh  && \
#     chmod  +x  /config/updatepubkeys.sh
```

```
WORKDIR /install/sensei
```

It is our hope that the scientific visualization community will benefit from this work and build on this material for future research.

References

1. Ahrens, J., Jourdain, S., O'Leary, P., Patchett, J., Rogers, D.H., Petersen, M.: An image-based approach to extreme scale in situ visualization and analysis. In: SC 2014: Proceedings of the International Conference for High Performance Computing, Networking, Storage and Analysis, pp. 424–434. IEEE (2014)
2. Ahrens, J., et al.: In situ mpas-ocean image-based visualization. In: Proceedings of the International Conference for High Performance Computing, Networking, Storage and Analysis, Visualization & Data Analytics Showcase (2014)
3. Argonne Leadership Computing Facility. https://alcf.anl.gov, Accessed Mar 2022
4. Ayachit, U., et al.: Performance analysis, design considerations, and applications of extreme-scale in situ infrastructures. In: SC 2016: Proceedings of the International Conference for High Performance Computing, Networking, Storage and Analysis, pp. 921–932. IEEE (2016)
5. Ayachit, U., et al.: Paraview catalyst: Enabling in situ data analysis and visualization. In: Proceedings of the First Workshop on In Situ Infrastructures for Enabling Extreme-Scale Analysis and Visualization, pp. 25–29 (2015)
6. Cobalt HPC management suite. https://github.com/ido/cobalt, Accessed Mar 2022
7. Docker open platform for developing, shipping, and running applications. https://www.docker.com, Accessed Mar 2022
8. Docker tmpfs mounts. https://docs.docker.com/storage/tmpfs/, Accessed Mar 2022
9. Kubernetes: Production-Grade Container Orchestration. https://kubernetes.io, Accessed Mar 2022
10. LAAMPS Lennard Jones Benchmark. https://www.lammps.org/bench.html, Accessed Mar 2022
11. McMillan, S.: Making containers easier with hpc container maker (2018). https://github.com/HPCSYSPROS/Workshop18/blob/master/Making_Containers_Easier_with_HPC_Container_Maker/ws_hpcsysp103.pdf
12. MPICH: High Performance Portable MPI. https://www.mpich.org, Accessed Mar 2022
13. Nealey, I.: https://github.com/inealey/cinema_transfer, Accessed Mar 2022
14. Nealey, I.: https://github.com/inealey/sensei/tree/lammps, Accessed Mar 2022
15. Nealey, I., Ferrier, N., Insley, J., Mateevitsi, V.A., Papka, M.E., Rizzi, S.: Artifacts for woiv (2022). https://doi.org/10.5281/zenodo.6336286
16. OpenSSH: https://www.openssh.com, Accessed Mar 2022
17. Pacific Research Platform. https://pacificresearchplatform.org, Accessed Sept 2021
18. Singularity open source container platform. https://github.com/sylabs/singularity, Accessed Mar 2022
19. Singularity Persistent Overlays. https://sylabs.io/guides/3.5/user-guide/persistent_overlays.html, Accessed Mar 2022

20. Snyder, P.: tmpfs: a virtual memory file system. In: Proceedings of the Autumn 1990 EUUG Conference, pp. 241–248 (1990)
21. Will, M., Wofford, Q., Patchett, J., Rogers, D., Lukasczyk, J., Garth, C.: Developing and evaluating in situ visualization algorithms using containers, pp. 6–11. Association for Computing Machinery, New York (2021). https://doi.org/10.1145/3490138.3490141

The 17th Workshop on Virtualization in High Performance Cloud Computing

Virtual Clusters: Isolated, Containerized HPC Environments in Kubernetes

George Zervas[1,2], Antony Chazapis[1(✉)], Yannis Sfakianakis[1,2],
Christos Kozanitis[1], and Angelos Bilas[1,2]

[1] Institute of Computer Science, FORTH, Heraklion, Greece
{georgzerb,chazapis,jsfakian,kozanitis,bilas}@ics.forth.gr
[2] Computer Science Department, University of Crete, Heraklion, Greece

Abstract. Today, Cloud and HPC workloads tend to use different approaches for managing resources. However, as more and more applications require a mixture of both high-performance and data processing computation, convergence of Cloud and HPC resource management is becoming a necessity. Cloud-oriented resource management strives to share physical resources across applications to improve infrastructure efficiency. On the other hand, the HPC community prefers to rely on job queueing mechanisms to coordinate among tasks, favoring dedicated use of physical resources by each application.

In this paper, we design a combined Slurm-Kubernetes system that is able to run unmodified HPC workloads under Kubernetes, alongside other, non-HPC applications. First, we containerize the whole HPC execution environment into a *virtual cluster*, giving each user a private HPC context, with common libraries and utilities built-in, like the Slurm job scheduler. Second, we design a custom Slurm-Kubernetes protocol that allows Slurm to dynamically request resources from Kubernetes. Essentially, in our system the Slurm controller delegates placement and scheduling decisions to Kubernetes, thus establishing a centralized resource management endpoint for all available resources. Third, our custom Kubernetes scheduler applies different placement policies depending on the workload type. We evaluate the performance of our system compared to a native Slurm-based HPC cluster and demonstrate its ability to allow the joint execution of applications with seemingly conflicting requirements on the same infrastructure with minimal interference.

Keywords: Cloud-native HPC · Kubernetes scheduling · Slurm

1 Introduction

Cloud and HPC computing environments are mostly similar in hardware specifications, but differ largely in the software stack and how it manages available resources. Cloud providers use virtualization mechanisms to facilitate sharing, valuing colocation of workloads to the point of overprovisioning, whereas in HPC clusters workloads are allocated exclusive resources, based on exact requirements

© Springer Nature Switzerland AG 2022
H. Anzt et al. (Eds.): ISC High Performance 2022 Workshops, LNCS 13387, pp. 347–357, 2022.
https://doi.org/10.1007/978-3-031-23220-6_24

given by the user when submitting the respective job. As the complexity of modern applications increases, it is not uncommon for deployments to include parallel provisioning of backend services, as well as on-demand execution of data analytics pipelines and HPC codes. For such workloads, it is essential to accommodate both resource allocation schemes on the same hardware infrastructure, exploiting resource sharing, but also avoiding interference as much as possible.

In this paper, we explore the convergence of Cloud and HPC in a common, container-based environment, backed by Kubernetes, the most prominent distributed container orchestration framework [3]. Containers are gaining ground as the preferred deployment method in the Cloud, as they implement a convenient packaging scheme for applications, they are lightweight when running, and provide isolation between instances for security purposes. Kubernetes provides abstractions for hardware resources and automatically scales service replicas to meet demand, while keeping redundancies to alleviate for unadvertised failures. The HPC world has cautiously been following the trend, primarily utilizing containers as a portable method to bundle applications with associated library dependencies. These containers are then typically submitted as jobs using Slurm, a popular workload manager responsible for coordinating the allocation of resources throughout the cluster, via shared submission queues.

To run HPC applications in Kubernetes, we introduce the concept of the *virtual cluster*, as a group of multiple container instances that function as a unified cluster environment from the user's perspective. Each node in a virtual cluster embeds all necessary libraries and utilities, as well as a private Slurm deployment; the user working inside a virtual cluster can only view and manage jobs submitted from within the same context. In practice though, each such Slurm setup is not independent. We extend the Slurm controller with a custom protocol, to communicate with the central Kubernetes scheduler when requiring resources, effectively placing Kubernetes in charge of resource allocations for the whole cluster. Moreover, we use *Genisys*, a custom Kubernetes scheduler that distinguishes between "HPC" and "data center" services (typical Kubernetes deployments that run in other containers), in order to apply different allocation policies and maximize overall usage. In cases where HPC workloads do not consume all node-local resources, Genisys colocates data center services, while constantly satisfying their user-defined performance targets. Therefore, HPC and data center workloads execute transparently on the same infrastructure, achieving high levels of CPU utilization.

This integration has several benefits: [(i)] Compatibility: Supporting Slurm inside virtual clusters is crucial in order to keep compatibility with existing Slurm scripts. [(ii)] Colocation: By containerizing the whole runtime environment and using Kubernetes as the substrate, we are able to run hybrid workloads on top of the same physical cluster, optimizing for high utilization and avoiding static cluster partitioning for HPC and data center tasks. [(iii)] Portability: The containerized environment offered with virtual clusters allows users to install different dependencies without polluting the bare metal infrastructure and avoid issues with conflicting versions of the same libraries. It also makes migrating to a different Kubernetes cluster possible, just by transferring the container images to the other system and deploying them using the same Kubernetes objects.

2   Related Work

The integration of HPC job management in the context of Kubernetes has been addressed in several studies. In [13], the authors use a utility called *hpc-connector* that acts as an HPC job proxy: Users submit respective Kubernetes jobs with the appropriate settings, and hpc-connector forwards them to the HPC cluster, monitors their execution, and collects their results. This solution can probably be used with containers to address portability issues. On the other hand, the main focus is on HPC job management with a Kubernetes-compatible interface; the HPC and cloud clusters are treated as two separate environments making it impossible to monitor and place cloud and HPC workloads over the same physical cluster. A similar approach is presented in [20], where a Kubernetes installation is interfaced to a Torque-based HPC cluster.

One critical aspect of the containerization of HPC workloads is runtime performance when compared to an actual physical cluster. Related work has measured the network performance of containerized HPC codes, and findings suggest that there is little to no performance overhead when an InfiniBand network is used [5]. In general, Docker containers do not introduce significant performance overheads, while in some cases they can provide better QoS due to the usage of cgroups resource limiting mechanisms when compared with a bare metal runtime environment [8–10].

There is a plethora of papers that handle the scheduling of workloads with the main goal of increasing the utilization in the infrastructure. Sparrow [16] and Eagle [7], handle the scheduling of application tasks in clusters. Sparrow focuses on speed, but can not handle workloads with conflicting goals as in our case. Eagle follows a hybrid approach, with a centralized component that performs careful placement of long-running tasks, and a distributed component emphasizing on quick placement. Our scheme is also hybrid, however, with different goals. Ursa [11] is a task scheduler for spark-monotasks [15] and Rhythm [19] is a data center scheduler that ensures the latency of latency-critical applications. Both works colocate "compatible" tasks to increase the utilization in the underlying infrastructure, but do not effectively guard against interference. In contrast, our approach constantly monitors application performance and adjusts container placement and resource allocations at runtime to achieve a user-defined performance target. Control loops for dynamically adjusting resources based on runtime performance have been used in systems such as SLAOrchestrator [14] and Skynet [17]. The former tries to optimize cost of services when running in the Cloud, while the latter optimizes hardware efficiency by colocating more applications on the same nodes, as long as they acheive their user-defined performance targets. Genisys's handling of data center tasks is based on Skynet, extended to allocate HPC tasks with different, placement-based constraints.

3 Design Overview

A *virtual cluster* is a group of container instances that virtualizes an environment to run HPC workloads that use MPI and other software frameworks. From the perspective of applications, virtual clusters are indistinguishable from physical nodes that execute instances of MPI processes in parallel, as all physical processing cores, RAM, the low-latency InfiniBand network, and accelerators are available in each container context. Each virtual cluster spans all physical nodes and multiple virtual clusters can co-exist over the same set of physical nodes, as shown in Fig. 1, which presents the high-level design concept.

Inside each virtual cluster, as part of the bundled software stack, we deploy a private Slurm context, so users can invoke existing scripts to run HPC workloads. One of the virtual cluster nodes acts as the Slurm controller, while all virtual cluster nodes run the Slurm agent and register with the controller. Configuration of the Slurm deployment is automatically done at virtual cluster initialization. Unmodified, the virtual-cluster-local Slurm would perform resource allocation and scheduling of Slurm jobs as if it were in control of the whole cluster. Each independent Slurm installation is isolated inside its own containers and does not account for the presence of other containers running and consuming computing resources; that being other virtual clusters or typical Kubernetes services.

To schedule and place workloads across multiple virtual clusters and prevent the interference introduced by overlapping jobs, we have modified the Slurm controller's placement mechanism to delegate all respective decisions to the external Kubernetes scheduler. The Kubernetes scheduler in this scheme is the central authority that has the full knowledge of the cluster's current resource allocations and acts as a global coordinator for new requests. Moreover, Genisys, our custom Kubernetes scheduler implementation (described in Sect. 4) distinguishes between "HPC" and "data center" type workloads, in order to improve the overall utilization of available hardware. Data center services do not use virtual clusters, but are deployed in Kubernetes as deployments, jobs, or other API objects that execute in containers running alongside the ones used by virtual clusters.

Genisys ensures each virtual cluster does not share resources with other virtual clusters or data center services. When a new service is deployed, Genisys iterates over an internal free resource list for each node and attempts to find which nodes can accommodate it. If *resource oversubscription* is not enabled Genisys will always place tasks on nodes with enough free resources to fit in. Furthermore, the scheduler supports two different placement policies: [(i)] The *Least Loaded Selection Policy* attempts to place tasks to the least loaded nodes on the cluster, effectively spreading out the load, allowing to fit more jobs on a given set of nodes to achieve higher cluster resource utilization. [(ii)] The *Max Loaded Selection Policy* attempts to pack as many services in nodes, allowing for higher energy efficiency, with the danger of not being able to fit as many tasks on the cluster (as some "loaded" nodes will not have enough free resources).

For data center workloads, Genisys allows sharing of resources, by estimating the aggregate resources that are required to achieve a user-defined performance objective (i.e., latency, throughput). It manages four types of resources: number of cores, memory size, I/O bandwidth, and network bandwidth. Genisys performs its estimations using a feedback control loop similar to Skynet. Afterwards, it decides on the size, the number, and the placement of containers in physical nodes according to the selected policy.

Colocating HPC tasks with the data center services is configurable. The default behaviour allows tasks of both types to use the same nodes and share resources. The other option is to perform type-based placement, implicitly partitioning the nodes by placing HPC tasks on some nodes and data center tasks on others. This approach may minimize interference introduced by task colocation, but also reduces efficiency, and is not used in this paper.

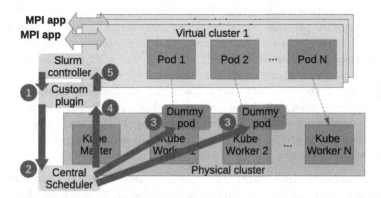

Fig. 1. Each container instance of a virtual cluster runs in a different physical machine, while multiple virtual clusters may run in parallel. The custom Slurm job placement plugin communicates with Genisys to perform job placement. These jobs are visible at the Kubernetes level as "dummy allocations".

Figure 1 illustrates the steps involved in the communication between virtual clusters and the cluster-wide Kubernetes scheduler for HPC workloads: 1. On job initialization Slurm sends an allocation request to the main Kubernetes controller via a custom plugin. In this request Slurm specifies the resources needed for the job (node count, CPU count, etc.). 2. The custom plugin forwards these allocations to Genisys, by allocating "dummy pods" in Kubernetes, with resource requirements matching the Slurm job's specifications. Dummy containers are practically idle; they consume no resources themselves, but act as placeholders for the allocation of resources that will be used by the actual jobs inside the virtual cluster. 3. On receiving a dummy allocation for a Slurm job placement, Genisys iterates over the available nodes and checks if enough resources are available. If so, it schedules the dummy containers for execution. 4. The allocation is communicated back to the custom Slurm plugin as a node list. 5. The plugin, in turn, forwards the response to the Slurm controller. The node list contains the selected nodes for the Slurm job deployment. If no suitable nodes are found, the controller puts the job on hold.

4   Implementation

Preparing and Deploying Virtual Clusters: Virtual cluster container images are prepared as "typical" Docker images, by starting from some base Linux distribution and adding layer after layer of development tools, libraries, and other software. Our reference images are based on CentOS and the Mellanox OpenFabrics Enterprise Distribution (OFED), which includes Open MPI with InfiniBand support as well as other libraries. In addition, we install several extra libraries and frameworks (i.e., CUDA, GROMACS, TensorFlow, Horovod), Slurm, as well as utilities to help in evaluating application performance. This base container recipe is available to our users, so they can tailor it to their needs, using different software versions or supplementary libraries and tools.

Upon instantiation, each virtual cluster container actually runs the SSH daemon as its primary process. The instance startup script first waits for all pods (nodes in the virtual cluster) to be ready and then creates all necessary configuration: keys for password-less SSH connectivity, MPI hostfile, and Slurm configuration at /etc/slurm.conf. As the last step, it starts Slurm (the Slurm controller runs in the first container). Each virtual cluster is deployed using a Kubernetes DaemonSet, which assigns one pod per physical machine. As HPC application developers usually assume similar capabilities and equal network-level distances across nodes, placing a single pod in each node is convenient and produces expected results.

Slurm-Kubernetes Interface: The Slurm controller uses a node bitmap in order to represent resource reservations in available HPC nodes and find candidates to place incoming jobs. For placement, Slurm uses the _job_test() function, which is called by the controller when a new job arrives. _job_test() receives the job's resource requirements and the node bitmap. It then checks if a set of computing nodes is available by calling _select_nodes(), which returns a list of selected nodes, so Slurm can proceed to mark them in the node bitmap and start the job. If the selection process returns an empty node list, then the job is rescheduled for later placement. To delegate all job placement decisions externally to Kubernetes, we first ignore the node bitmap returned by _select_nodes(). Instead, we implement a custom plugin written in Golang that receives the job's resource requirements (CPUs, RAM, node count) and creates a mirror Kubernetes allocation of "dummy pods" using the same resources. The plugin runs next to each Slurm controller communicating with Kubernetes via the API server. When the dummy pods are placed, we return the node list for the specified job back to the Slurm controller. On receiving the list, we trigger Slurm to modify the node bitmap and place the job.

Scheduling Extensions: The scheduling of dummy pods does not *require* a custom Kubernetes scheduler. However without special arrangements for HPC workloads, the default scheduler may place multiple HPC jobs on the same nodes, maximizing interference. To this end, we have extended our Genisys scheduler to support both "HPC" and "data center" workloads and enforce different types of placement policies. We label HPC workloads as "SLURM-JOB", in order to distinguish them from other workloads running on the same cluster. Allocations for Slurm applications happen in a static manner and Genisys can be configured to avoid colocating them with other jobs marked as "SLURM-JOB" for optimal performance. This policy may be selected because of the lack of available metrics offered by MPI applications and their sensitivity due to synchronization barriers.

On the other hand, data center workloads include a user-defined performance objective, which Genisys must achieve during their execution. Genisys monitors periodically the performance of each running data center service to get feedback about the effectiveness of its current resource allocation, using the Kubernetes Custom Metric Server and Prometheus [1]. In case of a performance violation in a workload, Genisys increases its resource allocation according to the measured drop in performance and vice versa. For new resource estimations, Genisys also considers the history of previous performance measurements, which is affected mainly by the workload mix.

5 Evaluation

We evaluate our system by running a mixture of MPI workloads and other services on the same cluster, and measuring the overall efficiency through the total runtime of all applications combined and the individual runtime per application. Our hardware setup consists of 5 servers, each with a single 32-core/64-thread AMD EPYC 7551P processor (running at 2.00 GHz) and 128 GB of memory, for 320 threads in total. All servers have SSD storage devices and are interconnected via 56 Gb/s InfiniBand. We run Kubernetes 1.19.7 on CentOS 7.6.

We have created a multi step MPI workload using benchmarks from the NAS Parallel Benchmark Suite [4]. We choose realistic HPC task sizes and their distribution by following traces outlined in [18], which analyzes the HPC workloads run on the Lomonosov-2 supercomputer, categorized according to resource allocation sizes and CPU consumption. We allocate 5% of the workload's CPU time to 16 thread (small), 20% to 32 thread (medium), 65% to 64 thread (medium-large), and 10% to 128 thread (large) jobs. The "data center" workload consists of: [(i)] 5 Nginx servers offering static content, each allocating 6 CPU threads. The servers are hit with 200,000 total requests from Apache Bench [2]. [(ii)] 5 memcached servers, each allocating 6 CPU threads. The servers are hit with a 200 million operation workload generated by YCSB [6]. [(iii)] Spark benchmarks from the Spark-Bench [12] performance suite, using 5 Spark workers, each allocating 20 CPU threads as a Kubernetes job.

As a baseline, we first run the full HPC workload on all nodes exclusively and then the data center tasks, representing the typical scenario where Slurm and Kubernetes time-share the same resources. For the other scenarios, we deploy both workloads concurrently, colocating them over the same physical resources, in 6 different configurations: [(i)] *Genisys Least Loaded Policy:* We use the Genisys scheduler and our modified version of Slurm that communicates with Genisys for placement decisions. In Genisys we select the *Least Loaded Policy.* [(ii)] *Genisys Max Loaded Policy:* Same as the previous configuration, but using Genisys's *Max Loaded Policy*. [(iii)] *Unmanaged:* We use the default Kubernetes scheduler and unmodified Slurm in virtual clusters. [(iv)] *Partitioned:* Like Unmanaged, but we statically partition the nodes into a 2-node Kubernetes and a 3-node Slurm cluster. [(v)] *Thread Partitioned 50%:* Like Unmanaged, but we partition the cluster's nodes by giving 50% of each node's CPU capacity to Kubernetes and the rest 50% to Slurm. Kubernetes and Slurm are configured to each use half of the CPU resources of each node. [(vi)] *Thread Partitioned 75%:* Same as the previous configuration, but by giving 75% of each node's CPU capacity to Kubernetes and 75% to Slurm. The HPC and data center workloads partially overlap over the same physical resources, as Slurm and Kubernetes see a total of (150%) of each node's capacity available.

The execution time of each workload step for the different scenarios is shown in Fig. 2. In the first graph we show the individual execution times of each workload step. The execution time is normalized to the execution of the workloads when running in dedicated Slurm and Kubernetes installations. The last bar group shows the execution time of the whole workload. In the second graph we show the cluster's CPU utilization over time for each different scenario.

Effect of Different Policies in Genisys: In general, the Least Loaded scenario is able to run more tasks in parallel and achieve higher cluster utilization, as spreading the tasks to the least loaded nodes allows for more efficient fitting when compared to choosing the most loaded nodes. In the case of the Max Loaded scenario, filling the most loaded nodes first, often leads to situations where tasks that request a specific number of nodes cannot fit into the cluster. Some nodes of the cluster are fully loaded and the number of nodes with enough space is smaller than the requested number of nodes. The Least Loaded policy achieved (14%) lower total execution times when compared to Max Loaded.

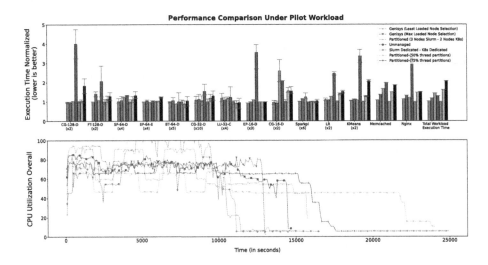

Fig. 2. Performance comparison of the different configurations

There was also a (4%) higher individual task performance. In the next sections we use the Least Loaded Policy in order to evaluate Genisys in contrast to other configurations.

Genisys vs Unmanaged: The Unmanaged setup introduces high interference between the tasks as Kubernetes and Slurm are not able to coordinate placement, which leads to resource over-subscription (both Kubernetes and Slurm see each individual node's resources as 100% available). Especially in the case of MPI tasks, this has catastrophic results in their performance, as threads running in congested nodes will slow down the whole job. During the runs, we observe that Slurm selects nodes serially, so jobs are packed in the first cluster nodes, which leaves other nodes underutilized. The Kubernetes default scheduler, on the other hand, places tasks in a round-robin fashion. The total execution time needed by Genisys's Least Loaded Policy to complete the combined workload is 11200 s, which is 25% faster when compared to Unmanaged (14633 s). On average the individual execution times are 28% faster when using Genisys compared to Unmanaged. Also, Genisys achieves higher average CPU utilization (90%), compared to Unmanaged (71%).

Genisys vs Partitioned: The Partitioned approach allows both HPC and data center tasks to have optimal performance as there is no resource overlapping, sacrificing, however, overall utilization. Due to restricting workloads into their corresponding partition, Slurm can not leverage resources from the Kubernetes cluster even when the execution of the data center tasks finishes. This results in a higher total workload execution time of 15800 s, 34% slower when compared to Genisys (11200 s). The average individual task completion time is 4% lower in the Genisys case. We assume that this is because Genisys spreads the tasks across all the cluster nodes and is able to better utilize the RDMA network. Again, Genisys achieves higher average CPU utilization (90%) compared to Partitioned (75%).

Genisys vs Thread Partitioned: While partitioning the cluster at the CPU level is an uncommon approach, it is interesting to compare it to Genisys, as Genisys allows resource sharing between data center and HPC tasks over the same physical nodes in a similar manner. The main goal of this experiment is to show that with Genisys we are going to have better resource utilization as workloads are not restricted to their respective partitions, so when one partition is underutilized the other will be able to leverage the free resources. The Thread Partitioned 50% scenario results in higher total workload execution time, 44% slower when compared to Genisys. The average individual task completion time is 4.5% lower in the Genisys case. Genisys achieves higher average CPU utilization (82%), compared to Thread Partitioned 50% (56%). In the Thread Partitioned case, when the data center workload finishes, Slurm is not able to utilize the Kubernetes nodes. Also due to the smaller number of threads available to both Slurm and Kubernetes, the tasks can not fit as efficiently as when running with Genisys. Similar results are obtained when overprovisioning, by assigning 75% of the resources to each partition. In Thread Partitioned 75%, the average individual task completion time is 28% lower in the Genisys case, which we attribute to even higher interference in congested nodes.

6   Conclusion

This paper presents a method to run HPC workloads in Kubernetes using portable and extensible containerized environments called *virtual clusters*. Virtual clusters include Slurm, so users can run existing scripts unmodified, and are deployed alongside other Kubernetes services on the same physical nodes. Without any additional changes, the resulting hybrid resource allocation environment would have individual Slurm instances operating within their virtual cluster constraints, unaware of what is happening at the overall cluster-level, where decisions are made by Kubernetes. To avoid resource allocation conflicts, we integrate Slurm with Kubernetes, by extending the Slurm controller to delegate placement decisions to Genisys, our custom Kubernetes scheduler.

Our evaluation results indicate that it is not only possible to colocate data center tasks with HPC jobs when remaining CPU cycles are available, but with appropriate scheduling it can be beneficial to overall performance. Overall, Genisys is able to integrate Slurm into the Kubernetes ecosystem with minimal performance overhead across different task categories. The evaluation shows that with the use of Genisys it is possible to reduce the execution time of combined workloads compared to unmanaged and partitioned approaches.

Acknowledgement. We thankfully acknowledge the support of the European Commission under the Horizon 2020 Programme through projects HiPEAC (GA-871174) and EVOLVE (GA-825061).

References

1. An open-source monitoring solution. https://prometheus.io/
2. The apache software foundation. apache http server benchmarking tool. https://httpd.apache.org/docs/2.2/programs/ab.html
3. VMware: The State of Kubernetes 2020. https://k8s.vmware.com/state-of-kubernetes-2020/
4. Bailey, D., et al.: The nas parallel benchmarks. Int. J. High Perform. Comput. Appl. **5**(3), 63–73 (1991)
5. Beltre, A.M., Saha, P., Govindaraju, M., Younge, A., Grant, R.E.: Enabling hpc workloads on cloud infrastructure using kubernetes container orchestration mechanisms. In: 2019 IEEE/ACM International Workshop on Containers and New Orchestration Paradigms for Isolated Environments in HPC (CANOPIE-HPC), pp. 11–20 (2019)
6. Cooper, B.F., Silberstein, A., Tam, E., Ramakrishnan, R., Sears, R.: Benchmarking cloud serving systems with YCSB. In: Proceedings of the 1st ACM Symposium on Cloud Computing, p. 143–154. SoCC 2010, ACM, New York, NY, USA (2010)
7. Delgado, P., Didona, D., Dinu, F., Zwaenepoel, W.: Job-aware scheduling in eagle: divide and stick to your probes. In: Proceedings of the Seventh ACM Symposium on Cloud Computing, pp. 497–509. SoCC 2016, ACM, New York, NY, USA (2016)

8. Felter, W., Ferreira, A., Rajamony, R., Rubio, J.: An updated performance comparison of virtual machines and linux containers. In: 2015 IEEE International Symposium on Performance Analysis of Systems and Software (ISPASS), pp. 171–172 (2015)
9. Herbein, S., et al.: Resource management for running hpc applications in container clouds, pp. 261–278, June 2016
10. Higgins, J., Holmes, V., Venters, C.: Orchestrating docker containers in the hpc environment, pp. 506–513, July 2015
11. Jin, T., Cai, Z., Li, B., Zheng, C., Jiang, G., Cheng, J.: Improving resource utilization by timely fine-grained scheduling. In: Proceedings of the Fifteenth European Conference on Computer Systems, pp. 1–16 (2020)
12. Li, M., Tan, J., Wang, Y., Zhang, L., Salapura, V.: Sparkbench: a comprehensive benchmarking suite for in memory data analytic platform spark. In: Proceedings of the 12th ACM International Conference on Computing Frontiers. CF 2015, ACM, New York, NY, USA (2015)
13. López-Huguet, S., Segrelles, J.D., Kasztelnik, M., Bubak, M., Blanquer, I.: Seamlessly managing HPC workloads through Kubernetes. In: Jagode, H., Anzt, H., Juckeland, G., Ltaief, H. (eds.) ISC High Performance 2020. LNCS, vol. 12321, pp. 310–320. Springer, Cham (2020). https://doi.org/10.1007/978-3-030-59851-8_20
14. Ortiz, J., Lee, B., Balazinska, M., Gehrke, J., Hellerstein, J.L.: Slaorchestrator: reducing the cost of performance slas for cloud data analytics. In: 2018 USENIX Annual Technical Conference (USENIX ATC 18), pp. 547–560. USENIX Association, Boston, MA, July 2018
15. Ousterhout, K., Canel, C., Ratnasamy, S., Shenker, S.: Monotasks: architecting for performance clarity in data analytics frameworks. In: Proceedings of the 26th Symposium on Operating Systems Principles, pp. 184–200 (2017)
16. Ousterhout, K., Wendell, P., Zaharia, M., Stoica, I.: Sparrow: distributed, low latency scheduling. In: Proceedings of the Twenty-Fourth ACM Symposium on Operating Systems Principles, pp. 69–84. ACM (2013)
17. Sfakianakis, Y., Marazakis, M., Bilas, A.: Skynet: performance-driven resource management for dynamic workloads. In: 2021 IEEE 14th International Conference on Cloud Computing (CLOUD). IEEE (2021)
18. Shvets, P., Voevodin, V., Nikitenko, D.: Approach to Workload Analysis of Large HPC Centers, pp. 16–30, July 2020
19. Zhao, L., et al.: Rhythm: component-distinguishable workload deployment in datacenters. In: Proceedings of the Fifteenth European Conference on Computer Systems, pp. 1–17 (2020)
20. Zhou, N., Georgiou, Y., Zhong, L., Zhou, H., Pospieszny, M.: Container orchestration on HPC systems. In: 2020 IEEE 13th International Conference on Cloud Computing (CLOUD), pp. 34–36 (2020)

Analyzing Unikernel Support for HPC: Experimental Study of OpenMP

Pierre Jacquot[1], Pierre Olivier[2], Christian Perez[1], and Abdulrahman Azab[3]([✉])

[1] Univ. Lyon, Inria, CNRS, ENS Lyon, UCBL, Lyon, France
{pierre.jacquot,christian.perez}@inria.fr
[2] The University of Manchester, Manchester, UK
pierre.olivier@manchester.ac.uk
[3] Division of Research Computing, University Center for Information technology
(USIT), University of Oslo, Oslo, Norway
abdulrahman.azab@usit.uio.no

Abstract. Unikernels are single-application operating systems designed to run as virtual machines. They are popular in the cloud domain and are considered as a good alternative to containers due to the benefits they provide in terms of performance, low resource consumption, and security. This paper investigates the use of unikernels as a platform for HPC applications. The performance and stability of two unikernel platforms (HermitCore and HermiTux) are experimentally evaluated over standard representative HPC OpenMP benchmarks. We observe that unikernels remarkably reduce the overhead due to system calls, leading to a significant speedup (up to 77%) in system-bound applications. For applications that are not system-intensive, there are a few performance differences between the unikernel and the vanilla Linux execution. It should be remarked that modern unikernel projects are not yet fully mature, and exhibit stability issues running some OpenMP benchmarks.

1 Introduction

The last decade saw the birth and growth of unikernels, a new field of systems software research. Unikernels [16,18] are virtualized, lightweight, single-address-space Operating System images. They are library operating systems (LibOSes) developed mainly for cloud and networking applications [17]. They fit into small Virtual Machine (VM) images, have low memory footprints, and boot in less than a second. They also present performance benefits, such as low-latency system calls, that have been demonstrated to significantly speed up cloud and networking applications [9,11,12,16]. In addition, Unikernels offer security advantages [19,25], including a reduced attack surface and strong isolation through hardware-assisted virtualization. Unikernels are thus seen as a potential future alternative to containers [20], and are a popular research topic in the systems community. They are mostly explored in the cloud domain [3,8,9,11–13,16,21].

© Springer Nature Switzerland AG 2022
H. Anzt et al. (Eds.): ISC High Performance 2022 Workshops, LNCS 13387, pp. 358–370, 2022.
https://doi.org/10.1007/978-3-031-23220-6_25

Although many of the benefits they provide seem attractive in the field of HPC, unikernels have not been much explored in this domain. The few related studies either do not focus on performance [21] or present only microbenchmarks [13].

This paper investigates the applicability of unikernels to execute HPC applications. We start by reviewing the high-level strengths and limitations of the unikernel OS design in the context of HPC. We identify the strengths in terms of performance (fast system calls, reduced OS noise), security (strong isolation) and lightweightness (low memory footprint). Concerning the limitations, we note that unikernels are still at the state of prototypes and suffer from a lack of maturity: they have a relatively poor degree of compatibility regarding hardware (Symmetric Multiprocessing and GPU/Infiniband devices support) and software [14,21] (programming languages, applications, libraries, toolchains) components. This lack of maturity also translates into stability issues with some applications at runtime. Finally, the fact that most unikernel models are developed by small teams of volunteers/academics raises questions regarding the long-term maintenance of these projects. Focusing on shared-memory multithreaded HPC applications (OpenMP), we study the existing unikernels models and identified the best candidates for running such programs: HermitCore [13] and HermiTux [21].

Using standard OpenMP benchmarks, we evaluate the performance of unikernels by comparing the execution times on HermitCore and HermiTux compared to vanilla Linux. We observe that the fast system calls feature of unikernels can bring significant speedups to the OpenMP applications for which are frequently calling the operating system mainly through scheduler-related system calls. For applications that are not OS-intensive, i.e. not performing frequent system calls, the performance difference between unikernel and Linux execution is relatively negligible.

Finally, we evaluate the stability of unikernels over the Bots [6] and Rodinias [4] benchmarks and highlight the issues of crashes and deadlocks.

To sum up, this paper proposes the following contributions:

- A review of the current unikernel benefits and limitations in the context of HPC applications.
- Based on that review and focusing on shared-memory multithreading, the identification of the most suitable unikernel models to execute OpenMP programs: HermitCore [13] and HermiTux [21].
- A stability evaluation of these two unikernels highlighting maturity issues with some programs.
- A performance evaluation of HermitCore and HermiTux over standard OpenMP benchmarks demonstrating performance improvement for OS-intensive applications.

This paper is organized as follows: Sect. 2 gives some background about unikernels. Section 3 presents our experimental setup. Section 4 deals with the experimental stability evaluation while Sect. 5 focuses on experimental performance evaluation. Finally, Sect. 6 concludes the paper.

2   A Background on Unikernels

The idea behind unikernels originates from the observation that in many virtualization use cases, a full-fledged VM is deployed for the sole reason of running a single application (e.g. a web server, a database, etc.). The vast amount of software that is included in the VM, but that is not necessary to the application's execution represents as many software bloats [24]. Software bloat, also known as bloatware, refers to unneeded software that is pre-installed (e.g. libraries, executables) and running (e.g. deamons) in a traditional distribution, but also from the large monolithic guest kernel (Linux), of which only a small subset of the services are needed for the executed application. This software bloat impacts performance as well as resource usage and thus costs. In terms of security it also represents a wide attack surface. Although the use of containers [20] may partially solve these issues, for security reasons practitioners do not fully trust inter-container isolation [19] as shown by the current trend of running containers within VMs [22]. Originally proposed in the MirageOS seminal paper [16] in 2013, with the unikernel OS model, an application is statically compiled into a binary with only the necessary libraries and a thin OS layer, in order to be executed as a virtualized guest on top of a hypervisor. The unikernel OS layer is a LibOS [7], and as such when the unikernel is built at compile time, only the necessary OS services are included [11]. Figure 1 illustrates how unikernels tackle the previously mentioned issues By running only the necessary software. Unikernels reduce resource consumption, increase efficient (i.e. application) resource usage, and lower the attack surface. From the security standpoint, a unikernel instance is in effect a VM and hence does not suffer from the isolation issues of containers [19].

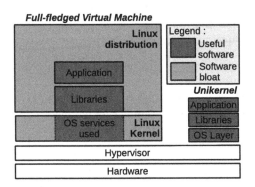

Fig. 1. Illustration of a traditional VM (left) and a unikernel (right).

A unikernel instance executes a single application within a single address space. As such, within a guest OS the unikernel does not need to maintain inter-application isolation. This removes the need for user-kernel isolation and

Table 1. List of Bots benchmarks, and their respective OpenMP variants.

Implementation	Alignment	FFT	Fib	Floorplan	Health	NQueens	Sort	SparseLU	Strassen
omp-tasks		✓	✓	✓	✓	✓	✓		✓
omp-tasks-tied		✓	✓	✓	✓	✓	✓		✓
omp-tasks-if_clause			✓	✓	✓	✓			✓
omp-tasks-if_clause-tied			✓	✓	✓	✓			✓
omp-tasks-manual			✓	✓	✓	✓			✓
omp-tasks-manual-tied			✓	✓	✓	✓			✓
for-omp-tasks	✓							✓	
for-omp-tasks-tied	✓							✓	
single-omp-tasks	✓							✓	
single-omp-tasks-tied	✓							✓	

all the code in a unikernel instance, including user code, executes on the processor with full privileges (supervisor mode i.e. protection ring 0 for x86-64). This has the interesting effect of transforming system calls into common function calls. A traditional system call is a costly operation [23] that is involving an interrupt and a world-switch. Function calls' latency being one to several orders of magnitude faster, and thus unikernels can bring significant speedups to OS-intensive applications [9,11,12]. It should be noted that the isolation between different unikernel instances (i.e. different applications) running on the same host is still maintained by the hypervisor. With their minimalist design, unikernels represent a form of lightweight virtualization: their memory and disk footprints can be as low as a few megabytes [11], and their boot time is in the order of a few milliseconds [21]. There exist several unikernel platforms [3,5,8,11–13,16,21,27], which can broadly be classified into two categories: *Language-based*, and *POSIX-Like* unikernels. Language based unikernels support running applications which are written in a high level memory-safe language. Examples include MirageOS [16] (OCaml), LING [5] (Erlang) or HalVM [26] (Haskell). Although this provides some benefits in terms of security and optimizations, a major downside of language-based unikernels is the high cost of porting legacy applications which are not originally written in the associated language. On the other hand, POSIX-like unikernels aim at offering legacy application compatibility to some extent. Some of those unikernels (e.g. Rumprun [8] and HermitCore [13]) are source-level compatible, i.e. generally interfacing with the application at the level of the C library. Others are binary-compatible in order to avoid recompilation, which means that they can run unmodified binaries from a popular OS, Linux. Binary compatibility can be achieved at the system call level as with HermiTux [21] and Unikraft [11] or, in a more restrictive way, at the libc level as with OSv [9] and Lupine Linux [12].

3   Experimental Setup

Hardware Description. For the experimental evaluation, we have make use of two nodes of two clusters of Grid'5000 [2]. The nova node is a Dell PowerEdge R430 node equipped with two 8-core Intel Xeon E5-2620v4 Broadwell CPU (2.10GHz). The gros node is a Dell PowerEdge R640 equipped with a 18-core Intel Xeon Gold 5220 Cascade Lake-SP CPU (2.20GHz). The hyper-threading feature was disabled.

Unikernel Models. We use the HermitCore and HermiTux[1] unikernels, and a Debian 10 distribution (Linux kernel version 4.19.0-14-amd64) to have a base reference.

Due to unikernels limitations regarding OpenMP and compilers, we have been forced to compile specific executables for Linux and each unikernels. HermitCore executables are compiled with HermitCore's toolchain (GCC v6.3), and Hermit-Core's OpenMP Intel runtime (v5.0) compiled with GCC v6.3. Note that the use of HermitCore's toolchain is mandatory with this unikernel, forcing the use of these relatively outdated compiler and OpenMP versions. HermiTux executables are compiled with Clang/LLVM version 11, and linked with the LLVM OpenMP runtime version 11 (compiled with Clang v11) thanks to HermiTux' GCC wrapper. For our Linux baseline, executables are compiled with Clang/LLVM version 11, and use the LLVM OpenMP runtime version 11 (compiled with Clang v11).

Benchmarks. Experiments have been made with two set of benchmarks.

Bots Benchmarks. The Bots benchmarks [6] have been developed by the Barcelona Supercomputing Center. They are used for evaluating various OpenMP tasking implementations for some given problems. We make use of the 8 codes: alignement, fft, fib, floorplan, health nqueens, sort, sparselu, as well as strassen. These codes have several OpenMP implementation variants (from 2 to 6 versions). We are using all the variants to evaluate whether they have an impact. Table 1 sumps up these variants.

To compile the Bots benchmarks for HermitCore, two modifications were performed on the sources as HermitCore does not support the utsname structure and the basename(). As they are not critical, we remove their usage. Compiling for HermitCore further required to update the benchmarks' build infrastructure to make use of the unikernel specific toolchain. On the other hand, building for HermiTux was as simple as a standard Linux build and required no source modifications, demonstrating the benefits of binary-compatibility [21].

---

[1] The commit used for HermiTux is: d92b5bd from https://github.com/ssrg-vt/HermiTux; and for HermitCore the commit is: 2ff4836 from https://github.com/hermitcore/libhermit.

Rodinias Benchmarks. The Rodinias benchmarks [4] are designed to evaluate different accelerators for compute-intensive applications: OpenMP, OpenCL, and CUDA. They are composed of existing codes and come from many scientific domains. Note that some of the Rodinia's benchmarks showed some crashes and strange behavior, and as such we present results here for the stable ones: Lud (LU Decomposition) and LavaMD (3D Molecular Dynamics). These represent long and compute-intensive applications. We only used the OpenMP versions.

4 Stability Evaluation

This section illustrates the stability evaluation of the HermitCore and HermiTux unikernels on the Bots benchmarks.

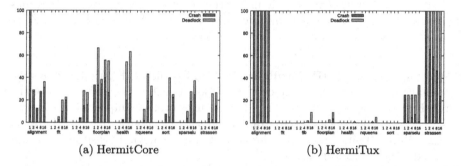

(a) HermitCore   (b) HermiTux

Fig. 2. Percentage of crashes and deadlocks of all Bots benchmarks for HermitCore and HermiTux, averaged across all variants, in function of the number of core.

While experimenting with these unikernels, we observed two types of faults: crashes and deadlocks. A crash occurs when a program aborts its execution prematurely through an exception such as a page fault or a general protection fault. A deadlock occurs when a program's execution seems stuck for an abnormal amount of time. This limits has been arbitrarily fixed at the time measured on our Linux baseline plus 20 s. Still on the baseline, please note that all benchmarks considered here execute without any crash or deadlock on Linux (Debian 10).

For this study, we consider three parameters: the OS kernel type, the number of cores, and the program. The three kernel types have been considered: HermitCore, HermiTux and a Linux baseline (a Debian 10 distribution with Linux v4.19). The number of cores varies from 1 to 16 cores. With respect to programs, we make use of all the variants of the Bots benchmarks.

Stability Improvements of HermiTux. Preliminary experiments highlighted two major bugs in HermiTux' kernel. A first issue was a bug in the memory management subsystem, that occurred for a particular use case of the mmap system call. The second issue was a thread management bug that caused deadlocks.

After filing a bug report, these issues were fixed by HermiTux' main developer and in the rest of this section we give result for the version of HermiTux with these bug fixes.

Impact of the Number of Cores on Stability. Figure 2 shows that Hermit-Core and HermiTux have some differences in stability. For HermitCore, there is at least one configuration that leads to a crash and/or a deadlock for all benchmarks. However, there is only one situation (`alignement`, 1 core) that systematically crashes. For other benchmarks, increasing the number of cores, usually leads to a higher probability of crash and/or deadlocks. One and two core execution do not show crash or deadlocks but for `alignement`.

For HermiTux, there are two benchmarks (`alignement` and `strassen`) that are not able to complete (due to either crash or deadlock) in all configurations. For `strassen` and `sparselu`, it is interesting to note that the crash probability decreases with the number of cores. For the other benchmarks, HermiTux experienced very few crashes and few deadlocks.

Impact of the OpenMP Parallelization on Stability. Figure 3 displays the percentage of crashes and deadlocks for all Bots benchmarks in function of the parallelization variants (c.f., Table 1). For HermitCore, the impact of the variant is not very relevant but for `floorplan`, where there is a huge difference between the `if_clause` (tied or nod) and the `manual` (tied or not). This situation is not observed in other benchmarks.

The situation for HermiTux is very similar as the variants do not impact stability but for `floorplan` and `sparselu` where each code has a variant that crashes and/or deadlocks, respectively `omp-task` and `single-omp-tasks`.

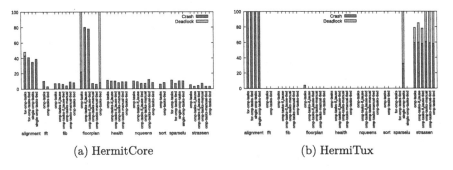

(a) HermitCore   (b) HermiTux

Fig. 3. Percentage of crashes and deadlocks of all Bots benchmarks for HermitCore and HermiTux, averaged across the number of cores, in function of the OpenMP variants.

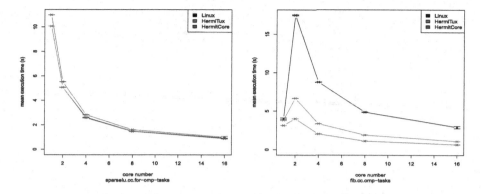

Fig. 4. Execution times for `sparselu` and `fib` benchmarks, omp-tasks variant.

5   Performance Evaluation

Overview. In this section, we evaluate the performance of the HermitCore and HermiTux unikernels on a subset of the Bots and Rodinias benchmarks. Two main metrics are used in the experiments: the execution time and the number of systems calls executed. As this latter is difficult to measure with Unikernels, we measure it on the vanilla Linux with the `strace` command.

We consider four parameters: the OS kernel version, the number of cores (1 to 16 cores), the program, and the CPU model (`nova` or `gros` node). Note that we only use the omp-tasks variant as the goal is to study the impact of unikernels. For executables that experienced some crashes or deadlocks, we execute as many times it is required to obtained 20 successful executions. For the Bots benchmarks, we mainly report the results for `fib` and `sparselu` as they are representative of the rest of the benchmarks. From the Rodinias benchmarks, as discussed above we select `LavaMD` and `Lud`.

Performance Results: Bots Benchmarks. The results fall into two classes. For space constraints, we only present one typical example for each class: Fig. 4 displays the execution time for `sparselu` and `fib`. For `sparselu`, both unikernels and Linux have similar and classical performance. In fact, this is the case for most of the benchmarks. HermitCore tends to be slightly slower than HermiTux. A potential explanation is that HermitCore's executables are compiled with an older compiler compared to HermiTux' (GCC v6.3 vs. clang/LLVM 11).

For two particular benchmarks (`fib` and `nqueens`– not displayed), unikernels dramatically accelerate execution time when the number of cores increases. With 16 cores, `fib.omp-tasks` and `nqueens.omp-tasks` benchmarks are two times faster when they are executed with a unikernel than with Linux. This is due to the fast system calls feature of unikernels: indeed we observed that these particulars benchmarks make very frequent scheduling-related system calls. Our Linux' baseline presents a high system call latency, while the unikernels significantly reduce it. We also observe that HermitCore is faster than HermiTux.

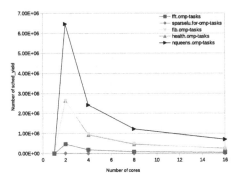

Fig. 5. Systems calls performed during the execution of the benchmarks.

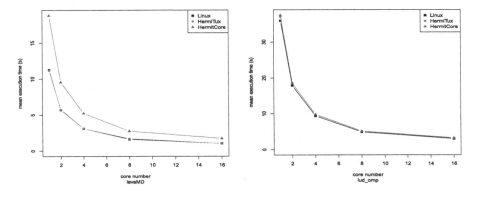

Fig. 6. LavaMD and Lud Rodinias benchmarks, executed on a `gros` node.

This is due to the fact that in HermitCore, system calls are pure function calls, while HermiTux still uses a trap-based mechanism to provide binary compatibility [21]. Still in HermiTux that operation is significantly optimized compared to Linux' system calls, which explains why HermiTux is much faster than the baseline for these OS-intensive benchmarks.

We traced the system calls made by these benchmarks using `strace`. Figure 5 displays a graph where the number of `sched_yield` systems calls performed by an execution of the benchmarks on Linux is plotted in function of the number of cores. As the number of system calls invoked other than `sched_yield` is negligible, we do not display them. Some benchmarks clearly stand out by performing a lot of `sched_yield` system calls. These benchmarks are `fib.omp-tasks` and `nqueens.omp-tasks` where we observed a better performance on unikernels than on vanilla Linux. Hence, we can infer that the execution time improvement comes from the high number of `sched_yield` performed. In addition, we note that for benchmarks where we observe similar performance between unikernels and Linux, we also observe a much smaller number of `sched_yield` which also seem coherent.

The source of these high numbers of `sched_yield` system calls seems to be the LLVM OpenMP runtime that use this system call for its task stealing paradigm. `fib` and `nqueens` are not compute intensive: they do no generate not enough tasks hence leading to many yield operations.

Since the discovery of the SPECTRE [10] and Meltdown [15] side-channels in Intel processors, the cost of system calls have greatly increased on most CPU models due to the introduction of the corresponding software mitigation, *Kernel Page Table Isolation* (KPTI), involving an additional page table switch introduce upon invocation and return from system calls. The `nova` node we used to run the benchmarks is equipped with an Intel CPU requiring KPTI. More recent Intel CPUs include a hardware-based mitigation that negates the need for KPTI, significantly improving system call latency with Linux. To verify if the impact of system calls on the time execution was due KPTI, a costly software fix that we deem temporary in terms of processor generations, we ran the benchmarks on a `gros` node that includes the hardware fix and does not require KPTI. Still, experiments show that the performance profile is similar when the benchmarks are executed on the new CPU. Hence, the fix of these vulnerabilities does not show to have an impact on the behavior of the performance, and it is likely that the fast system call feature of unikernel will be beneficial versus traditional Linux system calls in the long term.

Performance Results: Rodinias Benchmarks. Figure 6 shows the execution time for two Rodinias benchmarks: `LavaMD` and `lud_omp`. The execution times of unikernels and Linux are very similar to compute intensive benchmarks of the Bots benchmarks.

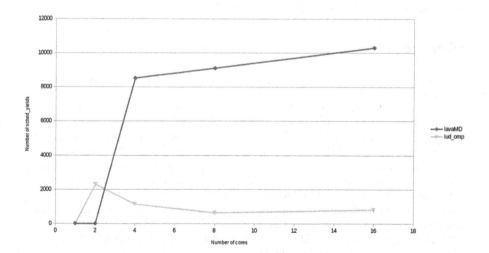

Fig. 7. Systems calls performed for lavaMD and Lud benchmarks

Figure 7 shows that the number of `sched_yield` system calls performed by the two benchmarks are low. This confirms the fact that unikernels take advantage when Linux is slowed down by the many systems calls performed by a program or a runtime. When a program is compute-intensive, unikernels does not stand out by accelerating its execution.

6   Conclusion

In this paper we conduct a stability and performance evaluation of two unikernels using OpenMP benchmarks. We highlight performance improvements (up to 77%) for applications making frequent system calls. We also demonstrate the lack of maturity of unikernels, in the form of stability issues (deadlocks, crashes) on our benchmarks. We conclude that, although unikernels do have benefits to bring in the domain of HPC, they are still facing many limitations that will undoubtedly hinder a wide adoption for the time being. Still, we believe that addressing these issues is a matter of engineering. Most of these problems are in the process of being solved, and the emergence of unikernel projects backed up by major industrial actors (e.g. Unikraft) gives hope for a growing adoption in the years to come.

Acknowledgments. This work was financially supported by the PRACE project [1] funded in part by the EU's Horizon 2020 Research and Innovation programme (2014–2020) under grant agreement 823767. Olivier's work is partly funded by the UK's EPSRC New Investigator Award grant EP/V012134/1. Experiments presented in this paper were carried out using the Grid'5000 testbed, supported by a scientific interest group hosted by Inria and including CNRS, RENATER and several Universities as well as other organizations (see https://www.grid5000.fr).

References

1. Partnership for advanced computing in Europe. http://www.prace-project.eu. Accessed 16 Dec 2019
2. Bolze, R., et al.: Grid'5000: a large scale and highly reconfigurable experimental grid testbed. Int. J. High Perform. Comput. App. **20**(4), 481–494 (2006)
3. Bratterud, A., Walla, A.A., Haugerud, H., Engelstad, P.E., Begnum, K.: IncludeOS: A minimal, resource efficient unikernel for cloud services. In: 2015 IEEE 7th International Conference on Cloud Computing Technology and Science (CloudCom), pp. 250–257. IEEE (2015–11). https://doi.org/10.1109/CloudCom.2015.89, http://ieeexplore.ieee.org/document/7396164/
4. Che, S., et al.: Rodinia: a benchmark suite for heterogeneous computing. In: 2009 IEEE International Symposium on Workload Characterization (IISWC), pp. 44–54. IEEE, December 2009. https://doi.org/10.1109/IISWC.2009.5306797, http://ieeexplore.ieee.org/document/5306797/
5. Cloudozer LLP: Ling/erlang on xen website (2017). http://erlangonxen.org/. Accessed 20 Nov 2017

6. Duran, A., Teruel, X., Ferrer, R., Martorell, X., Ayguade, E.: Barcelona OpenMP tasks suite: a set of benchmarks targeting the exploitation of task parallelism in OpenMP. In: 2009 International Conference on Parallel Processing, pp. 124–131. IEEE, Sep 2009. https://doi.org/10.1109/ICPP.2009.64, http://ieeexplore.ieee.org/document/5361951/

7. Engler, D.R., Kaashoek, M.F., O'Toole, J.: Exokernel: an operating system architecture for application-level resource management. In: Proceedings of the Fifteenth ACM Symposium on Operating Systems Principles, pp. 251–266. SOSP 1995, Association for Computing Machinery, New York, NY, USA (1995). https://doi.org/10.1145/224056.224076, https://doi.org/10.1145/224056.224076

8. Kantee, A., Cormack, J.: Rump kernels : No OS? no problem! (2014)

9. Kivity, A., et al.: Osv—optimizing the operating system for virtual machines. In: USENIX Annual Technical Conference (USENIX ATC 2014), pp. 61–72. USENIX Association, Philadelphia, PA, June 2014. https://www.usenix.org/conference/atc14/technical-sessions/presentation/kivity

10. Kocher, P., et al.: Spectre attacks: exploiting speculative execution. In: 2019 IEEE Symposium on Security and Privacy (SP), pp. 1–19. IEEE (2019)

11. Kuenzer, S., et al.: Unikraft: fast, specialized unikernels the easy way. In: Proceedings of the Sixteenth European Conference on Computer Systems, pp. 376–394. ACM, Apr 2021. https://doi.org/10.1145/3447786.3456248, https://dl.acm.org/doi/10.1145/3447786.3456248

12. Kuo, H.C., Williams, D., Koller, R., Mohan, S.: A Linux in unikernel clothing. In: Proceedings of the Fifteenth European Conference on Computer Systems, pp. 1–15. ACM, Apr 2020. https://doi.org/10.1145/3342195.3387526, https://dl.acm.org/doi/10.1145/3342195.3387526

13. Lankes, S., Pickartz, S., Breitbart, J.: HermitCore: a unikernel for extreme scale computing. In: Proceedings of the 6th International Workshop on Runtime and Operating Systems for Supercomputers, pp. 1–8. ACM, June 2016. https://doi.org/10.1145/2931088.2931093, https://dl.acm.org/doi/10.1145/2931088.2931093

14. Lefeuvre, H., et al.: Unikraft and the coming of age of unikernels. In: USENIX; login: (2021). https://www.usenix.org/publications/loginonline/unikraft-and-coming-age-unikernels

15. Lipp, M., et al.: Meltdown: Reading kernel memory from user space. In: 27th USENIX Security Symposium (USENIX Security 2018), pp. 973–990 (2018)

16. Madhavapeddy, A., et al.: Unikernels: library operating systems for the cloud. SIGARCH Comput. Archit. News **41**(1), 461–472 (2013). https://doi.org/10.1145/2490301.2451167, https://doi.org/10.1145/2490301.2451167

17. Madhavapeddy, A., et al.: Unikernels: library operating systems for the cloud. ACM SIGPLAN Notices **48**(4), 461–472 (Apr 2013). https://doi.org/10.1145/2499368.2451167, https://doi.org/10.1145/2499368.2451167

18. Madhavapeddy, A., Scott, D.J.: Unikernels: rise of the virtual library operating system. Queue. **11**(11), 30–44 (2013). https://doi.org/10.1145/2557963.2566628, https://doi.org/10.1145/2557963.2566628

19. Manco, F., et al.: My VM is lighter (and safer) than your container. In: Proceedings of the 26th Symposium on Operating Systems Principles, pp. 218–233 (2017)

20. Merkel, D.: Docker: lightweight Linux containers for consistent development and deployment. Linux J. **2014**(239), 2 (2014)

21. Olivier, P., Chiba, D., Lankes, S., Min, C., Ravindran, B.: A binary-compatible unikernel. In: Proceedings of the 15th ACM SIGPLAN/SIGOPS International Conference on Virtual Execution Environments - VEE 2019, pp. 59–73. ACM Press (2019). https://doi.org/10.1145/3313808.3313817, http://dl.acm.org/citation.cfm?doid=3313808.3313817

22. Randazzo, A., Tinnirello, I.: Kata containers: an emerging architecture for enabling MEC services in fast and secure way. In: 2019 Sixth International Conference on Internet of Things: Systems, Management and Security (IOTSMS), pp. 209–214. IEEE (2019)

23. Soares, L., Stumm, M.: FlexSC: flexible system call scheduling with exception-less system calls. In: 9th USENIX Symposium on Operating Systems Design and Implementation (OSDI 2010), p. 14. USENIX Association, Vancouver, BC, October 2010. https://www.usenix.org/conference/osdi10/flexsc-flexible-system-call-scheduling-exception-less-system-calls

24. Soto-Valero, C., Harrand, N., Monperrus, M., Baudry, B.: A comprehensive study of bloated dependencies in the Maven ecosystem. Empir. Softw. Eng. **26**(3), 1–44 (2021). https://doi.org/10.1007/s10664-020-09914-8

25. Sung, M., Olivier, P., Lankes, S., Ravindran, B.: Intra-unikernel isolation with intel memory protection keys. In: Proceedings of the 16th ACM SIGPLAN/SIGOPS International Conference on Virtual Execution Environments, pp. 143–156 (2020)

26. Wick, A.: The HalVM: A simple platform for simple platforms. Xen Summit (2012)

27. Zhang, Y., et al.: KylinX: a dynamic library operating system for simplified and efficient cloud virtualization. In: Proceedings of the 2018 USENIX Annual Technical Conference (2018)

On the Use of Linux Real-Time Features for RAN Packet Processing in Cloud Environments

Luca Abeni[1]([✉]), Tommaso Cucinotta[1], Balázs Pinczel[2], Péter Mátray[2],
Murali Krishna Srinivasan[3], and Tobias Lindquist[3]

[1] Scuola Superiore Sant'Anna, Pisa, Italy
{luca.abeni,tommaso.cucinotta}@santannapisa.it
[2] Ericsson, Budapest, Hungary
{balazs.pinczel,peter.matray}@ericsson.com
[3] Ericsson, Stockholm, Sweden
{murali.krishna.xk.srinivasan,tobias.lindquist}@ericsson.com

Abstract. This paper shows how to use a Linux-based operating system as a real-time processing platform for low-latency and predictable packet processing in cloudified radio-access network (cRAN) scenarios. This use-case exhibits challenging end-to-end processing latencies, in the order of milliseconds for the most time-critical layers of the stack. A significant portion of the variability and instability in the observed end-to-end performance in this domain is due to the power saving capabilities of modern CPUs, often in contrast with the low-latency and high-performance requirements of this type of applications. We discuss how to properly configure the system for this scenario, and evaluate the proposed configuration on a synthetic application designed to mimic the behavior and computational requirements of typical software components implementing baseband processing in production environments.

1 Introduction

Networking infrastructures are experiencing a huge paradigm shift, with an ever-increasing need to support, among others, mobile scenarios with higher and higher performance requirements, both in terms of networking bandwidth and of predictable or ultra-low latency. This requires a great degree of flexibility and adaptation in the management of physical resources, where a number of lessons learnt from the domain of cloud computing are being applied in the context of networking infrastructures. For example, this is witnessed by the recent rise of network function virtualization (NFV) [3,4] (often coupled with software-defined networking (SDN) [9]).

A NFV infrastructure hosts a number of Virtualized Network Functions (VNFs) that need to process packets with low latency. In 5G mobile scenarios, this latency has to be controlled even in the milliseconds-scale, to support properly ultra-reliable low-latency communications (URLLC) [2,7], one of the

© Springer Nature Switzerland AG 2022
H. Anzt et al. (Eds.): ISC High Performance 2022 Workshops, LNCS 13387, pp. 371–382, 2022.
https://doi.org/10.1007/978-3-031-23220-6_26

key characteristics of 5G architectures enabling mobile communications in modern and future use-cases in such areas as industrial manufacturing and factory automation, robotics and automotive. For example, individual VNF components hosted in an NFV infrastructure may sometimes have available a "budget" in terms of processing latency [6] that can become as little as $1ms$, which is the case of baseband packet processing, the use-case we focus on in the present paper.

One of the advantages of applying cloud principles to NFV infrastructures, is the ability to host a diverse set of workloads with heterogeneous requirements within a shared physical infrastructure. This is a geo-distributed and multi-site data center equipped with flexible storage solutions and general-purpose servers, where different VNF components are often co-located on the same physical servers in the form of virtual machines or containers.

However, due to the strict timing requirements of the scenarios mentioned above, it is of paramount importance to be able to guarantee that the end-to-end performance of hosted applications is not impaired by: a) the virtualization layer, often used to achieve the needed flexibility in management of the physical resources throughout the NFV infrastructure; b) the temporal interferences due to the co-location of multiple VNF components onto the same servers.

The second problem is well-known and often referred to as the "noisy neighbour" problem. It is generally tackled in both general cloud and NFV infrastructures by recurring to a number of custom configurations of the virtualized or containerized environment for hosting guests, typically by [10]: disabling over-provisioning in the virtual to physical CPU allocation, and applying a static mapping among them (core pinning); similarly, disabling memory over-commitment and dynamic allocation (ballooning); deploying data-intensive components with greater risks of interference in different NUMA nodes, so to minimize the interferences among their data paths in the hierarchical memory subsystem, i.e., preventing contention at the L2-cache access and memory-controller levels; disabling hyperthreading. However, some of these configurations (such as, for example, disabling hyperthreading) are not recommended in cloud environments because they end up decreasing the CPU throughput and the possibility to run multiple applications on the cloud nodes.

This paper provides an experimental evaluation of the impact of various hardware and OS tuning features mentioned above. We focus on an industrial use-case scenario tied to low-latency packet processing for 5G/URLLC, namely baseband packet processing. The results show that with careful tuning of the hardware and software configuration it is possible to remove most of the sources of interference and tail-latency (making it possible to host such an application with the required level of time-predictability) without compromising the CPU throughput and the performance of other applications running in the cloud. While previous works [5] disabled features like hyperthreading to achieve more predictable response times, this work shows how hyperthreading can be left enabled without compromising the real-time performance of the baseband software.

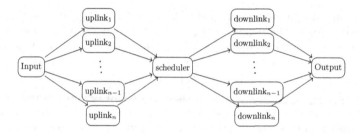

Fig. 1. Model of the baseband application as a DAG.

2   Scheduling the BaseBand Application

In RAN packet processing, multiple frequencies of the available spectrum are used to handle communications, where the time is divided into Transmission Time Intervals (TTIs) all having the same duration. In each TTI, data is received by the various radio cells, and new data is prepared to be transmitted to them.

The baseband software considered as a test-case for this work is designed to serve n cells and is a multi-threaded application, described by the directed acyclic graph (DAG) shown in Fig. 1. This is composed of: an I/O thread, responsible for communications with the remote radio units ("Input" and "Output" nodes in the figure); n uplink threads processing data received from one of the cells; a scheduler thread, coordinating the use of the spectrum and time slots within each TTI; n downlink threads preparing data to be sent to one of the cells. In practice, there is an uplink thread and a downlink thread per cell.

For the sake of simplicity, assume that the I/O thread periodically activates all the uplink threads at the beginning of each TTI. After executing for some time, each uplink thread sends an activation to the scheduler thread and then blocks until the beginning of the next TTI (next activation from the I/O thread). After receiving an activation from all the n uplink threads, the scheduler thread wakes up, executes for some time, and then activates all the downlink threads. If the end of the TTI arrives before all the uplink threads sent an activation to the scheduler thread, a timeout fires and the scheduler thread is activated anyway. Each downlink thread, after being activated by the scheduler thread, executes for some time and then terminates; all the n downlink threads should terminate before the end of the period.

Hence, we measure an end-to-end response time from the activation of the first uplink thread to the termination of the last downlink thread. This end-to-end response time should be smaller than an end-to-end relative deadline D which is equal to the TTI duration. If such a deadline is seldom missed, then higher-layer protocols can recover by re-transmits, but if this occurs too frequently, then the transmissions degrade in quality or even fail. Looking at Fig. 1, we can see that if C_{ul}, C_{sched}, and C_{dl} are the WCETs (worst case execution times) of the uplink, scheduler and downlink threads, then the maximum end-to-end response time, equal to the longest path from I/O to the downlink termination (maximum makespan of the DAG), is $C_{ul}+C_{sched}+C_{dl}$. So, the parallel task will respect the deadline D if $C_{ul} + C_{sched} + C_{dl} \leq D$. This response time can be obtained by scheduling all the threads as soon as they are activated, and using n CPU cores (a core sequentially executes an uplink thread, the scheduler thread and a downlink thread, the other $n - 1$ cores execute an uplink thread and a downlink thread). Hence, the end-to-end response time can be minimized by having only one active real-time thread per core, avoiding temporal scheduling; in this case, a SCHED_FIFO scheduling policy is considered to be the best option to run this application: if each thread is assigned the maximum real-time priority, then it is scheduled as soon as it activates, as required. More advanced scheduling policies such as SCHED_DEADLINE [1,8] could be useful when the CPU scheduler has to schedule multiple real-time threads on the same CPU core, or when it is necessary to limit the fraction of CPU time consumed by a real-time application. Pinning real-time threads to specific CPU cores can be useful to avoid migrations and reduce the scheduling overheads, or to cope with the unpredictabilities caused by hyperthreading, as shown in Sect. 3.

When there are no uplink/scheduler timeouts, the scheduler executes only after all the uplink threads are finished, and the downlink threads execute only after the scheduler thread is finished; so, if the total end-to-end time is smaller than $1\,TTI$, then this property is respected using n cores only. If an uplink thread takes more than $1\,TTI$ (scheduler timeout) or the total end-to-end response time is larger than $1\,TTI$ (uplink threads are activated while downlink threads are still active), then $2n$ cores could potentially be needed.

For certain scenarios, a typical pattern of execution times could look like the following: the execution times of the uplink threads are generally shorter than $500\,\mu s$ (except for a few rare outliers), the execution times of the scheduler thread are generally smaller than $100\,\mu s$, and the execution times of the downlink threads are generally smaller than $300\,\mu s$. However, there are a few sources of non-determinism causing fluctuations in these numbers, i.e., radio link quality, channel coding, cell load, and others. Assuming $C_{ul} = 500\,\mu s$, $C_{sched} = 100\,\mu s$, and $C_{dl} = 300\,\mu s$, we have $C_{ul} + C_{sched} + C_{dl} = 900\,\mu s$, so a TTI of $1\,ms$ can be supported using n CPU cores.

If, instead, execution times distributions with longer tails are assumed, then $2n$ CPU cores might be needed.

3   CPU Configuration

The goal of this work is to run a virtual baseband application on a large server based on multiple Intel x86 CPUs with a large number of cores. These modern CPUs are designed to maximize the average performance/throughput and reduce power consumption by using various mechanisms. The three most important ones are Dynamic Voltage and Frequency Scaling (DVFS), CPU idle states, and hyperthreading. In particular, DVFS and idle states allow reducing power consumption when the server is not fully loaded, while hyperthreading allows doubling the number of *logical* CPU cores seen by applications.

The hyperthreading technology allows the OS kernel to see a single CPU core (referred to as *hardware core* in the following) as two *siblings* (also referred to as *logical cores* or *hardware threads*). This means that if a CPU is composed of n hardware cores the OS can use $2n$ siblings to schedule the application tasks. Technically, this result is achieved by duplicating the hardware resources that store the state of each core (such as the CPU registers). Other hardware resources such as the ALU, the caches, and similar, instead, are not duplicated and are shared by the siblings executing on the same physical core. The two siblings executing on the same physical core risk competing for the execution resources that are not duplicated; hence, running an application on a sibling can slow down the execution of applications on the other one. This makes the execution unpredictable, and this is why hyperthreading is often disabled when real-time performance and determinism are important.

When a CPU is idle (it has no tasks to execute), some hardware components can be turned off to save some energy. Modern CPUs allow to achieve this result by entering different *idle states*; for example, Intel CPUs can be in different "C-states" (named, C0, C1, etc.). Increasing the state number, a C-state is said to be "deeper", stops more hardware components, and allows saving more energy. Returning from an idle state to C0 takes some time, which increases with the state number (deeper C-states have longer exit and entry latencies). This is why modern operating system kernels such as Linux allow disabling some (or all) of the idle states. When all the idle states are disabled and a CPU is idle, it executes a busy loop in the idle task.

In Intel CPUs, C-states are per physical core (so, a hardware thread cannot enter an idle state if the other sibling of the physical core is executing machine instructions), however, Linux allows disabling C-states for individual logical cores. When a sibling is idle and can enter an idle state, it is stopped (so, a single sibling remains active on the physical core) but the C-state of the physical core does not change until its other sibling also needs to enter an idle state.

Finally, the DVFS mechanism allows lowering the working frequency of CPU cores (and consequently the voltage at which the CPU is driven) to save some energy. Obviously, the frequency of a core should be reduced when the core is not fully loaded. Generally, the OS is responsible for selecting the most appropriate working frequency for the various CPU cores, based on an estimation of the system workload or on some constraints imposed by the applications running in the system. The various frequency/voltage configurations supported by a CPU are often known as Operating Performance Points (OPP) or Power States (P-states); even if in modern Intel CPUs the P-state concept is more advanced than a simple frequency/voltage configuration, the Linux kernel internally maps P-states to CPU frequencies, making it possible to give the CPU hints regarding the frequencies at which its cores should work. Obviously, when the DVFS mechanism is active the CPU speed becomes less predictable: even if the frequency scaling algorithm is configured to always select the maximum possible speed when a real-time task is active, the time needed to switch frequency can

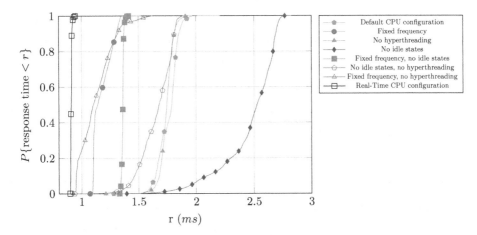

Fig. 2. CDF of the end-to-end response time with deterministic execution times and various CPU configurations.

negatively affect the real-time performance. This is why DVFS is generally disabled (and the CPU is driven at an almost constant frequency—even disabling mechanisms such as the *"turbo mode"*) when real-time performances need to be guaranteed.

As mentioned, the general guidelines for executing real-time applications on modern CPUs recommend to disable frequency scaling, idle states and hyperthreading. Some preliminary results (see below) confirm that with this configuration (named "Real-Time CPU" configuration in the following) the CPU can support deterministic execution of the baseband real-time application. However, in a cloud environment it would be useful to keep hyperthreading enabled, to give more CPU time to non-real-time applications running in background.

To experiment with various possible hardware and software configurations using a deterministic and reproducible real-time workload, we implemented a synthetic application that, from a task scheduling perspective, behaves similarly to a softwarized baseband software (same number of threads and synchronization among them), but allows users to control the execution times of the various threads. Basically, the synthetic application reproduces the thread synchronization used by the real baseband software, but the various threads consume CPU time by executing busy loops instead of decoding/encoding the radio signal (the loop counters are calibrated so that each thread executes for the desired amount of time). All the tests have been performed on a server equipped with a dual Intel(R) Xeon(R) CPU E5-2640 v4 running at 2.40 GHz (having 10 physical cores per CPU; with hyperthreading enabled there are 40 siblings).

First of all, we tested various CPU configurations with the synthetic application configured for 2 cells (2 uplink threads and 2 downlink threads) and deterministic execution times $C_{ul} = 500\,\mu s$, $C_{sched} = 100\,\mu s$, and $C_{dl} = 300\,\mu s$. Figure 2 reports the Cumulative Distribution Function (CDF) of the end-to-end response times measured with different CPU configurations ranging from the "Default CPU" configuration (DVFS, turbo mode, idle states and hyperthreading are enabled) to the "Real-Time CPU" configuration (DVFS, turbo mode, idle states and hyperthreading are all disabled).

Looking at the figure, there are some interesting results to be noticed. First of all, it can be seen that the "Real-Time CPU" configuration works as expected, and the response times are always very close to the theoretical value of $900\,\mu$s (the CDF plots the probability to measure an end-to-end response time smaller than the value r on the x-axis, hence an almost vertical line indicates almost deterministic response times). Another interesting fact to be noticed is that the "Fixed Frequency no idle states" configuration also exhibits deterministic response times, but they are larger than the theoretical value (around $1350\,\mu$s instead of $900\,\mu$s). All the other plots show a much larger execution-time variation, and the result changes from run to run, while the "Real-Time CPU" and "Fixed Frequency no idle states" configurations generate reproducible results.

Another interesting thing to be noticed in the figure is the "No idle states" curve, which looks strange since it shows that disabling the CPU idle states increase the response times and make them less deterministic. This strange behaviour can be explained by noticing that this configuration disables all the idle states (C-states deeper than C0) for all the CPUs seen by the Linux kernel (which, in this case, are logical cores). In this configuration, all the idle siblings will execute a busy loop in the idle task. Hence, if the real-time application is executing on the first sibling of a physical core and the second sibling of such physical core is idle, then the real-time application will experience the interference of the idle loop running on the second sibling!

This also explains the increased response times incurred when using the "Fixed frequency no idle state" configuration. To address this issue, *idle states should be disabled only on the logical cores executing real-time applications* (in this way, when the other sibling is idle, it is stopped and does not interfere with the execution of the real-time application). To do this, the real-time application has to be pinned to a limited number of siblings (so that it is possible to know in advance on which siblings the real-time application will execute and to disable idle states only on them). This configuration will be referred to as "Fixed frequency no idle states on RT cores" in the following.

Of course, the "Fixed frequency no idle states on RT cores" configuration can improve the real-time performance when some cores are idle, but does not offer significant advantages when all the logical cores are heavily loaded. To get good real-time performance in this situation (without resorting to disabling hyperthreading completely) it would be necessary to make sure that while a real-time thread is executing on a sibling nothing is scheduled on the second sibling of its physical core. This result can be achieved by using a functionality that has been recently introduced in the Linux kernel, named *Core Scheduling*[1].

---

[1] https://www.kernel.org/doc/html/latest/admin-guide/hw-vuln/core-scheduling.html.

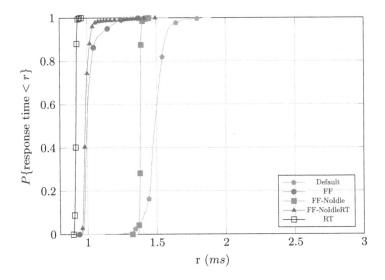

Fig. 3. CDF of the end-to-end response time with deterministic execution times.

With Core Scheduling it is possible to assign *"cookies"* to threads, and the kernel CPU scheduler will make sure that only tasks with the same cookie executes simultaneously on the same physical core (so, if a thread with cookie $\mathcal{C}$ is executing on the first sibling of a physical core, then only threads with cookie $\mathcal{C}$ can execute on the second sibling—if no other thread with cookie $\mathcal{C}$ is ready for execution, the second sibling is left idle).

Although Core Scheduling has been originally developed to address security issues (mitigating hardware bugs such as L1TF[2]), it can be used to increase the predictability of real-time applications. By assigning unique cookies to the real-time threads (and leaving non-real-time threads with no cookies), it is possible to make sure that real-time threads do not share their physical cores with any application (and hence do not suffer of any interference due to hyperthreading). This configuration will be named "Core Scheduling" in the following.

4   Experimental Results

An extensive set of experiments has been performed on the server described in Sect. 3 to evaluate the previously discussed configurations and the effectiveness of the core scheduling mechanism.

Figure 3 reports the CDFs of the end-to-end response times for the most stable CPU configurations when the threads execution times are assumed to be deterministic (and equal to the worst-case values). For the sake of simplicity, from now on "FF" represents the "Fixed Frequency" CPU configuration, "FF-NoIdle" represents the "Fixed frequency, no idle states" configuration, and

---

[2] https://www.kernel.org/doc/html/latest/admin-guide/hw-vuln/l1tf.html.

Table 1. Summary of the naming used for various CPU configurations.

Name	Description
Default	DVFS, turbo mode, idle states and hyperthreading enabled
FF	Fixed Frequency (DVFS and turbo mode disabled)
FF-NoIdle	Fixed Frequency, no idle states (DVFS, turbo mode and idle states disabled)
FF-NoIdleRT	Fixed Frequency, no idle states on RT cores (DVFS and turbo mode disabled, idle states disabled only on the cores where the real-time threads execute)
Core	Core scheduling (as above, but core scheduling is used to ensure that when a real-time thread executes on a physical core, no other thread can execute on the other sibling of the physical core)
RT	Real-Time CPU configuration (DVFS, turbo mode, idle states and hyperthreading disabled)

"FF-NoIdleRT" represents the "Fixed frequency, no idle states on RT cores" configuration (Table 1 summarizes these symbols). In this experiment, the baseband software is the only application running in the server, which is otherwise idle, hence most of the response times are lower respect to Fig. 2. As already noticed in Sect. 3, the Real-Time CPU configuration is very effective in providing deterministic response times near to the theoretical value of 900 μs. "FF-NoIdle" also results in deterministic response times, but introduces an additional delay due to the interference of the idle loop with the siblings where the real-time threads are executing. Notice that the "RT" and "FF-NoIdle" curves are identical to the ones of Fig. 2, confirming the determinism of these configurations. "FF-NoIdleRT" reduces the response times of "FF-NoIdle" by pinning the real-time threads on siblings 0 and 2, and disabling the CPU idle states only on these two siblings (as previously described).

The experiment has also been repeated using randomly-distributed execution times for the real-time threads, instead of considering their worst-case values (see Fig. 4). To account for some outliers executing for more than the expected WCETs, the probability distributions of the execution times[3] have some tails larger than C_{ul}, C_{sched} and C_{dl} (hence, the average execution times are smaller than in the previous experiments while the maximum execution times are larger—although very infrequent).

When the system is loaded with some background non-real-time applications, things look more interesting and both "FF" and "FF-NoIdleRT" result in response times comparable with the "FF-NoIdle" configuration (so, not good for real-time). This is where core scheduling can help. To investigate this setup, we executed some more experiments pinning the real-time threads to siblings 0

---

[3] In this case, gaussian distributions have been used for the sake of simplicity.

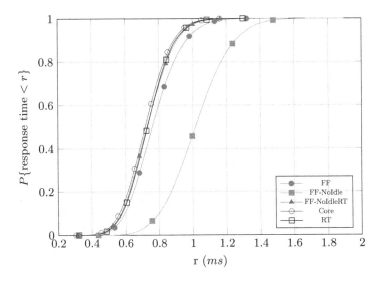

Fig. 4. CDF of the end-to-end response time with gaussian execution times and no additional load.

Table 2. CPU throughput for non-real-time applications running in background.

	ffmpeg4	ffmpeg2	Prime4	Prime2
FixFreq	1496 (100%)	897 (100%)	84794 (100%)	69091 (99.9%)
No idle states	1001 (61.9%)	853 (95%)	70390 (83%)	69102 (100%)
No idle on RT cores	1253 (83.7%)	886 (98.7%)	78168 (92.2%)	69084 (99.9%)
Core scheduling	1195 (80%)	837 (93.3%)	76117 (89.7%)	67780 (98%)
Real-Time CPU	917 (61.3%)	789 (88%)	61882 (72.9%)	58417 (84.5%)

and 2 and running a CPU-intensive application on siblings 20 and 22 (the two hardware threads sharing physical cores with siblings 0 and 2). We selected two different CPU-intensive applications to run in background: a synthetic benchmark using n threads to compute prime numbers and a more realistic application transcoding some audio and video in background (using ffmpeg). The results are reported in Fig. 5 and show that the "RT" and the "Core" configuration result in very similar response times (which are basically identical to the ones shown in Fig. 4). All the other configurations result in large response times due to the interference of the non-real-time application caused by hyperthreading.

To evaluate the "cost" of this isolation Table 2 reports the total number of frames transcoded by the ffmpeg instance or the total number of prime numbers found by the synthetic application. Two different setups have been tested: non-real-time application scheduled on siblings 0, 2, 20 and 22 (indicated as "Prime2" and "ffmpeg2") or scheduled on siblings 4, 6, 20 and 22 (indicated as "Prime4" and "ffmpeg4"). Notice how core scheduling allows to find a good

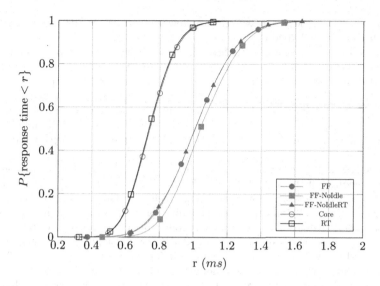

Fig. 5. CDF of the end-to-end response time with gaussian execution times and non-real-time load in background.

trade-off between real-time and non-real-time performance, increasing the CPU throughput respect to the Real-Time configuration without compromising real-time performance.

5   Conclusions

This paper evaluated the performance of a cloud node when serving a cRAN application characterized by strict temporal constraints. While the current approach to cloudify this kind of baseband applications relies on disabling hyperthreading and reducing the CPU time left to other applications running in the cloud, this paper showed how it is possible to find a reasonable trade-off between real-time performance and cloud throughput without disabling hyperthreading, by properly using advanced kernel features such as Core Scheduling.

As a future work, we will investigate scalability issues and power consumption. In this regard, some preliminary results seem to indicate that core scheduling allows to find a good trade-off between real-time performance and power consumption. We also plan to take advantage of more advanced scheduling policies, such as `SCHED_DEADLINE`, to reduce the number of CPU cores used by real-time threads and to host multiple real-time applications on the same node.

References

1. Abeni, L., Balsini, A., Cucinotta, T.: Container-based real-time scheduling in the Linux kernel. SIGBED Rev. **16**(3), 33–38 (2019)

2. Ericsson: 5G wireless access: an overview - Ericsson White Paper 1/28423-FGB1010937, April 2020
3. ETSI: Network Functions Virtualisation - Introductory White Paper - An Introduction, Benefits, Enablers, Challenges & Call for Action. Technical report, SDN and Openflow World Congress, Darmstadt, Germany (2012). https://portal.etsi.org/nfv/nfv_white_paper.pdf
4. ETSI: Network Functions Virtualisation (NFV) - Update White Paper - Network Operator Perspectives on Industry Progress. Technical report, SDN and Openflow World Congress, Frankfurt, Germany (2013). http://portal.etsi.org/nfv/nfv_white_paper2.pdf
5. Foukas, X., Radunovic, B.: Concordia: Teaching the 5 g VRAN to share compute. In: Proceedings of the 2021 ACM SIGCOMM 2021 Conference, pp. 580–596. SIGCOMM 2021, Association for Computing Machinery, New York, NY, USA (2021)
6. Giannone, F., et al.: Impact of ran virtualization on fronthaul latency budget: an experimental evaluation. In: IEEE Globecom Workshops, pp. 1–5, December 2017
7. Le, T.K., Salim, U., Kaltenberger, F.: An overview of physical layer design for ultra-reliable low-latency communications in 3 g pp releases 15, 16, and 17. IEEE Access 9, 433–444 (2021). https://doi.org/10.1109/ACCESS.2020.3046773
8. Lelli, J., Scordino, C., Abeni, L., Faggioli, D.: Deadline scheduling in the Linux kernel. Softw. Pract. Exp. 46(6), 821–839 (2016)
9. Open Networking Foundation (ONF): ONF SDN Evolution. ONF TR-535, ONF (2016). http://www.opennetworking.org/wp-content/uploads/2013/05/TR-535_ONF_SDN_Evolution.pdf
10. Suchánek, M., Navrátil, M., Bailey, L., Boyle, C.: Performance Tuning Guide - Monitoring and optimizing subsystem throughput in RHEL 7, August 2021. https://access.redhat.com/documentation/en-us/red_hat_enterprise_linux/7/html/performance_tuning_guide/index

eBPF-based Extensible Paravirtualization

Luigi Leonardi$^{(\boxtimes)}$ (iD), Giuseppe Lettieri (iD), and Giacomo Pellicci

University of Pisa, Pisa, Italy
luigi.leonardi@phd.unipi.it, giuseppe.lettieri@unipi.it,
g.pellicci2@studenti.unipi.it

Abstract. High performance applications usually need to give many hints to the OS kernel regarding their needs. For example, CPU affinity is commonly used to pin processes to cores and avoid the cost of CPU migration, isolate performance critical tasks, bring related tasks together, and so on. However, when running inside a Virtual Machine, the (guest) OS kernel can only assign virtual resources, e.g., pinning a guest process to a virtual CPU thread (vCPU); the vCPU thread, however, is still freely scheduled by the host hypervisor, which is unaware of the guest application requests. This *semantic gap* is usually overcome by statically allocating virtual resources to their hardware counterparts, which is costly and inflexible, or via *paravirtualization*, i.e., by modifying the guest kernel to pass the hints to the host, which is cumbersome and difficult to extend. We propose to use host-injected eBPF programs as a way for the host to obtain this kind of information from the guest in an extensible way, without modifying the guest (Linux) kernel, and without statically allocating resources. We apply this idea to the example of CPU affinity and run some experiments to show its effect on several microbenchmarks. Finally, we discuss the implications for confidential computing.

Keywords: eBPF · Paravirtualization · Virtualization · CPU Pinning

1 Introduction

Performance-critical applications often cannot rely on the resource scheduling decisions of general purpose kernels. Kernels have evolved to meet the special requirements of these applications by either accepting resource-usage hints (e.g., via the `madvice()` system call), providing means to let the applications override the kernel's scheduling decisions (e.g., in CPU pinning [4,6] or IRQ affinity [5]) or implementing ways to completely bypass some of the kernel's abstractions [10]. The unifying idea of these advanced kernel APIs is that applications may benefit from direct access to hardware resources, with as little kernel intervention as possible. However, inside a Virtual Machine, the guest kernel itself has no direct access to the host hardware, and the traditional implementation of these APIs may not achieve the intended effect.

The issue is particularly clear for CPU pinning. Applications pin their threads to specific CPU cores for a number of performance-related reasons: avoid the

© Springer Nature Switzerland AG 2022
H. Anzt et al. (Eds.): ISC High Performance 2022 Workshops, LNCS 13387, pp. 383–393, 2022.
https://doi.org/10.1007/978-3-031-23220-6_27

cost of CPU migration, isolate performance critical tasks, bring related tasks together, or place them closer to critical hardware resources. When running in a virtual machine, however, the guest kernel is only able to pin application threads to *virtual* CPUs, which are usually implemented as software threads scheduled by the VM hypervisor. The hypervisor is still free to migrate the CPU threads among available hardware cores or to time-share several threads on a single core. Moreover, virtual resources that look "close" to the guest (e.g. hyperthreads of the same virtual core) may still be scheduled on "far" hardware resources (e.g., on two separate cores). This behaviour effectively negates most or all the performance gains that the guest applications where trying to achieve. The problem is that the relevant information is split between two distinct subsystems: the application needs are only known by the guest kernel, while the hardware resource state is only known to the hypervisor. The traditional way to address this problem is to partly remove the distinction by virtual and hardware resources, e.g., by statically pinning each virtual CPU thread to an isolated hardware CPU thread. This solution, while effective, may be unnecessarily costly, if the application workload is subject to changes. A different, more dynamic approach is suggested by Lee and Eom [7]: here, suitable hypercalls are inserted in the guest kernel to pass the scheduling decisions down to the hypervisor, which will then apply them on the host system. This is an example of *paravirtualization* [2], where the guest system is made aware of running inside a virtual machine.

The typical way to achieve paravirtualization, as also exemplified here, is to modify the guest kernel in an *ad hoc* way to solve the particular problem of interest. This is unsatisfying for several reasons: modifying the kernel is a complex undertaking; new modifications must be devised whenever new needs arise; the choices of guest software may be subject to limitations (e.g., particular kernel versions where the modification is available).

In recent years, eBPF [9] has emerged as a generic solution to extract information, or customize the behaviour of unmodified Linux kernels, and work to support it in Windows is also underway [3]. Using the eBPF framework, userspace applications can inject programs in the running kernel and attach them to specific tracepoints. The programs, run by the kernel whenever the tracepoint is reached, have controlled access to kernel data structures and can pass informations to interested userspace programs. In this paper we propose to reuse eBPF technology for paravirtualization purposes, i.e., by having the virtual machine monitor inject eBPF programs in the guest kernel, in order to extract any information that may be relevant for the efficient, dynamic allocation of hardware resources based on guest application requests.

2   eBPF

eBPF is a flexible and efficient technology, available in the Linux kernel, that is composed of an instruction set, storage objects, and helper functions. Its instructions are executed by a Linux kernel BPF runtime, which includes an interpreter and a JIT[1] compiler for efficiency.

This technology enables dynamic tracing: the ability to insert tracing points into live software, and costs zero overhead when not in use, as software runs unmodified.

An eBPF program is "attached" to a designated code path in the kernel. When the code path is traversed, any attached eBPF programs are executed. Code paths can be of various kind, allowing programs to be attached to trace-points, kprobes, and perf events. Since eBPF programs can access kernel data structures, developers can write and test new debugging code without having to recompile the kernel.

One really important aspect of eBPF is that it is verifiable: There are inherent security and stability risks with allowing user-space code to run inside the kernel. For this reason, there are some limitations to the instruction set, like loops. The verifier has an important role and is asked to detect the eBPF program type, to restrict which kernel functions can be called from eBPF programs and which data structures can be accessed.

3 Extensible Paravirtualization

This work aims to create a generic mechanism that allows to have a certain degree of paravirtualization in a system that uses hardware-assisted virtualization. This must be done transparently, meaning that the guest operating system should not be modified.

The approach that has been followed is the following: A remote client injects a payload into the virtual device on the host side, and the guest daemon, through the device driver regulating the access to the device, obtains such message and consumes it accordingly to its content. Note that the payload content might be whatever, from a simple command to a more complex payload, for instance, an eBPF program containing a kprobe

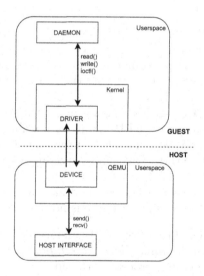

Fig. 1. Generic extensible paravirtualiza-tion mechanism architecture

ready to be loaded into the guest kernel. Any information obtained by this eBPF program might be used inside or outside the guest system and possibly being propagated up to host hypervisor or even to the client that initiated the communication.

---

[1] Just in Time.

The proposed architecture, shown in Fig. 1, is simple and linear. This choice was made to favor integration with existing technologies such as QEMU and the Linux kernel. Note that no specifications on the communication channel are given, meaning that can be either simplex or duplex. In the general case, it is assumed that this communication is duplex. Although a QEMU guest agent exists, it has not been used in this work and has been re-implemented for simplicity and to better fit this project's needs.

To summarize a system that allows communication between host and guest has been created. This communication happens through messages structured as header and payload, whose meaning is associated with their message type.

4 Virtual to Physical CPUs Affinity

CPU affinity, also known as CPU pinning, is a technique that allows to set the affinity of a process or thread with a set of CPUs. By doing so the process or thread will only run on the designated CPU(s), ignoring the others. The main advantage of pinning a process or a thread to one single CPU is that it cannot move to other CPUs, never losing the content of its cache as it happens when a process or thread is moved to another CPU. There are several reasons why a program might want to control this aspect of the system:

- Considering a pair of coupled processes or threads like in a typical producer-consumer system: If the communication protocol is non-blocking, there are some performance benefits when two processes or threads are running on different CPUs. Note that, in the default way in which Linux handles it, no guarantees are given about the two sharing the same CPU, while the other CPUs are idle. Even though this is a rare event but may happen, on the other hand with CPU affinity is possible to ensure that two processes or threads are never scheduled on the same CPU.
- In NUMA[2] machines accessing resources like RAM or I/O has different costs from different CPUs. Forcing a process or thread on the CPU that has "local" access to the most used memory zones can have beneficial effects on performance. This last case is not covered in this work.

On Linux, the CPU affinity of a process can be altered with the *taskset* program, while the *sched_setaffinity* system call can be used to modify the CPU affinity of a process or thread.

Note that the usage of CPU affinity to boost performance depends heavily on the program structure. Different benefits can be achieved depending on whether the program is CPU bound or if it makes extensive use of cache.

In this work, the environment is composed of a host system and one or more virtual machine(s) that are called guest(s). Inside the guest, an operating system will manage the underlying virtualized hardware and provide system calls to the guest userspace applications. The latter system can be started with one or more

---

[2] Non-Uniform Memory Architecture.

CPUs that are virtual, or vCPUs for short, and in reality are host userspace threads which in this case are created by QEMU. Setting the CPU affinity inside the guest operating system, that binds a guest userspace thread to a guest CPU, means nothing because the latter is just a representation of a physical CPU. In other words it is binding the guest thread to the host thread that represent the guest virtual CPU.

It would be useful in some applications to be able to apply CPU affinity also outside the guest system, resulting in a real CPU pinning.

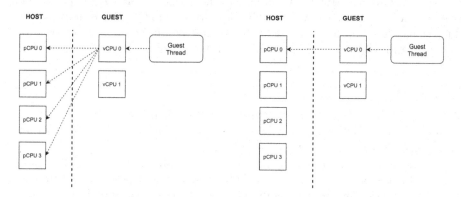

Fig. 2. Dashed arrows represent affinity. No pinning is performed on vCPU by the host system.

Fig. 3. Dashed arrow represent affinity. Pinning is performed correctly on pCPU 0.

4.1   Implementation

The general idea is to have an eBPF program that will track calls to the *sched_setaffinity* system calls and notify the guest agent. This agent will then send to the QEMU virtual device the requested affinity masks through the device driver. Once the affinity masks arrive in the QEMU virtual device, they can be used to call *sched_setaffinity* on the host side. Affinity mask remapping can be enabled from the host side depending on whether Hyper-threading is supported, sending a specific message which has been defined for this purpose.

The aforementioned eBPF program, which contains a Kprobe to be installed on *sched_setaffinity()*, is loaded into the kernel. Then, whenever the probed function is called, the eBPF program will fire and the affinity mask, which is provided as an argument, is written in an eBPF map.

In addition if the device is enabled for affinity mask remapping, a remapping is then performed, otherwise, the unmodified affinity mask is applied on the QEMU threads that represent the virtual CPUs that the guest uses to run its code.

To summarize: the eBPF program, which uses the *"kprobe/sched_setaffinity"* hook, writes the affinity masks inside an eBPF map every time that syscall is invoked. The guest agent constantly checks this map for changes, if any, and uses the *ioctl* system call to notify the guest driver when new affinity masks are available so that it can start the transfer. In the host system, these masks can be used to invoke *sched_setaffinity*, according to some host-defined allocation policy. In this work for simplicity, no particular policy has been enforced and the host's vCPU(s) process(es), inside the affinity mask, are pinned to their relative pCPU(s).

Hyper Threading. Hyper-threading has different CPU ordering depending on whether the system is a native one or if it is started from QEMU. To fully support HT a remapping function is needed. Every time an affinity mask is received and has to be applied to the host system, it will be remapped if the flag is set.

4.2   Tests

The testing phase aims at understanding the performance difference between virtual machines that exploit hardware-assisted virtualization with and without the extensible paravirtualization mechanism.

The application used as a benchmark is a simplified version of the system presented in the article "Cache-aware design of general-purpose Single-Producer-Single-Consumer" queues [8]. Lamport queues have been picked. In the system, there are two threads, one producer and one consumer, that are pinned to different CPUs, so that they can run in parallel.

Performance in the system has been evaluated and the Mpps[3] metric has been chosen. The host system is subjected to different types of loads, from fully unloaded CPUs to multiple processes running on each CPU. To simulate the workload in the host system the Linux command *yes* is used.

Producer-consumer systems like SPSCQ benefit from parallelization and interaction in a non-blocking way. The Linux scheduler does nothing to prevent two threads from being scheduled one after the other on the same CPU. The latter is not a frequent scenario because the scheduler will try to balance the workload among the available CPUs; However, in a system under load, there is the possibility that the two threads: producer and consumer, are scheduled one after the other on the same processor, introducing a serialization condition, which drastically degrades the performance of the entire system.

By introducing this mechanism that allows applying CPU affinity requests on the host system as well, there is the guarantee that the producer and consumer threads will never be serialized on the same CPU, avoiding this kind of slowdown.

Two types of tests have been carried out to evaluate the benefits of this extension:

- **Virtual CPU pinning.** In this testing scenario, the performance difference between a hardware-assisted virtualization system with and without the extensible paravirtualization extension is evaluated. The SPSCQ system

---

[3] Mega packets per second.

throughput is shown when these two parameters vary: the host system load and the fraction of test time in which the two threads, producer and consumer, are serialized. For this test an Intel Core i5-6600 CPU @ 3.30GHz has been used, which does not implement Hyper-threading.

- **Virtual Hyper-thread pinning.** During this test, the performance differences are evaluated between using standard *sched_setaffinity()* behaviour and Hyper-thread pinning extensions, in guest machines. Moreover, differences in throughput between running an SPSCQ application directly on the host system and running SPSCQ within a guest system are also evaluated. For this test, an Intel Core i7-6700K CPU @ 4.00GHz has been used, which implements Hyper-threading.

5   Results

Results are obtained through repeated experiments and plotted with their 90% confidence intervals.

5.1   Virtual CPU Pinning

In this test, the throughput in a standard guest system is compared with one that uses the extension made for this purpose. This comparison is performed by varying two elements: the load on the host system and the fraction of time during which the two threads, producer and consumer, are scheduled on the same CPU. Note that the host load refers to how many *yes* processes are being executed in the background on the host system.

Inside the guest machine, two threads are created: one producer P and one consumer C. Those threads will request to be pinned to different CPUs: P on vCPU0 and C on vCPU 1. In the 'no load' scenario, without vCPU pinning what happens in the host system is that the QEMU threads associated with their vCPUs are freely scheduled on all available CPUs. The host system, being idle, will result in those threads running on any host CPU with a low probability of being moved to another CPU, because no other process or thread is likely to preempt them. Instead, pinning vCPU 0 to pCPU 0 and vCPU 1 to pCPU 1 will guarantee that the QEMU threads responsible for vCPU 0 and 1 will not be moved to any other host physical CPU. And as is possible to see in Fig. 4. The advantage is negligible as shown in the 'no load' section of the graph.

As the load starts to intensify in the host system, 'low load' in Fig. 4, different behaviour is shown. The host system is forced to execute 8x yes processes in addition to the P and C threads. So, for this reason, without vCPU pinning performance is reduced with regard to the 'no load' case. With vCPU pinning instead, the performance remains similar as P and C, which are scheduled on vCPU 0 and vCPU 1, can only be assigned on pCPU 0 and pCPU 1, while the yes processes will share the other physical CPUs.

Another scenario worthy of mention is what can be called the serialization one. This situation is represented, on the plot, by the serialization variable, whose

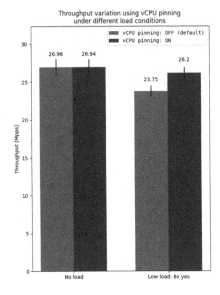

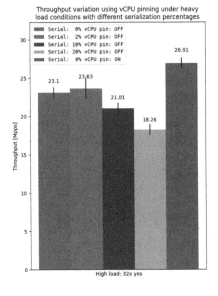

Fig. 4. Throughput on a standard system and vCPU pinning. No load and low load conditions.

Fig. 5. Throughput on standard system and vCPU pinning. High load conditions with serialization scenarios.

range starts from no serialization (0%) and goes up to high serialization (20%). The use of vCPU pinning guarantees that P and C will never be scheduled on the same physical CPU as long as they are pinned on two different vCPUs that are assigned to two different pCPUs.

This behaviour can be seen in Fig. 5 in which the host system is under high load conditions (32× yes processes running on the host). Overall, serialization significantly degrades performance in standard systems, while the others that use vCPU pinning, are not affected by this problem.

5.2   Virtual Hyper-thread Pinning

This test is a comparison of the throughput obtained by a standard guest system with one that uses the Hyper-thread pinning technique, which is a further extension of the vCPU pinning mechanism. For this test, an Intel Core i7-6700K was used; It implements Hyper-threading and has 8 logical processors. For this reason, host load indicators are now multiplied by 8.

The SPSCQ test program creates two threads, P and C, and performs high-speed operations on a lockless queue while varying the load in the host system. Then all performances with Hyper-thread pinning and the standard behaviour are compared. Finally, the performance penalty is analyzed, which is introduced by running the SPSCQ program within a virtual machine, with and without Hyper-thread pinning, with regard to executing it directly on the host machine.

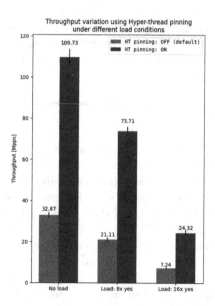

Fig. 6. Throughput on a standard system and Hyper-thread pinning. No load and low load conditions.

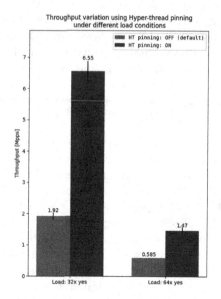

Fig. 7. Throughput on a standard system and vCPU pinning. High load conditions.

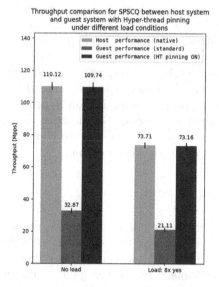

Fig. 8. Throughput on host system and guest system with Hyper-thread pinning

In Figs. 6 and 7 is plotted the comparison between standard system throughput and on a system using Hyper-thread pinning technique. Results are interesting: using HT pinning throughput is about 3.4 times higher than what is achieved in a traditional guest system. There is a small drop, in terms of throughput gain, when the load on the host system is very high i.e. 64× yes processes. Note that unlike many programs, SPSC benefit a lot from this technology, because running on the same core, processes can easily share resources such as caches.

In Fig. 8 a comparison between native and virtualized performance is shown. What is clear, is that SPSCQ performance on a standard guest system, that does not use Hyperthreading correctly is much lower than what you get by running SPSCQ directly on the host. This shows that the theoretical 'near-native' speed is not achieved by the guest system. On the other hand, using Hyper-thread pinning, the guest system can pin P and C threads on the same host physical core, thus obtaining near-native performance as hardware-assisted virtualization claims, but cannot be guaranteed in this special case, without modifications.

6   Confidential Computing

Confidential Computing techniques allow Virtual Machines (or processes) to run on untrusted hypervisors (or kernels). The VM can run in an "enclave" where most memory is hardware encrypted, with a decryption key that is available only while the guest software controls the CPU. Since the hypervisor has no access to the decryption key, the guest can protect its confidential data even if all of the software running outside the VM is compromised.

Confidential computing creates difficulties for paravirtualization solutions, which have always assumed that the host had free access to all of the guest memory. For example, consider *hyperupcalls* as proposed in [1]. The motivation for hyperupcalls is similar to our own: improve performance by granting the host access to some guest kernel state. Hyperupcalls achieve this aim by having the *guest* download programs in the *host*. The host runs these programs when needed, to correctly interpret the data structures living in the guest memory. In a confidential computing setting this is not easily done, since these programs would run in a context that has no access to the decryption key. In our proposed solution, instead, the programs are injected in the opposite direction and are run in the *guest*, where they have access to the decrypted guest memory.

We think that our solution, with respect to the alternatives, is also more compatible with the spirit of confidential computing. In systems, where confidential computing is used, security is a major concern. For this reason, using an ad-hoc modified version of the kernel, to introduce the paravirtualization hypercalls, can be considered a possible weak link in the root-of-trust. On the other hand, using our proposed method, the guest can formally verify the injected code, and according to some policies, decide whether to load that code or not.

7   Conclusions and Future Work

In conclusion, in this work we realized an extensible paravirtualization mechanism that makes use of eBPF programs. It allows programmers to add specific capabilities to host-guest systems. Overcoming the limitation introduced by running the guest system in a virtualized environment and realizing CPU affinity. This showed substantial performance gains, especially when Hyper-threading is available and a program that can benefit from is used. Future work should consider implementing a whitelist of eBPF's hook inside the guest user agent to enforce security policies and other potential applications of this extensible mechanism.

References

1. Amit, N., Wei, M.: The design and implementation of Hyperupcalls. In: 2018 USENIX Annual Technical Conference (USENIX ATC 2018), pp. 97–112. USENIX Association, Boston, MA (2018)
2. Barham, P., et al.: Xen and the art of virtualization. ACM SIGOPS Oper. Syst. Rev. **37**(5), 164–177 (2003)
3. eBPF for Windows (2022). https://github.com/microsoft/ebpf-for-windows
4. Ghatrehsamani, D., Denninnart, C., Bacik, J., Amini Salehi, M.: The art of CPU-pinning: evaluating and improving the performance of virtualization and containerization platforms. In: 49th International Conference on Parallel Processing - ICPP. ICPP 2020. Association for Computing Machinery, Edmonton, AB, Canada (2020). https://doi.org/10.1145/3404397.3404442
5. Gutiérrez, C.S.V., Juan, L.U.S., Ugarte, I.Z., Vilches, V.M.: Real-time Linux communications: an evaluation of the Linux communication stack for real-time robotic applications. arXiv preprint arXiv:1808.10821 (2018)
6. Krzywda, J., Ali-Eldin, A., Carlson, T.E., Östberg, P.-O., Elmroth, E.: Powerperformance tradeoffs in data center servers: DVFS, CPU pinning, horizontal, and vertical scaling. Futur. Gener. Comput. Syst. **81**, 114–128 (2018)
7. Lee, T., Eom, Y.I.: VCPU prioritization interface for improving the performance of latency-critical tasks. In: 2020 14th International Conference on Ubiquitous Information Management and Communication (IMCOM), pp. 1–4 (2020). https://doi.org/10.1109/IMCOM48794.2020.9001717
8. Maffione, V., Lettieri, G., Rizzo, L.: Cache-aware design of general-purpose single-producer-single-consumer queues. Softw. Pract. Exp. **49**, 748–779 (2018). https://doi.org/10.1002/spe.2675
9. Vieira, M.A., Castanho, M.S., Pacífico, R.D., Santos, E.R., Júnior, E.P.C., Vieira, L.F.: Fast packet processing with EBPF and XDP: concepts, code, challenges, and applications. ACM Comput. Surv. (CSUR) **53**(1), 1–36 (2020)
10. Zhang, I., Liu, J., Austin, A., Roberts, M.L., Badam, A.: I'm not dead yet! The role of the operating system in a kernel-bypass era. In: Proceedings of the Workshop on Hot Topics in Operating Systems, pp. 73–80 (2019)

Correction to: Compiler-Assisted Instrumentation Selection for Large-Scale C++ Codes

Sebastian Kreutzer⬤, Christian Iwainsky⬤, Jan-Patrick Lehr⬤,
and Christian Bischof⬤

Correction to:
**Chapter "Compiler-Assisted Instrumentation Selection
for Large-Scale C++ Codes" in: H. Anzt et al. (Eds.):**
High Performance Computing, **LNCS 13387,**
https://doi.org/10.1007/978-3-031-23220-6_1

Chapter "Compiler-Assisted Instrumentation Selection for Large-Scale C++ Codes" was previously published non-open access. It has now been changed to open access under a CC BY 4.0 license and the copyright holder updated to 'The Author(s)'. The book has also been updated with this change.

The updated original version of this chapter can be found at
https://doi.org/10.1007/978-3-031-23220-6_1

Author Index

Abeni, Luca 371
Acquaviva, Andrea 262
Ahrens, James 283
Alias, Christophe 20
Ardebili, Mohsen Seyedkazemi 262
Arima, Eishi 206
Azab, Abdulrahman 358

Baiz, Abdulaziz 317
Barrett, Gregg 47
Bartholomew, Paul 33
Bartolini, Andrea 262
Belikov, Evgenij 233
Benini, Luca 262
Bilas, Angelos 221, 347
Bischof, Christian 5
Brown, Nick 233
Bruchertseifer, Jens 295
Bukhanov, Nikita 317

Cancelliere, Michel 317
Carretero, Jesus 129, 190
Cascajo, Alberto 129
Caspart, René 108
Castelló, Adrián 65, 176
Catalán, Sandra 176
Charara, Marwan 317
Chazapis, Antony 221, 347
Comprés, A. Isaías 206
Criado, Joel 162
Cucinotta, Tommaso 371

Debus, Charlotte 108
Demiralp, Ali C. 295
Der Chien, Wei 233
Dutta, Soumya 283

Egan, Hilary 251
Emani, Murali 47

Fecht, Jan 147
Ferrier, Nicola 324
Flatken, Markus 233
Fox, Geoffrey 47

Garcia-Blas, Javier 190
Garcia-Gasulla, Marta 162
Gerndt, Andreas 233
Gerrits, Tim 295
Geveci, Berk 283
Gibb, Gordon 233
Gibbs, Tom 47
Götz, Markus 108

Hayashi, Akihiro 90
Hey, Tony 47
Holmes, Daniel J. 147
Huang, Jian 306

Igual, Francisco D. 176
Insley, Joseph 324
Isensee, Fabian 108
Iwainsky, Christian 5

Jacquot, Pierre 358

Kanterakis, Alexandros 221
Kimura, Keiji 20
Kirkpatrick, Christine 47
Klasky, Scott 306
Kozanitis, Christos 347
Kreutzer, Sebastian 5
Krüger, Marcel 295
Kuhlen, Torsten W. 295

Lapworth, Leigh 33
Lehr, Jan-Patrick 5
Leonardi, Luigi 383
Lettieri, Giuseppe 383
Lindquist, Tobias 371
Lipsa, Dan 283
Lopez, Victor 162
Luszczek, Piotr 47

Maliaroudakis, Evangelos 221
Marazakis, Manolis 221
Markidis, Stefano 233
Martínez, Héctor 65
Mateevitsi, Victor A. 324
Mátray, Péter 371
Moreland, Kenneth 306

Nash, Rupert   233
Nealey, Isaac   324
Nolden, Marco   108
Novikov, Pavel   317

Obermaier, Holger   108
Oehrl, Simon   295
Olivier, Pierre   358

Papay, Juri   47
Papka, Michael E.   324
Parsons, Mark   33
Paul, Sri Raj   90
Pellicci, Giacomo   383
Perez, Christian   358
Pinczel, Balázs   371
Podobas, Artur   233
Pritchard, Howard   147
Pugmire, David   306
Purkayastha, Avi   251

Quintana-Ortí, Enrique S.   65, 176

Raffeiner, Simon   108
Ramírez, Cristian   65
Ramirez-Miranda, Guillem   162
Rashed, Fahad   317
Reinartz, Ines   108
Rizzi, Silvio   324
Rodríguez-Sánchez, Rafael   176

Sabitov, Denis   317
Sarkar, Vivek   90
Scholtyssek, Jan   108

Schreiber, Martin   147
Schuhmacher, Leon Pascal   108
Schulz, Martin   147, 206
Sfakianakis, Yannis   347
Shankar, Mallikarjun   47
Sickinger, David   251
Singh, David E.   129, 190
Spreizer, Sebastian   295
Srinivasan, Murali Krishna   371

Teruel, Xavier   162
Thievenaz, Hugo   20
Thiyagalingam, Jeyan   47
Tiwari, Manasi   77
Trofimova, Darya   108
Tsaris, Aristeidis   47
Turton, Terece L.   283

Vadhiyar, Sathish   77
Vinyals-Ylla-Catala, Joan   162
Vishwanath, Venkatram   47
von Laszewski, Gregor   47

Wang, Feiyi   47
Weiland, Michèle   33
Weyers, Benjamin   295
Weyrauch, Arvid   108

Yin, Junqi   47

Zarins, Justs   33
Zervas, George   347
Ziegler, Sebastian   108

Printed in the United States
by Baker & Taylor Publisher Services